POINT-COUNTERPOINT

Readings in American Government

POINT

COUNTERPOINT

Readings in American Government

Herbert M. Levine
University of Southwestern Louisiana

Scott, Foresman and Company. **Glenview, Illinois**
Dallas, Tex. Oakland, N.J. Palo Alto, Cal. Tucker, Ga. London, England

For Albert, Louise, and Philippe Boudreau

Library of Congress Card Number 79-64135

Copyright © 1979 Scott, Foresman and Company.

All Rights Reserved.

Printed in the United States of America.

ISBN   0-673-15297-9

2 3 4 5 6 7 8 9 10 -B- 85 84 83 82 81 80 79

Preface

When Democratic presidential candidate Jimmy Carter and Republican presidential incumbent Gerald Ford agreed to a debate on television during the campaign of 1976, public interest ran high on the issues and personalities involved. At last, it was believed, the American electorate would learn the differences between the two major candidates so that they could make a more rational voting choice.

In the opinion of many Americans, the debates were less than outstanding in presenting differences. Some critics contended that the candidates treated the issues superficially. Others said that the debates were dull and put television viewers to sleep, rather than informing Americans about the issues. Critics also charged that the candidates were more concerned with avoiding making any serious mistakes, which would cost votes, rather than with enlightening the electorate. Although the candidates did not clarify their differences on every issue, they did reveal—at least to the satisfaction of some—the basic positions uniting and dividing them.

Whether or not successful in educating the electorate, the Carter-Ford debates served as one example of a debate tradition as old as the Republic itself. Soon after American colonists achieved independence from British rule, they debated issues as fundamental as slavery, tariffs, and the policy of the United States toward the French Revolution. Some debates in American history—Lincoln-Douglas and Kennedy-Nixon—have become part of the national memory.

Although these presidential campaign debates were dramatic, every debate strengthens the democratic tradition. It is with this in mind that the present text has been developed. *Point-Counterpoint* is a collection of readings that reveal the pro and con aspects of American government. It is designed to contribute to a democratic tradition in which vigorous controversy is regarded as both proper and desirable.

To provide students with a better understanding of the great diversity of controversial political issues, *Point-Counterpoint* contains articles dealing with the basic structure of the American political system, influences by nongovernmental institutions on government, the power of policy makers, and the direction of public policy. Topics were selected on the basis of their inherent controversial nature.

On structure, questions deal with the power structure, the Constitution, federal government-state relations, and civil liberties. Topics include, for example, the ability of the states to solve vital domestic problems and the regulation of pornography versus freedom of speech and press.

On influences of nongovernmental institutions on government, a variety of subjects is also treated, such as the influence of the media on society and the dangers of interest groups in a democracy.

On policy makers, topics include the desirability of a strong president, the uniqueness of the Nixon presidency, the ability of a government agency—such as the Central Intelligence Agency—to resist congressional control, and judicial activism by the Supreme Court.

Public-policy issues are debated in the areas of domestic policy, national security, and foreign policy. Among the domestic issues discussed are the best solutions for solving urban problems and the desirability of gun control. National security and foreign policy questions deal with some of the most lively controversies of the day, such as the military strength of the United States, human rights, and détente.

The format of the book, then, encourages critical thinking. The *chapter introduction* provides important background information and gives a brief synopsis of major points in each article. For each *debate question* offered, one "Yes" and one "No" article are given. *Notes, questions for discussion,* and *suggested readings* follow each debate. These questions help students formulate their own answers to the debate question. If the conflicting views on any issue both seem convincing, students can then turn to the suggested readings, which provide general background information as well as pro and con arguments.

Three cautionary points are in order. First, students will find that the issues cannot be broken down into one neat classification, such as a liberal-conservative dichotomy. The material has been selected from a variety of sources—socialist and anti-socialist; liberal and conservative; idealist and realist; Marxist and anti-Marxist; and "Establishment" and "anti-Establishment."

Second, space limitations and the format of the book dictate that only two views—"Yes" and "No"—are given for each question. More often than not, other answers could be presented, such as "Yes, but . . . ," "No, but . . . ," or even "Maybe." In the process of debate, refinements can be developed. The yes-no approach, however, should at least provide a beginning toward understanding problems of American government.

Third, the book does not present a single ideological perspective. As a whole, it does not take a side on every issue but presents, instead, many views. If there is one ideological commitment, however, it is implicit in the nature of the format of the book: a commitment to vigorous debate as befits the democratic tradition.

I am grateful to the many people who offered suggestions for improving this anthology. Their comments ranged from recommending particular readings to urging revisions of the introductory notes. I found their assistance invaluable.

I want to thank my colleagues at the University of Southwestern Louisiana—the late Walter Craddock, Charles Dunn, Philip Dur, Burk Foster, Patricia Harris, Paul Edward Joubert, Ronald Labbé, John Meriwether, Jeremy Millett, Henry Pitchford, Thomas Schoonover, and Joseph Zentner. Donn M. Kurtz II, head of the Department of Political Science, protected me from excessive administrative responsibilities during my work on this book. J. Norman Heard, Acting Director of Dupré Library, solved numerous library problems for me.

I also wish to express appreciation to Ryan Barilleaux, a student at the University of Southwestern Louisiana; Susan Davis, a recent graduate of Georgetown University; Marvin Maurer, Professor of Government at Monmouth College in New Jersey; Robert Schuettinger, editor of *Policy Review*; and Anne L. Simon, an attorney with Mestayer and Simon.

No one has been of more help to me in my work for this book than Thomas Ferrell, my colleague in the Department of Political Science. I believe I made excessive demands upon his time. He made valuable suggestions about the introductory material and the selections, and I want to take this opportunity to tell him how much I appreciate his criticisms and his time.

My editors at General Learning Press—Judy Green, Walter Kossmann, and Edith Vann—have been most helpful on this project. I have profited from their recommendations and criticisms. I also wish to thank Anita Samen for her excellent copy editing.

Herbert M. Levine

Contents

PART THREE • ARE POLICY MAKERS TOO INFLUENTIAL?   217

9. Is the American Presidency Too Powerful?   218

10. Is the Bureaucracy Acting in a Responsible Manner?   256

PART ONE

How Democratic
Is the
American
Political System?

1.

Is the United States Undemocratic?

When protest movements formed in the 1960s to criticize the policies of American political and economic institutions, no serious challenge to the American creed of democracy was asserted. Unlike the depression years of the 1930s, when some critics of the system turned to fascism and rejected even the principle of democracy, most protesters of the 1960s were not against democracy but rather in favor of it, although they defined democracy in different ways.

Civil rights groups, for example, contended that black Americans did not have equal access to the American Dream. They demanded the promise of democracy—full political rights and the economic power that could be derived from political power.

Student activists denounced university institutions as undemocratic. They called for democratization of the university, which to them meant more student participation in decision making in such areas as curriculum, hiring of faculty members, and even university investment portfolios.

Civil libertarians argued for the implementation of the Bill of Rights. Governmental institutions, they contended, should live by the laws they professed. Government should be more democratic, which to them meant eliminating such practices as illegal wiretapping, surveillance of dissenters, unauthorized searches and seizures, and police infiltration of radical organizations.

When President Lyndon Johnson called for a war on poverty, supporters of the poor asked for a democratizing element to the program. They wanted poor people to have a role in creating and administering any program the government might institute in its Great Society. Popular involvement, they argued, was a necessary component of democracy.

Democracy was acclaimed by the protest movement in foreign and national security matters as well. The "movement" opposed United States' participation in the war in Vietnam for many reasons, among them issues of democracy. South Vietnam, they contended, was led by a dictatorship, and the United States had no business supporting dictatorships. They also claimed that a small and conspiratorial military-industrial complex in the United States was responsible for American involvement in an Asian war to the detriment of the masses of American people. The protesters, moreover, criticized the military draft, which they saw as an undemocratic institution, because individual freedom was restricted.

Although the protest movement of the left accepted democracy, so, too, did the protest movement of the right, for the most part. Members of such a right-wing organization as the John Birch Society blamed a conspiracy of a small group of communists and communist sympathizers—rather than the American people themselves—for America's problems. Young Americans for Freedom (YAF), a conservative group, was as vocal in its advocacy of democracy as its left-wing counterparts. For example, YAF argued during the Vietnam War that the Viet Cong would establish a communist dictatorship that would be far more undemocratic than the existing South Vietnamese government.

The Establishment—the president, Congress, the courts, and state and local governments—contended that they, too, accepted democracy. For example, Establishment critics of the more militant protesters argued that tactics of resistance—such as bombing government buildings, taking over university offices, and fomenting civil disorder—were undermining the laws, which were themselves the expression of majority will.

The fact that so many people with such different views accepted the principle of democracy highlights the problem of using the term *democracy*. For democracy has had such a long history that not only is its very meaning ambiguous, but an evaluation of whether or not a political system is, in fact, applying democratic principles is controversial—even when a definition is accepted. Although there are differences in defining democracy, the principal contemporary uses of *democracy* are political and economic. Political democracy is generally described in two ways: (1) direct, or participatory, or (2) indirect, or representative.

POLITICAL DEMOCRACY

In a direct, or participatory, democracy all citizens participate in the political process, serving directly as judges and law makers. This form of democracy, in which all citizens participate in the political life of the community, was practiced centuries ago in ancient Athens. The bulk of the population—which included women, slaves, children, and foreigners—was excluded from the citizenry, however. Only male property owners were considered citizens. But for its time, there was more popular participation in Athenian democracy than in any other political system. In present-day America, the New England town meeting is a modern example of direct democracy.

Indirect, or representative, democracy is more characteristic of communities larger than the Greek city-states. Officials are elected periodically in these systems and are accountable to the people for their actions. These officials make laws that are binding upon the people.

Whether direct or indirect, political democracy is concerned with procedures rather than policies. The main components of these procedures in a political democracy are popular sovereignty, political equality (one person, one vote), majority rule, and minority rights. A basic premise of this kind of democracy is that so long as groups are free to compete in the political process, the key to governmental rule is through winning majority coalitions. Policy is influenced by changing attitudes or shifting majorities. So long as the procedures of political democracy are maintained, government can respond to popular needs.

ECONOMIC DEMOCRACY

Another approach to democracy focuses on economic rather than political elements. According to left-wing partisans, unless some material benefits accrue to the masses of people, democracy is meaningless. "What good is it that minority-group members can vote," they ask, "if they cannot find jobs or achieve basic economic security?"

Democratic socialists contend that a political system cannot be considered truly democratic unless wealth is more equitably dispersed than capitalism has demonstrated a capacity to accomplish. The way to achieve economic equality, consequently, is to elect into office advocates of socialist policies. The late Norman Thomas, an American Socialist party leader, asserted such a view. Many communists who advocate Marxism-Leninism, however, focus their attention almost entirely on the economy. For them, the existing state in noncommunist societies is really nothing more than a sinister capitalist organization. According to this view, political procedures—so vital to the democratic socialists—are not regarded as crucial to freeing the oppressed. Only when capitalism is destroyed, they feel, will the masses of people be free.

Many anticommunist radicals, too, argue that democratic procedures in the United States are rigged for the benefit of the propertied classes. America, they contend, is ruled by elites who manipulate elections and the media in order to thwart the will of ordinary people. These critics would be as hostile to communism as they are to any power elite that prevents popular control.

CHALLENGES TO THE EXISTENCE OF DEMOCRACY IN AMERICA

The question of whether or not American government is truly democratic focuses on the foundations of our governmental system. Some advocates of the view that American government is undemocratic point to the structure of power at home and covert operations abroad as evidence for their contention. This chapter deals with these two subjects by asking these questions: (1) does a power elite prevent the people from ruling? (2) can the United States engage in covert operations abroad and still be considered a democracy?

Power Elite: Fact or Fiction?

Some social scientists have argued that the masses of the people in a political democracy are prevented from ruling because of the activities of a power elite. Sociologist C. Wright Mills is one of the more prominent proponents of this view. He argues that an elite composed of military officers, politicians, and capitalists really runs America. According to Mills, the military seeks promotions and big defense budgets, politicians strive for reelection, and capitalists pursue profits. Together they control policy making. The manipulatory control of the elite is so complete, Mills asserts, that the public cannot even recognize the "real issues," much less develop opinions on them. Political scientist Robert A. Dahl, in contrast, argues that the elite theorists make too much of the persistence of inequalities in power and influence in all associations and societies. The premise that inequalities in power and resources exist, he contends, does not warrant the conclusion that there is a ruling class.

Covert Operations: Safeguards or Threats?

When studying democracy, classical political philosophers have tended to focus their attention on domestic politics. Particularly in the twentieth century, however, foreign policy and national security have played important roles in the preservation or destruction of democratic institutions. Democratic institutions may be lost through conquest by dictatorial powers; they may also be destroyed by internal changes necessitated by external dangers.

Particularly since the end of World War II, United States policy makers have feared a threat to American democratic institutions from the Soviet Union. The United States, consequently, became involved in global politics on a grand scale, which was reflected in wars, foreign aid programs, and intelligence activities. Widespread American fear of the Soviet Union made anticommunism a fundamental tenet of American policy.

Dissatisfaction with the war in Vietnam and revelations arising from Watergate activities contributed to a growing mood of despondency about America's activities abroad. Newspaper accounts and congressional investigations revealed United States' complicity in plotting assassinations of public officials abroad, interference in the internal affairs of other governments, and bribery of foreign leaders. Most of the information about these activities had been kept secret from Congress and the American people for years.

The Central Intelligence Agency (CIA), particularly, was criticized by Congress and the media. The morality of a democratic government engaging in covert operations abroad became one issue of the debate about the proper role of that agency.

Former Director of the CIA William E. Colby became a principal supporter of the use of intelligence agents in secret operations abroad. He argues that democracies do not have the information needed to make accurate assessments of an adversary's strengths and weaknesses if that adversary is a dictatorship and that a democracy must engage in these operations if it is to survive.

Morton H. Halperin, a former foreign-policy advisor in the Nixon Administration, has challenged the necessity of engaging in such activities. He argues primarily on philosophical grounds. According to Halperin, secret operations are contrary to two basic requirements of democracy: the free flow of information that enables citizens to make choices, and the accountability of the bureaucracy to elected officials. Consequently, he asks for an end to these covert activities.

Does a Power Elite Prevent the People from Ruling?

YES

C. WRIGHT MILLS
*The Structure of Power in American Society**

I

Power has to do with whatever decisions men make about the arrangements under which they live, and about the events which make up the history of their times. Events that are beyond human decision do happen; social arrangements do change without benefit of explicit decision. But insofar as such decisions are made, the problem of who is involved in making them is the basic problem of power. Insofar as they

* From C. Wright Mills, "The Structure of Power in American Society," *The British Journal of Sociology* 9 (March 1958):29–41. Reprinted by permission of Routledge & Kegan Paul Ltd.

could be made but are not, the problem becomes who fails to make them?

We cannot today merely assume that in the last resort men must always be governed by their own consent. For among the means of power which now prevail is the power to manage and to manipulate the consent of men. That we do not know the limits of such power, and that we hope it does have limits, does not remove the fact that much power today is successfully employed without the sanction of the reason or the conscience of the obedient. . . .

II

The power to make decisions of national and international consequence is now so clearly seated in political, military, and economic institutions that other areas of society seem off to the side and, on occasion, readily subordinated to these. The scattered institutions of religion, education and family are increasingly shaped by the big three, in which history-making decisions now regularly occur. Behind this fact there is all the push and drive of a fabulous technology; for these three institutional orders have incorporated this technology and now guide it, even as it shapes and paces their development.

As each has assumed its modern shape, its effects upon the other two have become greater, and the traffic between the three has increased. There is no longer, on the one hand, an economy, and, on the other, a political order, containing a military establishment unimportant to politics and to money making. There is a political economy numerously linked with military order and decision. This triangle of power is now a structural fact, and it is the key to any understanding of the higher circles in America today. For as each of these domains has coincided with the others, as decisions in each have become broader, the leading men of each—the high military, the corporation executives, the political directorate—have tended to come together to form the power elite of America.

The political order, once composed of several dozen states with a weak federal center, has become an executive apparatus which has taken up into itself many powers previously scattered, legislative as well as administrative, and which now reaches into all parts of the social structure. The long-time tendency of business and government to become more closely connected has since World War II reached a new point of explicitness. Neither can now be seen clearly as a distinct world. The growth of executive government does not mean merely the "enlargement of government" as some kind of autonomous bureaucracy: under American conditions, it has meant the ascendency of the corporation man into political eminence. Already during the New Deal, such men had joined the political directorate; as of World War II they came to dominate it. Long involved with government, now they have moved into quite full direction of the economy of the war effort and of the postwar era.

The economy, once a great scatter of small productive units in somewhat automatic balance, has become internally dominated by a few hundred corporations, administratively and politically interrelated, which together hold the keys to economic decision. This economy is at once a permanent-war economy and a private-corporation economy. The most important relations of the corporation to the state now rest on the coincidence between military and corporate interests, as defined by the military and the corporate rich, and accepted by politicians and public. Within the elite as a whole, this coincidence of military domain and corporate realm strengthens both of them and further subordinates the merely political man. Not the party politician, but the corporation executive, is now more likely to sit with the military to answer the question: what is to be done?

The military order, once a slim establishment in a context of civilian distrust, has become the largest and most expensive feature of government; behind smiling public relations, it has all the grim and clumsy efficiency of a great and sprawling bureaucracy. The high military has gained decisive political and economic relevance. The seemingly permanent military threat places a premium upon it and virtually all political and economic actions are now judged in terms of military definitions of reality: the higher military has ascended to a firm position within the power elite of our time.

In part at least this is a result of an historical fact, pivotal for the years since 1939: the attention of the elite has shifted from domestic problems—centered in the 'thirties around slump—to international problems—centered in the 'forties and 'fifties around war. By long historical usage, the government of the United States has been shaped by domestic clash and balance; it does not have suitable agencies and traditions for the democratic handling of international affairs. In considerable part, it is in this vacuum that the power elite has grown.

(i) To understand the unity of this power elite, we must pay attention to the psychology of its several members in their respective milieux. Insofar as the power elite is composed of men of similar origin and education, of similar career and style of life, their unity may be said to rest upon the fact that they are of similar social type, and to lead to the fact of their easy intermingling. This kind of unity reaches its frothier apex in the sharing of that prestige which is to be had in the world of the celebrity. It achieves a more solid culmination in the fact of the interchangeability of positions between the three dominant institutional orders. It is revealed by considerable traffic of personnel within and between these three, as well as by the rise of specialized go-betweens as in the new style high-level lobbying.

(ii) Behind such psychological and social unity are the structure and the mechanics of those institutional hierarchies over which the political directorate, the corporate rich, and the high military now preside. How each of these hierarchies is shaped and what relations it has with the others determine in large part the relations of their rulers. Were these hierarchies scattered and disjointed, then their respective elites might tend to be scattered and disjointed; but if they have many interconnections and points of coinciding interest, then their elites tend to form a coherent kind of grouping. The unity of the elite is not a simple reflection of the unity of institutions, but men and institutions are always related; that is why we must understand the elite today in connection with such institutional trends as the development of a permanent war establishment, alongside a privately incorporated economy, inside a virtual political vacuum. For the men at the top have been selected and formed by such institutional trends.

(iii) Their unity, however, does not rest solely upon psychological similarity and social intermingling, nor entirely upon the structural blending of commanding positions and common interests. At times it is the unity of a more explicit coordination.

To say that these higher circles are increasingly coordinated, that this is *one* basis of their unity, and that at times—as during open war—such coordination is quite wilful, is not to say that the coordination is total or continuous, or even that it is very surefooted. Much less is it to say that the power elite has emerged as the realization of a plot. Its rise cannot be adequately explained in any psychological terms.

Yet we must remember that institutional trends may be defined as opportunities by those who occupy the command posts. Once such opportunities are recognized, men may avail themselves of them. Certain types of men from each of these three areas, more farsighted than others, have actively promoted the liaison even before it took its truly modern shape. Now more have come to see that their several interests can more easily be realized if they work together, in informal as well as in formal ways, and accordingly they have done so.

The idea of the power elite is of course an interpretation. It rests upon and it enables us to make sense of major institutional trends, the social similarities and psychological affinities of the men at the top. But the idea is also based upon what has been happening on the middle and lower levels of power, to which I now turn.

III

There are of course other interpretations of the American system of power. The most usual is that it is a moving balance of many competing interests. The image of balance, at least in America, is derived from the idea of the economic market: in the nineteenth century, the balance was thought to occur between a great scatter of individuals and enterprises; in the twentieth century, it is thought to occur between great interest blocs. In both views, the politician is the key man of power because he is the broker of many conflicting powers.

I believe that the balance and the compromise in American society—the "countervailing powers" and the "veto groups," of parties and associations, of strata and unions—must now be seen as having mainly to do with the middle levels of power. It is these middle levels that the political journalist and the scholar of politics are most likely to understand and to write about—if only because, being mainly middle class themselves, they are closer to them. Moreover these levels provide the noisy content of most "political" news and gossip; the images of these levels are more or less in accord with the folklore of how democracy works; and, if the master image of balance is accepted, many intellectuals, especially in their current patrioteering, are readily able to satisfy such political optimism as they wish to feel. Accordingly, liberal interpretations of what is happening in the United States are now virtually the only interpretations that are widely distributed.

But to believe that the power system reflects a balancing society is, I think, to confuse the present era with earlier times, and to confuse its top and bottom with its middle levels.

By the top levels, as distinguished from the middle, I intend to refer, first of all, to the scope of the decisions that are made. At the top today, these decisions have to do with all the issues of war and peace. They have also to do with slump and poverty which are now so very much problems of international scope. I intend also to refer to whether or not the groups that struggle politically have a chance to gain the positions from which such top decisions are made, and indeed whether their members do usually hope for such top national command. Most of the competing interests which make up the clang and clash of American politics are strictly concerned with their slice of the existing pie. Labor unions, for example, certainly have no policies of an international sort other than those which given unions adopt for the strict economic protection of their members. Neither do farm organizations. The actions of such middle-level powers may indeed have consequence for top-level policy; certainly at times they hamper these policies. But they are not truly concerned with them, which means of course that their influence tends to be quite irresponsible.

The facts of the middle levels may in part be understood in terms of the rise of the power elite. The expanded and centralized and inter-locked hierarchies over which the power elite preside have encroached upon the old balance and relegated it to the middle level. But there are also independent developments of the middle levels. These, it seems to me, are better understood as an affair of intrenched and provincial demands than as a center of national decision. As such, the middle level often seems much more of a stalemate than a moving balance.

(i) The middle level of politics is not a forum in which there are debated the big decisions of national and international life. Such debate is not carried on by nationally responsible parties representing and clarifying alternative policies. There are no such parties in the United States. More and more, fundamental issues never come to any point or decision before the Congress, much less before the electorate in party campaigns. In the case of Formosa, in the spring of 1955, the Congress abdicated all debate concerning events and decisions which surely bor-dered on war. The same is largely true of the 1957 crisis in the Middle East. Such decisions now regularly bypass the Congress, and are never clearly focused issues for public decision.

The American political campaign distracts attention from national and international issues, but that is not to say that there are no issues in these campaigns. In each district and state, issues are set up and watched by organized interests of sovereign local importance. The professional politician is of course a party politician, and the two par-ties are semifeudal organizations: they trade patronage and other fa-vors for votes and for protection. The differences between them, so far as national issues are concerned, are very narrow and very mixed up. Often each seems to be forty-eight parties, one to each state; and accordingly, the politician as campaigner and as congressman is not concerned with national party lines, if any are discernible. Often he is not subject to any effective national party discipline. He speaks for the interests of his own constituency, and he is concerned with national issues only insofar as they affect the interests effectively organized there, and hence his chances of reelection. That is why, when he does speak of national matters, the result is so often such an empty rhetoric. Seated in his sovereign locality, the politician is not at the national summit. He is on and of the middle levels of power.

(ii) Politics is not an arena in which free and independent organi-zations truly connect the lower and middle levels of society with the top levels of decision. Such organizations are not an effective and major part of American life today. As more people are drawn into the political arena, their associations become mass in scale, and the power of the individual becomes dependent upon them; to the extent that they are effective, they have become larger, and to that extent they have become less accessible to the influence of the individual. This is a central fact about associations in any mass society: it is of most consequence for political parties and for trade unions.

In the 'thirties, it often seemed that labor would become an insurgent power independent of corporation and state. Organized labor was then emerging for the first time on an American scale, and the only political sense of direction it needed was the slogan, "organize the unorganized." Now without the mandate of the slump, labor remains without political direction. Instead of economic and political struggles it has become deeply entangled in administrative routines with both corporation and state. One of its major functions, as a vested interest of the new society, is the regulation of such irregular tendencies as may occur among the rank and file.

There is nothing, it seems to me, in the makeup of the current labor leadership to allow us to expect that it can or that it will lead, rather than merely react. Insofar as it fights at all it fights over a share of the goods of a single way of life and not over that way of life itself. The typical labor leader in the USA today is better understood as an adaptive creature of the main business drift than as an independent actor in a truly national context.

(iii) The idea that this society is a balance of powers requires us to assume that the units in balance are of more or less equal power and that they are truly independent of one another. These assumptions have rested, it seems clear, upon the historical importance of a large and independent middle class. In the latter nineteenth century and during the Progressive Era, such a class of farmers and small businessmen fought politically—and lost—their last struggle for a paramount role in national decision. Even then, their aspirations seemed bound to their own imagined past.

This old, independent middle class has of course declined. On the most generous count, it is now 40 percent of the total middle class (at most 20 percent of the total labor force). Moreover, it has become politically as well as economically dependent upon the state, most notably in the case of the subsidized farmer.

The *new* middle class of white-collar employees is certainly not the political pivot of any balancing society. It is in no way politically unified. Its unions, such as they are, often serve merely to incorporate it as hanger-on of the labor interest. For a considerable period, the old middle class *was* an independent base of power; the new middle class cannot be. Political freedom and economic security *were* anchored in small and independent properties; they are not anchored in the worlds of the white-collar job. Scattered property holders were economically united by more or less free markets; the jobs of the new middle class are integrated by corporate authority. Economically, the white-collar classes are in the same condition as wage workers; politically, they are in a worse condition, for they are not organized. They are no vanguard of historic change; they are at best a rear guard of the welfare state.

The agrarian revolt of the 'nineties, the small-business revolt that has been more or less continuous since the 'eighties, the labor revolt of the 'thirties—each of these has failed as an independent movement which could countervail against the powers that be; they have failed as politically autonomous third parties. But they have succeeded, in varying degree, as interests vested in the expanded corporation and state; they have succeeded as parochial interests seated in particular districts, in local divisions of the two parties, and in the Congress. What they would become, in short, are well-established features of the *middle* levels of balancing power, on which we may now observe all those strata and interests which in the course of American history have been defeated in their bids for top power or which have never made such bids.

Fifty years ago many observers thought of the American state as a mask behind which an invisible government operated. But nowadays, much of what was called the old lobby, visible or invisible, is part of the quite visible government. The "governmentalization of the lobby" has proceeded in both the legislative and the executive domain, as well as between them. The executive bureaucracy becomes not only the center of decision but also the arena within which major conflicts of power are resolved or denied resolution. "Administration" replaces electoral politics; the maneuvering of cliques (which include leading senators as well as civil servants) replaces the open clash of parties.

The shift of corporation men into the political directorate has accelerated the decline of the politicians in the Congress to the middle levels of power; the formation of the power elite rests in part upon this relegation. It rests also upon the semiorganized stalemate of the interests of sovereign localities, into which the legislative function has so largely fallen; upon the virtually complete absence of a civil service that is a politically neutral but politically relevant, depository of brainpower and executive skill; and it rests upon the increased official secrecy behind which great decisions are made without benefit of public or even of congressional debate. . . .

IV

. . . The top of modern American society is increasingly unified, and often seems wilfully coordinated: at the top there has emerged an elite whose power probably exceeds that of any small group of men in world history. The middle levels are often a drifting set of stalemated forces: the middle does not link the bottom with the top. The bottom of this society is politically fragmented, and even as a passive fact, increasingly powerless: at the bottom there is emerging a mass society.

These developments, I believe, can be correctly understood neither in terms of the liberal nor the Marxian interpretation of politics and history. Both these ways of thought arose as guidelines to reflection about a type of society which does not now exist in the United States. We confront there a new kind of social structure, which embodies elements and tendencies of all modern society, but in which they have assumed a more naked and flamboyant prominence.

That does not mean that we must give up the ideals of these classic political expectations. I believe that both have been concerned with the problem of rationality and of freedom: liberalism, with freedom and rationality as supreme facts about the individual; Marxism, as supreme facts about man's role in the political making of history. What I have said here, I suppose, may be taken as an attempt to make evident why the ideas of freedom and of rationality now so often seem so ambiguous in the new society of the United States of America.

Does a Power Elite Prevent the People from Ruling?

NO

ROBERT A. DAHL
*Rule by the Few as a Solution**

. . . The idea that representative institutions conceal a ruling elite has long been popular in the United States among observers disillusioned by the visible shortcomings of the American political system. Americans with unconventional and unpopular views who feel thwarted in their efforts to change "the system" sometimes attribute their defeats to a half-hidden ruling class. Thus Socialists and Populists have thought

* From Robert A. Dahl, "Rule by the Few as a Solution," in *Democracy in the United States: Promise and Performance*, 3d ed. (Skokie, Ill.: Rand McNally, 1976), pp. 35–40. © 1976 Rand McNally College Publishing Company. Reprinted by permission.

the country to be run by Wall Street bankers. Many extreme conservatives believe that a small eastern "liberal establishment" dominates communications, education, religion, finance, the Department of State, and, indeed, government generally. In recent years, the position of a dominant elite has often been assigned to "the military-industrial complex." In 1970, half the people in a national survey agreed with the statement that "the government is pretty much run by a few big interests looking out for themselves." Only 14 percent agreed that "it is run for the benefit of all the people."[1]

SOURCES OF OLIGARCHIC TENDENCIES

The view that in practice rule by the people means oligarchy draws a good deal of its strength from certain general characteristics of political life; for example, one of the writers quoted a moment ago seems to have been outraged to discover that his own Socialist party preached democracy but practiced oligarchy. How was it possible that parties dedicated to democratic ideals could be so undemocratic in their own internal government? His answer stressed a number of persistent sources for the tendency to oligarchy. These included:

- The need for organization, which in turn enhances the power of an organization's leaders.
- The impossibility of direct government among large numbers of persons, hence the need for representation, which increases the power of the representatives in comparison with the voters.
- Certain psychological tendencies among "the masses": their desire to be led, gratitude toward their leaders, and a tendency to revere their leaders and magnify their virtues and capacities.
- Greater skills and competence of leaders, the inability of organizations to function without them, the incompetence of the mass of the people in most organizations.
- The financial power of the leaders, and their control over the organization's bureaucracy and technical services.
- Psychological changes in the leaders, particularly their increased sense of their own indispensability and their enhanced desire for power.[2]

Probably the strongest aspect of this theory—and as we shall see, its weakest, too—is its focus on persistent inequalities in power and influence that can be seen in every political system, including "democratic" systems. Thus the theory fastens on a problem that, as we have already seen, is definite and serious.

CAUSES OF INEQUALITIES   R-S-I

. . . equality and consent are threatened by persistent inequalities. We noted that among the causes of political inequalities are social arrangements, individual characteristics, and in representative governments, the very process of representation itself. These factors in turn help to produce differences in political *resources, skills,* and *incentives.*

Resources

Political resources consist of all the means available to one for influencing the behavior of other people. In this country, political resources include access to money, hence wealth, income, and credit. They also include control over jobs; the ballot; popularity, friendships, reputation, and esteem in the eyes of others; knowledge or access to knowledge; control over mass media and other means of communication; and many other things.

One important political resource easily lost sight of is *time*. If you have no time left over from your other affairs to try to change the conduct of government, you are unlikely to be in a position to exercise much influence over it. Conversely, the more time you have available, the better your chances. Time is one of the most critical resources that professional politicians have. By hook or crook they manage to spend almost full time at the game of politics, while most of us devote only a few hours out of the year.

Still another resource which is unevenly distributed—inevitably so—is *officiality*. Constitutional rules, law, and practice allow officials to do things that ordinary citizens cannot. A major difference between the policeman and the man he arrests is that the office of the policeman entitles him to make arrests, using force if necessary. Official position invariably allocates to officials some resources that are denied to others: thus only judges can decide legal cases and only legislators can pass laws. By conferring officiality on the winner and denying it to the loser, elections award extra resources to the winner. In 1876, one electoral vote—a rather dubious one at that—was enough to confer the presidency on Rutherford B. Hayes rather than on Samuel J. Tilden. Even in that age of weak presidents, the presidency gave to Hayes important legal authority, such as the veto, that was denied to Tilden.

Allied to officiality as a resource, but not identical with it, is _legitimate authority_: the widespread view that an individual or an office ought to be obeyed. Thus the president is powerful not only because of what the Constitution authorizes him to do but also because of what history and tradition authorize him to do.

Except perhaps for the ballot, and that only recently, all these resources are unequally distributed among adult American citizens. Hence it should not be too surprising if various citizens exert unequal influence on the conduct of government.

Skills

Even if two individuals had practically identical resources, they might, nonetheless, be unable to exercise equal influence over the conduct of government if one of them were politically more _skillful_. (Political skill might be considered, of course, as a special kind of resource, but it seems more illuminating to think of it as a capacity for using one's resources efficiently.) Although almost all political observers agree with the political philosopher Niccolò Machiavelli (1469–1527) that differences in political skills exist and are important, political skills, unlike military, entrepreneurial, artistic, and scientific skills, are hard to pin down and not well understood.

Incentives

Even if two individuals had identical resources and skills, one might exercise more influence over government than another simply because he or she _wanted_ to influence the government and the other did not. If you do not care what the government is doing, you probably will not use your resources and skills to influence it; the more you care, the more of your resources you will be willing to invest and the harder you will try to acquire the necessary skills. Thus, your influence is partly dependent on your goals and estimates of the best strategies for obtaining them. We might call this third factor _incentives_ for acquiring political skills and for employing resources to influence the conduct of government.

While some causes of political inequalities can be reduced or removed, others seem impossible to uproot. Can we ever get rid of all differences in political incentives? Should we even try to? Will differences in incentives not inevitably lead to differences in skills? Will not appointed and elected officials to whom authority is delegated inevitably have access to more political resources than do ordinary citizens?

Extreme advocates of the view that all political systems are dominated by a ruling group argue that so much inequality in resources, skills, and incentives is bound to persist as to make rule by the people impossible and rule by a particular class, stratum, or elite inevitable. However, to leap from the premise of inequality to the conclusion that all political systems are ruled by an elite entails some highly questionable assumptions.

A COMMON ERROR IN POLITICAL THINKING

In fact to equate all politics with oligarchy is to fall into the common error of dividing things into two mutually exclusive categories: good-bad, we-they, saints-sinners, Americans-foreigners, democracy-dictatorship. This is sometimes called the "fallacy of dichotomous thinking."

Most of us know that outside the domain of politics things can often be thought about as if they were located along a continuous line. Thinking in continuities is more flexible and more subtle than dichotomous thought. I think most of us would agree that it is not necessary, and is often unprofitable, to divide human beings, for example, into just two groups: tall-short, lean-fat, blond-brunette, healthy-sick, nice-vicious, etc. We all recognize that while it is convenient for some purposes to dichotomize, for others it is senseless. Imagine an insurance company that divided applicants for life insurance into young-old; a judicial system that knew only the categories guilty of murder or innocent; an educational system in which students were catagorized as either idiots or geniuses!

Yet for many people it evidently seems reasonable to believe that if a country is not an ally, it is an enemy; if a political system is not a democracy, it is a dictatorship. And if the people do not rule, there must be a ruling elite.

The difficulty with two exclusive categories like these is that they often rob us of important distinctions. Even if the people do not rule, and political equality and consent are by no means fully achieved, are there not significant differences in political systems? Would it not make sense to say that while no country has a truly "democratic" political system, some systems are *significantly more* democratic than others? An alternative interpretation, which answers in the affirmative, is the theory of polyarchy—a political system with important democratic elements which also contains some nondemocratic elements.

SUMMARY

1. An important line of thought argues that rule by the people is impossible and in practice every political system, whatever its forms, is ruled by an elite.

2. This line of argument draws strong support from the observable facts that (a) inequalities in power and influence seem to persist in all associations and societies despite their professed ideals, and (b) some of the causes of these inequalities seem extremely difficult, perhaps impossible, to remove.

3. However, the premise that inequalities in power and resources exist does not warrant the conclusion that a ruling class exists.

4. If we are to avoid the fallacy of dichotomous thinking, we need to consider the possibility that even if the people do not rule, and even though political equality and consent are by no means fully achieved, there may, nonetheless, be significant differences in the extent to which these goals are achieved in different political systems.

NOTES

1. Arthur H. Miller, "Political Issues and Trust in Government: 1964–1970," *The American Political Science Review* 68(September 1974):951–972, Table 1, 973.
2. Robert Michels, *Political Parties* (New York: The Free Press, 1966).

QUESTIONS FOR DISCUSSION

1. What are the social, economic, and political criteria for determining whether or not a power elite exists in American society?

2. What criticisms can be made of Mills' theory of power in America?

3. Mills' book, *The Power Elite,* was published in 1956. How would you evaluate the validity of his theory in terms of the behavior of the corporations, the military, and the politicians in the past two decades?

4. Is there a power elite in fascist or communist political systems? If so, what are the similarities to the American power elite? If not, what are the differences?

5. Study a particular policy area (taxation, public housing, environmental protection, racial integration, or energy) or event (the Vietnam war, the resignation of President Nixon, or the cancellation of the B-1 bomber program). Evaluate it in terms of the power elite theory. Does the theory offer a plausible explanation for what happened in your case study?

SUGGESTED READINGS

Dahl, Robert A. "A Critique of the Ruling Elite Model." *The American Political Science Review* 52(June 1958):463–469.

Domhoff, G. William. *Who Rules America?* Englewood Cliffs, N.J.: Prentice-Hall, 1967.

——, and Hoyt B. Ballard, eds. *C. Wright Mills and the Power Elite*. Boston: Beacon Press, 1968.

Mayo, Henry B. *An Introduction to Democratic Theory*. New York: Oxford University Press, 1960.

Mills, C. Wright. *The Power Elite*. New York: Oxford University Press, 1956.

Olsen, Marvin E., ed. *Power in Societies*. New York: Macmillan, 1970.

Parenti, Michael. *Democracy for the Few*. New York: St. Martin's Press, 1974.

Rose, Arnold M. *The Power Structure: Political Process in American Society*. New York: Oxford University Press, 1967.

Walker, Jack L. "A Critique of the Elitist Theory of Democracy." *The American Political Science Review* 60(June 1966):285–295.

Wolfe, Alan. *The Seamy Side of Democracy*. New York: David McKay, 1973.

Can the United States Engage in Covert Operations Abroad and Still Be Considered a Democracy?

YES

WILLIAM E. COLBY
*The View from Langley**

If I said I am happy to be here, my statement might be used to challenge the credibility of the Intelligence Community. But I am happy to serve under a Constitution which, in my view, brings me here. While I might have constructed the program of this conference somewhat differently, it reflects the workings of our free society. It is thus incum-

* From *The CIA File*, Robert L. Borosage and John Marks, editors, pp. 181–187. Copyright © 1975, 1976 by the Center for National Security Studies. Reprinted by permission of Grossman Publishers.

bent upon our government officials to explain to the public the functions and activities of their particular organizations, and I include in this, as you can see by my presence here, the Central Intelligence Agency [CIA] and the Intelligence Community.

Our military forces must be responsive to our public, but our public does not demand that our war plans be published. Our judicial system must meet the public's standards of justice, but our judicial conferences and grand-jury proceedings are not conducted in public. It is even necessary for the Congress to conduct some of its business in executive session, while remaining accountable to the voters for the legislation it passes. Similarly, I believe it is feasible to explain to the American people the functions and activities of CIA and the Intelligence Community while at the same time maintaining the necessary secrecy of the sources and methods of our intelligence, which would dry up if publicized.

In part, I can respond to legitimate public inquiry through general discussions of our activities, omitting the critical names and details. In other respects, I believe I can respond to the public's need for assurance by reporting fully to congressional committees or other bodies appointed by the public's representatives to receive and retain this sensitive information and to make value judgments about our functions and activities. Another test of our effectiveness lies in the opinions of those in the executive and legislature who are provided the intelligence results of our operational and analytical efforts, but not how these were obtained and produced. There is a final control, of course, in the fact that some of our activities, if badly handled, come to public attention in a somewhat clamorous way.

There have been some "bad secrets" concerning intelligence; their exposure by our academic, journalist, and political critics certainly is an essential part of the workings of our Constitution. There have been some "nonsecrets" which did not need to be secret; I have undertaken a program of bringing these into the open. But I think that responsible Americans realize that our country must protect some "good secrets." It is for this reason that I am proposing legislation which will impose penalties on those who take upon themselves the choice of which secrets to reveal, rather than relying on the established declassification procedures of our government. I might clarify that my proposal would not apply to the news media or any other persons than those who consciously assume the obligation to respect the secrecy to which they are admitted as government employees or similar, and that the reasonableness of the classification would be subject to judicial review.

If our laws provide for criminal penalties for the unauthorized disclosure of certain census information, income-tax information, Selective Service information, and cotton and other agricultural statistics, I think it reasonable that there should also be penalties for the unauthorized disclosure of foreign-intelligence sources and methods upon which the safety of the nation could well depend.

The title of this conference is "The CIA and Covert Action." In my letter accepting Mr. [Robert] Borosage's* invitation to appear here, I commented that I was somewhat surprised that there was no attempt in the agenda to examine the need for the contribution that objective and independent intelligence can make to policy decisions. In fact, however, I note that there has been considerable discussion of our intelligence activities, such as the U-2, in addition to our covert-action role.

In this regard, I would like to clarify that the predominant focus of CIA and the Intelligence Community today is clearly on our information and analytical responsibilities. In this field, we endeavor to serve the executive branch by providing intelligence on the facts of the world about us and our assessments of likely future developments. We also try to serve the Congress and the public by providing the output of the intelligence investment made by the United States, to support them in their role in American decision making. Thus, CIA has appeared before eighteen committees on twenty-eight occasions this year (Armed Services, Appropriations, Foreign Affairs, Atomic Energy, and Economics), testifying on a variety of subjects. We have cleared for publication some of this testimony on the economies of the Soviet Union and China and on the Soviet presence in the Indian Ocean. We also produce a number of unclassified publications and distribute them through the Library of Congress to over two hundred libraries and institutes around the country, as well as making publicly available our reports of foreign broadcasts and translated documents. In addition, I have talked with 132 newsmen in the past year, and about 100 have come to CIA for briefings by our analysts on substantive questions involving foreign countries, thus benefiting from our accumulated information from our most sensitive sources.

It is a strange anomaly that our country makes publicly available vast amounts of material on the United States, whereas the corresponding material about our potential adversaries must be collected by intelligence techniques at a cost of hundreds of millions of dollars. In this situation, if we cannot protect our intelligence sources and methods, I fear we may reach a situation in which our adversaries profit from our openness while we are blinded by their secrecy.

Dr. [Herbert] Scoville [a former Deputy Director of the CIA] has quite properly indicated the revolution in intelligence which has been

---

* Robert Borosage is Director of the Center for National Security Studies.

achieved through the growth of technology over the past two decades. This intelligence, however, is still limited to what physically exists. It does not give us the intentions, the research ideas, and the decision-making dynamics of the countries which might pose a threat to the United States. In today's accelerating technology, we are condemned always to be well behind if we rely only on what has appeared in the marketplace instead of on what is planned for the future. In addition, in a world which can destroy itself through misunderstanding or miscalculation, it is important that our leaders have a clear perception of the motives, intentions, and strategies of other powers so that they can be deterred, negotiated about, or countered in the interests of peace or, if necessary, the ultimate security of our country. These kinds of insights cannot be obtained only through technical means or analysis. From closed societies they can only be obtained by secret intelligence operations, without which our country must risk subordination to possible adversaries.

To turn to *covert action,* which is included in those "other functions and duties related to intelligence affecting the national security as the National Security Council may from time to time direct," as stated in the National Security Act, there is debate as to the degree Congress intended CIA to engage in these actions when passing the legislation in 1947. The [Office of Strategic Services, 1942–1945] OSS precedent, the National Security Act's clear authorization of functions "related to intelligence" by reason of secret techniques and frequent use of the same assets, and the periodic briefings given to the Congress over the years through its authorized committees clearly establish the agency's authority to perform these functions.

The agency conducts such activities only when specifically authorized by the National Security Council. Thus, CIA covert actions reflect national policy. National policy has been in a state of change, and CIA's involvement in covert action has correspondingly changed. In the early days of the "Cold War," when national policy makers believed it essential to confront an aggressive Communist subversive effort in many areas of the world and in the international-organizational sphere, there was a great deal of this sort of effort. Some was revealed in the 1967 disclosures of our relationships with various American groups which helped their country to present the American position and support America's friends in this arena during the 1950s and 1960s. The record is clear that the assistance given to these institutions by the CIA was to enable them to participate in *foreign* activities; there was no attempt to interfere in internal American domestic activities. CIA aid helped such groups as the National Student Association to articulate the views of American students abroad and meet the Communist-subsidized effort to develop a panoply of international-front organizations. I might quote Ms. Gloria Steinem, one of those so assisted, who commented that the CIA "wanted to do what we wanted to do—present a healthy, diverse view of the United States. . . . I never felt I was being dictated to at all."

There have also been, and are still, certain situations in the world in which some discreet support can assist America's friends against her adversaries in their contest for control of a foreign nation's political direction. While these instances are few today compared to the 1950s, I believe it only prudent for our nation to be able to act in such situations, and thereby forestall greater difficulties for us in the future.

In other situations, especially after Nikita Khrushchev's enthusiastic espousal of the thesis of "wars of national liberation," the United States believed it essential to provide paramilitary support to certain groups and nations. In 1962 President Kennedy, for national-policy reasons, did not want to use the uniformed forces of the United States in Laos, but also did not want to be limited to a mere diplomatic protest against the continued presence of five thousand North Vietnamese troops in Laos in violation of the Geneva Accords, and their expansion of control over communities who wished to resist them.

Thus CIA was directed to provide support to those communities, a duty which grew to a major effort, known and approved by the Lao government, but not confronting North Vietnam and its allies with a direct and overt U.S. challenge. Mr. [Fred] Branfman [Director of the Indochina Resource Center] has told you of some of the terrible human problems involved in any war when it grows to a conventional scale involving artillery, air bombardment, and so forth. What has perhaps not been fully perceived is that the American assistance to this effort involved a small commitment of CIA Americans and a small expenditure over the many years in which this action was undertaken; and that, as a result of the defensive efforts of the forces supported by CIA, the battle lines at the end of the period were essentially unchanged from those at the opening.

As with the Bay of Pigs, when the activity became too large, it no longer remained secret. But I think the CIA people who conducted this effort deserve the praise of our citizens for the effective but modest manner in which President Kennedy's mission was carried out—a mission, by the way, that cost the lives of eight CIA officers there. This activity was reported to and appropriated for on a regular basis by the authorized elements of the Congress—the war was no secret from them.

But it is clear that American policy today is different from when it was confronting world-wide Communist subversion in the 1950s or Communist insurgency in the 1960s. Our involvement has been reduced in many areas, in part, I might add, by the fact that many of the

Communist efforts during those years were unsuccessful. CIA's covert actions in many of these instances thus assisted in laying the groundwork for the new period of détente which we pursue in our relationships with the Communist world today. As a result, CIA's involvement in covert action is very small indeed compared to those earlier periods. I do not say that we do not now conduct such activities; I merely state that they are undertaken only as directed by the National Security Council, they are frankly and regularly reported to the appropriate committees of the Congress, and they require only a small proportion of our effort at this time.

I am not being more precise on these various covert actions. Some you are aware of because of exposure, leak, or failure—such as the Bay of Pigs. Some you are not aware of because they have been effectively handled and have achieved their objectives. I abide by what one president said about CIA, that our successes are unheralded and our failures trumpeted.

It is advocated by some that the United States abandon covert action. This is a legitimate question, and in light of current American policy, as I have indicated, it would not have a major impact on our current activities or the current security of the United States. I believe, however, that a sovereign nation must look ahead to changing circumstances. I can envisage situations in which the United States might well need to conduct covert action in the face of some new threat that developed in the world.

In 1924 we sank the brand new battleship *Washington* as a demonstration of our belief in disarmament. At about the same time, we disbanded an intelligence element in the Department of State on the thesis that "gentlemen do not read each other's mail." During the same period, we declined the international burdens of membership in the League of Nations. I believe our post-World War II history, with all its costs, constituted an improvement on our post-World War I policies and did avoid a World War III during these thirty years. I thus would think it mistaken to deprive our nation of the possibility of some moderate covert-action response to a foreign problem and leave us with nothing between a diplomatic protest and sending the marines.

Bills in Congress today would amend the National Security Act of 1947 to clarify a requirement that the Congress be kept informed "in such manner as the Congress may prescribe" of any "functions and duties related to intelligence affecting the national security" carried out by CIA. I fully support this change in the CIA's basic legislative charter, which would establish in law the practice we follow today.

In Mr. Borosage's announcement with respect to this conference, he expressed the concern that untrammeled secret power poses a threat to our liberties and that our program of covert activities abroad must be reexamined before similar techniques are employed to subvert our democracy at home. I have indicated that I do not believe that CIA's covert actions abroad constitute "untrammeled secret power" in view of our responsibilities to the executive and to the legislature.

With respect to the second part of Mr. Borosage's concern about these techniques being employed in the United States, I again point to a bill being considered in the Congress which would make it crystal clear that CIA's activities lie only in the field of *foreign* intelligence by adding the word "foreign" wherever the word "intelligence" appears in the National Security Act. I fully support this wording and, in fact, originally suggested it in my confirmation hearings. My predecessors and I have admitted that CIA did exceed its authority in several instances with respect to Watergate. We have taken steps within the Agency to ensure that such actions do not occur again. The proposed change in our legislative charter would make this a matter of statutory direction. But the fact that a retired CIA employee becomes involved in some illegal activity in the United States should no more eliminate a function essential to our nation than should the fact that a Vietnam veteran commits a crime be used as the basis to deprive the United States Army of its pistols. And the concern of all of us that CIA not be used against U.S. citizens should not bar it from lawfully collecting that foreign intelligence available within the United States.

Can the United States Engage in Covert Operations Abroad and Still Be Considered a Democracy?

NO

MORTON H. HALPERIN
   Covert Operations*

Mr. Chairman, I consider it an honor and a privilege to be invited to testify before this committee on the question of covert operations. From this committee's unprecedented review of the activities of our

* From U.S., Congress, Senate, Select Committee to Study Government Operations with Respect to Intelligence Activities, *Intelligence Activities*, Senate Resolution 21, Hearings, 94th Cong., 1st sess., 1975, vol. 7: *Covert Action*, pp. 57–60.

intelligence agencies must come a new definition of what the American people will permit to be done in their name abroad and allow to be done to them at home. No problem is more difficult and contentious than that of covert operations.

It appears that I have been cast in the role of the spokesman on the left on this issue. It is an unaccustomed position and one that I accept with some discomfort. It should be clear to the committee that there are a great many thoughtful and articulate Americans whose views on this question are considerably to the left of mine, at least as these terms are normally used. I would not presume to speak for them. Nor, Mr. Chairman, am I speaking for the organizations with which I am now affiliated. I appear, as you requested, as an individual to present my own views.

I believe that the United States should no longer maintain a career service for the purpose of conducting covert operations and covert intelligence collection by human means.

I believe also that the United States should eschew as a matter of national policy the conduct of covert operations. The prohibition should be embodied in a law with the same basic structure as the statute on assassinations which the committee has already recommended.

These proposals are not put forward because I believe that no covert operation could ever be in the American interest or because I could not conceive of circumstances where the capability to conduct a covert operation might seem to be important to the security of the United States. I can in fact envision such circumstances. However, I believe that the potential for covert operation has been greatly overrated and in my view the possible benefits of a few conceivable operations are far outweighed by the costs to our society of maintaining a capability for covert operations and permitting the executive branch to conduct such operations.

The revelations made by this committee in its report on assassinations are in themselves sufficient to make my case. I will rely on these illustrations not because there are not many others of which we are all aware but rather to avoid any dispute over facts.

The case against covert operations is really very simple. Such operations are incompatible with our democratic institutions, with congressional and public control over foreign policy decisions, with our constitutional rights, and with the principles and ideals that this Republic stands for in the world.

Let me begin with the last point. The CIA operations described in this committee's assassination report are disturbing not only because murder was planned and attempted, but also because the operations went against the very principles we claim to stand for in the world. In Cuba, the Congo, and Chile we intervened in the internal affairs of other countries on our own initiative and in the belief that we had the right to determine for others what kind of government their country needed and who posed a threat to their welfare. We acted not because we believed those that we opposed were the tools of foreign powers kept in office by outside intervention; rather we acted in the face of assertions by the intelligence community that the leaders we opposed were popular in their own lands.

In the Congo our efforts were directed at keeping [Patrice] Lumumba [a left-wing nationalist leader in the Democratic Republic of the Congo, 1960–1961] from speaking and keeping the parliament from meeting because we believed that allowing him to speak or allowing the parliament to meet would have meant that Lumumba would be back in office. In Chile we preached to the military the need to ignore the constitution and to overthrow a democratically elected government. We warned that the alternative was deprivation and poverty for the Chilean people.

All of these things were undertaken in the name of the United States but without the knowledge or consent of the Congress or the public. Nor could such consent have been obtained. Can you imagine a president asking the Congress to approve a program of seeking to reduce the people of Chile to poverty unless their military, in violation of the constitution, seized power; or the president seeking funds to be used to keep the Congolese parliament out of session so that it could not vote Lumumba back into office; or the authority to promise leniency to Mafia leaders if they would help to assassinate Castro? These programs were kept covert not only because we would be embarrassed abroad, but also because they would not be approved if they were subjected to the same congressional and public scrutiny as other programs. That is one major evil of having a covert capability and allowing our presidents to order such operations. The assassinations themselves may have been an aberration; the means and purposes of our interventions were not.

Another inevitable consequence of conducting covert operations is that it distorts our democratic system in ways that we are only beginning to understand. Covert operations by their nature cannot be debated openly in ways required by our constitutional system. Moreover, they require efforts to avoid the structures that normally govern the conduct of our officials. One obvious area is lying to the public and the Congress.

We should not forget that the erosion of trust between the government and the people in this Republic began with the U-2 affair and has continued through a series of covert operations including Chile. Whether or not perjury was committed—and I see little doubt that it was—it is surely the case that the Congress and the public were systematically deceived about the American intervention in Chile. Such deception must stop if we are to regain the trust needed in this nation; it cannot stop as long as we are conducting covert operations. Given the current absence of consensus on foreign policy goals, such operations will not be accorded the deference they were given in the past. Critics will press as they do now on Angola and Portugal. And administrations will feel the need and the right to lie.

Surely at this point in time it is not necessary to remind ourselves of the certainty that the techniques that we apply to others will inevitably be turned on the American people by our own intelligence services. Whether that extends to assassination has sadly become an open question but little else is.

The existence of a capability for covert operations inevitably distorts the decision-making process. Presidents confronted with hard choices in foreign policy have to face a variety of audiences in framing a policy. This in my view is all to the good. It keeps us from straying far from our principles, from what a majority of our citizens are prepared to support, from a policy out of touch with reality. The overt policies of the American government ultimately come under public scrutiny and congressional debate. Long before that they have been subject to bureaucratic struggles in which the opponents of the policy have their day in court.

Our intelligence analysts are free to explain why the policy will not work. With covert policies none of this happens. Intelligence-community analysts were not told of the plans to assassinate Castro and so they did not do the careful analysis necessary to support their view that it would make no difference. The Assistant Secretary of State for Latin America was kept in the dark about Track II [a plan initiated by the Nixon Administration to foment a military coup against Salvadore Allende, the leftist leader who became President of Chile] in Chile so he was not able to argue against it and inadvertently deceived the public.

In fact, I would argue that the route of covert operations is often chosen precisely to avoid the bureaucratic and public debate which our presidents and their closest advisers come to despise. That is precisely what is wrong with them. Our presidents should not be able to conduct in secret operations which violate our principles, jeopardize our rights, and have not been subject to the checks and balances which normally keep policies in line.

You will hear, I am sure, various proposals to cure these evils by better forms of control. Such proposals are important, well-intentioned, and certainly far better than the status quo, but I have come to believe that they cannot succeed in curing the evils inherent in having a covert capability. The only weapon that opponents of a presidential policy, inside or outside the executive branch, have is public debate. If a policy can be debated openly, then Congress may be persuaded to constrain the president and public pressure may force a change in policy. But if secrecy is accepted as the norm and as legitimate, then the checks put on covert operations can easily be ignored.

Let me conclude by violating my self-imposed rule to draw only on cases in the assassination report and discuss some rumored current covert operations. I ask you to assume (since I assume that the committee is not prepared to confirm) that the United States now has underway a major program of intervention in Angola and a plan to create an independent Azores Republic should that prove "necessary." I ask you to consider how the Congress and the public would treat these proposals if they were presented openly for public debate. Congress could, in principle, vote publicly to send aid to one side in the Angolan civil war as other nations are doing and we could publicly invite the people of the Azores to choose independence and gain our support. But because we maintain a covert operations capability and because such operations are permitted, the president can avoid debate in the bureaucracy and with the Congress and the public. We can be drawn deeply into commitments without our consent and have actions taken on our behalf that we have no opportunity to stop by public pressure or to punish at the polls.

Mr. Chairman, in response to the position I have outlined briefly this morning, one is confronted with a parade of hypothetical horribles—the terrorists with the nuclear weapons, a permanent oil embargo and the like. To these I would reply in part that such scenarios seem implausible and should they occur the likelihood that covert capabilities could make an important difference also seems remote. As to the consequences of legislating a total prohibition in light of the possible unexpected catastrophe, I am content to call your attention back to the committee's excellent treatment of this issue in your assassination report.

This country is not, in my view, in such dangerous peril that it need continue to violate its own principles and ignore its own constitutional system to perpetuate a capability which has led to assassination attempts, to perjury, and to the subversion of all that we stand for at home and abroad. We are secure and we are free. Covert operations have no place in that world.

QUESTIONS FOR DISCUSSION

1. What arguments are used to justify covert operations abroad?
2. What are the dangers to a democracy when a government engages in covert operations abroad?
3. Should any limits be placed on covert operations? If so, what should these limits be? If not, why should there be no limits?
4. Was the United States acting in an undemocratic manner when it engaged in covert operations against Germany and Japan in World War II?
5. Do dictatorships have advantages over democracies in the conduct of foreign policy?

SUGGESTED READINGS

Borosage, Robert, and John D. Marks, eds. *The CIA File.* New York: Grossman, 1976.

Cline, Ray S. *Secrets, Spies and Scholars: Blueprint of the Essential CIA.* Washington, D.C.: Acropolis Books, 1976.

Copeland, Miles. *Without Cloak or Dagger.* New York: Simon & Schuster, 1974.

Frank, Thomas M., and Edward Weisband, eds. *Secrecy and Foreign Policy.* New York: Oxford University Press, 1974.

Halperin, Morton H., et al. *The Lawless State: The Crimes of the U.S. Intelligence Agencies.* New York: Penguin Books, 1976.

Report to the President by the Commission on CIA Activities Within the United States (The Rockefeller Report). Washington, D.C.: Government Printing Office, 1975.

Rositzke, Harry. *The CIA's Secret Operations: Espionage, Counterespionage and Covert Action.* New York: Reader's Digest Press, 1977.

Ross, Thomas B., and David Wise. *The Invisible Government.* New York: Vintage, 1974.

U.S. Congress. House. Select Committee on Intelligence. *U.S. Intelligence Agencies and Activities.* Hearings, vols. 1–6, 94th Cong., 1st sess., July–December 1975. (The *Village Voice* published the Committee's secret report on February 16 and 23, 1976.)

U.S. Congress. Senate. Select Committee to Study Governmental Operations with Respect to Intelligence Activities. *Covert Action in Chile: 1963–1973.* Staff Report, 94th Cong., 1st sess., 1975.

U.S. Congress. Senate. Select Committee to Study Governmental Operations with Respect to Intelligence Activities. *Final Report.* 94th Cong., 1st and 2nd sess., 1976.

2.

Are the Fundamental Rules of the American Political System Fair?

The Constitution establishes the ground rules governing the American political system. What the Founding Fathers believed and how they acted at the Constitutional Convention at Philadelphia in 1787 reveal much about the establishment of the "rules of the game" in the late eighteenth century and suggest questions about the effect these rules might have on political behavior thereafter.

Historians disagree sharply about the Framers of the Constitution. Some have challenged the view that the men who met at Philadelphia were idealists. Their characterizations of the Framers range from that of self-serving leaders seeking to promote the interests of their own economic class to that of pragmatic people encompassing profound differences of economic interest and political philosophy.

The basic facts about the Constitution, however, are generally accepted. The Constitutional Convention was called after six years under the Articles of Confederation. That document established a league of friendship among the states, rather than a national government. The period under the Articles of Confederation was marked by an inability to negotiate commercial treaties, widespread debt, Shays' rebellion (a revolt of poor Massachusetts farmers), and economic decay. Most of the Framers, moreover, were young, politically experienced, and financially comfortable. In addition, the delegates met in secret. Although they shared some assumptions about government and society, their differences were profound.

It is generally accepted that without compromise the convention would have failed. One important conflict was between the large states, who wanted representation based on population, and the small states, who wanted each state to have equal representation. This conflict was resolved by the establishment of a House of Representatives constituted on the basis of population and a Senate organized on the principle of state equality. Another conflict involved popular participation in the election process. This division was resolved by permitting the House of Representatives to be elected by popular vote and the Senate to be elected by the state legislatures (this was changed in 1913 to allow for popular vote).

The Constitution provided for a stronger central government than had existed under the Articles of Confederation. That new government was to be a republic in which president and Congress would be selected directly or indirectly by the people. The Constitution also provided for the establishment of the basic institutions of the national government: president, Congress, and Supreme Court. Specific provisions were made for how leaders would be chosen for these offices and how their authority would be limited.

The Founding Fathers feared the concentration of power in the hands of a few. A fundamental feature of the new Constitution, therefore, was a system of shared power. Each branch of the federal government has primary power in one area, but that power is not total. Congress, consequently, has primary legislative power; the president, primary executive power; and the Supreme Court, primary judicial power.

Each of these powers, however, is shared. The president exercises some judicial power (the nomination of judges to the Supreme Court) and some legislative power (the vetoing of legislation). Congress has some executive power (Senate confirmation of executive appointments) and some judicial power (impeachment by the House of Representatives). The courts, too, have some legislative power (the interpretation of laws) and some executive power (the administration of laws to ensure compliance with judicial decisions).

The Constitution also establishes the system of federalism by which power is distributed between a central government and state governments. Some powers are given exclusively to the central government (the coining of money), some are shared (taxation), and some reserved to the states (education). On the last point, the Tenth Amendment declares that all powers not delegated to the federal government are reserved to the states or the people. The powers of the central government have, however, expanded at the expense of the state governments through exercise of the implied powers of the Congress. Education serves as one example. Although education was regarded as the primary concern of the states, the federal government has intervened to promote integration in the schools. It is clear, however, that there have been problems concerning the demarcation of governmental authority over the years. The constitutional Framers did not try to delineate all government powers; hence, the conflict over states' rights. That conflict, however, is not as characteristic of the American federal system as is the sharing of power.

The basic facts about the Constitution, then, are not much in debate. Controversy continues, however, about the forces at work at Philadelphia in 1787 and about the enduring effect of the "rules of the game." Two questions often asked about the Constitution are (1) did the Founding Fathers believe in democracy? and (2) is American democracy only for the rich?

THE FOUNDING FATHERS: DEFENDERS OF PEOPLE OR PROPERTY?

Political scientist Martin Diamond contends that the Founding Fathers created the most democratic document of the day when they wrote the Constitution. According to him, the document must be understood by eighteenth- rather than twentieth-century standards. The progressive character of the document can then be better appreciated.

Diamond contends that the Founders believed in popular rule, a modern idea for their time. He takes issue with the notion that the Constitution was a retreat from the democratic principles asserted in the Declaration of Independence. It was, rather, consistent with the Declaration. Features of the Constitution, such as the amendment process, suffrage requirements, the electoral college, and the indirect election of the Senate, were all reflections of popular sovereignty.

Political scientist Michael Parenti, in contrast, argues that the Founding Fathers wrote a constitution to defend property rights rather than to provide for the needs of the masses. Disagreements were between the haves and the haves, not between the propertied classes and the poor.

According to Parenti, the very structure of government established by the Constitution prevented the masses from exercising power. The system of separation of powers and checks and balances ensured that power was fragmented, not democratized, by the Constitution. The original Constitution, moreover, contained no Bill of Rights, and property qualifications required for citizens to vote in the states made even the House of Representatives less responsive to popular control than would have been the case in a truly democratic political system. Finally, the Constitution mentioned nothing about economic rights, such as guarantees for employment, good health, and material security.

THE RULES: FAIR OR UNFAIR?

Even if the Founding Fathers rigged the system to benefit the property owners and merchants, it is still possible for the Constitution to be used differently today. The Constitution, it is often said, is a living document. It may be altered in many ways: through amendment, statute, judicial interpretation, political developments, and custom. Political scientist Duane Lockard argues that the rules of politics continue to favor the affluent classes. The basic rules influence or determine who shall have formal authority, what recourse any person involved in a political decision may possess, and how much participation an individual may legitimately have in determining policy. According to Lockard, the rules—constitutional, judicial, statutory, and administrative—have tended to work against those without prestige and power.

Criticisms about the bias of the rules have been made since the adoption of the Constitution. Particularly since the early 1960s, however, much attention has been directed towards the effect of the rules on black people. Supporters of social reform pointed to many examples of the disadvantaged position of blacks with respect to white people in America—higher infant mortality rate, lower life expectancy, lower income, poorer housing, and higher unemployment.

The portrait of a disadvantaged group of Americans was used by supporters of President Johnson's Great Society programs in many areas—jobs, housing, education, and health. This portrait, moreover, was used by advocates of affirmative action to redress the pattern of discrimination by engaging in active efforts to hire members of minority groups in public and private employment.

Social scientists and journalists have debated the degree of progress that has been made since the civil rights and Great Society legislation of the 1960s. Ben J. Wattenberg, a former political aide to President Johnson, contends that although there is still discrimination in the United States, blacks have made considerable progress and are becoming members of the Establishment. He provides statistics in income, employment, and education to show that the gap between whites and blacks in these areas is narrowing. If Wattenberg is correct, then the rules set forth in the Constitution have not served to keep the poor and weak in perpetual bondage.

Did the Founding Fathers Believe in Democracy?

YES

MARTIN DIAMOND
Democracy and The Federalist: *A Reconsideration of the Framers' Intent**

It has been a common teaching among modern historians of the guiding ideas in the foundation of our government that the Constitution of the United States embodied a reaction against the democratic principles

* From Martin Diamond, "Democracy and *The Federalist:* A Reconsideration of the Framers' Intent," *The American Political Science Review* 53 (March 1959): 52–68. Reprinted by permission.

espoused in the Declaration of Independence. This view has largely been accepted by political scientists and has therefore had important consequences for the way American political development has been studied. I shall present here a contrary view of the political theory of the Framers and examine some of its consequences. . . .

I

Our major political problems today are problems of democracy; and, as much as anything else, the *Federalist* papers are a teaching about democracy. The conclusion of one of the most important of these papers states what is also the most important theme in the entire work: the necessity for "a republican remedy for the diseases most incident to republican government."[1] The theme is clearly repeated in a passage where Thomas Jefferson is praised for displaying equally "a fervent attachment to republican government and an enlightened view of the dangerous propensities against which it ought to be guarded."[2] *The Federalist,* thus, stresses its commitment to republican or popular government, but, of course, insists that this must be an enlightened commitment.

But *The Federalist* and the Founding Fathers generally have not been taken at their word. Predominantly, they are understood as being only quasi- or even antidemocrats. Modern American historical writing, at least until very recently, has generally seen the Constitution as some sort of apostasy from, or reaction to, the radically democratic implications of the Declaration of Independence—a reaction that was undone by the great "democratic breakthroughs" of Jeffersonianism, Jacksonianism, etc. This view, I believe, involves a false understanding of the crucial political issues involved in the founding of the American Republic. Further, it is based implicitly upon a questionable modern approach to democracy and has tended to have the effect, moreover, of relegating the political teaching of the Founding Fathers to the predemocratic past and thus of making it of no vital concern to moderns. The Founding Fathers themselves repeatedly stressed that their Constitution was wholly consistent with the true principles of republican or popular government. The prevailing modern opinion, in varying degrees and in different ways, rejects that claim. It thus becomes important to understand what was the relation of the Founding Fathers to popular government or democracy.

I have deliberately used interchangeably their terms, "popular government" and "democracy." The Founding Fathers, of course, did not use the terms entirely synonymously and the idea that they were less than "democrats" has been fortified by the fact that they some-

times defined "democracy" invidiously in comparison with "republic." But this fact does not really justify the opinion. For their basic
view was that *popular government was the genus, and democracy and
republic were two species* of that genus of government. What distinguished popular government from other genera of government was that
in it, political authority is "derived from the great body of the society,
not from . . . [any] favored class of it."[3] With respect to this decisive
question of where political authority is lodged, democracy and
republic—as *The Federalist* uses the terms—differ not in the least. Republics, equally with democracies, may claim to be wholly a form of
popular government. This is neither to deny the difference between the
two, nor to depreciate the importance *The Federalist* attached to the
difference; but in *The Federalist's* view, the difference does not relate to
the essential principle of popular government. Democracy means in
The Federalist that form of popular government where the citizens "assemble and administer the government in person."[4] Republics differ in
that the people rule through representatives and, of course, in the
consequences of that difference. The crucial point is that republics and
democracies are equally forms of popular government, but that the one
form is vastly preferable to the other because of the substantive consequences of the difference in form. Those historians who consider the
Founding Fathers as less than "democrats" miss or reject the Founders' central contention that, while being perfectly faithful to the *principle* of popular government, they had solved the *problem* of popular
government. . . .

II

The Declaration has wrongly been converted into, as it were, a super-
democratic document; has the Constitution wrongly been converted in
the modern view into an insufficiently democratic document? The only
basis for depreciating the democratic character of the Constitution lies
in its Framers' apprehensive diagnosis of the "diseases," "defects" or
"evil propensities" of democracy, and in their remedies. But if what
the Founders considered to be defects *are* genuine defects, and if the
remedies, without violating the principles of popular government, *are*
genuine remedies, then it would be unreasonable to call the Founders
anti- or quasi-democrats. Rather, they would be the wise partisans of
democracy; a man is not a better democrat but only a foolish democrat
if he ignores real defects inherent in popular government. Thus, the
question becomes: are there natural defects to democracy and, if there
are, what are the best remedies?
   In part, the Founding Fathers answered this question by employ-

ing a traditional mode of political analysis. They believed there were several basic possible regimes, each having several possible forms. Of these possible regimes they believed the best, or at least the best for America, to be popular government, but only if purged of its defects. At any rate, an unpurged popular government they believed to be indefensible. They believed there were several forms of popular government, crucial among these direct democracy and republican—or representative—government (the latter perhaps divisible into two distinct forms, large and small republics). Their constitution and their defense of it constitute an argument for that form of popular government (large republic) in which the "evil propensities" would be weakest or most susceptible of remedy. . . .

What are some of the arrangements which have been considered signs of "undemocratic" features of the Constitution? The process by which the Constitution may be amended is often cited in evidence. Everyone is familiar with the arithmetic which shows that a remarkably small minority could prevent passage of a constitutional amendment supported by an overwhelming majority of the people. That is, bare majorities in the thirteen least populous states could prevent passage of an amendment desired by overwhelming majorities in the thirty-six most populous states. But let us, for a reason to be made clear in a moment, turn that arithmetic around. Bare majorities in the thirty-seven least populous states can pass amendments against the opposition of overwhelming majorities in the twelve most populous states. And this would mean in actual votes today (and would have meant for the thirteen original states) constitutional amendment by a minority against the opposition of a majority of citizens. My point is simply that, while the amending procedure does involve qualified majorities, the qualification is not of the kind that requires an especially large numerical majority for action.

I suggest that the real aim and practical effect of the complicated amending procedure was not at all to give power to minorities, but to ensure that passage of an amendment would require a *nationally* distributed majority, though one that legally could consist of a bare numerical majority. It was only adventitious that the procedure has the theoretical possibility of a minority blocking (or passing) an amendment. The aim of requiring nationally distributed majorities was, I think, to ensure that no amendment could be passed simply with the support of the few states or sections sufficiently numerous to provide a bare majority. . . .

Consider next the suffrage question. It has long been assumed as proof of an antidemocratic element in the Constitution that the Founding Fathers depended for the working of their Constitution upon a substantially limited franchise. Just as the Constitution allegedly was ratified by a highly qualified electorate, so too, it is held, was the new government to be based upon a suffrage subject to substantial property qualifications. This view has only recently been seriously challenged, especially by Robert E. Brown, whose detailed researches convince him that the property qualifications in nearly all the original states were probably so small as to exclude never more than twenty-five percent, and in most cases as little as only five to ten percent, of the adult white male population.[5] That is, the property qualifications were not designed to exclude the mass of the poor but only the small proportion which lacked a concrete—however small—stake in society, i.e., primarily the transients or "idlers."

The Constitution, of course, left the suffrage question to the decision of the individual states. What is the implication of that fact for deciding what sort of suffrage the Framers had in mind? The immediately popular branch of the national legislature was to be elected by voters who "shall have the qualifications requisite for electors of the most numerous branch of the State Legislature." The mode of election to the electoral college for the presidency and to the Senate is also left to "be prescribed in each State by the legislature thereof." At a minimum, it may be stated that the Framers did not themselves attempt to reduce, or prevent the expansion of, the suffrage; that question was left wholly to the states—and these were, ironically, the very hotbeds of postrevolutionary democracy from the rule of which it is familiarly alleged that the Founders sought to escape.[6]

In general, the conclusion seems inescapable that the states had a far broader suffrage than is ordinarily thought, and nothing in the actions of the Framers suggests any expectation or prospect of the reduction of the suffrage. Again, as in the question of the amending process, I suggest that the Constitution represented no departure whatsoever from the democratic standards of the Revolutionary period, or from any democratic standards then generally recognized.[7]

What of the Senate? The organization of the Senate, its term of office and its staggered mode of replacement, its election by state legislatures rather than directly by the people, among other things, have been used to demonstrate the undemocratic character of the Senate as intended by the Framers. Was this not a device to represent property and not people, and was it not intended therefore to be a nonpopular element in the government? I suggest, on the contrary, that the really important thing is that the Framers thought they had found a way to protect property *without* representing it. That the Founders intended the Senate to be one of the crucial devices for remedying the defects of democracy is certainly true. But *The Federalist* argues that the Senate, as actually proposed in the Constitution, was calculated to be such a device as would operate only in a way that "will consist . . . with the genuine principles of republican government."[8] I believe that the claim is just. . . .

The great claim of *The Federalist* is that the Constitution represents the fulfillment of a truly novel experiment, of "a revolution which has no parallel in the annals of society," and which is decisive for the happiness of "the whole human race."[9] And the novelty, I argue, consisted in solving the problems of popular government by means which yet maintain the government "wholly popular."[10] . . .

Did the Founding Fathers Believe in Democracy?

NO

MICHAEL PARENTI
*What the Founding Fathers Did**

. . . The American Constitution was framed by financially successful planters, merchants, lawyers, bankers and creditors, many of them linked by ties of family and acquaintance and by years of service in the Congress, the military, or diplomacy. They congregated in Philadelphia in 1787 for the professed purpose of revising the Articles of Confederation and strengthening the powers of the central government. They were impelled by a desire to build a nation and by the explicit and often repeated intent of doing something about the increasingly insurgent spirit evidenced among poorer people.

The rebellious populace of that day has been portrayed by many historians and textbook writers as consisting of irresponsible spendthrifts who never paid their debts and who believed in nothing more than timid state governments and inflated paper money. Little has been said about the actual plight of the common people, the great bulk of whom lived at a subsistence level. While concentrations of landed

* From Michael Parenti, *Democracy for the Few* (New York: St. Martin's Press, 1974), pp. 43–55. Reprinted by permission.

and commercial wealth were growing among the few, the poorer farmers were burdened by the low prices offered for their crops by traders and merchants, the high costs for merchandised goods and regressive taxes. They often bought land at inflated prices, only to see its value collapse and to find themselves unable to meet their mortgage obligations. Their labor and their crops usually were theirs in name only. To survive, they frequently had to borrow money at high interest rates. To meet their debts they mortgaged their future crops and went still deeper into debt. Large numbers were caught in that cycle of rural indebtedness which is the common fate of agrarian peoples in many countries to this day. The underpaid and underemployed artisans and workers (or "mechanics," as they were called) in the towns were not much better off.

Among the poor there grew the feeling that the revolution against the king of England had been fought for naught. When large numbers of debtors were jailed in Massachusetts early in 1787 and others were threatened with foreclosures on their farms, many of the poor began gathering at the county towns to prevent the courts from presiding over debtor cases. By the winter of 1787, farmers in western Massachusetts led by Daniel Shays had taken up arms. But their rebellion was forcibly put down by the state militia after a series of ragged skirmishes.

The specter of Shays' Rebellion hovered over the men who gathered in Philadelphia three months later. It confirmed their worst fears about the unreliable and irresponsible nature of the populace. They were determined that persons of birth and fortune should control the affairs of the nation and check the leveling impulses of that propertyless multitude which composed the "majority faction." "To secure the public good and private rights against the danger of such a faction," announced James Madison at the Philadelphia Convention, "and at the same time preserve the spirit and form of popular government is then the great object to which our inquiries are directed."

The Founding Fathers were of the opinion that things had become, in the words of one, "too democratic." They deemed the state legislatures too responsive to the people and not respectful enough of the needs of the prosperous. . . .

The Framers spent many weeks debating their differences, but these were the differences of merchants, slave owners, and manufacturers, a debate of haves versus haves in which each group sought certain safeguards within the new Constitution for its particular regional interests. Added to this were the inevitable disagreements that arise among men who are not certain what are the best means of achieving agreed-upon ends. One major question was how to erect a sturdy national government while preserving some kind of state representation. Questions of structure and authority occupied a good deal of the delegates' time: How much representation for the large and small states? How might the legislature be organized? How should the executive be selected? What length of tenure for the different officeholders? But certain questions of enormous significance, relating to the new government's ability to protect the interests of commerce and wealth, were agreed upon with surprisingly little debate. For on these issues there were no dirt farmers, dockworkers, indentured servants, or poor artisans attending the Convention to proffer an opposing viewpoint. The debate between haves and have-nots never took place.

The portions of the Constitution which give the federal government the power to support commerce and protect property were decided upon after amiable deliberation and with remarkable dispatch considering their importance. Thus all of Article I, Section 8 was adopted within a few days.[11] This section delegated to Congress the power to (a) regulate commerce among the states and commerce with foreign nations and Indian tribes, (b) lay and collect taxes, duties and tariffs on imports but not on commercial exports, (c) establish a national currency and regulate its value, (d) "borrow Money on the credit of the United States"—a measure of special interest to creditors,[12] (e) fix the standard of weights and measures necessary for trade, (f) protect the value of securities and currency against counterfeiting, (g) establish "uniform Laws on the subject of Bankruptcies throughout the United States," (h) "pay the Debts and provide for the common Defense and general Welfare of the United States." Congress was to be limited to powers which either were specifically delegated to it by the Constitution or could be implied as "necessary and proper" for the performance of the delegated powers. Over the years, under this "implied power" clause, federal intervention in the private economy grew to an extraordinary magnitude and came to include activities unknown to and undreamed of by the Framers.

Among the delegates at the convention were some who speculated in land and who expressed a concern about western holdings; accordingly, Congress was given the "Power to dispose of and make all needful Rules and Regulations respecting the Territory or other Property belonging to the United States. . . ." Some of the delegates were speculators or holders of highly inflated and nearly worthless Confederation securities. Under Article VI, all debts incurred by the Confederation were valid against the new government, a provision that allowed speculators to make generous profits when their securities matured and were honored at face value.[13]

In the interest of merchants and creditors, the states were prohibited from issuing paper money or imposing duties on imports and exports or interfering with the payment of debts by passing any "Law impairing the Obligation of Contracts." The Constitution guaranteed "Full Faith and Credit" in each state "to the Acts, Records, and judicial Proceedings" of other states, thus allowing creditors to pursue their debtors more effectively. The property interests of slave owners were looked after. To give the slave-owning states a greater influence, three fifths of the slave population were to be counted when calculating the representation deserved by each state in the lower house. The importation of slaves was allowed to continue until 1808. And under Article IV, slaves who fled from one state to another to escape bondage had to be delivered up to the original owner upon claim, a provision that was unanimously adopted at the Convention.

The Framers believed the states acted with insufficient force against the agitations of the day, so Congress was given the task of "organizing, arming, and disciplining the Militia" and calling it forth, among other things, to "suppress Insurrections." The federal government guaranteed to every state in the Union a "Republican Form of Government" and protection against invasion and "against domestic Violence." Provision was also made for "the Erection of Forts, Magazines, Arsenals, dock-Yards and other needful Buildings," and for the maintenance of an army and navy for national defense and to police unsettled American territories. To protect overseas trade, Congress could take steps to "punish Piracies and Felonies committeed on the high Seas, and Offenses against the Law of Nations."

CONTAINING THE SPREAD OF DEMOCRACY

In keeping with their desire to divest the majority of its alleged propensity toward self-aggrandizement, the Founding Fathers inserted "auxiliary precautions" *designed to fragment power without democratizing it.* By separating the executive, legislative, and judiciary functions and then providing a system of checks and balances among the various branches, including staggered elections, executive veto, Senate confirmation of appointments, and ratification of treaties, bicameralism, etc., they hoped to dilute the impact of popular sentiments. To the extent that it existed at all, the majoritarian principle was tightly locked into a system of minority vetoes, making swift and sweeping actions nearly impossible.

The propertyless majority, as Madison was to point out in *Federalist* No. 10, must not be allowed to concert in common cause against the established social order.[14] First, it was necessary to prevent a unity of public sentiment by enlarging the polity and then compartmentalizing it into geographically insulated political communities. The larger the nation, the greater the "variety of parties and interests" and the more difficult it would be for a majority to find itself and act in unison. As Madison argued, "A rage for paper money, for an abolition of debts, for an equal division of property, or for any other wicked project will be less apt to pervade the whole body of the Union than a particular member of it. . . ." Thus an uprising of impoverished farmers may threaten Massachusetts at one time and Rhode Island at another, but a national government will be large and varied enough to contain each of these and insulate the rest of the nation from the contamination of rebellion.

Second, not only must the majority be prevented from finding horizontal cohesion, but its vertical force—that is, its upward thrust upon government—should be blunted by interjecting an essentially nonmajoritarian and indirect form of representation. Thus the senators from each state were to be elected by their respective state legislatures. The chief executive was to be selected by an electoral college voted by the people but, as anticipated by the Framers, composed of political leaders and men of substance who would gather in their various states and choose a president of their own liking. Most probably, they would be unable to muster a majority for any one candidate, it was believed, and the final selection would be left to the House, with each state delegation therein having only one vote.* The Supreme Court was to be elected by no one, its justices being appointed to life tenure by the president and confirmed by the Senate. In time, of course, the electoral college proved to be something of a rubber stamp, and the Seventeenth Amendment, adopted in 1913, provided for the direct election of the Senate.

The only portion of government that was initially "left to the people" in the Constitution was the House of Representatives. Many of the Framers would have preferred excluding the public entirely from direct representation: John Mercer observed that he found nothing in the proposed Constitution more objectionable than "the mode of election by the people. The people cannot know and judge of the characters of Candidates. The worst possible choice will be made." Others were concerned that the people would sell their votes to ambitious adventurists and demagogues, who would ride into office on a populist tide only to pillage the treasury and wreak havoc on all. "The time is not distant," warned Gouverneur Morris, "when this Country will abound with mechanics and manufacturers [industrial workers] who will re-

---

* The delegates did anticipate that George Washington would be overwhelmingly elected the first president, but they believed that after that the electoral college would seldom be able to decide on one man.

ceive their bread from their employers. Will such men be the secure
and faithful Guardians of liberty? . . . Children do not vote. Why? Because they want prudence, because they have no will of their own. The
ignorant and dependent can be as little trusted with the public
interest."[15]

Several considerations mitigated the Framers' hostility toward
the common people. First and most important, the delegates restrained
themselves out of an anticipation that there were limits to what the
states would accept. Second, some of the delegates feared not only the
tyranny of the many but the machinations of the few. It was Madison
who reminded his colleagues that in protecting themselves from the
multitude, they must not reintroduce a "cabal" or a monarchy and thus
err in the opposite direction. Third, a few of the Framers, notably men
like George Mason and Benjamin Franklin, felt less hostility toward the
democratic principle than did their colleagues. If they said nothing in
support of extending the franchise, they did speak out against limiting
it. Franklin lauded "the virtue and public spirit of our common people;
of which they displayed a great deal during the war" and noted that
when they were treated decently they were likely to be loyal and faithful citizens.

In any case, when the delegates agreed to having "the people"
elect the lower house, they were referring to a somewhat select portion
of the population. Property qualifications disfranchised the poorest in
various states. Half the adult population was denied suffrage because
they were women. About one fourth, both men and women, had no
vote because they were held in bondage, and even among blacks who
had bought their freedom, in both the North and the South, none was
allowed to vote until the passage of the Fourteenth Amendment after
the Civil War. . . .

AN ELITIST DOCUMENT

Whatever conjectures we might make about the motivations of the
Framers, the more important task is to judge the end product of their
efforts. And the Constitution they fashioned tells us a good deal about
their objectives. It was and still is largely an elitist* document, more

---

* "Elitist" refers to interests or persons deemed to be socially select and superior and therefore
deserving of positions of rule, at least according to those who apply the elitist description to themselves. "Elites" in the politicoeconomic system are those close to the loci of decision making who
exercise a special initiative in public policy or who occupy top command positions within our political, social, and economic institutions. These elites may not always work with perfect cohesion and
sometimes they come into conflict with each other over policy particulars, but generally they share a
common commitment to the ongoing social order.

concerned with the securing of property interests than with personal liberties. Bills of attainder and ex post facto laws are expressly prohibited, and Article I, Section 9 assures us that "the Privilege of the Writ of Habeas Corpus shall not be suspended, unless when in Cases of Rebellion or Invasion the public Safety may require it," a restriction that still leaves authorities with a good measure of discretion. Other than these few provisions and similar ones imposed on the states, the Constitution that emerged from the Philadelphia Convention gave no attention to civil liberties. When Colonel Mason suggested to the convention that a committee be formed to draft "a Bill of Rights," a task that could be accomplished "in a few hours," the representatives of the various states offered little discussion on the motion and voted unanimously against it. Guarantees of individual rights—including freedom of speech and religion; freedom to assemble peaceably and petition (i.e., urge, remonstrate and demonstrate) for redress of grievances; the right to keep and bear arms; freedom from unreasonable searches and seizures, from self-incrimination, double jeopardy, cruel and unusual punishment, and excessive bail and fines; and the right to a fair and impartial trial and other forms of due process—were tacked on in the form of the first ten amendments (the Bill of Rights) only after the Constitution was ratified and the first Congress and president had been elected.

The twentieth-century concept of social justice, involving something more than formal and procedural liberties, is afforded no explicit place in our eighteenth-century Constitution. The Constitution says nothing about those conditions of life which have come to be treated by many people as essential human rights—for instance, freedom from hunger, the right to decent housing, good medical care, and education regardless of ability to pay, the right to regular and gainful employment, safe working conditions, decent recreational facilities, a clean, nontoxic environment. Under the Constitution the right to equality is treated as a *procedural* right without a *substantive* content. Thus "equality of opportunity" means equality of opportunity to move ahead competitively and become unequal to others; it means an equal chance to get in the game and best others rather than an equal chance to enjoy an equal distribution and use of the resources needed for the maintenance of community life.

Some people, like the philosophy professor Sidney Hook, have argued that democracy is simply a system of rules for playing the game which allows some measure of mass participation and government accountability, and the Constitution is a kind of rule book. One should not try to impose particular public policies, class relations, economic philosophies or other substantive arrangements on this open-ended game. This position certainly does reduce democracy to a game. It overlooks the inextricable relationship between substance and procedure and presumes that procedural rules can exist in a meaningful way independently of substantive realities. But whether procedural rights are violated or actually enjoyed, whether one is treated by the law as pariah or prince, depends largely on material realities that extend beyond a written constitution or other formal guarantees of law. The law in its majestic equality, Anatole France once observed, prohibits rich and poor alike from stealing bread and sleeping under the bridges. And, it might be added, in so doing the law becomes something of a farce, a fiction that allows us to speak of "the rights of all persons" divorced from the class conditions that place rich and powerful corporations above the law and poor individuals below it. In the absence of certain substantive conditions, legalistic and procedural rights are of little value to millions who suffer the miseries of hunger and poverty and who have neither the time, money nor opportunity to make a reality of their formal rights.

Take the "right of every citizen to be heard." In its majestic equality the law allows both the rich and the poor to raise high their political voices: both are free to hire the best-placed lobbyists and Washington lawyers to pressure and manipulate public officeholders; both are free to shape public opinion through the use of a privately owned and privately financed press; and both rich and poor have the right to engage in multimillion-dollar election campaigns in order to pick the right persons for office or win office themselves. But again, this formal political equality is something of a fiction. Of what good are the rules of the game for those millions who never get a chance to play?

NOTES

1. *The Federalist,* No. 10, p. 62. All references are to the Modern Library edition, ed. E. M. Earle.
2. *The Federalist,* No. 49, p. 327.
3. *The Federalist,* No. 39, p. 244. Here Madison speaks explicitly of the republican form of government. But see on the same page how Madison compares the republican form with "every *other popular* government." Regarding the crucial question of the lodgement of political authority, Madison speaks of republic, democracy, and popular government interchangeably. Consider that, in the very paper where he distinguishes so precisely between democracies and republics regarding direct versus representative rule, Madison defines his general aim both as a search for "a republican remedy" for republican diseases *and* a remedy that will "preserve the spirit and the form of *popular* government" (p. 58). Interest-

ingly, on June 6 at the Federal Convention, Madison's phrasing for a similar problem was the search for "the only defense against the inconveniences of democracy consistent with the *democratic* form of government." Madison, *Writings*, ed. G. Hunt, Vol. 3 (G. P. Putnam's Sons, New York, 1902), p. 103. Italics supplied throughout.

4. *The Federalist*, No. 10, p. 58.

5. *Middle Class Democracy and the Revolution in Massachusetts, 1691–1780.* (Cornell University Press, Ithaca, 1955).

6. Madison must have thought that he had established this point beyond misinterpretation in *The Federalist*, No. 57. "Who are to be the electors of the federal representatives? Not the rich, more than the poor; not the learned, more than the ignorant; not the haughty heirs of distinguished names, more than the humble sons of obscurity and unpropitious fortune. The electors are to be the great body of the people of the United States. They are to be the same who exercise the right in every State of electing the corresponding branch of the legislature of the State." (P. 371.)

7. This is not to deny the importance of the existing property qualifications for the understanding of the Founders' political theory. The legal exclusion from the franchise of even a very small portion of the adult population may have enormous significance for the politics and life of a country. This is obvious in the case of a racial, ethnic or religious minority. And the exclusion of otherwise eligible adult males on the grounds of poverty may be equally important. The property qualification clearly praises and rewards certain virtues, implies that the voter must possess certain qualities to warrant his exercise of the franchise, and aims at excluding a "rabble" from the operations of political parties. But important, therefore, as the property qualification was, it does not demonstrate that the Founding Fathers departed radically from the most important aspects of the principle of majority rule.

8. *The Federalist*, No. 62, p. 403.

9. *The Federalist*, No. 14, p. 85.

10. Ibid., p. 81.

11. John Bach McMaster, "Framing the Constitution," in his *The Political Depravity of the Founding Fathers* (New York: Farrar, Straus, 1964), p. 137. Originally published in 1896. Farrand refers to the consensus for a strong national government that emerged after the small states had been given equal representation in the Senate. Much of the work that followed "was purely formal" albeit sometimes time-consuming. See Max Farrand, *The Framing of the Constitution of the United States* (New Haven: Yale University Press, 1913), pp. 134–135.

12. The original wording was "borrow money and emit bills." But the latter phrase was deleted after Gouverneur Morris warned that "The Monied interest will oppose the plan of Government if paper emissions be not prohibited." There was much strong feeling about this among creditors. In

any case, it was assumed that the borrowing power would allow for "safe and proper" public notes should they be necessary. See Farrand, *The Framing of the Constitution*, p. 147.

13. The classic study of the economic interests of the Founding Fathers is Charles A. Beard, *An Economic Interpretation of the Constitution* (New York: Macmillan, 1913). Critiques of Beard have been made by Robert E. Brown, *Charles Beard and the American Constitution* (Princeton, N.J.: Princeton University Press, 1956), and Forrest McDonald, *We the People—The Economic Origins of the Constitution* (Chicago: Chicago University Press, 1958).

14. *The Federalist* No. 10 can be found in any of the good editions of *The Federalist Papers*. It is one of the finest essays on American politics ever written by a theorist or practitioner. With clarity and economy of language it explains, as do few other short works, how a government may utilize the republican principle to coopt the people and protect the propertied few from the propertyless many, and it confronts, if not solves, the essential question of how government may reconcile the tensions between liberty, authority, and dominant class interest. In effect, the Tenth Federalist Paper maps out a method of preserving the politico-economic status quo which is relevant to this day.

15. Max Farrand, ed., *Records of the Federal Convention of 1787*, Vol. 2 (New Haven: Yale University Press, 1927), pp. 200 ff.

QUESTIONS FOR DISCUSSION

1. What were the principal ideas put forth by the Founding Fathers on the subjects of government, the economy, and liberty?

2. What are the provisions of the Constitution that support the contention that the Constitution is a document concerned with protecting the privileges of the well-to-do at the expense of the poor?

3. What are the provisions of the Constitution that suggest that the Founding Fathers were concerned with establishing a democratic political system?

4. Does an analysis of the political, social, and economic conditions existing in America at the time of the Constitutional Convention support the arguments of either author?

5. How would you rewrite the Constitution to meet Parenti's criticisms?

SUGGESTED READINGS

Beard, Charles. *An Economic Interpretation of the Constitution*. New York: Macmillan, 1913.

Brown, Robert E. *Charles Beard and the Constitution: A Critical Analysis of*

"An Economic Interpretation of the Constitution." Princeton: Princeton University Press, 1956.

Farrand, Max. *The Framing of the Constitution.* New Haven: Yale University Press, 1913.

————, ed. *The Records of the Federal Convention of 1787.* 4 vols. New Haven: Yale University Press, 1911. Rev. ed., 1937.

Hamilton, Alexander, James Madison, and John Jay. *The Federalist Papers.* Introduction by Clinton Rossiter. New York: New American Library, 1961.

Hofstadter, Richard. *The American Political Tradition.* New York: Vintage, 1955, Ch. 1.

Lipset, Seymour Martin. *The First New Nation: The United States in Historical and Comparative Perspective.* Garden City, N.Y.: Doubleday, 1967.

McDonald, Forrest. *We the People: The Economic Origins of the Constitution.* Chicago: University of Chicago Press, 1958.

Roche, John P. "The Founding Fathers: A Reform Caucus in Action." *The American Political Science Review* 55(December 1961):799–816.

Rossiter, Clinton. *1787: The Grand Convention.* New York: Macmillan, 1966.

Is American Democracy Only for the Rich?

YES

W. DUANE LOCKARD
*The Rules of Politics as Determinants of Power**

Discussing political decision making, Charles E. Lindblom has said that ". . . the power of various social groups like the rich or the whites is less a determinant of policy outcomes than itself a result of the rules that men have made to govern the policy-making process."[1] In view of the other sources of muscle that the rich and the well-placed have at their command, this may exaggerate the importance of the rules for the political effectiveness of the advantaged, but it neverthe-

* Reprinted with permission of Macmillan Publishing Co., Inc. from *The Perverted Priorities of American Politics,* 2nd ed., by W. Duane Lockard. Pp. 31–43. Copyright © by W. Duane Lockard.

less gives appropriate emphasis to the ways in which the rules can be utilized by those who have the advantages. The rules of the political process were not written by the have-nots and the severely disadvantaged, after all, but predominantly by the politically well-off. It is no surprise to find that the rules serve best the interests of the kind of people who write them. As I shall argue, a vitally important aspect of those rules is the opportunity to say "No" to policy initiatives, and to those who have advantages the opportunity to say "No" with impunity is a major source of strength. As many observers have noted, the American constitutional system is notoriously warped in the direction of weakness and delay—inaction in a word—and the rules contribute mightily to that result. . . .

. . . When Congress establishes an Un-American Activities Committee or a Federal Trade Commission, or lays down rules on automobile safety, it thereby determines some basic rules. It not only asserts that such a power exists for Congress to exercise, but it also grants someone an official capacity to give orders to others and sets the standards for compliance, the procedures for raising objections, and the like. Each of these decisions establishes rules by which questions of subversiveness, competition, or safety are to be decided. Those empowered to act under these resolutions or statutes make the next set of determinations of the rules, often establishing subordinate codes that are just as much binding rules as the statutes to which they owe their origin. And so, down the line of political decisions, there are many interests significantly involved in setting the rules: the president or cabinet member who pushes for legislation in a specific form, the interest groups that battle to defend their positions, even marginally political parties that may take positions on issues and perhaps help round up the necessary votes for passage of a bill in a certain form.

In short, the basic rules influence or determine who shall have formal authority, they partially decide what recourse any person involved may possess (whether he is a beneficiary or a person disadvantaged by the decision in question), and they facilitate participation in determining policy for certain elements or prevent others from participating. For example, it was, as it turned out, important that the Antipoverty Law said there should be "maximum feasible participation" of the poor in the conduct of local programs. The clause in the statute appears to have gone unnoticed in the legislative stage by those who subsequently objected bitterly to its application, but, however it got there, it helped decide power allocation under the law. If the Office of Economic Opportunity [OEO] (which administers that law) had been rigid about it, there might have been more opportunity for actual participation of the poor; but the OEO was flexible in applying the rule. As a consequence, the opportunity for the affected clientele to participate in any meaningful way in the making of policy was much weakened.[2]

A good illustration of the point is to be found in the controversy that broke out during the last months of the Johnson Administration concerning the administration of federal highway grants to the states. Federal officials wanted to require two public hearings to be held by state highway departments before all federally supported highways could be constructed. One hearing would announce tentative alignments of the road and invite public comment; the second hearing would present the finally determined route and permit the public a second round of (inevitable) criticism. State highway commissioners bitterly objected to these requirements. In their view it was an invitation to trouble; and insofar as it facilitated the opportunity for affected parties to muster opposition to highway locations, it no doubt would involve difficulty for highway men, who feel a compulsion to build roads as cheaply, efficiently, and expeditiously as possible. And inviting local opposition is no way to simplify road building. These requirements, finally adopted in the last days of the Johnson Administration, do significantly affect the way the highway location game is played. Those who oppose the location of a highway in their backyards use publicity as a prime means of attack, and there is nothing like a rowdy, emotional hearing to arouse wide antipathy to the highway bulldozer and its tendency to plow furrows eight lanes wide. In short, a simple administrative ruling can have a tremendous impact on the way the actors in a controversy will be able to use their resources.[3]

The rules can alter power relationships completely. Thus, to use the antipoverty program as an example again, the mayors of the major cities of the country and the leaders of big-city political party organizations insisted in 1967 that Congress repeal the option the national OEO had of funding local independent groups to carry out OEO programs. Urban leaders insisted that only city agencies should be funded. Because the OEO could choose to work with privately organized groups concerned with welfare, manpower training, legal services to the poor, and the like, city hall politicians saw a real threat. The mayors' reasoning was perfectly clear: if we lack control over the patronage and operations of these private groups, they may become a challenge to our political hegemony. Of course, that was not the argument they used publicly—the announced reasons concerned proper coordination of agencies and their programs and other such sublime rationalizations, but at the heart of the matter was power. The rules decided who could have cash to spend on programs, and he who has cash can fill jobs and gain community standing for services offered—can, in short, gain some power. In the ultimate struggle over whether the mayors would force

Congress to grant them authority to require that only public agencies receive OEO money, the inevitable happened: those who had the greater pull prevailed. Thus the Edith Green Amendment became law in 1967: it did not prohibit funds from going to a private group, but permitted a local administration to rule that only public bodies could participate in the program.[4]

It is important to note that the rules of politics not only allocate power, but also create understandings of what is right and what should be accepted, like it or not. To be sure in this political system there is much objection—in various forms from pickets to lawsuits, riots, and referenda, to mention but a few—but there is also a strong inclination to accept the official edicts of government. The regime has legitimacy, to use a term much favored by political scientists. It is undoubtedly true that the events of the 1960s—from assassinations to Vietnam to Watergate—have undercut that legitimacy, but it would be wrong to assume it has deteriorated greatly for most people. The public, that is to say, respects the right of those in official positions to issue rulings: social norms endorse compliance, not resistance, and if there is objection, it is almost always to the particular rule and not to the general rightness of the authority issuing the order. It is obvious that the legitimacy of the system serves well those who have the greatest political influence. For acceptance of decisions without organized objection—partly on grounds of legitimacy—obviously aids most those who have the best resources for persuasion. This is a logical necessity, for if they prevail most often, then they are pushed least often to have to organize dissent.

The tendency to accept government as legitimate on the part of the disadvantaged is reinforced by their sense of defeatism about using government to achieve their goals; that is, those who are only marginally or not at all involved in government, who are unskilled in the use of political techniques, and who also lack confidence in their capacity to win justice for themselves have become apathetic toward politics. A comparative study of political attitudes in five nations, done by Gabriel Almond and Sidney Verba, does show that the American lower class feels somewhat more confidence in its ability to affect government than the lower classes in other nations, but the difference between the top and the bottom groups in this country are also significant. Among United States citizens in professional and managerial occupations, 96 percent expressed such optimism. And of those with the least education in the United States only a third expected that they would be given serious consideration in a government office or from the police if they made complaints; among those with higher education no less than 85 percent expressed confidence in their capacity to get attention.[5]

There is much in our culture that encourages the feeling that equitable treatment might be expected and that any citizen has a right to a hearing and due consideration. But there is also much that would discourage the lower class from taking advantage of what the beliefs and propaganda tell him is available. The literate and informed person has no qualms about going to a public official and making a complaint or request. He will have no fear that his attire, speech, demeanor would result in his own humiliation; he will not suspect that the police will take a jaundiced view of him because he makes an appeal; and he will know the relevant rules and procedures—or can readily find out what they are. From experience, either his own or that of others, he will expect a reasonable response. The poor, the undereducated, the chronically disadvantaged have none of these expectations. The poor are aware of the clear difference between themselves and those who work in government offices—in contrast to the middle- or upper-class person who may look down upon them as mere civil servants. The language of the poor is usually markedly different and so is their attire; they are ignorant of procedures and suspicious of officials. They feel less like equals and more like supplicants. If they have had to go to a hospital clinic or a welfare office or most any other kind of public institution dealing with the poor, they know the kind of neglect and rudeness that characterizes relations between the "public servant" and the client. (If this is doubted, dress in untidy clothes, sit in a welfare office for an hour, and observe the treatment the indigent routinely get.)

Indeed, as Hannah Arendt has pointed out, the impersonal, remote rules and those who apply them can develop the "Rule of Nobody";[6] that is, a Kafkaesque atmosphere can tyrannize just as much as a despot because the person caught in the web of seeming objectivity and rigid application of rules is as dominated as the victim threatened by an arbitrary superior.[7] For example, consider the slum dweller who has been without heat and running water for weeks and then tries to get bureaucratic relief for his complaint. The law may require the landlord to supply these minimal housing amenities, but getting the bureaucracy to respond may be more than a roomful of tenants can achieve. Joe Lyford in *The Airtight Cage* makes this point tellingly as he describes the runaround he got when reporting conditions in his upper Westside New York neighborhood.[8] He was sent from one office to another, left waiting at the office endlessly, and then shunted to another official, who, in turn, claims to lack jurisdiction or for some reason is unable to remedy the problem. If this happened to Lyford, a highly educated, articulate, and aggressive man determined to make the system respond, what should one expect for the lower class "left out" ones?

Not only this prevalent sense of "being out of it" restrains the poor and the uneducated from trying to use the government more effectively in their own behalf. There is also the set of myths that convinces many victims of these conditions that in some subtle way they are personally responsible for the troubles they are experiencing—that, indeed, government should not involve itself in personal problems of individuals, for some of the older, isolated poor are among the few who still have any belief in laissez-faire ideas. (Business tycoons believe in it only to get the government off their backs; laissez-faire is the farthest thing from their minds when they want a subsidy, contract, or government service). Mockery though it is, many of those who need help feel that any man who cannot make his own way independently is not indeed a real man at all; this despite the rapacious behavior of coal, timber, and other extractive interests that raise the hopes of people today and smash them to despair tomorrow because the resources are depleted or have become uneconomical to exploit—or can be exploited in some simpler way that needs the work of one man, not ten.

This then offers some reasons why the rules—constitutional, judicial, statutory, and administrative—can have an enormous effect on political contesting. Unhappily, one of the fundamental consequences of the rules, as they now exist and tend to be interpreted, is that those without prestige and power tend to be even more pushed outside the comfortable gambits of American life by the character of those rules and their interpretation.

Is American Democracy Only for the Rich?

NO

BEN J. WATTENBERG
Black Progress and Liberal Rhetoric (Race)＊

THE GOOD NUMBERS

Amid all the rhetoric of a split and racist nation, behind the lusty statements of black power, black rage, and black identity, co-mingled with all the cries for compensatory action and freedom now—

＊ "Black Progress and Liberal Rhetoric" by Ben J. Wattenberg from *The Real America*. Copyright ©
1974 by Ben J. Wattenberg. Used by permission of Doubleday & Company, Inc.

something remarkable has happened since 1960. Blacks are still well behind whites, but there has been a major racial catching-up going on. *And for the first time in the history of the republic, "middle class"* —as measured by criteria of income, occupation, and education—*became the adjective to describe the majority of black Americans.*

Acknowledging that the *gap* between white and black is still a national disgrace, acknowledging too that the condition of middle classitude is more prevalent outside of the South than in the South and more prevalent among younger blacks than older blacks, *it is the contention here that the emergence of such a substantial number of blacks into the American middle class is nothing less than a revolutionary development.*

America, it should not be forgotten, is a nation to which blacks came in chains. After a Civil War that did away with slavery, blacks were still subjected to economic servitude and social segregation, most cruelly in the South, where upward of 75 percent of the blacks lived until 1940. Not until the mid-1960s were blacks in the South (where still more than 50 percent of the blacks reside today) given a full voting franchise or access to the most elementary of social amenities.

Against that backdrop of chains and servitude we may now consider the new phenomenon—the emerging black middle class—and consider what it means in America today and what it portends for America in the future. In passing, and not surprisingly, it will be noted that the rhetoric of recent years has not conformed to the reality of recent years.

The bottom line in any real mass ranking of status in American life is *money*. And it is to money that we will look first to show the broad outlines of stark upward mobility.

The 1970 Census reveals that during the 1960s, that infamous decade of "deteriorating" conditions for blacks (how many times did we hear that during the riots?), the following income changes took place:

• Income for white families in America went up by 69 percent.

• Income for black families in America went up by 99.6 percent.*

Of course, if one rounds the 99.6 percent figure it can be stated that black family income *doubled* during a single decade.†

This striking increase in black family income led to this changing

---

* Actual figures for that and other numbers in this chapter, unless otherwise specified, are for "Negroes and Other Races" as defined by the Census Bureau. As "Negroes" comprise 90 percent of the "Negroes and Other Races" category, this is a relatively good index of all Negroes in America.

† That, however, would be accurate only if inflation had not eroded *everyone's* income. If one deflates the income statistics to account for inflation white income increased by 34 percent in the decade and black income by 54 percent.

ratio of black family income compared to white family income:

Average Ratio: Black Median Family Income to White

1950–1954	55%
1955–1959	53
1960–1964	54
1965–1969	61
1970	64
1971	63
1972	62
1974	62

It is true that 62 percent is a long way from 100 percent and still scandalously low. It may be argued that the numbers have plateaued during the early 1970s and have even dipped a point or two. But what is open to little argument is that there was sharp progress—a catching up—for black families during the 1960s, which was not apparent during the 1950s, and, as of now, most of this income gain has been held. Remember, these are *ratios*; incomes for *both* races went *up* sharply, but more sharply for nonwhites. . . .*

The march of blacks into the middle class can be seen even more clearly if one looks at the data at levels less than for all blacks:

About half (52 percent in 1972) of the blacks in America now live in the South—a stark change from 1950 when more than two thirds (68 percent) of the blacks lived in the South.

When we look at black life in the South and outside of the South, there is a sharp difference. Thus, in 1972, black family income in the South was 55 percent of white family income, but outside of the South, black family income was *68 percent* of white income.

A second variable within black-white income ratios concerns family status. As we shall note later, black families are much more likely

---

* An argument has been made that the critical income numbers were not *ratios,* but *absolute dollar* figures. The absolute dollar gap, it is true, *widened* slightly ($3,958 in 1971 versus $3,788 in 1961 in constant 1971 dollars) between black and white families. But in our judgment, the relative rate of closure is far more important than the absolute rate. Suppose, for example, that black income were $5,000 a year and white income were $10,000 a year in a given year. Suppose then that a decade later black income had increased to $40,000 and white income had increased to $50,000. Given such data, the absolutists could claim that the absolute dollar gap had doubled. In point of fact, in the decade of the 1960s, white income went up by 69 percent and black income went up by 100 percent, and this seems to be a fairly decent rate of closure. Were black income to have fully held the line on the absolute dollar gap, it would have had to go up by 136 percent; were black income to reach total white-income levels, black income would have had to *triple,* an unlikely occurrence over the course of a single decade.

In short, what we are saying, is: You can't get there without passing through here. Even a substantial rate of catch-up would, for a certain time, have to proceed relatively, not absolutely. That is an unfortunate law of mathematics, not of race, but it is a law nonetheless.

to be "female headed." But when they are *not*—when the families are "husband-wife" families—incomes are much more likely to be closer to "equality." Among black husband-wife families all over America in 1971, income was *74 percent* of comparable white husband-wife family income. Outside of the South, it was *87 percent*.

Perhaps that most encouraging and most meaningful cross-tabulation of the income data concerns *young* blacks. As we shall see subsequently, younger blacks have made striking educational gains in recent years and subsequent gains in "occupation"—i.e., the *sorts* of jobs they hold. Accordingly, some fraction of these gains have reached the bottom line—income. Thus, young black males age twenty-five to thirty-four earned 70 percent of what their white counterparts earned, and young black females earned 96 percent of their white counterparts—compared to the total ratio of 62 percent.

When one *combines* all these attributes—youth, nonsouthern residence and unbroken family—a striking statistic emerges:

**Median Income of Husband-Wife Families, in the
North and West, with Head of Family Under 35
Years of Age, as Percent of White Income**

1959	*1971*
78%	93% (!)
of white income	of white income

There is an equally striking word that comes very close to describing that number: *parity*. Among young, nonsouthern, unbroken black families income parity has *almost* been achieved. As a matter of fact, if one adds a fourth variable to the equation—looking at black families and white families where *both* the husband and wife were working—these are the numbers that appear:

**Median Income of Husband-Wife Families with Head Under
35, in North and West When Husband and Wife
Both Worked, as a Percent of White Income**

1959	*1971*
85%	105% (!) (!)

If there is a word "super-parity," the number 105 percent would probably qualify.*

Finally, to conclude this brief view of the black movement into the American middle-income brackets, one more index that reveals both the progress made and the distance left to go:

Black Families in Poverty

1959	48%
1972*	29

* 1974 data: 28 percent.

In thirteen years, it can be said, an enormous change has occurred. From almost *half* in poverty at the dawn of the 1960s, we now have somewhat between a *quarter* and a *third* in poverty. As statistical changes go, that is a substantial difference. But this tragic fact remains, a fact that spells out one of the key aspects of the still smoldering resentments in the black community: 29 percent of the black families today are in poverty. The white percentage is only 7 percent—and that too is a substantial difference.

Employment

For about two decades the reality of the black-white employment situation was summed up this way: black unemployment rates have been *twice* as high as white rates. That is still the unhappy case.

But there has been a massive shift in *who* the black unemployed are. Thus, a cross-tabulation of black *married men* reveals a far sharper drop than for the population as a whole, as this comparison of two early years of the Sixties with two early years of the Seventies shows:

---

* Some, but by no means all, of these remarkable husband-wife family gains are due to the fact that young black wives outside of the South are somewhat more likely to work *year round* than young white wives (51 percent vs. 39 percent). However, it is important to note that in those young black families in the North and West where wives worked, the husbands were also progressing mightily. They earned 76 percent of comparable white husbands in 1959—and 90 percent of comparable white husbands in 1970. Moreover, regardless of the fact that black wives do contribute somewhat disproportionately to young black nonsouthern unbroken families, the money, extra money, *is* getting to the family, and that would seem to be what's most important, despite the harder and longer work involved. The family has the money.

Unemployment Rate and Ratio, Black to White
for Married Men, 20 Years Old and Over,
with Spouse Present, 1962–1972

	Negro and Other Races	White	Ratio
1962	7.9%	3.1%	2.5 to 1
1963	6.8	3.0	2.3 to 1
1971	5.0	3.0	1.7 to 1
1972*	4.5	2.6	1.7 to 1

* 1974 ratio: the same

The drop in the ratio from 1962 to 1972 is 53 percent (from 2.5 to 1 to 1.7 to 1—with 1 to 1 representing parity).

Again, then, one can observe a steady and powerful movement into the middle class. Black *family* men are—like white family men— "at work," that is, at least ninety-five out of a hundred even during recessionary times.

At the same time, however, teenage unemployment has gone up. Among black teenagers (sixteen to nineteen), unemployment rates in 1960 were 24 percent—apparently strikingly high. In 1970, the rate had climbed to 29 percent—substantially higher, and by 1972 it was 34 percent. In each case the rate for white teenagers was between 13 percent and 15 percent.*

But there is something to be said about black teenage unemployment that is not generally understood. These numbers, from 1972, tell the story:

- In all there were 2.2 million teenagers sixteen to nineteen.

- Of these, 1.43 million were "not in the labor force," about two thirds. (About 1.2 million of these are *students*; most of the balance are housewives.) They were neither "at work" nor "looking for work." They are not tabulated in unemployment statistics. They are doing what most teenagers in America do—going to school or tending house.

- That leaves about 770,000. These are the black teenagers "in the labor force"—either "at work" or "looking for work." About *two thirds*—about 510,000—are at work.

- That leaves about 260,000 who are actually unemployed, i.e., "looking for work." (The fraction of 260,000 over 770,000 yields the high unemployment rate—the percentage *without* jobs who are actively looking for work. If one were to put the 260,000 over the de-

* 1975 data: up a couple of points for both races.

nominator of the 2.2 million total teenagers, the resultant percentage would be about 12 percent, which is a far cry from the 34 percent "unemployment" figure.)

- But even of the 260,000 unemployed black teenagers, about 45 percent—116,000—*are in school* and about 83 percent of these are looking for *part-time work*.

- That leaves about 144,000 black teenagers—males and females—who are *out of work, out of school, and looking for work,* a condition that would somewhat more closely approach the popular perception of what "teenage unemployment" actually represents.

- The out-of-school out-of-work component represents *6.6 percent* of the total number of black teenagers!

That is a far cry from the stereotype of hordes of young blacks hanging around street corners staring vacant-eyed toward a dead-end future, remembering a dead-end past. About 70 percent of black teenagers are in school. About another 25 percent are at work or at home as housewives. The rest—about 6 percent—may well be perceived as hard-core teenage unemployed.

Why then the stereotype of massive black teenage unemployment? Part of the fault lies in the statistical reportage system. The "unemployment rate" is defined as the percentage of those "in the labor force" who are "looking for work." But among young people almost two thirds are "not in the labor force," although they are usefully occupied, typically as either students or housewives. "Unemployed" also involves students seeking part-time work, surely an important consideration, sometimes a critical consideration for a family, sometimes a necessity to be able to stay in school, but also surely not generally in tune with the notion of desolated young men hanging around on street corners with no future before them. They are students. They are going someplace.

The second reason for the stereotype is the high visibility—and the dangerous potential—of such young, unemployed, black males as there are. Of particular significance in this connection is the ominous—and terrifying—rise in the crime rate generally and specifically the very high rate of young black criminals, particularly in urban areas.

On balance: teenage unemployment rates are up, adult male rates down, particularly so among married males. The teenagers are mostly in school. The adults are mostly supporting families. The net result would seem to be a social and economic plus despite the continuing "two to one" ratio of black to white unemployment rates.

Middle classness, of course, concerns itself with more than just "income" and more than just "unemployment." Part of the mosaic of middle-class life concerns what *kind* of jobs people hold.

Looking now at that slice of life we see a major march by blacks into the middle-class occupations. If one uses the grouping "white collar workers," "craftsmen" and "operatives"* as the one representing the better (middle class) jobs in America, then we see this progression over the decade:

Numbers of White Collar Workers, Craftsmen
and Operatives

	Negro	White
1960	2.9 million	46.1 million
1970	5.1	57.0
1972	5.2	58.3
Percentage Increase 1960–1972	79%	26%

Over the same dozen years the numbers of Negroes in "other" work—primarily low paying jobs in private households, as service workers, farm workers and laborers—*decreased from 4.0 million to 3.5 million.*

Compare, then, the *balance* of occupational status for blacks in America in 1960 and in 1970. In 1960, blacks in "good" jobs totaled 2.9 million while blacks in "not good" jobs totaled 4.0 million. Far more blacks had "not good" jobs. But by 1972, the number of blacks with "good" jobs totaled 5.2 million, while those with "not good" jobs totaled 3.5 million.

The 1960 data works out to 42 percent of the blacks holding the "good" (i.e., middle-class) jobs—less than half. By 1972, the rate haa climbed to 60 percent—about three fifths in middle-class jobs.†

In 1970, there were 196,000 black "construction craftsmen" of whom, for some examples, 26,000 were "brickmasons and stonemasons" and 14,000 were electricians (up almost 100 percent since 1960).‡ There were 183,000 black "truck drivers" and 73,000 black "automobile mechanics and repairmen, including body." And there were 223,000 black "teachers except colleges and universities," 9 percent of

---

* A grouping used by the Census Bureau in *The Social and Economic Status of the Black Population in the U.S., 1971*.

† 1974 data: 63 percent.

‡ Many of the new and better jobs held by blacks are union jobs, and many of these are in the much-discussed construction trades. Of particular interest are the apprenticeship figures, for these

the total in America. Back in 1960, there were 4,378 blacks who were engineers. And in 1970, there were 13,000. Some other changes:

Black Males, Selected Occupations, 1960–1970

	1960	1970
Accountants	5,434	9,177
Foremen	20,944	52,894
Printing craftsmen	3,306	8,049
Police	10,803	22,254
Welders and flame cutters	24,787	46,994

Education

Along with higher incomes and better jobs, the 1960s also saw a great breakthrough in the educational realm. Thus in 1960, a little more than a third—only 38 percent—of young Negro males (aged twenty to twenty-nine) had finished at least four years of high school. By 1967, the rate was more than half—*52 percent*. By 1972, it was almost two thirds—*64 percent*. Among young women the increase was about as great—from 43 percent in 1960 to 56 percent in 1967 and to 66 percent in 1972.

If one were to set an educational level that would accurately separate the American society into "middle class" and "nonmiddle class," probably the criteria of "completed high school education" serves best. For young blacks, in a dozen years, the rate of finishing high school went from about 40 percent to about 65 percent!

There is an even longer range perspective available. Here is the progression of "median school years completed" for *all* young Americans since 1940:

Median School Years Completed, All Races, Aged 25–29

1940	10.3 years
1950	12.1
1960	12.3
1970	12.6
1972*	12.7

* 1974 data: 12.5 years.

---

signal the way of the future. In 1972, 13 percent of the total number of apprentices in the construction trades, and 20 percent of those enrolled in the first half of 1972, were nonwhite—rates above the nonwhite proportion of the population as a whole. Curiously, despite all the talk about blacks and unions, one central fact is generally ignored: Blacks are slightly more likely, not less likely, to belong to unions than are whites. In 1970, black workers were 12 percent of all union members. (Blacks are 11 percent of the total population.)

Twelve years of schooling equals a completed high school education. Thus, young Americans (i.e., *white* Americans) moved into the
"educational middle class" during the 1940s: In 1940, the typical young
American was still a "high school dropout," by 1950, the typical young
American was a "high school graduate."

Twenty years later the same sort of great leap forward took place
for blacks in America:

Median School Years Completed, Negroes, Aged 25–29

1940	7.0 years
1950	8.6
1960	10.8
1970	12.2(!)
1972	12.4

In 1940, the young black was typically an *elementary school dropout*. A decade later he could be described only as an *elementary school
graduate*. Not until 1960 did the young American black typically reach
even the level of *high school dropout*. And not until 1970 did he typically
become a *high school graduate*—a bona fide member of the educational
middle class.

And there is a shorter range perspective also available to show
that the progress hasn't stopped: The high school dropout rate for
blacks aged fourteen to twenty-four in 1967 had come down to 24
percent for males and 22 percent for females—from about 36 percent in
1960. By 1972, the dropout rate was 18 percent for males and 17 percent for females. In a dozen years, then, a halving!

To give a flavor of the speed with which a major degree of "catching up" came about, we can note that the gap between young whites
and young blacks in 1950 was 3.5 years of completed school years.
(The young white in 1950 was already a high school graduate—12.1
years of school completed. The young black—with 8.6 years of school
completed was an elementary school graduate.) Twenty years later the
gap was .4 of a year—12.6 years vs. 12.2 years.*

The leap into the educational middle class can also be seen in the
college enrollment statistics. Here are the data showing black-white
comparisons over a short seven-year period—from 1965 to 1972.

---

* For Americans of *all ages*, there is still a major disparity, reflecting earlier years of inequity. Median
school years completed for *all adult* Negroes was 10.1 years in 1971, compared to 12.2 years for all
adult whites.

Percent of Persons Aged 18–24 Enrolled in College 1969–1972

	1965	1972
Negro	10%	18%
White	26	26
"Gap"	16	8
Ratio	2.6 to 1	1.4 to 1

Again the gap remains—but it has narrowed considerably.

Viewed in a somewhat different way: In 1967, there were 370,000 blacks in college; by 1972, the number had gone up by 97 percent (!) to 727,000. In the same time period, white enrollment in college went up by just 26 percent. Blacks today comprise about 9 percent of the total college population, not too far off from their relation to the population as a whole (11 percent). . . .

There it is: By most of the standards by which America has in the past calculated what is middle class, Negroes in the last decade have made mighty strides, both absolutely and relatively to whites. If this sounds as if what is being said here is that the stereotype of the black in America must be changed from an earlier portrait of an uneducated, ill-employed, poverty-stricken slum dweller to a new stereotype—that is correct. If it sounds as if we are saying that the new black stereotype involves an individual earning a living wage at a decent job, with children who stay in school and aspire to still better wages and still better jobs, living out of a slum but still in a ghetto, in a decent but unelaborate dwelling, still far "behind" whites but catching up—that too is correct. This new stereotype, it is suggested, represents a middle-class life-style and it can be appropriately applied to about half the black population. That is a striking change in the American scene—better by far than what it replaces. . . .

NOTES

1. Charles E. Lindblom, *The Policy-Making Process* (Englewood Cliffs, N.J.: Prentice-Hall, 1968), p. 34.
2. See John C. Donovan, *The Politics of Poverty* (New York: Pegasus, 1967), especially Ch. 3. See also, particularly for his criticism of the participatory rule, Daniel Patrick Moynihan's *Maximum Feasible Misunderstanding* (New York: The Free Press, 1969).
3. Significantly, the pressure of state officials forced the removal of a provision for appeals from decisions and released the highway departments from an

obligation to consider alternative means of transportation, such as mass transit systems. See *The New York Times,* Jan. 17, 1969.

4. See the article reviewing the legislative history of the Green Amendment, *The New York Times,* Dec. 25, 1967. Significantly, the amendment also bars use of OEO money for voter registration drives!

5. Gabriel Almond and Sidney Verba, *The Civic Culture* (Princeton, N.J.: Princeton University Press, 1963), pp. 210, 219. See also Sidney Verba and Norman H. Nie, *Participation in America* (New York: Harper, 1972).

6. Hannah Arendt, *Eichmann in Jerusalem* (New York: Viking, 1964), p. 289.

7. Franz Kafka, *The Castle* (New York: Knopf, 1930).

8. Joseph Lyford, *The Airtight Cage* (New York: Harper, 1966).

QUESTIONS FOR DISCUSSION

1. What are the differences between Lockard and Wattenberg? What are the similarities?

2. Do the rules established in the Constitution work against the poor?

3. Take one area of public policy—such as environmental protection, education, occupational safety, taxation, affirmative action, or public health—and evaluate whether or not the constitutional rules were rigged for the benefit of the well-to-do.

4. If Wattenberg's analysis that the economic and social conditions of black people in America are improving is correct, what conclusions should be drawn about the bias of the American political system?

5. Would you consider Wattenberg to be a conservative or a liberal? Why?

SUGGESTED READINGS

Banfield, Edward C. *The Unheavenly City Revisited: A Revision of "The Unheavenly City."* Boston: Little, Brown, 1974.

Beichman, Arnold. *Nine Lies About America.* New York: Library Press, 1972.

Dellinger, Dave. *More Power Than We Know: The People's Movement Toward Democracy.* Garden City, N.Y.: Anchor, 1975.

Etzkowitz, Henry, and Peter Schwab, eds. *Is America Necessary? Conservative, Liberal and Socialist Perspectives of United States Political Institutions.* St. Paul, Minn.: West, 1976.

Harrington, Michael. *The Other America: Poverty in the United States.* Baltimore: Penguin Books, 1962.

Keech, William R. *The Impact of Negro Voting: The Role of the Vote in the Quest for Equality*. Skokie, Ill.: Rand McNally, 1968.

Novack, George. *Democracy and Revolution*. New York: Pathfinder Press, 1971.

Parenti, Michael. *Democracy for the Few*. New York: St. Martin's Press, 1974.

Report of the National Advisory Commission on Civil Disorders. Introduction by Tom Wicker. New York: Bantam, 1968.

3.

Has Federalism Outlived Its Usefulness?

Which is closer to the people: the state or national government? Americans differ about the correct answer. Some argue that the states are closer to the people. The national government in Washington, D.C., is far away, they contend, while the state government is located nearby. Bureaucrats in Washington, moreover, are never as familiar with the special problems of the states and cities as are state officials.

Other Americans, however, answer that the national government is closer to the people. They argue that more people can identify national leaders than state or local ones. Moreover, participation in presidential elections is greater than in state and local contests. The media, too, devote more attention to national than to state news. The national bureaucracy is not only located in Washington, they add, but in towns and cities throughout the United States as well.

Divided loyalties between national and state government are as much a problem today as they were when the Constitution was written in 1787. Then the Framers of the Constitution differed as to how much power the national and state governments should have and what the relationships of each division of government should be to the people. Most of them, however, agreed that a *federal* rather than a *unitary* system be established.

The Framers' decision to establish a federal system was put into the Constitution. At that time, America was an agricultural country of only thirteen states and was a small power in the world arena. In spite of the many changes that have occurred since 1787—among them the expansion of the United States to fifty states and its emergence as a major industrial nation and a world power—the federal system has endured.

An understanding of the federal system today requires, first, an examination of what federalism is, why it was established, and how it has evolved. Federalism is a system of government under which power is distributed between central and regional authorities in a way that provides each with important power and functions. The United States is but one of many federal systems around the world; Canada, India, and West Germany are all examples of nations that have federal systems. In the United States the central authority is the *federal government* and the regional authorities are the *state governments.*

A federal system, then, divides power. A unitary system, in contrast, concentrates power. In a unitary system, power is controlled by the central authorities as, for example, in Great Britain and France. In Britain, regional governing authorities are created, abolished, or rearranged by the central government at Westminster. In the federal system of the United States, however, state governments cannot be so restructured. No state boundary can be changed by the government in Washington acting on its own authority. (One exception occurred during the Civil War when the state of West Virginia was created out of Virginia. That case, however, was a product of the special conditions of the Civil War.)

A federal system was adopted in 1787 because a unitary structure would have been unacceptable to the American people, who had strong loyalties to their states. In addition, the Framers of the Constitution wanted a government that would be stronger than the one existing under the Articles of Confederation, but they feared a government that was too powerful. The federal system allowed for a compromise between those who favored a strong central government and those who supported a weak central government.

The central government was given some exclusive powers (e.g., the power to coin money and to establish tariffs). The states and federal government shared some powers (e.g., the power to tax and to spend money). The Tenth Amendment to the Constitution provided that the powers not delegated to the United States by the Constitution, nor prohibited by it to the states, "are reserved to the states respectively, or to the people."

The Constitution, however, is not so clear about where the powers of the central government end. Two centuries of conflict over this issue of states' rights have marked American history. In general, the trend has been away from states' rights and toward national supremacy.

Those who argue for states' rights contend that the Constitution must be interpreted strictly. Congress should legislate only in those areas that are specifically delegated to it in the Constitution, and should leave all those powers not mentioned to the states.

Those who argue for national supremacy, however, maintain that the Constitution establishes a strong central government with vast authority. They support a broad interpretation of federal government powers.

National supremacy proponents have won victories although they have always been under attack by states' rights advocates. In 1819, for example, in *McCulloch* v. *Maryland,* the Supreme Court upheld the power of the federal government to create a bank in spite of the fact that the Constitution does not grant an expressed power to the national government for this purpose. Congress was granted broad scope through Article I, Section 8, Clause 18 of the Constitution that gives Congress the right to select whatever means are necessary and proper to carry out its delegated powers.

As the character of American society has changed, so, too, have the institutions of government. The relationship between the states and national government has been influenced by these changes. In commerce the states were unable to deal with the problems of the big corporations whose activities transcended state boundaries. Economic problems such as unemployment and inflation could not be solved satisfactorily at the state level and required national attention.

States' rights became the slogan of groups who benefited from decentralized control—such as big business and segregationalists—while national supremacy was heralded by those groups who received strong support from Washington—such as labor unions and civil rights advocates. In those instances in which the states were unable or unwilling to meet the demands of a changing industrial economy and the welfare state, the national government asserted its authority—often at the expense of the states. The courts have upheld the right of the federal government to move into areas previously dominated by the states—such as integration, education, housing, commerce, and employment.

Because the issue of states' rights has become so prominent in the course of American history, it would be wrong to conclude that the relationship between the federal government and the states is best categorized as a zero-sum game: that is, whatever one side gains, the other side loses. Today, *cooperation* rather than *conflict* characterizes the relations between the two levels of government, as may be seen from the kinds of federal assistance given to the states.

The federal government has been increasing its support of the states through programs of federal aid to state governments. The federal government has been collecting taxes and disbursing its revenues to the states to be used for a variety of purposes, such as housing, education, health, transportation, highways, and law enforcement. Interestingly, the states have not asserted the doctrine of states' rights to prevent the money from flowing to their own coffers, but rather have encouraged and lobbied for more aid.

Three basic types of economic assistance have been most prominent: categorical grants, block grants, and revenue sharing. Each type has advantages and disadvantages that are loudly proclaimed by the groups and agencies who benefit the most from one rather than the other aid forms.

A categorical grant is an allocation for a specific purpose, such as hospital equipment or school lunches. Under this type of grant, the state may administer a program but must comply with rigid federal guidelines dealing with policies and expenditures. Sometimes the federal grant depends on the state providing matching funds (that is, contributing state money) in amounts ranging from 10 percent to 50 percent of the federal contribution.

A block grant is an allocation of money to the states for broad rather than narrow functions. Unlike the categorical grant, with its rather specific designation of programs, the block grant is allocated for such general policy areas as education, transportation, and law enforcement. A block grant for education can be used for any kind of educational assistance decided upon by state authorities, although it is subject to general federal regulations. State agencies have much more flexibility in using block grants than they have with categorical grants.

Revenue sharing is a recent innovation in grants and was probably the Nixon Administration's major achievement in domestic policy. Under revenue sharing, the federal government provides a general grant to the states and localities to be used by them as they see fit, but with certain restrictions. In 1972 Congress approved legislation providing $5.3 billion of general revenue sharing for the first year, and a total of $30.1 billion over a period of five years. Two thirds of the funds were reserved for the localities and one third for the states. The areas in which the states and localities could spend the money were limited to such fields as transportation, law enforcement, libraries, environmental protection, social services, public safety, recreation, and financial administration.

In 1976 Congress approved a $25.6 billion extension of the federal revenue-sharing program through fiscal year 1980. These funds were to be distributed over a forty-five month period. The basic entitlement of fiscal year 1977 was $6.65 billion. For fiscal years 1978 through 1980, it would be $6.85 billion each year. The law adhered to the principle of "no-strings" by removing the limitations of the 1972 law in which the money could only be used for certain general areas of policy. It strengthened civil rights features, including a timetable for establishing equality and a mechanism for closing off funds to localities found to be discriminatory. The law also provided for increased popular participation in deciding how the money would be used.

Two questions about federalism are asked in this chapter: (1) can the states be trusted to meet the most important domestic priorities? and (2) is revenue sharing more effective than categorical grants in benefiting the poor and minorities?

TRUSTING THE STATES

Daniel J. Elazar, Director of the Center for the Study of Federalism at Temple University, argues that the states can be trusted to meet important domestic priorities. He contends that criticisms against the states are based on beliefs that may have had some validity in the past but that are no longer accurate assessments of state practices. Specifically, he directs his criticism against five myths: (1) the states are unmindful of local—particularly big-city—needs, while the cities distrust the states and refuse to cooperate with them; (2) the states and localities are administratively incapable of properly utilizing any additional powers that might be transferred to them; (3) even if the states and localities now have enough in common and sufficient administrative skills to handle the additional powers, corruption and vested interests will prevent them from utilizing those powers well; (4) the states and localities have failed to assume their proper fiscal obligations, and there is no reason why the federal government should bail them out; and (5) the states and localities will dissipate federal money given them without any strings attached instead of using the funds where they are most needed.

Historian Arthur Schlesinger asserts a modern liberal view of the role of the states. He charges that state governments are not responsive to the people, but rather are dominated by the locally powerful.

According to Schlesinger, the national government—rather than state governments—is better suited to deal with the problems of industrial society. The national government, moreover, has vindicated racial justice, strengthened civil liberties, civilized industries, protected natural resources, and helped labor and farmers.

GRANTS-IN-AID

Even when there is agreement that the federal government should provide funds to the states, controversy surrounds the kind of aid to be offered. This controversy stems in part from the fact that different government agencies, legislators, interest groups, and individuals may benefit from revenue sharing rather than categorical grants-in-aid.

The pros and cons of revenue sharing are discussed in an article by Michael D. Reagan, a leading scholar of federalism. That article was written prior to the enactment of the 1976 law that made some revisions in revenue sharing. It reveals, however, the most important arguments for and against this kind of assistance.

Reagan asserts the following arguments for revenue sharing: (1) It has been politically successful in that governors, mayors, city councils, and the appointed officials who help spend the money all enjoy receiving the quarterly checks. (2) Its public notification requirements contribute to increased citizen participation in at least some cities. (3) The absence of federal red tape makes it simple to administer. (4) In the short run, revenue sharing provides a proportionate shift in decision-making power from federal to local hands. (5) It provides aid that can be used for the central functions of local governments. (6) The hand of elected leaders of local government may be strengthened vis-à-vis their functional department heads. (7) Revenue sharing provides greater evenness and predictability in the flow of funds than does the present project-grant system in many localities.

Reagan also notes the arguments against revenue sharing: (1) There are a number of identifiable national objectives to be obtained through domestic public policies. These specific objectives are better served through grants-in-aid that allow for accountability. (2) Three problem categories—problems of the poor, problems of ethnic minorities, and problems of the cities—suffer the most under revenue sharing. (3) The rise of revenue sharing has been used as an excuse for cutting back on the other kinds of aid. (4) Federal leverage to promote a merit personnel system so that states would have better administrators is weakened. (5) The institution-building function of many federal demonstration grant and pilot-program grants is now almost entirely ended. (6) The nondiscrimination provisions of the law are inadequate. (7) The beneficiary user groups are the nonpoor, non-minority residents.

Although providing arguments for and against revenue sharing, Reagan concludes that categorical grants and revenue sharing each have strengths and weaknesses. He recommends a compromise that would "focus on block grants, while permitting perhaps 10 percent of the funds in any grant program to be available on a very broad, open-ended competitive proposal basis."

Can the States Be Trusted to Meet the Most Important Domestic Priorities?

YES

DANIEL J. ELAZAR
The New Federalism: Can the States Be Trusted?∗

. . . I propose to evaluate state and local government, not by citing a few extreme examples, but by looking at the general record which state and local governments as a whole have built in each of the areas their critics have pointed to.

∗ From Daniel J. Elazar, "The New Federalism: Can the States Be Trusted?" *The Public Interest*, No. 35 (Spring 1974), pp. 91–102. © 1974 by National Affairs, Inc. Reprinted by permission.

THE MYTH OF URBAN-RURAL WARFARE

Criticism #1: The states are unmindful of local—particularly big-city— needs, while the cities distrust the states and refuse to cooperate with them. This argument had considerable merit during the two generations or so the country took to make the transition from rural to urban living. Not unreasonably, declining rural populations were reluctant to give up their dominance of state governments to the new urbanites, particularly since so many of the former genuinely believed in the moral superiority of rural life and so many of the latter belonged to ethnic or racial groups with decidedly different mores. Indeed, much of what posed as urban-rural conflict was really interethnic conflict set in a discreet juridical framework—one confirmation of which can be found in the voting support those city dwellers who came from the same ethnic, cultural, and religious backgrounds gave their rural brethren.

Since the rural-urban transition took place at different times in different parts of the country, different states have been undergoing its pains since the late nineteenth century. Consequently, in the memories of those now living there have always been horrible examples of rural-dominated state political systems interfering with the burgeoning cities within their borders, and these examples have obscured the ever-growing number of states that were politically responsive to their cities.

By 1970 few, if any, states had yet to enter the transition period. Put simply, the record reveals that the transition begins when at least 40 percent of a state's population is urban and is completed when urban places account for over 60 percent of the population total. No state is now below that 40 percent figure, and only 11 (seven of them in the South) are less than 50 percent urban, but these contain only a bit more than 10 percent of the country's population. Another nine fall between 50 and 60 percent. Before the 40 percent mark is attained, big cities find it very difficult to gain consideration in their state capitols. This is hardly surprising in a democracy, where majorities rule and overwhelming majorities tend to rule easily. After the 40 percent figure is reached, the cities can begin to bargain with increasing success. Georgia is a case in point, having passed the 40 percent mark in 1960 and closed on the 50 percent mark in 1970.

Past 60 percent, there is no longer any real contest. Minnesota and Indiana are good examples. Since they passed 60 percent their legislatures, each in its own way, have opened up to every kind of prometropolitan legislation that has been proposed. Ten of the 50 states, containing some 79.4 million people (or nearly 40 percent of the country's total population), are 75 percent urban or more, which means that urban and state interests are essentially identical.

Cities—of varying sizes and with varying interests, to be sure—are in the saddle in virtually all of the states today, and rural-urban conflict has given way to new interurban conflicts in whose resolution the state government plays a legitimate and not unfair role, even if the losers, in the great tradition of American politics, holler "foul" at every opportunity. Today the old myth is perpetuated by such phenomena as the political squabbles between New York City and New York State (85 percent urban)—which are the logical outcome of the inevitable clash between a powerful mayor and an equally powerful governor, both of whom, in the natural course of things, are likely to harbor national political ambitions—and the difficulties Washington, D.C., has because it belongs to no state. Not only are both these cases exceptional, but the squabbling obscures the substantial, if quiet, day-to-day intergovernmental cooperation that prevails even in these jurisdictions.

Even more significant than the fact of urban hegemony in contemporary state-city relations is the fact that state expenditures have grown extraordinarily since World War II, and that most of those expenditures, particularly in the last decade, have been funneled into urban areas, especially big cities. Unfortunately, the great fixed-cost programs such as public welfare, in which the fixed costs keep rising, have absorbed the greater part of these funds so that they are largely unavailable for more innovative uses. Worse for the public image of the states, the funds are so quickly absorbed in this manner that the public is not even aware that they have been increased—but this does not change the fact that they have been. . . .

THE MYTH OF ADMINISTRATIVE INCOMPETENCE

Criticism #2: The states and localities are administratively incapable of properly utilizing any additional powers that might be transferred to them. This myth also has its roots in a partial truth of the past. When the role of government in American society underwent drastic expansion in the 1930s, Washington did indeed set the pace in the development of a proper bureaucracy to manage the new government programs. Many of the states and localities were either unprepared or too impoverished by the Depression to respond in kind, and some were still too small in size to require so extensive an administrative apparatus. Nevertheless, most states laid the foundations during the Depression years for an administrative system appropriate to the mid-twentieth century, and then built on those foundations after World War II, when the resources denied them by circumstances for fifteen years or more became available again.

Today, in my own talks with officials of federal agencies that work with their state and local opposite numbers I have found, even among those not particularly disposed to turn their functions over to other planes of government, a growing consensus affirming the competence of state and local administration. These insiders' arguments in favor of retaining a strong federal presence are based on real or perceived policy differences between them and the states and localities, not on the question of competence. Nor should this cause any great surprise. The investigations of political scientists over the past decade—totally ignored by the mythologists, of course—have consistently found no substantial difference among the three groups of bureaucrats with respect to background, capability, and dedication to their respective programs. All the studies have shown that, in most program areas, the administrative officials of all three planes of government are drawn from the same professional backgrounds and are committed to the same professional goals.

Perhaps most important, within the past decade the executive agencies of general government in both the states and localities—that is, the offices of the governors and mayors—have generally been strengthened in a manner reminiscent of the strengthening of the president's office in the 1920s and 1930s. State planning agencies are being developed as arms of the office of governor; executive office staffing has improved in cities as well as in states; and mayors and governors are increasingly using their planning staffs as resources for controlling and coordinating the multifarious activities of their governments, much as our presidents use the Office of Management and Budget. . . .

None of the foregoing is intended to suggest that there are no problems facing state and local administrations or that all business is efficiently conducted in the states and localities; but by the same token, no one is about to claim that the federal administration is without its serious problems either. Not many Americans would deny Washington the wherewithal to administer programs because of the TFX scandal [in which a Department of Defense decision in 1962 to build a tactical fighter aircraft—TFX, later named F-111—became embroiled in controversy about the military effectiveness of the airplane, spiraling costs, choice of contractor, and civil-military relations] or the Post Office mess or the lack of coordination within HEW [Health, Education, and Welfare]. No government has a monopoly on efficiency—or inefficiency—in the United States today. Consequently, decisions as to where to locate responsibility must hinge on other criteria.

THE PROBLEM OF CORRUPTION

Criticism #3: Even if the states and localities now have enough in common and sufficient administrative skills to handle the additional powers, corruption and vested interests will prevent them from utilizing those pow-

ers well. The "local corruption" argument, another favorite myth in the American political repertoire, has at least two serious inadequacies. One is a question of fact. As a group, state and local governments today are far less corrupt in the usual sense of the term than at any time in the past hundred years. When it comes to "conventional" corruption, the same can be said of the federal government. (The kind of corruption represented by Watergate is something new—and it is far more dangerous than old-fashioned graft and influence peddling.) A whole host of factors having to do with changes in American society have operated to reduce at all planes of government the relatively crude forms of political payoff common at the turn of the century and earlier.

This is not to suggest that there is no longer any old-fashioned corruption in government in the United States. The real question here, however, is whether Bobby Baker's style of corruption is somehow less pernicious or objectionable than that of the ex-mayor of Newark? I doubt it. Payoffs, slush funds, and links with organized crime are no more defensible when they involve federal officials than when they involve state or local ones. For that matter, there is little to be said for private corporations in this connection either, particularly in the wake of the scandal surrounding the Penn Central [Railroad] bankruptcy and other such examples of corporate malfeasance. . . .

A second weakness of the "local corruption" argument is its tendency to overestimate the extent to which corruption, where it exists, affects the delivery of governmental services. There are many indications that corruption has far less influence on governmental performance today than it did eighty or one hundred years ago. This is because the nature of corruption has changed; the old days of straightforward bribery and "buying" of public officials have generally disappeared. Today, practices are more subtle; characteristically, they involve rewarding one's friends with favors rather than blocking proposed government activities. The lucrative business today is in the awarding of contracts for the delivery of services, a system which more or less guarantees that services will be delivered one way or another. Consequently, whether corruption exists or not, the services will.*

Corruption is a perennial governmental problem, and it is usually related to norms rooted in the local culture. By all accounts, states like Michigan, Minnesota, Virginia, and Utah are far less corrupt than the

---

* Massachusetts may well be a case in point. While its politics are often described as seamy, its governmental record actually makes it by any measure one of the most progressive governments in the Union, and in pioneering new programs or setting higher standards it often outdoes Washington. In the case of the Bay State, the combination of the moralistic commitment to "good government" stemming from its Puritan heritage and the desire to utilize politics to gain material advantage which is strong among many of its "ethnic" politicians has served to enhance the progressive character of that commonwealth when it comes to the delivery of services, even as it maintains its reputation for shady politics.

federal government. New York, North Carolina, and Pennsylvania are probably on a par with Washington in this respect, while Indiana, Louisiana, New Jersey, and Texas are probably more corrupt. Even the above list indicates that there is no simple correlation between corruption and the quality of government.

Much the same argument can be made in the case of waste. There are clearly no grounds for believing that one plane of government is more wasteful than the others, though the way in which their wastefulness is manifested may differ. Personal deficiencies of public officials cause waste and inefficiency in some of the smaller states and localities, but no more than is generated by red tape in very large bureaucracies like the federal government today.

Nor do vested interests in the states and localities cause more "distortions" of public policy than those in Washington. This proposition has been well tested in recent years as the federal government has extended its regulatory powers over coal mining, boating, flammable clothes, and, most recently, industrial safety, supposedly in response to state "failures." It has become increasingly apparent that federal regulation has meant not higher standards in these areas but an adjustment of standards toward a national mean that suits the interests of the parties being regulated, often to the dismay of those who championed federal intervention in the first place on the ground that federal action would obviously mean higher standards.

WHY ARE FEDERAL FUNDS NEEDED?

Criticism #4: The states and localities have failed to assume their proper fiscal obligations, and there is no reason why the federal government should bail them out. If the truth be known, the states and localities have borne the brunt of the effort to cope with increased demand for domestic services since the end of World War II. No matter what base period is used, the fiscal data confirm this. Since 1946, state and local revenues from their own sources have risen from under $10 billion to over $100 billion, or by more than 10 times, while federal revenues have only quadrupled. Between 1960 and 1969—a decade of great expansion of federal activities—federal expenditures rose 69 percent, including increases for the Vietnam war, but state and local expenditures rose 76 percent. For only a few brief years during the mid-1960s at the height of the Great Society did federal expenditures increase at the same rate as those of the states and cities.

In 1969, three fifths of the states with their local governments spent over $2 billion annually. Approximately two fifths spent over $4 billion. No state (with its localities) spent less than $0.5 billion. The present administration has announced that California and New York stand to gain half a billion dollars each from revenue sharing, yet the state and local governments of each now spend in the vicinity of *$30 billion annually*. . . .

Even the argument about the regressiveness of state taxes has lost potency in the last decade. Forty-five states now collect a state income tax, and several of the remaining states, which rely exclusively on the sales tax, have made that tax a far less regressive instrument than it once was by exempting such necessities as food, clothing, and medicine. As Dick Netzer [Professor of Economics at New York University] has shown, a properly constructed sales tax can be less regressive than some income taxes. Only in the case of local reliance on property taxes is serious regressiveness still built into the system, but even here many states are now providing some relief for low-income taxpayers to the extent that they are fiscally able to do so. In fact, additional states are moving toward the adoption of statewide income taxes every year. What seems to be holding them back (and holding others back from substantially increasing their rates) is the already onerous burden of the federal income tax, which has virtually preempted the field.

There are good reasons for utilizing federally collected funds for increasing state and local revenues in a manner that provides some inter-state equalization and does not penalize the more progressive states in competing for new industry. But the need for revenue sharing does not mean that the states (with two or three exceptions) have been negligent or remiss in bearing the fiscal burdens placed upon them by their Constitutional responsibility for most of the domestic functions of government.

WILL FEDERAL MONEY BE WISELY USED?

Criticism #5: The states and localities will dissipate federal money given them without any strings attached instead of using the funds where they are most needed. The governmental functions which generate the heaviest drains on the country's fiscal resources—education, welfare, health, transportation—are precisely the ones whose necessity is generally accepted in all parts of the country or which have well-established clientele and interest-group support. The chances that any state or locality could easily ignore that public support is exceedingly slight. It has become entirely clear, in the study of federal aid programs, that once a program becomes routinized, there is rarely any difference of opinion among the planes of government as to the necessity for maintaining it. If anything, there is a tendency to freeze such programs in. There is absolutely no reason to doubt that the bulk of any shared revenues would be used to meet well-defined, well-established, and well-supported needs in these essential areas. . . .

I do not doubt that, in some places, greater local responsibility for making and administering public policy will engender results that liberals and persons whose concern for a particular program is unmodified by other interests will find disagreeable. In other places, the result will be just as disturbing to conservatives and to those whose opposition to particular programs is untempered by any other interest. This is the price of democracy. No doubt it is a price worth arguing about. But those who choose to discuss the issue should do so on its merits, not on the basis of the myths which have hitherto obscured them. Today there is simply no justification for thinking that the states and localities, either in principle or in practice, are less able to do the job than the federal government. In fact, there is some reason to believe that, even with their weaknesses, they will prove better able to restore public confidence in America's political institutions.

Can the States Be Trusted to Meet the Most Important Domestic Priorities?

NO

ARTHUR SCHLESINGER, JR.
Is It Jeffersonian? *

For American historians, President Nixon's State of the Union Message had an agreeably nostalgic ring. "The further away government is from people," he said, "the stronger government becomes and the weaker people become. . . . Local government is the government closest to the people and more responsive to the individual person; it is

* From Arthur Schlesinger, Jr., "Is It Jeffersonian?" *The New York Times,* January 30, 1971, p. 27. ©
1971 by The New York Times Company. Reprinted by permission.

people's government in a far more intimate way than the government in Washington can ever be."

This is the purest Jeffersonian gospel, and the familiar phrases strike deep and reassuring chords in all our sensibilities. On the other hand, our national experience has seen a steady movement away from Jeffersonian localism. Does this mean that American history was all a mistake? Or did Jeffersonianism in practice turn out to have fatal flaws? This is not just a question for the Nixon administration. It is a question for those on the left who denounce the national government and cry "all power to the people."

The reason why Jeffersonianism has receded through our history, it may be suggested, is precisely because government has *not* been, most of the time, "responsive to the individual person"—because it has *not* been, in fact, "people's government." For local government is characteristically the government of the locally powerful, not of the locally powerless; and the best way the locally powerless have found to sustain their rights against the locally powerful is through resort to the national government. Jeffersonianism, in short, has ordinarily meant in practice a system by which the strongest local interests, whether planters, landlords, merchants, bankers, or industrialists, have been able to consolidate their control. Local government is generally the last refuge of reaction. This is why liberals have long since abandoned Jeffersonian localism—and why conservatives, from the American Liberty League to President Nixon, like to flourish the Jeffersonian standard.

Seventy years ago Theodore Roosevelt explained that the national government was the only means by which we could correct injustices in a national society. He knew that industrialism had long since destroyed the rural utopia of Jefferson and that Hamiltonian means were now required. Woodrow Wilson even insisted that Jefferson himself would have changed his mind. "I feel confident," Wilson said, "that if Jefferson were living in our day he would see what we see. . . . Without the watchful interference, the resolute interference of the government, there can be no fair play."

It is the national government, for example, that has vindicated racial justice against local bigotry. It is the national government that has protected the Bill of Rights against local vigilantism. It is the national government that has preserved natural resources. It is the national government that has civilized our industry, that has secured the rights of labor organization, that has defended the farmer. The growth of national power, far from producing government less "responsive to the individual person," has given a majority of Americans far more dignity and freedom than they could win in a century of localism.

It is little wonder that those who dislike civil rights and civil liberties, who want to loot our timber lands and break our unions and dismantle our regulation of business, should propagate the fraud of local government as the only true "people's government." It is a little harder, though, to see why the New Left should join in this crusade.

Other considerations argue against Mr. Nixon's neo-Jeffersonianism. It demands, for example, a really stupefying act of faith to suppose local government more incorruptible, more efficient or more expert than national government. The national authority is less vulnerable to selfish local pressures, more flexible in the transfer of resources, more economical in the use of trained personnel.

To say this is not to say, as Mr. Nixon suggests, that "a bureaucratic elite in Washington knows what is best for people everywhere." Obviously more money should go to cities and states, though under stringent national standards; obviously we need a great deal more of what David Lilienthal [former director of the Tennessee Valley Authority] used to call the "decentralized administration of centralized authority."

But decentralization on the Nixon model—decentralization that would simply turn money and power over to local government and private business—would only defeat the humane purposes of contemporary America.

Mr. Nixon's notion that this would be "government that truly is by the people" and would give people "a bigger voice in deciding for themselves those questions that so greatly affect their lives" is refuted by American history. As for Mr. Nixon's proposition that inadequate enthusiasm for local government "is really a contention that you cannot trust people to govern themselves," this is sheer demagoguery.

The national government is just as "truly . . . by the people," just as legitimate an instrument of self-government, as local government—and an instrument that, through our history, has served individual freedom and social justice a good deal more consistently than the currently fashionable nostrum of all power to the neighborhood oligarchs.

QUESTIONS FOR DISCUSSION

1. Which is closer to the people: the state governments or the federal government?

2. What are the arguments for strengthening state governments at the expense of the federal government?

3. Are state governments more corrupt than the federal government? If so, why? If not, why?

4. If you were the leader of a group concerned with aiding poor people in America, would you advocate more power to (a) state governments, (b) the federal government, (c) both state and federal governments, or (d) none of these? Why?

5. How has the character of state governments changed since the beginning of the twentieth century?

SUGGESTED READINGS

Campbell, Alan K., ed. *The States and the Urban Crisis.* Englewood Cliffs, N.J.: Prentice-Hall, 1970.

Graves, W. Brooke. *American Intergovernmental Relations.* New York: Charles Scribner's Sons, 1964.

Grodzins, Morton. *The American System: A New View of Government in the United States,* ed. Daniel J. Elazar. Skokie, Ill.: Rand McNally, 1966.

Hamilton, Alexander, James Madison, and John Jay. *The Federalist Papers.* Introduction by Clinton Rossiter. New York: New American Library, 1961.

Jacob, Herbert, and Kenneth S. Vines, eds. *Politics in the American States: A Comparative Analysis,* 3rd ed. Boston: Little, Brown, 1976.

Kenyon, Cecilia M., ed. *The Antifederalists.* Indianapolis, Ind.: Bobbs-Merrill, 1966.

Leach, Richard. *American Federalism.* New York: Norton, 1970.

Lockard, Duane, ed. *Governing the States and Localities.* New York: Macmillan, 1969.

Mason, Alpheus T. *The States Rights Debate: Antifederalism and the Constitution,* 2nd ed. Englewood Cliffs, N.J.: Prentice-Hall, 1972.

Reagan, Michael D. *The New Federalism.* New York: Oxford University Press, 1972.

Riker, William H. *Federalism: Origin, Operation, Significance.* Boston: Little, Brown, 1964.

Sanford, Terry. *Storm over the States.* New York: McGraw-Hill, 1967.

Sharkansky, Ira. *The Maligned States: Policy Accomplishments, Problems, and Opportunities.* New York: McGraw-Hill, 1972.

Does Revenue Sharing Benefit the Poor and Minorities in the Way Categorical Grants-in-Aid Were Intended?

YES AND NO

MICHAEL D. REAGAN
*Revenue Sharing: The Pro and Con Arguments**

There is an interesting change in the character of arguments about the value of a public policy program as it moves from the status of a gleam in the eye of the interest groups and political leaders who propose it to that of an ongoing program having observable, real-world consequences. At the earlier stage, discussion focuses heavily on what the proposal should or should not accomplish; ideological points are prominent. Factual assertions are in part necessarily speculative extrapolations from some analogous precedents. Once a policy proposition has been legislated and implemented for a couple of years, however, the pros and cons become a good deal more practical. The arguments refer increasingly to specific evidence, and the pattern of who favors and who opposes increasingly reflects the realities of who is gaining and who is losing. Interest becomes more important than ideology, though the latter never disappears.

General revenue sharing—which will almost certainly stand as the most notable domestic policy initiative of the Nixon administration—was enacted as the State and Local Fiscal Assistance Act of 1972. At the time of this writing, it had been operating for two years. Long range effects remain necessarily uncertain (although we are not without some clues), but some of the short-run patterns of utilization and immediate impacts, political as well as fiscal, are already becoming apparent. An analysis of the arguments based upon evaluations or experience—which are growing hotter in anticipation of the debate in Congress regarding extension of the original five-year authorization—will therefore differ in significant respects from the prepassage arguments.[1]

* Reprinted from "The Pro and Con Arguments" by Michael D. Reagan in volume no. 419 of *The Annals* of the American Academy of Political and Social Science, May 1975, pp. 24–35. Reprinted by permission.

ARGUMENTS IN FAVOR

In this context, the strongest single argument in favor of revenue sharing is no longer Richard Nixon's (or Gerald Ford's) "New Federalism" notion of turning back the tide of history to re-create state-local government autonomy, on the rather naive assumption that doing so would automatically give greater political power (policy determining voice) to the average local citizen; nor is it the liberals' (led by economist Walter Heller) calculation that a once-projected but never reached federal surplus could be channeled into enlargement of the public sector while avoiding the obstacle of conservative objection to enlargement of the specifically national segment. The primary argument now—and it is likely to be a successful one in the renewal debates—is the bread-and-butter political one: governors, mayors, city councils, and the appointed officials who help spend the money all enjoy receiving the quarterly checks.

Some recipients are considerably disillusioned because the inauguration of what they had been led to expect would be an augmentation of discretionary income, supplementing existing grants-in-aid, coincided instead with a decrease in sometimes greater proportion in categorical grant funds. However, the formulae for revenue sharing are working in such a way that a large number of local jurisdictions are being pleasantly surprised to discover that their shares are large, relative to their existing budgets and needs, and can therefore be devoted to one-time special capital projects. That is a delightful situation for any politician, of course; thus the city fathers of hamlets, villages, and small towns are now the supporters of revenue sharing as a bulwark of localism—and those small towns are still a most salient factor in the political lives of congressmen. . . .

A second major argument that has emerged more prominently in the practice of revenue sharing than in prepassage discussions is the contribution that its public notification requirements seem to be making for increased citizen participation in at least some cities. One early study reported that about 50 percent of all cities held hearings on revenue sharing to provide an opportunity for citizens to be heard individually and through special interest groups regarding preferred areas of expenditure.[2] In some cities, hearings on the use of revenue-sharing funds were, or would have been, almost meaningless. When every available cent has to be used to maintain such basic services as police and fire protection and street maintenance, little room is left for discretionary judgment on the basis of citizen preferences. On the other hand, outside of the largest cities the fiscal situation was perhaps not sufficiently desperate to foreclose completely the making of choices, and the hearings could therefore be of substantive significance. Where special hearings were held on revenue-sharing funds—apart from standard general hearings on a city's entire budget—there seems to have been a great deal of interest elicited.

What remains to be seen is whether increased citizen interest— that is, citizen interest as expressed through leaders of private and public interest groups—which was clearly evident in the early months of revenue sharing, would fade as the early winners in the allocation struggle came to be seen as vested interests no longer amenable to shifting, or whether a true reawakening of a feeling of citizen power was being evidenced. One may speculate that individual and group participation was greater than it might otherwise have been simply because revenue sharing came along at a time when environmental and consumer protection activities had made citizen activism much more common than it had been for some time.

Finally, it should be noted that much of what can be said on this score falls in the realm of speculation, since the experience of revenue sharing is still a new one. It is interesting to note, even on that basis, that a greater percentage of revenue-sharing funds—though still a very small percentage—was spent on social services and health services in cities which held public hearings than in those which did not. This is possible evidence of the impact that citizen groups may have, if they stick to their guns. A carryover to general city budgets of the interest generated in direct public input into city budgeting processes would be particularly exciting as a presumably unanticipated spinoff from general revenue sharing. Life would become more hectic for city council members and budget analysts in the offices of city managers, but local democracy would be at least partly revitalized along the rhetorical lines used in the original advocacy of revenue sharing as a part of New Federalism.

Yet another element of revenue sharing that has clearly met with great approbation on the part of local governments is the administrative simplicity of the program: the absence of federal red tape as compared with the grantsmanship efforts that local governments have to engage in to receive funds under most of the project type grant-in-aid programs. There is a dilemma here, because the intent behind the bureaucratic requirements of the grant-in-aid programs is, quite properly, to ensure that federal funds are expended in accordance with the specific priorities embedded in the legislation under which Congress has authorized categorical grants; and accountability in the spending of public funds is not easily achieved without some reporting requirements. On the other hand, accountability requirements may largely defeat their own purpose if they ask for an amount or other precise information from the local level that cannot reasonably be attained, or if they involve attempts at control of local minutiae by officials some distance removed. As one close observer of federal aid programs has commented, the "amount of federal administrative regulation has been way out of proportion to the realization of federally prescribed values."[3] . . .

Whether revenue sharing constitutes in the long run a decentralization and return of power to state-local levels, or the creation of a much broader (not restricted to specific categories) dependency of those levels on Washington than has ever existed, is an open question.[4] In the short run, however, and at a yearly budget level of decision making within the context of the existing rules of the game, it is true that revenue sharing provides a proportionate shift in decision making power from federal to local hands. Receiving jurisdictions, under general revenue sharing, are required to report to the Office of Revenue Sharing in the Treasury Department their planned pattern of expenditures for the next revenue-sharing period and also to show ex post facto expenditures. They do so in a standardized format, but with no directions whatsoever as to where the emphasis in expenditures shall be placed, with the one exception that they are not permitted to spend revenue-sharing funds on school operation and maintenance, although they can use these monies for capital outlay of benefit to education. Since this is the only programmatic "string" attached to general revenue sharing, it does indeed give local jurisdictions greater choice in determining what human values will be given priority in the programs of a particular community.

Some other arguments in favor of revenue sharing remain much the same now as they were when the policy was first discussed. Revenue sharing provides aid that can be used for the central functions of local governments—police, fire, health and sanitation, for example—that have been hardest to get categorical aid for, perhaps because they have always been seen as the major local responsibility areas and perhaps because they lack political appeal. The basic housekeeping functions of local governments are, however, at the heart of what makes urbanization possible and hopefully pleasant. Certainly without these core activities, more sophisticated amenities of civilization would be worth little. Yet in many jurisdictions that have not had great need for the special programs funded by Washington through categorical grants, there has nevertheless been a need for improved basic services.

Two additional advantages of revenue sharing may appeal to the elected leaders of local governments particularly. First, the hand of such leaders may be strengthened vis-à-vis their functional department heads. The reasoning here is that under categorical grants the generalist leadership of a city had to rely very heavily upon the specialized skills and specialized contacts of functional department heads, who could bring these skills and contacts to bear in the process of seeking federal grants-in-aid for sewage plants, park and recreation facilities, urban renewal projects, airport construction, or whatever other purpose. Under general revenue sharing, however, it is the generalized elected leadership of mayors and city councils, governors and legislators who hold the purse strings and discretionary authority. Functional department heads must therefore make their cases to local generalist leadership if they are to obtain their share of revenue-sharing funds. Thus the direction of dependency is changed about. Another possible consequence of this change is that the department heads may have to become local politicians to a greater degree than previously; that is, they must develop skills in mobilizing electoral and interest group support locally to back up their requests at city hall.

The second advantage of revenue sharing for local leadership is that it provides greater evenness and predictability in the flow of funds than does the project grant system, so far as many localities are concerned. At least during the five-year term of the system, every community can use the official formula to project within reasonably close terms what its revenue-sharing income will be each year. Granted that the uncertainty of renewal at the end of five years has been a significant cause for complaint and hesitancy on the part of cities regarding areas that they fear they could not continue to finance if revenue sharing were dropped, it is still a good deal more reliable and predictable than the flow of funds under a project system in which all that is known is that the amount of funds available for each program annually will be considerably less than the amount requested in the form of competitive proposals. Under a project system, some cities do not get anything, and others do not know what they will get until administrative officials of the national government have approved or denied applications. While revenue sharing will almost certainly be continued, though probably not expanded proportionately to other forms of federal grants, the predictability advantage will presumably increase.

ARGUMENTS AGAINST REVENUE SHARING

Perhaps the most basic group of arguments in favor of specific grants-in-aid as the means the federal government uses to help states and localities financially—and equally the most basic set of arguments against general revenue sharing—revolves around the ideas that there are a number of identifiable national objectives to be obtained through domestic public policies; that the concept of national citizenship establishes an intellectual and ethical base for national criteria of equity in the provision of public services and a national minimum standard of living; that nationally raised funds should not be utilized without some accountability to national criteria; and that proven inefficiency of state and local governments and proven lack of concern of middle-class political majorities for the needs of ethnic minorities and the poor require that the national government use financial leverage if equity is to be attained and national social responsibility is to be served. All of these reasons together constitute a very strong argument against simply handing out money with no strings attached.

These arguments continue to be made, but now that revenue sharing has been implemented, certain argumentative aspects stand out more strongly and warrant additional emphasis. That is to say, the particular form of the arguments is now affected by the particular provisions and formulae of the legislation as enacted.

With a total of more than 400 categorical grant-in-aid programs at the peak of the trend, before consolidation into larger block grants got underway at the beginning of the 1970s, it might be said that there were almost as many programs as there were domestic problems. In the shift toward general revenue sharing, it becomes clear that the three broad problem categories which, in de facto political terms, had been most clearly identified as having priority status—namely, problems of the poor, problems of ethnic minorities, and problems of the cities—are the ones which suffer most. This negative rather than positive effect is due to cutbacks in the funding of specific urban-oriented categorical grant programs, such as Model Cities, simultaneously with the start of revenue sharing. In any case, urban minorities who are poor and have for a decade constituted a priority target group for public policies aimed at creating a more equitable society, and the largest cities, with their increasing need for human services simultaneous with a decline in the tax base, are clearly the major losers under general revenue sharing.

Their loss has two primary components: (1) the loss of national leverage for ensuring that state and local governments direct their efforts toward solving public problems rather than reducing the local tax level or the provision of nonpriority amenities; and (2) a revenue-sharing formula that distributes money too much in accordance with population and not enough in accordance with local finances and local needs as related specifically to *national* problem-solving criteria. Closely related to these concerns is the fact that, to the extent that urban problems are partly those of fragmented governmental jurisdictions (which enable the suburbs to have the advantages of the central city without paying an equitable share of the burden), revenue sharing makes things worse: first, by providing funds that enable minor suburban townships to stay afloat (whereas financial pressures might otherwise have induced them to join in metropolitan area governments); and, second, because the totality of funds going to all governments in a metropolitan area cannot under this system be directed toward a single major use, but rather is subject to fragmentation resulting from as many different utilization judgments as there are townships sharing the money. . . .

Clearly there is something wrong when a central city has absolutely no maneuverability and its revenue-sharing funds disappear in the desperate attempt to maintain existing inadequate levels of basic services, while adjoining suburbs solicit ideas for the spending of money that is beyond need or expectation. Ironically, general revenue sharing appears to reward exactly those jurisdictions that were least innovative and least active in attempting to avail themselves of the categorical grant system—whether because of lack of imagination or lack of need. If a city had not been obtaining much or any grant-in-aid money, then it gains from revenue sharing in two ways, in comparison with cities that had become heavily dependent on categorical grants: (1) it suffers no loss from displaced categorical grants, and (2) it obtains new funds that can be used in new ways.

The situation of the central cities is further exacerbated by the extent to which the influx of revenue-sharing money was matched by a simultaneous reduction in funds previously obtained on a project grant basis to meet specific central city needs. It is probably not correct, fiscally or politically, to charge that the inauguration of revenue sharing was itself a cause of decline in funding for major urban-oriented grant-in-aid programs. However, it is almost certainly accurate to state that the rise of revenue sharing has been used as an excuse for cutting back on the other kinds of aid. . . .

Probably even more important than the maldistribution of funds, and certainly at least as important, is the argument that for whatever sums of money it distributes, general revenue sharing lacks the clout that would come from federal priority specifications in the use of the monies. . . .

While the dream of many observers of the urban scene that suburbs and central cities might be fused into single metropolitan-wide governments seems unlikely, some other approaches to the diminution of the consequences of governmental jurisdiction fragmentation seem to have been making some headway, from the "workable plan" requirement of the 1949 urban renewal legislation, through the "701 Comprehensive Planning Assistance" of the Housing Act of 1954 and the Circular A-95 requirement of the Office of Management and Budget for metropolitan area and regional coordination on federally assisted projects. Essentially these were all devices by which a particular local jurisdiction had to pay at least some attention to the relation of its plans to those of neighboring jurisdictions and to some overall conception of the needs and logical development pattern of the metropolitan region as a whole. Under general revenue sharing, all of this stimulus is lost. Worse, a new stimulus is created that necessarily works specifically toward the maintenance of fragmentation, for the jurisdiction that is receiving new monies without having to prove its need through a competitive grant proposal process is confirmed in its autonomy from its own metropolitan area needs.

Another argument against general revenue sharing that relates indirectly to the special needs of very large cities is that, although those needs are still very pressing and can be expected to continue unabated, the more general fiscal crisis of state and local government may well be receding. Melville J. Ulmer has pointed out that education, public welfare, and highway construction now account for more than two-thirds of all state and local expenditures, but that educational expenditures are leveling off because of changes in the birth rate, and huge capital expenditures on school buildings will not be the large drain that they were for the past twenty years. Also, the National Highway Program is nearing completion, and public assistance programs seem to be well on the way toward totally national financing.[5] The state-local fiscal crisis will therefore be ameliorated through these demographic and economic changes.

Critics of unfettered state-local discretion in the use of federal money cite not only the fact that political power may determine which groups are likely to benefit from the expenditures, but they also have great doubts about the administrative capacity of those governments. Except for a few states, the spoils system of personnel appointments, for example, remains amazingly strong. Even where adequate merit systems exist, the salary levels of many cities and counties and some states cannot compete effectively for the best talent among city managers, finance officers, health and welfare officers, housing planners, and the like. For that matter, the rate of increase in federally aided programs over the past ten years has been so much faster than the rate of production of skilled manpower in many of the needed fields that, regardless of salary level, it would be impossible for all jurisdictions to obtain equally competent persons.

The need for developmental efforts, for technical assistance from the higher jurisdiction with its easier claim to the best talent, and for the use of leverage to ensure that at least minimal professional practices are followed is therefore quite clear. Awareness of this need has produced some of the red tape in federal grant programs in order to ensure effective administration by the receiving governments. General revenue sharing would have been a particularly strategic opportunity for enlarging the scope of requirements along these lines, inasmuch as the leverage would run to all governments of general jurisdiction. That opportunity was completely lost, however. Similarly, there was an opportunity for stimulating fiscal reform at the state and local level, and it too was missed.

Revenue-sharing funds could be withheld from any state that had not enacted a personal income tax, or they could be withheld from any state or local jurisdiction that did not have a merit personnel system. Since both of these provisions could be enacted without interfering in any way with the shared revenues principle of letting states and localities decide how to spend their funds, it is to be hoped that renewal of the revenue sharing program will not again pass up the opportunity to stimulate improved capacity, fiscal and administrative, of the lower jurisdictions. If this were achieved, a major argument against revenue sharing would be eliminated.

Another problem with revenue sharing, one which was not very much alluded to in advance but is becoming increasingly apparent, is that the institution-building function that many federal demonstration grant and pilot program grants had performed is now almost entirely ended. Institution-building and demonstration-grant programs provide an opportunity for pulling together a critical mass of the best talent available with regard to a specific function, whether it be urban planning, gerontology, the analysis of poverty problems, or defense analyses. . . .

One further major argument has developed against revenue sharing as specifically legislated in 1972, although this argument is not inherent in the general revenue-sharing concept. Under the existing legislation the civil rights, or nondiscrimination, provision has been held by many critics to be totally inadequate and indeed quite regressive as compared with nondiscrimination enforcement provisions in many other pieces of legislation. The Fair Housing Act and the Equal Employment Opportunity Act, for example, have had detailed regulations and specific procedures for acting against alleged violations of the nondiscrimination provision. The general revenue-sharing act, however, lacks detailed procedures and even is vague in its definitions of discrimination and "such corrective action as may be appropriate." The enforcement burden is placed largely on the states in the first instance, but obviously it is from some of the states that the greatest unwillingness to honor civil rights has come; and the sanctions for violation of the nondiscrimination provision are minimal in that the

ultimate sanction of termination of entitlement payments applies only
to the particular program in which noncompliance is found, rather than
to the entire unit of government in which it occurs. Although some
revisions of a strengthening nature were promulgated in February 1973,
an analysis done for the RAND Corporation concluded that discrimination may still be prevalent under revenue sharing.

Apart from the specific civil rights provisions of the revenue-
sharing act, the problem of discrimination exists in a larger sense. For
one thing, revenue sharing puts funds without strings attached in the
hands of state and local power structures that in many instances, and
not just in the deep South, are very narrowly based in the Anglo middle
class. This may result in hard-to-prove discrimination which is in principle subject to the official sanctions of the act but is almost certainly
what Nicki King refers to as implicit discrimination, or the use of
revenue-sharing monies for functions whose beneficiary user groups
are the nonpoor, nonminority residents of the area. . . .

While the prohibition against explicit racial discrimination can be
strengthened, and stronger enforcement measures devised, implicit
discrimination is not so easily dismissed as a problem, inasmuch as it is
the logical result of the essence of revenue sharing: to let the locus of
responsibility for priority determination in the spending of federal
funds be shifted from federal agencies operating under congressionally
authorized mandates to local officials operating on a carte blanche
basis.

CONCLUSION

Categorical grant-in-aid programs do a much better job than revenue
sharing of accommodating expenditures to national social priorities and
stimulating innovative programs in states and localities, which must
present competitive proposals in order to receive funds. However,
revenue sharing is superior to categorical grants in terms of reducing
bureaucratic red tape and permitting maximum freedom at the local
level to accommodate special needs, even if some of those needs do not
fit into the pattern expressed in appropriations priorities by Congress.

Can this dilemma be resolved? The resolution would seem to lie in
rational compromise that would focus heavily on block grants, while
permitting perhaps 10 percent of the funds in any grant program to be
available on a very broad, open-ended competitive proposal basis.
Where there was a real desire for innovation and a real sense of healthy
local discussion and program formulation in which broad segments of
the citizenry participated, providing funds apart from the normal

categorical programs would be very worthwhile. The system of fiscal federalism can and should accommodate whatever instances of real local initiatives exist; but the existing general revenue-sharing program goes too far in accommodating nonexistent local initiatives and local skills that are no more than the rhetorical dreams of conservative ideology.

NOTES

1. For examples and summaries of the prepassage arguments, see, U.S., Joint Economic Committee, *Revenue Sharing and Its Alternatives: What Future for Fiscal Federalism?* (a compendium, 3 vols.), 90th Cong., 1st sess., 1967; and Michael D. Reagan, *The New Federalism* (New York: Oxford University Press, 1972), Chap. 4.

2. David A. Caputo and Richard L. Cole, "The Initial Impact of Revenue Sharing on the Spending Patterns of American Cities," in *Public Policy Evaluation*, ed. Kenneth A. Dolbeare (Beverly Hills, Calif.: Sage Publications, 1975), Chap. 5.

3. Martha Derthick, Minority Statement in *Revenue Sharing and the Planning Process* (a report of the Subcommittee on the Planning Process and Urban Development of the Advisory Committee to the Department of Housing and Urban Development, Washington, D.C.: National Academy of Sciences, 1974), p. 90.

4. For a little further elaboration of this argument, see, Reagan, *The New Federalism*, pp. 102–105.

5. Melville J. Ulmer, "The Limitations of Revenue Sharing," in *The Annals* 397(September 1971), pp. 51–52.

QUESTIONS FOR DISCUSSION

1. What are the arguments in favor of revenue sharing?
2. What are the arguments against revenue sharing?
3. If you were the leader of a group concerned with the improvement of the quality of life for poor people in America, would you favor categorical grants rather than revenue sharing? Why?
4. If you were the mayor of New York City, would you favor categorical grants rather than revenue sharing? Why?
5. Does revenue sharing strengthen or weaken the power of the states in the federal system?

SUGGESTED READINGS

"Congress Clears Revenue Sharing Extension." *Congressional Quarterly Almanac: 94th Congress, 2nd Session.* . . . Washington, D.C.: Congressional Quarterly, 1976.

Etzioni, Amitai, and Marina Ottaway. "Revenue Sharing: The Next Domestic Disaster." *The Nation,* January 29, 1973, pp. 138–142.

Nathan, Richard P., et al. *Monitoring Revenue Sharing.* Washington, D.C.: The Brookings Institution, 1975.

————. *Where Have All the Dollars Gone?* Washington, D.C.: Department of Justice, Law Enforcement Assistance Administration, National Institute of Law Enforcement and Criminal Justice, 1976.

U.S. Congress. House. Committee on Government Operations. *State and Local Fiscal Assistance Act (General Revenue Sharing).* Hearings before a subcommittee on Government Operations on H.R. 6558 and related bills, 94th Cong., 1st sess., 1975.

U.S. Congress. House. Judiciary Committee. *Civil Rights Aspects of General Revenue Sharing.* Hearings before the subcommittee on Civil Rights and Constitutional Rights, 94th Cong., 1st sess., 1975.

U.S. Congress. House. Select Committee on Aging. *Government's Response to Elderly, Revenue Sharing as It Affects Elderly.* Hearings, 94th Cong., 1st sess., 1975.

U.S. Congress. Senate. Committee on Finance. *General Revenue Sharing.* Hearing on H.R. 13367, 94th Cong., 2d sess., 1976.

U.S. Congress. Senate. Government Operations Committee. *Revenue Sharing, 1975.* Hearings before subcommittee on Intergovernmental Relations, 94th Cong., 1st sess., 1975.

4.

Should Limits Be Placed on Civil Liberties and Civil Rights?

When Jimmy Carter became president, he called upon the United States to support a policy of human rights throughout the world. The new President was severely criticized for trying to apply principles of western democracy to the conduct of foreign policy. Had Carter confined his commentary to the strengthening of human rights in the United States, however, he would probably have elicited widespread support at home.

President Carter recognized the weak position of human rights in other nations. Communist governments and right-wing military regimes daily violate the freedoms that most Americans consider as commonplace as the air they breathe. Amnesty International, the London-based, Nobel Prize-winning group, calls attention every year to the violation of the fundamental human rights of large numbers of political prisoners in many countries.

Human rights are difficult to define. In western democracies, however, they usually include political rights, such as civil rights and civil liberties. Civil rights are specific rights derived exclusively from the state. Civil liberties are rights enjoyed without precise formulation in constitutions. There is, however, no universal acceptance of these distinctions, and both civil rights and civil liberties are mentioned in western democratic constitutions.

The human rights found in the body of the Constitution, the Bill of Rights (the first ten amendments to the Constitution), and subsequent amendments were designed to protect citizens not only from the acts of government but from the acts of private citizens as well. Human rights have, in fact, been violated by government and private citizens. For example, the United States government violated the rights of individuals by spying on dissidents, bugging phones of civil rights workers, and attempting to suppress radical opinion in the 1960s. White supremacists of the Ku Klux Klan, representing no government agency, moreover, violated the civil rights of black people after the American Civil War.

The basic human rights guaranteed by the Constitution—freedom of religion, freedom of speech, freedom of assembly, freedom of the press, and equality under the law—are considered by most Americans to be the foundation of a free society.

Freedom of religion refers to the right to believe in any religion and practice a religious faith. The Constitution asserts, moreover, that no religious requirement can be made of a public official.

Freedom of speech entitles each person to express his or her own opinion. Even ideas that are regarded as political heresies are protected. The basic premise of freedom of speech is that however unpopular a view is today, it must not be silenced by those people who do not agree with it.

Freedom of the press is a necessity in the view of most Americans. When Thomas Jefferson said that he would rather have newspapers without government than government without newspapers, he was calling attention to the important role of the press in a free society. The press reports the news so that citizens can assess events and make judgments. A press that is censored does not furnish the necessary information from which intelligent decisions can be made.

Equality under the law has come to mean that discrimination on the basis of religion, race, or sex is a violation of human rights. Developments in this area have been most rapid in the past two decades.

Although there is often agreement about what these rights are, difficulties arise in applying their principles. As we will see, one right may conflict with another. A right, moreover, may conflict with the need for public order. The umpire in reconciling right versus right and right versus public order is the Supreme Court. The fact that the court must deal with controversial and often "gray" areas makes that branch of government the target of criticism by those who are "losers" in the court decisions.

Many cases show the difficulty in applying rights to concrete situations. Freedom of religion is accepted, but may—under certain conditions—be limited. For example, the courts have upheld the legality of compulsory vaccination even when vaccination is considered against religious principles. The Supreme Court has also held that polygamy, which was an accepted practice of the Morman faith, is illegal.

Freedom of speech has been protected by the courts, but that freedom is not absolute. Freedom of speech does not permit the slander of an individual or the "right to shout fire in a crowded theater."

Freedom of the press gives special consideration to reporters in their attempts to gather the news. Freedom of the press, however, does not mean that journalists have the right to publish classified information about the movement of troops in wartime.

The courts have struck down laws that have denied equality to blacks and women. The problems of promoting equality, however, are complex and have been treated in different ways at different times by the court. In *Plessy* v. *Ferguson* (1896), the court accepted the principle of separate but equal. So long as public accommodations are the same for blacks as for whites, the court asserted, then the practice of segregation satisfies the Fourteenth Amendment guarantee that the states shall not deny to any person "the equal protection of the laws." In *Brown* v. *Board of Education* (1954), however, the Supreme Court contended that segregated public schools violated the equal protection clause of the Fourteenth Amendment. *Brown* v. *Board of Education* reversed *Plessy* v. *Ferguson*.

The issues discussed in the selections in this chapter reveal the continuing controversies surrounding human rights. These controversies deal with only a few of the many problems of human rights the Supreme Court faces each year.

PORNOGRAPHY

The increased availability and visibility of X-rated films and pornographic literature have prompted some individuals and groups who regard pornography as dangerous to moral standards to demand government suppression of such materials. In some communities the police have raided movie theaters that were showing pornographic films. When the editor of *Hustler* magazine was convicted of publishing and distributing pornographic literature, his case received national publicity.

Is pornography a form of freedom of expression? Author Gay Talese feels that it is and that government should not suppress pornography, but, rather, should allow the greatest of freedom. Talese argues that there are no suitable criteria for distinguishing pornography from art. He contends, moreover, that the individual, rather than society, should determine what kinds of films to see or magazines to read.

In opposition, Ernest van den Haag, adjunct professor of social philosophy at New York University, contends that government suppression of pornography is necessary. Pornography, he asserts, has nothing to do with freedom of expression. It is designed so that people are regarded purely as subjects of exploitation for sexual purposes, which, van den Haag claims, is detrimental to community values.

THE EQUAL RIGHTS AMENDMENT (ERA)

Many laws discriminating against women have been changed or declared unconstitutional. Reforms have been made in employment, salaries, and availability of credit, and many patterns of discrimination have been eliminated. Still, total equality has not been achieved—either in law or in practice. The key provision of the proposed Equal Rights Amendment states: "Equality of rights under the law shall not be denied or abridged by the United States or by any state on account of sex."

The League of Women Voters contends that the ERA will eliminate the last legal barriers to equality for women. In defense of this view, the League argues that although changes have taken place to improve the rights of women, the pace of change is too slow. The League denies that ERA will have a major impact on existing arrangements for alimony and child support, that labor laws protecting women will be invalidated, that federalism will be weakened, that laws protecting women from sex crimes will be ended, that unisex restrooms will be required, or that single-sex private schools will have to become coeducational. The League notes that the military draft issue is not valid because there is no draft today and, besides, family situations have always been a basis for exemption from the draft.

Former North Carolina Senator Sam J. Ervin, Jr., however, opposes the Equal Rights Amendment. He regards it as unrealistic because it commands Congress and all state legislatures to ignore sex when making laws. The ERA may be construed in such a way as to nullify every law making any distinction between men and women. Laws protecting wives, mothers, and widows, consequently, will be in jeopardy. Ervin states that recent Supreme Court decisions striking down acts of discrimination against women make the amendment unnecessary.

QUOTA SYSTEMS

Because members of minority racial groups and women have been denied the same chance to compete with white men for positions in the public and private sectors, government has implemented policies of affirmative action. These policies require that institutions make special efforts to provide jobs or grant admission to women and members of minority groups. Universities that receive federal government funds, for example, must show that they are complying with the laws forbidding discrimination on the basis of race, sex, and age. As a result of these policies, admission to professional schools has become a serious problem.

One means of increasing minority group representation in professional schools is to establish a system in which only members of minority groups may participate. The University of California Medical School at Davis attempted to increase minority enrollment in this way. It reserved 16 percent of its student admission places exclusively for members of minority groups. Is such a quota system valid under the Constitution? That was the issue before the Supreme Court of California in *Allan Bakke* v. *The Regents of the University of California* (1976).

Allan Bakke, a white student, applied for admission to the medical school at Davis. When he was rejected, he filed suit against the university. Bakke claimed he had been the victim of invidious discrimination because of his race, in violation of the equal protection clause of the Fourteenth Amendment of the Constitution. That clause prevents any state from denying "to any person under its jurisdiction the equal protection of the laws." In opposition to Bakke, the university contended that the purpose of the program was to expand medical educational opportunities to persons from economically or educationally disadvantaged backgrounds.

The Supreme Court of California ruled for Bakke. Speaking for the court, Justice Stanley Mosk rejected the notion that racial discrimination may be more easily justified against one race (a majority) than another (a minority). The court did not argue that a candidate's disadvantaged economic and educational background may not be taken into consideration as factors for admission, but a quota system is not constitutional.

In a vigorous dissent, Justice Matthew O. Tobriner argued that the use of racial classifications to promote integration or to overcome the effects of past discrimination is not necessarily unconstitutional. In this case, Justice Tobriner contended, racial classification was proper because alternative methods to the special program at Davis would not work.

On June 28, 1978, the United States Supreme Court ruled that Bakke must be admitted to the medical school. The Court struck down the particular system of reserving a fixed number of places exclusively for minority-group competition. The Court upheld, however, the constitutionality of educational admission programs that give special advantages to minorities to help remedy past discrimination.

BUSING

Although the Supreme Court asserted in *Brown* v. *Board of Education* that segregation is inherently unequal, actual integration of schools has been a slow process. Various plans have been drawn up to integrate public schools; the problem is to implement them. Busing has become one technique used by the courts to reverse the pattern of segregation.

Is busing of students to promote integration necessary? Irving Kristol, Henry Luce Professor of Urban Values at New York University, argues that the liberal premises underlying busing are not valid. According to Kristol, busing in most circumstances does not encourage interracial harmony, but instead is more likely to promote racial hostility and violence. Busing, moreover, does not improve anyone's educational achievements. Finally, Kristol asserts that the more busing we have, the less integrated our schools become because busing cannot prevent white migration to the suburbs.

Norman Goldfarb, an attorney involved in cases concerning desegregation of schools in Buffalo, New York, contends that busing is one means to end the pattern of segregation. He believes that busing is a useful device to end segregation in those instances in which there has also been purposeful residential segregation. Busing, moreover, becomes accepted quickly and rarely is the subject of long-standing controversy. According to Goldfarb, busing is not a panacea for problems of integration, but it does not have the deleterious effects that its critics assert.

Is Government Regulation of Pornography an Infringement of Civil Liberties?

YES AND NO

WALTER GOODMAN
What Is a Civil Libertarian to Do When Pornography Becomes So Bold?*

As pornography has proliferated across the land, from centers of sexual technology such as New York and Los Angeles to less advanced communities, a suspicion that something may be awry has begun to nag at even that enlightened vanguard which once strove to save Lady Chatterley from the philistines. Having opened the door to sex for art's sake, they have found that it is no longer possible to close it against sex for profit's sake.

Where does duty lie today for the dutiful civil libertarian confronted by efforts around the country to prosecute the purveyors of porn? One may wish that Al Goldstein, an avant-garde publisher of the stuff, would go away, but no civil libertarian can cheer the efforts by lawmen in Wichita, Kansas, to have him put away. One might doubt

* From Walter Goodman, "What Is a Civil Libertarian to Do When Pornography Becomes So Bold?" *The New York Times*, November 21, 1976, sec. 2, p. 1. © 1976 by The New York Times Company. Reprinted by permission.

that Harry Reems, who has filled many X-rated screens, is contributing much to the art of the cinema, yet no civil libertarian wants the assistant U.S. Attorney in Memphis, Tennessee, to clap him in irons. What to do?

To grapple with this matter, I brought together two figures known to have provocative—and sharply conflicting—views on the subject: author Gay Talese, whose ongoing research for a book about sex in America includes the management of two New York City massage parlors, and psychoanalyst Ernest van den Haag, adjunct professor of social philosophy at New York University and a favorite "expert witness" of pornography prosecutors everywhere.

Our conversation began with an effort by Professor van den Haag to identify the animal which he believes ought to be locked up:

van den Haag: I would call pornographic whatever is blatantly offensive to the standards of the community.

Talese: But does the public have the right to ban "Ulysses" because some people find it offensive?

van den Haag: I think anyone who reads "Ulysses" for the sake of pornographic interest ought to get a medal. The characteristic focus of pornography is precisely that it leaves out all human context and reduces the action to interaction between organs and orifices—and that I find obscene, degrading to sex, and dehumanizing to its audiences.

Talese: So if you have a picture of a girl, including the genitals, then that is pornographic.

van den Haag: Not necessarily.

Talese: But if she's making love it would be?

van den Haag: I'm not even opposed to that altogether. But, if the love-making picture focuses on the operation of the genitals. . . .

Talese: You mean if it shows the genitals while the love-making is going on?

van den Haag: If the genitals are shown incidentally, that does not greatly disturb me. But if it is clearly focused on the operation of the genitals and the persons are only shown incidentally, then I think the stuff is pornographic.

Talese: There's no agreement on a definition at all, even by the people who want to ban it. Obscenity is the one crime that cannot be defined. Unlike murder, burglary, forgery, the word means different things to different people—to judges, to newspaper editors, to pornographic film-makers.

van den Haag: That's why we have courts of law and lawyers.

Talese: And it means different things to different lawyers—it's the most imprecise of crimes.

van den Haag: Gay, if you were to see a man walking down the street, fully clothed except that his genitals were exposed, would you regard that as obscene?

Talese: On the issue of whether the cop on the beat has the right to stop public behavior that is unseemly and offensive we have no quarrel. But no policeman ought to have the right to stop two homosexuals in a Holiday Inn in Teaneck, New Jersey, from doing whatever they want together. They have that right, and I have the right to see a film or a play even if it is considered offensive by Sidney Baumgarten of the Mayor's Midtown Enforcement Project. I don't want policemen to tell me what is moral or immoral in my private life. I think we have too much government and where sex is concerned, I want next to no government.

van den Haag: I certainly agree, Gay, that you or I should be allowed to indulge in sexual acts in our homes. That's our business. I am not in the least disturbed about that. But when anyone can see the spectacle we are no longer dealing with a private matter, but with a public matter.

Talese: If I want to pay five dollars to go into a theater to go see "Deep Throat," that's a private matter.

van den Haag: Then you regard a public spectacle as a private act.

Talese: How about buying a book?

van den Haag: If it is publicly available to anyone who pays the price, it's a public matter.

Talese: So, according to you, I have the right to read *Ulysses* or *The Story of O* or *The Sex Life of a Cop* in my home—only I shouldn't be allowed to get it into my home in the first place.

van den Haag: The police should not come into your home and check what you're reading—but the police can accuse a seller of selling something pornographic. The matter can then be brought up before a jury, and if the jury feels that what the seller sold publicly is pornography, then the seller can be convicted.

Talese: So you'd ban such magazines as *Playboy* or *Oui* or *Screw?*

van den Haag: I have testified against *Screw* and I am in favor of banning it. As for *Playboy* and so on, I would leave those to juries in particular communities. If I'm invited as an expert to testify about the effects they will have on a particular community, I will testify that these effects are deleterious, but it is not for me to decide whether they should be prohibited or not.

Goodman: Ernest, why should it be any more the business of a jury what Gay likes to read or watch than it is what he likes to do in bed?

van den Haag: Gay's view—one that is widespread—is that soci-

ety consists of individuals, each independent of each other, and that the
task of the government is merely to protect one individual from interference by others. That is not my view. My view is that no society can
survive unless there are bonds among its members, unless its members
identify with each other, recognize each other as humans, and do not
think of each other simply as sources of pleasure or unpleasure. For
once they do, then they may come to think of people as kinds of
insects. If one disturbs you, you kill it. Once you no longer recognize
that a person is fully human, like yourself, you can do what the Germans did to the Jews—use the gold in their teeth. Human solidarity is
based on our ability to think of each other not purely as means, but as
ends in ourselves. Now the point of all pornography, in my opinion, is
that it invites us to regard the other person purely as a subject of
exploitation for sexual pleasure.

Goodman: Gay, am I right in assuming that you don't agree that
pornography has such dire consequences?

Talese: Government interference in these areas is usually justified
on the grounds that obscenity is harmful to the morals of society,
harmful to family life, harmful to juveniles. But in fact there is no proof
that exposure to pornography leads to antisocial behavior. There is no
proof that watching a pornographic movie leads anybody to go out
and commit rape.

van den Haag: You're not getting my point. I do not maintain that
reading pornography leads to an increase in crime. It may, but I don't
think there's conclusive evidence either way. I feel that the main damage pornography does is not to the individual but to the social climate.

Talese: Tell me how.

van den Haag: You and I both write books, and our books are
somehow meant to influence what people feel and think. Sexual mores,
you certainly will agree, have changed over the past century. Why
have they changed? Basically because of the ideas of people who write
books, make movies, produce things. The biology of sex hasn't
changed. What has changed is our perception of it and our reaction to
it. So I don't think it can be denied that books do have an influence. If
that is so, we come to the question of whether the government has the
right or duty to limit it. Here my point is a very simple one. Every
community has a right to protect what it regards as its important shared
values. In India, I would vote for the prohibition against the slaughter-
ing of cows. In Israel, I would vote for the prohibition against the
raising of pigs for slaughter. In the United States, where a certain
amount of sexual reticence has been a central value of traditional culture, I would vote for the rights of communities to protect their sexual
reticence.

Talese: And I'm saying that the government should not have the right to deal with this "crime" that it cannot define. The Supreme Court has never been able to define what is obscene to the satisfaction of most Americans. If you are going to give government the power to tell us what is obscene and to restrict our freedom to read books, see films or look at pictures, if you give government that kind of power over the individual, you are not going to maintain a democracy.

van den Haag: I am for freedom, too, but you ignore the fact that freedom can be used for good or bad. For instance, if the Weimar Republic had banned its political pornographers such as Hitler, then perhaps six million Jews would not have been killed. The dogmatic insistence on freedom as the only value to be protected by the government disregards such things as survival and community traditions which are essential to survival.

Talese: But you seem to forget that Hitler himself opposed pornography. Almost the first thing he did on taking power was to ban "Ideal Marriage," a classic work on sex and marriage.

Goodman: Would you put any limits at all on individual liberties in this area, Gay?

Talese: I believe there should be censorship—in the home. I have two daughters, and in my home I do exercise censorship. I subscribe to magazines and newspapers that I do not leave on the coffee table. But I do not want government to tell me what I can have in my house or what I can have my daughters read.

van den Haag: I congratulate you on having this family that you describe. Let me point out that many American families are not so structured. Not all parents are able to exercise such parental discipline.

Goodman: But isn't Gay's response to government intrusions into family life in accord with your own principles as a conservative?

van den Haag: In an ideal society, things that we now regulate by law, would be regulated by custom and by the authority of parents. We don't live in this ideal society. The authority of parents has been undermined by all kinds of things, starting with progressive education. If we could strengthen the hand of parents and integrate families more, that would be much better. I have found no way of doing so for the time being.

Talese: So you're willing to give this power to a policeman.

van den Haag: I am not proposing that we trust the government with the power of censorship. I'm opposed to censorship, opposed to prior restraint which is unconstitutional. I am in favor of traditional American legislation. Whereby each state, and more recently each community, may determine for itself what it wishes and what it does not wish to be publicly sold. In each case, Ralph Ginzburg or Al Goldstein or you or anyone can publish whatever he wishes. Until the bounds have been exceeded. . . .

Talese: What bounds? It's all so hypocritical. One night these people have been at an American Legion smoker enjoying hard-core porn and the next day they are deciding to put a pornographer in jail. What a member of the jury is likely to say in public has nothing to do with the way he behaves in private. That seems to me socially unhealthy. Many of the people who would go on record to have Times Square closed down because it has too many massage parlors patronize the places. We're dealing here with something very private—sexual desires. Very private.

Goodman: But is the expression of these desires around an area such as Times Square really all that private? It seems pretty public to me.

Talese: Sure, Times Square has always been a center of public entertainment. What some people can't stand is that it is today a center of entertainment for the working class instead of for the elite. There are two kinds of pornography. You have the pornography for the working man, like the Forty-second Street peep shows, and you have the "legitimate theater," where the elite can see "Let My People Come," "Oh, Calcutta!" or the works of Edward Albee or Arthur Miller or Tennessee Williams. The government does not as readily interfere with the pornography of the elite as it does with the pornography of the man who buys his magazine at the corner newsstand, which is the museum of the man in the street, or the man who pays twenty-five cents to see copulating couples in a coin-operated machine. Pornography is primarily denied to the blue-collar classes. That has always been the case. Strong government tries always to control the masses—just as much in China and Cuba as in Times Square. The people who get their pleasure from going to an art gallery to look at Goya's "The Naked Maja" aren't bothered by government.

Goodman: Ernest, under your definition of pornography, is there any difference between a picture of a copulating couple on a museum wall and in the centerfold of a girly magazine?

van den Haag: Yes, effect and intent are different, and I think the courts are correct in taking the context into consideration. That is, if Hugh Hefner had put "The Naked Maja" in Playboy a few years ago, it might have become pornographic in that context though Goya had not intended it that way.

Talese: So pornography is all right for the elite, but not for the working man.

van den Haag: It may appear that way, but the reason as you yourself pointed out, is that the working man gets his pornography in a more public way. A theater at which you've made a reservation and paid $10, is much less public than the twenty-five-cent arcade; therefore, there is more justification, if you are against pornography, to intervene against one than against the other.

Goodman: You don't deny, Gay, that Times Square has in fact become a place of public pornography.

Talese: Yes, our sensibilities are assaulted. I wish the Forty-second Street pornographer would be more subtle. But people have as much right to put a quarter in a machine as to pay five dollars for "Deep Throat" or ten dollars for "Let My People Come." I do not want to give to law-enforcement officials the right to clean up Times Square, to deny pornography to those who want it. If crimes are being committed, people being mugged, that should be prevented. But nobody is forced to go into a peep show or a massage parlor or to pay for sex with a prostitute.

Goodman: I take it you're opposed to laws against prostitution.

Talese: I would really like to see prostitution legalized, but I know that would be the worst thing for prostitution, because it would mean that women would have to be fingerprinted.

van den Haag: You would simply decriminalize it.

Talese: I would like to see that happen.

Goodman: And you, Ernest?

van den Haag: For call girls yes; for street prostitution no.

Goodman: Isn't that a trifle elitist, as Gay terms it?

van den Haag: No. A call girl is an entirely private proposition. You call her. In the case of the street prostitute, the initiative must come from the soliciting girl, and that makes a difference.

Talese: Have you ever been assaulted by a prostitute on the street? All the girls do is ask a question.

van den Haag: There's more to it than that. In the United States, for some reason, prostitution has always been connected with crime. The sort of thing that exists around Times Square attracts not only prostitutes and their customers, but people who prey on prostitutes and customers and make the whole area unsafe. I believe that crime must not only be prosecuted; it must also be prevented.

Talese: What offends the white New Yorker, the customer on his way to the bus terminal, about Times Square is that he walks through the neighborhood and sees the great number of blacks there—the black prostitutes and black pimps. That's what makes people fearful. There is more crime all over the country today, but it has nothing to do with prostitutes working Eighth Avenue. You see, I don't think it's a crime to have sex with a person. The prostitutes are there, on the street in great numbers, because men—not the children Ernest is legitimately concerned about but middle-class married white men—want them. For some reason, they find prostitutes necessary. That's their private affair. I don't want to have Times Square become acceptable to Franco's Spain. I don't want government to clean it up.

van den Haag: You're saying that people should be allowed to have what they want. But should people be forced to have what they don't want? Suppose that a town in Ohio votes that it doesn't want prostitutes on its streets or pornographic movies? You are in favor of pornography in principle, regardless of what the majority wants.

Talese: I am in favor of freedom of expression.

van den Haag: The men who wrote Article I of the Bill of Rights intended to make sure that the government would not suppress opposition. They did not intend to include such things as pornography.

Talese: They wrote that Congress shall make no law abridging freedom of speech or the press; they didn't add, "except when it comes to sexual expression."

Goodman: Gentlemen, I am not sure how much light we have shed on pornography but your respective positions are clear as day. And I thank you.

QUESTIONS FOR DISCUSSION

1. How would you distinguish pornography from art?
2. What are the arguments in favor of suppressing pornography?
3. Who should decide whether or not a pornographic film may be shown in a community?
4. What are the effects of pornography on society?
5. To what extent is the suppression of pornography "discrimination against the blue-collar classes?"

SUGGESTED READINGS

Brown, Marvin, Donald Amoroso, and Edward Ware. "Behavioral Effects of Viewing Pornography." *Journal of Social Psychology* 98(April 1976):235–245.

Fahringer, Herald Prince. "Censorship and Pornography." *The Humanist,* July/August 1977, pp. 30–33.

Pilpel, Harriet F., and Marjorie T. Parsons. "Dirty Decisions in Court." *Civil Liberties Review* 1(Fall 1974):30–41.

"Porno Plague." *Time,* April 5, 1976, pp. 58–63.

Rembar, Charles. *The End of Obscenity: The Trials of Lady Chatterley, Tropic of Cancer and Fanny Hill.* New York: Random House, 1968.

_____. "Obscenity—Forget It." *Atlantic,* May 1977, pp. 37–41.

Sparrow, John. "Freedom of Expression: Too Much of a Good Thing?" *American Scholar* 46(Spring 1977):165–180.

Steinem, Gloria. "Pornography—Not Sex but the Obscene Use of Power." *Ms.,* August 1977, pp. 43–45.

U.S. Commission on Obscenity and Pornography. *The Report.* Washington, D.C.: U.S. Government Printing Office, 1970.

Wills, Garry. "Measuring the Impact of Erotica." *Psychology Today,* August 1977, pp. 30 ff.

Will the Equal Rights Amendment Improve the Rights of Women?

YES

LEAGUE OF WOMEN VOTERS
*Cool Facts for the Hot-Headed Opposition**

WHAT THE ERA IS AND WHAT IT SAYS

The ERA is the proposed 27th Amendment to the United States Constitution. It says, in three simple statements, "Equality of rights under the law shall not be abridged by the United States or by any State on account of sex. The Congress shall have the power to enforce, by appropriate legislation, the provisions of this article. This amendment shall take effect two years after the date of ratification."

WHAT THE ERA WILL DO

It will create a greater range of *opportunities* for both men and women. It will stop federal and state sanction of discrimination against men and women on the basis of sex.

Specifically, it will:

- insure the legal right to equal educational opportunities in publicly supported schools for both men and women students and strengthen laws against sex discrimination in education
- strengthen laws against sex discrimination in employment so that workers will be hired and judged on the basis of individual merit
- reinforce laws against discrimination in credit backed by federal funds or insurance and assure that such credit is available on the basis of ability to pay, not on the basis of sex
- provide equal access to military service for men and women and guarantee equal eligibility for benefits
- insure that men and women get the same social security benefits
- erase laws that prohibit women from controlling property, mortagages, or insurance.

WHY THE ERA IS NECESSARY

Overwhelming evidence (thoroughly documented by congressional hearings) shows that sex discrimination under the law exists, particularly in areas of legal rights, credit, insurance, education, and employment. Discrimination in the area of legal rights is disturbing because it restricts basic rights and responsibilities of our democratic system. However, sex discrimination in education and employment is even more disturbing, because it affects the majority of women in this country and because these detrimental effects last for a lifetime.

ON THE SUBJECT OF WOMEN'S "PRIVILEGES" . . .

THE OPPOSITION CLAIMS that women's "privileges" will be taken away.

WE SAY that no one group speaks for all women—neither the League of Women Voters nor the ERA opposition. But it is clear that nothing is being taken away from women; rather, opportunities are being opened up in education, in the military services, and in the free-enterprise system.

These opportunities are badly needed by women. Forty-five percent of all women work; 18 million women* work because they have to.

---

* Those among the 35 million total women in the labor force in 1973 who, according to the Department of Labor Women's Bureau, are single, divorced, widowed or separated—or whose husbands earn less than $5,000 per year.

So-called protective labor laws have been designed so that they have excluded women from higher paying jobs they were willing and able to do. Discrimination in educational institutions has left many women less prepared for the future than their male counterparts.

Poor women have suffered the most. Of adults in poverty, 61 percent are women. The median income of working women who have not finished high school is less than $5000. Men with the same educational background earn over $7000. Discriminatory laws adversely affect poor women more than poor men.

TOO FAR-REACHING?

THE OPPOSITION CLAIMS that the ERA is unnecessary—that eliminating sex discrimination with a constitutional amendment is "trying to kill a fly with a sledge hammer."

WE SAY that flyswatters haven't been working very well. American women have been trying to knock out sex discrimination through individual court cases and single-law reforms for 350 years, but sex discrimination is still flagrant. Short of a comprehensive constitutional amendment, progress will follow the pattern of the past, a pattern that's too slow and that unfairly puts on individuals the burden of establishing the rights of half the human race.

Some Specifics

The Supreme Court got around to affirming in 1874 (*Minor* v. *Happersett*) that women are persons. What they gave with one hand they took away with the other: in the same decision, the court prohibited women *as a class* from voting! It took the Nineteenth Amendment to clear that up. *This* constitutional amendment would put an end to the business of treating women as a class, in *any* area of life in which sex is an irrelevant criterion.

This very minute, women are being forced to fight one by one for the right to be judged as individuals, instead of being treated as a class, when it comes to getting credit, getting mortgages, getting housing, getting jobs, getting insurance, getting into professional schools, ad infinitum. Case-by-case redress is painfully slow and piecemeal. We haven't time, as we move into the last quarter of the twentieth century, to build basic, self-evident human rights bit by bit, like a Byzantine mosaic. The ERA would forbid discrimination against women as a group or class.

ONLY A PSYCHOLOGICAL PROP?

THE OPPOSITION CLAIMS that ERA does very little. They say that the arguments in favor of the ERA boil down to the fact that women— not many, just a few—need the amendment for "psychological and symbolic reasons."

WE SAY that we're not sneering at the psychological and symbolic value of the ERA. Who says psychological support isn't important? But to say that they're the *only* point of the ERA and to say that only a few women have problems about discrimination is to pretend that an overwhelming body of evidence doesn't exist.

Some Specifics

When the ERA supports women's right to equal pay for equal work, that's not just a psychological or symbolic benefit. That's an economic benefit—the dollars and cents to support herself and her family, as 18 million American women are now trying to do under unfair handicaps. To cite a single example: Stewardesses certainly haven't been in the forefront of the pro-ERA movement. But they went to court to assert the right to wear glasses, and not to be bypassed by a new echelon of male "flight attendants." They won, but it's ridiculous to have to argue in court about such an evident injustice.

It isn't just equal pay for equal work that's at stake. It's access to educational opportunities, access to jobs without sex labels, the right to control the money one earns or inherits. Not to have these rights is to be deprived—deprived psychologically but also deprived of bread and butter, deprived of the right to full development as a person, deprived of the right to choose how to contribute to community life.

If the benefits of the ERA were only psychological and symbolic, individuals and groups as diverse as the president, the AFL-CIO [American Federation of Labor-Congress of Industrial Organizations], the AAUW [American Association of University Women] and the National Council of Churches wouldn't be agreeing that it's sorely needed.

ON THE SUBJECT OF WIVES' RIGHT TO SUPPORT . . .

THE OPPOSITION CLAIMS that the ERA would take away the "right of the wife to be in the home as a full-time wife and mother" because the ERA would invalidate "every one of the state laws which require the husband to support his wife."

WE SAY that this argument plays on fears by pointing at a needle of truth in a haystack of half-truths and distortions.

First, the ERA is in the business of establishing rights, not taking them away. It would affirm rights for women (and for men) that they do not now fully enjoy. Among those rights is the right to choose how to live one's life. That most emphatically includes the right to choose "to be in the home as a full-time wife and mother." ERA would have little or no impact on people who make this choice, for the simple reason that the ERA would not alter the institution of marriage in any direction.

Second, the state laws to which the opposition refers are a fragile prop at best. Yes, they're on the books, all right. But state supreme courts have ruled that ongoing marriages are out of bounds for the courts—so all those laws mean nothing, if a wife in an ongoing marriage seeks their protection through court action. *McGuire* v. *McGuire* is a case in point. The wife worked the fields, cared for the house, sold chickens and eggs, but her husband refused to buy on credit, to let her buy on credit, or to provide her with a bathroom, a kitchen sink, or money for clothing. The Nebraska Supreme Court denied the wife any recompense because "to maintain an action such as the one at bar the parties must be separated or living apart from each other." The practical fact is that it's only when a separation or divorce proceeding is brought that the issue of support comes before a court and the question of the legal right to support arises.

Third, the court cases which the opposition cites, in trying to demonstrate that husbands at present must support their wives, actually demonstrate quite another point. In one such case, a husband was required to pay a department store for a fur coat charged by his wife. The principle here is that a man is responsible for debts incurred *in his name;* not, please note, *by his wife,* but *in his name.* Though Phyllis Schlafly and others have been getting a lot of mileage out of what's come to be known vaguely as "the mink coat case," there's considerable irony in their choice of example. The elementary fact is that the wife could not have got credit from the store in the first place without her husband's signature. If that husband, or any husband of a nonworking wife, refuses to sign a credit application, his wife has no recourse. Some protection of a wife's rights! The case may have determined that a creditor can demand payment from a husband for a purchase made on credit established by a husband's signature. It emphatically did *not* say anything reassuring about a wife's right to ongoing support.

Fourth, there's a subtle threat buried in this opposition argument: that somehow the ERA will turn the tables overnight and force a wife who is not working, who may never have worked, to begin to support herself—and maybe her husband to boot. Simply not so. The ERA *will* require that support laws be written in sex-neutral language, but it *will not* require any changes in judicial enforcement of support laws. If that kind of change comes, it won't be the ERA that brings it.

ON THE SUBJECTS OF ALIMONY AND CHILD SUPPORT . . .

THE OPPOSITION SAYS that under the ERA women who were divorced or separated would be in big trouble. They call the ERA a "take-away" that will "do away with a woman's right to alimony" and child support.

THE FACT IS that the ERA will have little or no effect on existing arrangements about alimony and child support. True, the language of the laws will have to become sex-neutral. But after ERA, just as now, divorce settlements will be based on fault and on need. The spouse with the greater financial capacity will be required to contribute to the support of the spouse in need. Just as now, every case will be settled individually. All that will change after ERA is that more women might be in the now rare position of having a stronger financial base or greater earning power than her spouse. Child custody and child support would be determined, after ERA, just as it is now—on the basis of who can better meet the needs of the children.

Incidentally, statistics indicate that alimony and child support are rights more honored in the breach than in the observance. The Citizens' Advisory Council on the Status of Women cites one study which shows that one year after divorce two fathers in five (42 percent) had made no support payment at all; by the tenth year, four out of five (79 percent) were making no payments. These figures are particularly disturbing when one realizes that most support awards meet less than half the actual cost of supporting a child, to begin with.

ON THE SUBJECT OF "PROTECTIVE" LABOR LAWS . . .

THE OPPOSITION CLAIMS that the ERA would take away labor laws that protect women.
WE SAY:

1. Most protective labor legislation was instituted in another era and under different conditions.
2. Title VII of the Civil Rights Act, administered by the Equal Employment Opportunity Commission, has already invalidated that earlier legislation.
3. The dreadful consequences prophesied as a result of eliminating those "protective" labor laws have not come true.

4. The best evidence of the hollowness of this argument is the number of unions that support ratification of the ERA, including the AFL-CIO, the American Federation of Teachers, the Communications Workers of America, the Newspaper Guild, the Teamsters, the International Union of Electrical Workers and the United Auto Workers.

A Specific

Section 293.060 of the revised statutes of Missouri, 1969, states that "no female shall be employed in or about mines except in an office in a clerical capacity." It's an interesting example of a "protective" labor law that excludes women from earning higher pay. Not only does it exclude her from mine *labor;* it simultaneously excludes her from mine *management,* even though a mine management job is unlikely to be detrimental to a woman's physical well-being. The existence of this kind of law offers a clear example of the need for the ERA. If this law had not been challenged meanwhile under Title VII of the Civil Rights Act, it would have to be brought into conformity with the ERA within two years of ratification.

ON THE SUBJECT OF THE DRAFT . . .

THE OPPOSITION CLAIMS that under the ERA women would be drafted and have to serve in combat equally with men.

WE SAY that's another of those needle and haystack arguments. The needle of truth is that under the ERA the country's claim on citizens' military service would apply equally to women and men. But—

1. To begin with, there is no draft today.
2. Drafting women is not a novel idea. During World War II (June 1, 1944) Rep. Emanuel Celler introduced a bill to draft single women between ages 20 and 35. In 1948, General Eisenhower said, "I am convinced that in another war they [women] have got to be drafted just like the men."
3. All women would not serve in combat any more than all men do. In 1971, only 5 percent of eligible men were drafted and only 1 percent ever served in combat. There are physical requirements for combat; for instance, men with flat feet have never been eligible to fight. Presumably, whatever a particular woman was physically unable to do she would be exempt from doing—just as men now are.
4. Family situations have always been a basis for draft classification. Men with children were exempted in the Korean and Vietnam wars.

5. It should be pointed out that the armed forces also provide benefits that would become available to many more women than at present.

ON THE SUBJECT OF STATES' RIGHTS . . .

THE OPPOSITION CLAIMS that Section 2 of the ERA, which grants enforcement power to the Congress, makes the amendment "a grab for power at the federal level."

THE FACT IS that the power the ERA gives to Congress is no more and no less than that given by other constitutional amendments. The language of this section is similar to that in the Thirteenth, Fourteenth and Fifteenth Amendments. Since the very point of a constitutional amendment is to state a *national* principle, it must, for consistency, be enforceable nationally. But states constitutionally retain all powers not delegated to the federal government. And since the ERA does not grant the federal government *exclusive* enforcement powers, states retain their authority to implement the ERA's provisions.

It's interesting to note that at one point, before the amendment's passage by the Congress, the enforcement section of the ERA gave authority to the Congress and the states "within their respective jurisdictions." It was the interpretation of Paul Freund of the Harvard Law School that such delegation of authority was more restrictive than that found in any of the other amendments.

Additionally, once ERA's ratified, the states will have two years to review their laws and bring them into conformity.

ON THE SUBJECT OF RAPE LAWS . . .

THE OPPOSITION CLAIMS that the ERA will "knock out present laws protecting women from sex crimes such as statutory rape."

THE FACT IS, that's not true. Rape laws are based on real physical differences between men and women. Sexual assault laws will be extended to cover both sexes and statutory rape laws will be extended to cover statutory sexual assault on minors by both sexes.

ON THE SUBJECT OF SLEEPING QUARTERS
AND RESTROOMS . . .

THE OPPOSITION CLAIMS that women and men will be forced to share sleeping quarters and rest rooms under the ERA.

WE SAY to that, Senator Marlowe Cook (R. Ky.) calls this argument the "potty excuse."

The ERA will not interfere with the constitutional right of privacy. The right of privacy, as defined in the Supreme Court case, *Griswold* v. *Connecticut,* is the result of a combination of the specific rights guaranteed by the First, Third, Fourth, Fifth and Ninth Amendments. Because each citizen possesses these rights, i.e., freedom of speech and religion, freedom from search and seizure, freedom from self-incrimination, we possess the consequent right of privacy.

The same case clearly established that the right to privacy covers sexual relations. Because our society interprets disrobing and bodily functions to be sex related, it is clear that the ERA would not require coeducational restrooms or sleeping quarters.

ON THE SUBJECT OF PRIVATE SCHOOLS . . .

THE OPPOSITION CLAIMS the ERA will force single-sex private schools to become coeducational.

THE FACT IS that the ERA affects only state and federal laws and institutions. Its ratification will not require single-sex private schools to become coed.

It *is* possible that a future Supreme Court ruling may require those private schools that accept federal funding to open their doors to both sexes. If so, the ruling would flow from a judgment about the legal effect of accepting federal funds. (The 1972 Education Amendments, prohibit sex discrimination in public schools under certain circumstances.) It would be derived not from the ERA.

> # Will the Equal Rights Amendment Improve the Rights of Women?

NO

SAM J. ERVIN, JR.
The Equal Rights Amendment*

The Equal Rights Amendment is unrealistic because it commands Congress and all state legislatures to ignore sex when making laws.

America is the most law-ridden land on earth. This is so because

* From a statement presented to the North Carolina General Assembly on January 24, 1977.

whenever they are confronted by any problem, a substantial number of Americans demand the passage of a new law or the adoption of a new Constitutional amendment to solve the problem. All too often their legislators harken to this demand without pausing to determine whether or not laws or constitutional provisions already in existence are sufficient to cope with the problem or whether the proposed new law or constitutional amendment will create problems more serious than the problems it seeks to solve or whether the problem is one which must be solved by human cooperation or religion rather than by the law or the Constitution.

Laws are designed to regulate the conduct of men and women. Insofar as they engage in similar roles, they should have equal rights and responsibilities. It is otherwise, however, where they have incompatible functions. The Equal Rights Amendment is unrealistic because it constitutes an effort to convert men and women into identical legal beings having exactly the same rights and exactly the same responsibilities at all times and under all circumstances. In so doing, the Amendment emulates Procrustes, the fabled robber of ancient Greece, who stretched or mutilated his victims to make them conform to the length of his bed.

It is the height of folly to command legislative bodies to ignore sex in making laws. This is true because the continuation of life on earth is dependent upon sex. God gave men the capacity to beget children and women the capacity to bear them. He also decreed that a newborn child is the most helpless of his creatures and that children require many years of nurture and training to make them intelligent beings capable of functioning as adults.

Every intelligent society has taken these things into consideration in making its laws. Since the task of providing nurture to children ordinarily falls upon the housewife and mother, intelligent societies have imposed upon the husband and father the primary responsibility for supporting his wife and children. Moreover, they have decreed that the woman who devotes her life to housekeeping and motherhood shall receive some provision from the estate of her husband when she becomes his widow. Besides, all women need protection against such crimes as rape and seduction. If the Equal Rights Amendment is construed as its most militant advocates say it must be construed, i.e., to nullify every law making any distinction between men and women no matter how reasonable such distinction may be, wives, mothers, and widows will be robbed of these protections and laws relating to rape and seduction and other sexual crimes will be annulled.

The strongest advocates for the ratification of the Equal Rights Amendment are business and professional women. While some of them can undoubtedly cite discriminations which they have suffered on account of the customs of society, none of them can cite any law which gives to a business or professional man any right which they do not enjoy. This is so simply because business and professional women enjoy every legal right which the law confers upon business and professional men. Why any of them should desire to rob those women who elect to become wives and mothers, and unfortunately widows, of necessary legal protections or to rob all women of protection against crimes which can only be committed by men is past comprehending.

The Procrustean attempt of the amendment to solve the problems which life presents to men and women by conferring upon them exactly the same rights and exactly the same responsibilities at all times and under all circumstances, irrespective of differing roles in life, will raise more serious problems than it will solve. Moreover, it attempts to solve by law relationships which only can be solved satisfactorily by cooperation and religion.

Recent decisions of the Supreme Court interpreting the Due Process Clause of the Fifth Amendment, the Due Process Clause and Equal Protection Clause of the Fourteenth Amendment, and other constitutional provisions and recent federal and state laws nullifying invidious legal discriminations against women make it manifest that the Equal Rights Amendment is totally unnecessary.

Since 1971 the Supreme Court of the United States has made at least eight rulings which show that the ratification of the Equal Rights Amendment is totally unnecessary to remove any legal discriminations to which women may be subjected.

In these cases, the Supreme Court of the United States holds, in substance, that any law, federal or state, which makes any distinction whatever between the legal rights and responsibilities of men and women is unconstitutional unless the distinction is based upon reasonable grounds and is designed to protect women in some role they enact in life.

I respectfully submit that these holdings afford a far better way to satisfy the wishes of advocates of ratification of the Equal Rights Amendment, whose blunderbuss approach would invalidate any law making any legal distinction between the rights and responsibilities of men and women, no matter how reasonable the distinction might be, and no matter how necessary the distinction might be to protect women in roles which they may play in life.

Recent acts of Congress, recent executive orders of the President, and recent regulations of federal departments and agencies prohibit discrimination on the ground of sex in education, employment, financing, housing, public accommodations, and all other federal activities.

Moreover, these same acts, orders and regulations forbid states and their subdivisions and all private persons to discriminate on the basis of sex in any activity of any nature which is financed in whole or in part by federal funds. Since so many activities in America are financed in whole or in part by federal funds, these acts, orders, and regulations make invidious discriminations against women illegal in virtually all areas of American life.

Time and space do not permit me to analyze in detail these various acts, orders, and regulations. Inasmuch, however, as advocates of the Equal Rights Amendment complain loudly of discrimination against women in public and private employment, I will note that sections of Title 5 and Title 42 of the United States Code, and Executive Orders 11498 and 11521 forbid discrimination on the basis of sex in federal employment, and the Fair Labor Standard Act of 1938, the Equal Pay Act of 1963, and Title VII of the Civil Rights Act of 1964 outlaw discrimination on the ground of sex in respect to the employees and the employments covered by the acts.

The breadth of the prohibition against discrimination on the basis of sex is indicated by Section 703 of Title VII of the Civil Rights Act of 1964, which makes it illegal for any employer subject to the act "to fail or refuse to hire or to discharge any individual or otherwise to discriminate against any individual with respect to his compensation, or terms or conditions of employment because of such individual's sex."

Inasmuch as interstate commerce is now construed to embrace virtually all economic activities in America, these congressional acts may now be invoked by women in virtually all areas of our land to prevent or redress discrimination against them by private employers.

The states themselves have enacted multitudes of laws to buttress the federal laws, orders, and regulations outlawing discrimination on the basis of sex.

I believe that virtually all the states have repealed their former laws discriminating against women in major respects. I cannot affirm with finality, however, that all the insignificant laws of all the states discriminating against women in some minor respects have been expunged from their statute books. I am nevertheless satisfied that the legislatures of the several states where such insignificant laws may still remain will forthwith repeal them if they are called to their attention.

I do affirm, however, with absolute conviction that using the blunderbuss Equal Rights Amendment to nullify any such remaining laws would be even more foolish than exploding an atomic bomb to eradicate a few mice.

If it is ratified, the Equal Rights Amendment will transfer from the states to the federal government vast governmental powers which have been reserved to the states throughout our history. By so doing, the amendment will substantially thwart the purpose of the Constitution to create "an indestructible union composed of indestructible states" and reduce the states in large measure to powerless zeroes on the nation's map.

When the Founding Fathers drafted and ratified the Constitution, they divided governmental powers between the federal government and the states, delegating to the federal government the powers necessary to enable it to operate as a national government for all the states and reserving to the states all other governmental powers.

The chief governmental power reserved to the states by the Constitution has been the power to make the laws governing the rights and responsibilities of the men and women living within their respective borders.

By virtue of this reserved power, the states have made throughout our history the laws regulating marriage, the support of the family, the property rights of married people, the care and custody of children, divorce, alimony, and the myriad other aspects of relationships between men and women. As a consequence, each state has been able to conform its laws relating to these matters to the convictions of the people residing in its borders and to ignore the differing views entertained by people living in distant states.

Moreover, the power to interpret laws of this nature has resided in the state courts whose rulings concerning them have been exempt from reversal by the Supreme Court of the United States except in those comparatively rare instances where such laws deny individuals the equal protection of the laws or deprive them of due process of law in violation of the Fourteenth Amendment.

While its advocates may not so intend, all of these things will be drastically changed if the Equal Rights Amendment should be ratified. This is true because the Equal Rights Amendment will convert the states from sovereign authorities in the constitutional field now assigned to them into rather meaningless zeroes on the nation's map.

If ratified, the Second Section of the Equal Rights Amendment will play havoc with the legislative powers of the states. This is so because this section will transfer from the legislatures of all the states to the Congress the ultimate power to pass binding laws regulating the rights and responsibilities of men and women.

After ratification, a state legislature will be able to pass laws of this nature only by the forbearance of Congress, which can step in at any time and pass congressional acts nullifying and supplanting any and all State laws undertaking to regulate the rights and responsibilities of men and women.

If they are to be beneficial to society, constitutions and laws must be based on the realities of life and not on false pretenses concerning them.

The Equal Rights Amendment is based on the false pretense that the second of these inescapable realities does not exist. As a consequence, the Amendment imperils the welfare of wives and mothers and their children and the highest interests of society itself. This is true notwithstanding the beguiling and camouflaging name its advocates bestow upon the Amendment.

QUESTIONS FOR DISCUSSION

1. What effect would failure to ratify ERA have on the rights of women?
2. Would any privileges existing under law today be denied to women if ERA is adopted?
3. Does ERA discriminate against wives, mothers, and widows?
4. What effect would ERA have on federalism?
5. How would the Supreme Court interpret the ERA in dealing with such matters as the military draft, alimony, and laws pertaining to rape?

SUGGESTED READINGS

Amundsen, Kirsten. *A New Look at the Silenced Majority: Women and American Democracy.* Englewood Cliffs, N.J.: Prentice-Hall, 1977.

"The Continuing Controversy over the Women's Equal Rights Amendment: Pro & Con." *Congressional Digest,* June/July 1977.

Freeman, Jo. *The Politics of Women's Liberation: A Case Study of an Emerging Social Movement and Its Relation to the Policy Process.* New York: McKay, 1975.

Lear, Martha Weinman. "You'll Probably Think I'm Stupid." *The New York Times Magazine,* April 11, 1976, pp. 30 ff.

U.S. Congress. House. Committee on the Judiciary. *Equal Rights for Men and Women, 1971.* Hearings before subcommittee no. 4 of the Committee on the Judiciary on H. J. Res. 35, 208, and Related Bills, 92nd Cong., 1st sess., 1971.

U.S. Congress. Senate. Committee on the Judiciary. *Equal Rights 1970.* Hearings on S. J. Res. 61 and S. J. Res. 231, 91st Cong., 2nd sess., 1970.

U.S. Congress. Senate. Committee on the Judiciary. *The "Equal Rights Amendment."* Hearings before the subcommittee on Constitutional Amendments of the Committee on the Judiciary on S. J. Res. 61, 91st Cong., 2nd sess., 1970.

"What Does Equal Rights for Women Mean to You?" *Parents Magazine,* July
1976, pp. 12–13, 70.

Williams, Roger M. "Women Against Women: The Clamor over Equal
Rights." *Saturday Review,* June 25, 1977, pp. 7 ff.

Do Quota Systems Deny Constitutional Rights Under the Equal Protection Clause?

YES

JUSTICE STANLEY MOSK (for the majority)
Allan Bakke *v.* The Regents of the University of California*

In this case we confront a sensitive and complex issue: whether a
special admission program which benefits disadvantaged minority students who apply for admission to the medical school of the University
of California at Davis (hereinafter University) offends the constitutional rights of better qualified applicants denied admission because
they are not identified with a minority. We conclude that the program,
as administered by the University, violates the constitutional rights of
nonminority applicants because it affords preference on the basis of
race to persons who, by the University's own standards, are not as
qualified for the study of medicine as nonminority applicants denied
admission.

In 1973 and 1974, plaintiff Allan Bakke, a Caucasian, applied for
admission to the University, which is supported by public funds. There
were 2,644 applicants for the 1973 entering class and 3,737 for the 1974
class. Only one hundred places are available each year, of which sixteen are filled under the special admission program in dispute; applicants for the remaining eighty-four places are chosen by recourse to the
normal admission process.

Bakke, who did not apply for consideration under the special
program, was denied admission in both years, and was not admitted to
any other medical school. He filed a complaint against the University

---

* From *Allan Bakke* v. *The Regents of the University of California,* Sup. 132 Cal. Rptr. 680 (1976).

seeking mandatory, injunctive, and declaratory relief to compel the University to admit him, alleging he was qualified for admission and the sole reason his application was rejected was that he was of the Caucasian race. The complaint also alleged that all students admitted under the special program were members of racial minorities, that the program applied separate, i.e., preferential, standards of admission as to them, and that the use of separate standards resulted in the acceptance of minority applicants who were less qualified for the study of medicine than Bakke and other nonminority applicants not selected. He claimed he had been the victim of invidious discrimination because of his race, in violation of the equal protection clause of the Fourteenth Amendment to the United States Constitution.

The University filed a cross-complaint for declaratory relief, seeking a determination that the special admission program was valid. The cross-complaint averred that the University considers the minority status of an applicant as only one factor in selecting students for admission, and that the purposes of the special program were to promote diversity in the student body and the medical profession, and to expand medical education opportunities to persons from economically or educationally disadvantaged backgrounds. The cross-complaint did not allege that Bakke should be denied relief because of laches.

The trial court, after considering the pleadings, the deposition and declaration of Dr. George H. Lowrey, the associate dean of student affairs and chairman of the admissions committee, and the interrogatories submitted by the parties, found that the special admission program discriminated against Bakke because of his race and that he was entitled to have his application evaluated without regard to his race or the race of any other applicant. It found against the University on its cross-complaint for declaratory relief. However, the court determined that Bakke was not entitled to an order for admission to the University because, although he was qualified to be admitted in both years in which he applied, he would not have been selected even if there had been no special program for minorities. Thus the court denied Bakke's prayer for an injunction ordering his admission.

Both parties appeal from the ensuing judgment—Bakke from the portion of the judgment denying him admission, and the University from the determination that the special admission program is invalid and that Bakke is entitled to have his application considered without regard to his race or the race of any other applicant. Bakke renewed his application for admission subsequent to the judgment, but the University refused to evaluate his qualifications without regard to the special admission program. We transferred the cause directly here, prior to a decision by the Court of Appeal, because of the importance of the issues involved. (Cal.Const., art. VI, § 12; rule 20, Cal.Rules of Court.) . . .

The issue to be determined thus narrows to whether a racial classification which is intended to assist minorities, but which also has the effect of depriving those who are not so classified of benefits they would enjoy but for their race, violates the constitutional rights of the majority.

Two distinct inquiries emerge at this point; first, what test is to be used in determining whether the program violates the equal protection clause; and second, does the program meet the requirements of the applicable test. . . .

We cannot agree with the proposition that deprivation based upon race is subject to a less demanding standard of review under the Fourteenth Amendment if the race discriminated against is the majority rather than a minority. We have found no case so holding, and we do not hesitate to reject the notion that racial discrimination may be more easily justified against one race than another, nor can we permit the validity of such discrimination to be determined by a mere census count of the races.

That whites suffer a grievous disadvantage by reason of their exclusion from the University on racial grounds is abundantly clear. The fact that they are not also invidiously discriminated against in the sense that a stigma is cast upon them because of their race, as is often the circumstance when the discriminatory conduct is directed against a minority, does not justify the conclusion that race is a suspect classification only if the consequences of the classification are detrimental to minorities.

Regardless of its historical origin, the equal protection clause by its literal terms applies to "any person," and its lofty purpose, to secure equality of treatment to all, is incompatible with the premise that some races may be afforded a higher degree of protection against unequal treatment than others. . . .

We come, then, to the question whether the University has demonstrated that the special admission program is necessary to serve a compelling governmental interest and that the objectives of the program cannot reasonably be achieved by some means which would impose a lesser burden on the rights of the majority.

The University seeks to justify the program on the ground that the admission of minority students is necessary in order to integrate the medical school and the profession. The presence of a substantial number of minority students will not only provide diversity in the student body, it is said, but will influence the students and the remainder of the profession so that they will become aware of the medical needs of the minority community and be encouraged to assist in meeting those demands. Minority doctors will, moreover, provide role models for younger persons in the minority community, demonstrating to them that they can overcome the residual handicaps inherent from past discrimination.

Furthermore, the special admission program will assertedly increase the number of doctors willing to serve the minority community, which is desperately short of physicians. While the University concedes it cannot guarantee that all the applicants admitted under the special program will ultimately practice as doctors in disadvantaged communities, they have expressed an interest in serving those communities and there is a likelihood that many of them will thus fashion their careers.

Finally, it is urged, black physicians would have a greater rapport with patients of their own race and a greater interest in treating diseases which are especially prevalent among blacks, such as sickle cell anemia, hypertension, and certain skin ailments.

We reject the University's assertion that the special admission program may be justified as compelling on the ground that minorities would have more rapport with doctors of their own race and that black doctors would have a greater interest in treating diseases prevalent among blacks. The record contains no evidence to justify the parochialism implicit in the latter assertion. . . .

We may assume arguendo [for the sake of argument] that the remaining objectives which the University seeks to achieve by the special admission program meet the exacting standards required to uphold the validity of a racial classification insofar as they establish a compelling governmental interest. Nevertheless, we are not convinced that the University has met its burden of demonstrating that the basic goals of the program cannot be substantially achieved by means less detrimental to the rights of the majority.

The two major aims of the University are to integrate the student body and to improve medical care for minorities. In our view, the University has not established that a program which discriminates against white applicants because of their race is necessary to achieve either of these goals.

It is the University's claim that if special consideration is not afforded to disadvantaged minority applicants, almost none of them would gain admission because, no matter how large the pool of applicants, the grades and test scores of most minority applicants are lower than those of white applicants. In support of this assertion, the University declared that in the two years before the special admission program was instituted, only two blacks and one Mexican-American qualified for admission, whereas between 1970 and 1974, while the program was in operation, thirty-three Mexican-Americans, twenty-six blacks, and one American Indian were admitted. But this showing is insufficient to satisfy the University's burden. For there is no evidence as to the nature of the admission standards prior to 1969, when the special admission program began, and it may well be that virtually determinative weight was accorded to test scores and grades. Thus the fact that few minorities were accepted before 1969 was not necessarily the result of the absence of a preference for minorities on strictly racial grounds.

We observe and emphasize in this connection that the University is not required to choose between a racially neutral admission standard applied strictly according to grade point averages and test scores, and a standard which accords preference to minorities because of their race. . . .

In addition, the University may properly as it in fact does, consider other factors in evaluating an applicant, such as the personal interview, recommendations, character, and matters relating to the needs of the profession and society, such as an applicant's professional goals. In short, the standards for admission employed by the University are not constitutionally infirm except to the extent that they are utilized in a racially discriminatory manner. Disadvantaged applicants of all races must be eligible for sympathetic consideration, and no applicant may be rejected because of his race, in favor of another who is less qualified, as measured by standards applied without regard to race. We reiterate, in view of the dissent's misinterpretation, that we do not compel the University to utilize only "the highest objective academic credentials" as the criterion for admission.

In addition to flexible admission standards, the University might increase minority enrollment by instituting aggressive programs to identify, recruit, and provide remedial schooling for disadvantaged students of all races who are interested in pursuing a medical career and have an evident talent for doing so.

Another ameliorative measure which may be considered is to increase the number of places available in the medical schools, either by allowing additional students to enroll in existing schools or by expanding the schools. . . .

While a program can be damned by semantics, it is difficult to avoid considering the University scheme as a form of an education quota system, benevolent in concept perhaps, but a revival of quotas nevertheless. No college admission policy in history has been so thoroughly discredited in contemporary times as the use of racial percentages. Originated as a means of exclusion of racial and religious minorities from higher education, a quota becomes no less offensive when it serves to exclude a racial majority. "No form of discrimination should be opposed more vigorously than the quota system." (McWilliams, A Mask for Privilege (1948) p. 238.)

To uphold the University would call for the sacrifice of principle for the sake of dubious expediency and would represent a retreat in the struggle to assure that each man and woman shall be judged on the basis of individual merit alone, a struggle which has only lately achieved success in removing legal barriers to racial equality. The safest course, the one most consistent with the fundamental interests of all races and with the design of the Constitution is to hold, as we do, that the special admission program is unconstitutional because it violates the rights guaranteed to the majority by the equal protection clause of the Fourteenth Amendment of the United States Constitution.

BAKKE'S APPEAL

As set forth above, the trial court found that Bakke would not have been admitted to either the 1973 or 1974 entering class at the University even if there had been no special admission program. However, in reaching this conclusion the court ruled that the burden of proof remained with Bakke throughout the trial. He asserts that since he established that the University had discriminated against him because of his race, the burden of proof shifted to the University to demonstrate that he would not have been admitted even without the special admission program.

We agree. Under the general rule, the burden of proof would remain with plaintiff Bakke throughout the trial on the issue of his admission. . . .

By analogy to these decisions, we hold that the trial court should have ruled that since Bakke successfully demonstrated that the University had unconstitutionally discriminated against him, the burden of proof shifted to the University to establish that he would not have been admitted to the 1973 or 1974 entering class without the invalid preferences. In these circumstances, we would ordinarily remand the case to the trial court for the purpose of determining, under the proper allocation of the burden of proof, whether Bakke would have been admitted to the 1973 or 1974 entering class absent the special admission program. (See Haft v. Lone Palm Hotel (1970) 3 Cal.3d 756, 775, 91 Cal.Rptr. 745, 478 P.2d 465.) However, on appeal the University has conceded that it cannot meet the burden of proving that the special admission program did not result in Bakke's exclusion. Therefore, he is entitled to an order that he be admitted to the University.

The judgment is affirmed insofar as it determines that the special admission program is invalid; the judgment is reversed insofar as it denies Bakke an injunction ordering that he be admitted to the University, and the trial court is directed to enter judgment ordering Bakke to be admitted. Bakke shall recover his costs on these appeals.

WRIGHT, C. J., and McCOMB, SULLIVAN, CLARK and RICHARDSON, JJ., concur.

Do Quota Systems Deny Constitutional Rights Under the Equal Protection Clause?

NO

JUSTICE MATTHEW O. TOBRINER (dissenting)
Allan Bakke *v.* The Regents of the University of California*

. . . By today's decision, the majority deliver a severe, hopefully not fatal, blow to these voluntary efforts to integrate our society's institutions and to ameliorate the continuing effects of past discrimination. Contrary to the majority's assertion, time-honored constitutional principles and precedent by no means establish that the special admission program at issue in this case violates the Fourteenth Amendment. Indeed, as I explain, past decisions of both the United States Supreme Court and this court clearly demonstrate the constitutional propriety of the admission program instituted by the medical school to integrate its student body. . . .

Unless it can be said that the promotion of integration is a constitutionally illegitimate purpose—a proposition which the majority obviously do not intend to embrace—I cannot understand how the admission policy at issue in this case can properly be found less permissible than these other long-accepted admission practices. There is, indeed, a very sad irony to the fact that the first admission program aimed at promoting diversity ever to be struck down under the Fourteenth Amendment is the program most consonant with the underlying purposes of the Fourteenth Amendment.

* From *Allan Bakke* v. *The Regents of the University of California*, Sup. 132 Cal. Rptr. 680 (1976).

1. The use of racial classifications to promote integration or to overcome
the effects of past discrimination is neither "suspect" nor presumptively unconstitutional.

There is no denying that racial classifications have played an odi-
ous role throughout our nation's history. In the course of the past
two-hundred years, racial classifications have been utilized to subjugate racial and ethnic minorities to a separate and inferior existence in
American society. At first, courts struck down only the most blatant
use of racial classifications against minorities, invalidating laws which
directly denied blacks or similar minorities basic legal rights and
privileges enjoyed by the majority of citizens. . . .

The racial classifications embodied in the special admission program are not intended to, nor do they in fact, exclude any particular
racial group from participation in the medical school; on the contrary,
the program is aimed at assuring that qualified applicants of all racial
groups are actually represented in the institution. Moreover, the racial
classifications do not stigmatize any racial group as an "inferior" race,
but instead give realistic recognition to the continuing effects resulting
from several centuries of discriminatory treatment. Finally, the racial
classifications are not the instruments through which a majority's racial
prejudice has imposed inferior treatment upon an impotent minority,
but rather are remedial measures voluntarily implemented to give all
students the distinct educational benefits flowing from an integrated
education. . . .

Whenever there is a limited pool of resources from which
minorities have been disproportionately excluded, equalization of opportunity can only be accomplished by a reallocation of such resources; those who have previously enjoyed a disproportionate advantage must give up some of that advantage if those who have historically
had less are to be afforded an equitable share. This reality, however,
has not led courts to invalidate the remedial use of benign classifications. . . .

The majority are similarly in error in claiming that the instant case
can be distinguished from past benign racial classification cases on the
ground that prior cases only permit the use of such classifications as a
remedy for racial discrimination undertaken in the past.

In the first place, the medical school's special admission program
is, in a very real and important sense, intended to overcome the continuing effect of past discrimination in this country. As the United
States Supreme Court has acknowledged on numerous occasions, the
effect of our nation's sad legacy of racial discrimination runs deep and
wide, and is in no sense limited to those schools, or to those states,
which practiced de jure segregation. . . . Further, Supreme Court decisions specifically recognize that discrimination endured by minorities

in primary and secondary education will frequently result in later disadvantage to such minorities if educationally based tests are used as the primary criterion for conditioning access to a benefit. . . . The medical school took this continuing discriminatory impact into account in concluding that the continuation of its traditional admission policies was unfair to disadvantaged minorities and in deciding to implement the special admission program.

The majority appear to suggest, however, that the medical school was not free to implement benign racial classifications because there is no evidence that the medical school had itself engaged in racial discrimination in the past. Initially, such a requirement is, on its face, completely illogical. The fact that a governmental institution has not itself engaged in discrimination affords no reason for precluding such an institution from taking into account, through remedial classifications, the present effects of past discrimination by other bodies. The rule proffered by the majority, moreover, would "penalize" precisely the wrong institutions. It must be remembered that the medical school here has *voluntarily* decided that it is in its educational interest to maintain an integrated medical school; the effect of the majority's suggestion would be to deny Davis medical school the right to implement such a judgment, and to grant that opportunity only to institutions that have practiced racial discrimination in the past. No one can seriously maintain that such a result is dictated by the Constitution. . . .

> **2.** The racial classifications embodied in the special admission program relate directly, and in a reasonable fashion, to the compelling state interest in promoting integration and are thus constitutional.

As discussed above, the remedial racial classifications at issue here cannot properly be viewed as presumptively unconstitutional and thus should not be tested against the standard applied to invidious racial classifications, the exacting, "seemingly insurmountable" strict scrutiny standard. . . .

There are sound reasons for the judiciary to take a somewhat cautious approach in reviewing ostensibly benign racial classifications. In light of the historical misuse of racial classifications in this country, it is important that courts carefully and realistically assess the purpose and effect of any racial classification to assure that the classification is actually devised for legitimate remedial purposes rather than as a covert method for imposing invidious racial discrimination. In undertaking such a realistic review, however, a court must also be mindful that remedies for the continuing effects of past discrimination have proven distressingly elusive, and that it is therefore important that entities attempting in good faith to promote integration be given reasonable leeway in experimenting with various methods to achieve this compelling societal objective. Accordingly, once a court is convinced that differential racial treatment has been adopted in a good faith attempt to promote integration, it should uphold a benign racial classification so long as it is directly and reasonably related to the attainment of integration. Under this standard, the racial classifications at issue here are clearly constitutional.

The background of the Davis special admission program demonstrates that its racial classifications were clearly devised as a realistic attempt to promote integration. . . .

First, as the chairman of the school's admission committee explained, disadvantaged minorities were accorded differential treatment in part because the school concluded that the "objective" academic credentials on which the school had largely relied in the past did not accurately predict such minority applicant's qualifications and did not provide an equitable basis for comparison with other applicants. To the extent that the differential treatment of minority applicants was thus based on the school's determination that its traditional criteria were "culturally biased" against minorities, it seems incontrovertible that the school, at the very least, was entitled voluntarily to adjust its standards to overcome any built-in bias. (Cf. *Griggs* v. *Duke Power Co., supra,* 401 U.S. 424, 91 S.Ct. 849.)

Indeed, the medical school's decision to deemphasize MCAT [Medical College Admission Test] scores and grade point averages for minorities is especially reasonable and invulnerable to constitutional challenge in light of numerous empirical studies which reveal that, among qualified applicants, such academic credentials bear no significant correlation to an individual's eventual achievement in the medical profession. The findings of these studies are not surprising when one considers all of the nonacademic qualities—energy, compassion, empathy, dedication, dexterity, and the like—which make for a "successful" physician. As medical school admissions officials themselves acknowledge, these studies raise questions of the most serious order as to the propriety of the continuing use of traditional admission criteria.

. . . Thus, given the race and ethnic background of the great majority of students admitted by the medical school, minority applicants possess a distinct qualification for medical school simply by virtue of their ability to enhance the diversity of the student body.

In addition to promoting diversity in the medical school itself, the special admission program was aimed at alleviating the largely segregated nature of the medical profession generally. There is no question but that during the years in question here minorities were grossly underrepresented in the medical profession. . . . Realizing that a segregated medical profession might well remain largely oblivious to the realities of life of disadvantaged minorities and the nature and scope of their medical problems, the medical school established the special admission program in part in recognition of its obligation to meet the broad needs of the medical profession at large.

One of the most pressing medical problems in the country, of course, is the paucity of medical services available to residents in poor minority neighborhoods. The medical school tailored its special admission program specifically to meet this problem; all of the minority students accepted under the program came from a disadvantaged background and all expressed their intent to return to practice in poor, minority communities upon completion of their medical training.

The majority, at one point, suggest that this purpose of the special admission program is somehow improper, and that the medical school has, by its approach, committed itself to the illegitimate task of producing, for example, "black [doctors] for blacks." This simplistic characterization of the special admission process surely does a grave disservice to the medical school. The medical school has by no means undertaken to train black doctors simply to treat blacks, or to train chicano doctors simply to treat chicanos; a minority doctor's medical degree is not, of course, a license only to treat minorities. In my view, however, it was neither unreasonable nor improper for the medical school to conclude that at least one of the reasons for the deplorable lack of effective medical services in minority communities is the shortage of minority physicians, and to determine that an increase of disadvantaged minority doctors might play at least some role in improving the situation. . . .

Finally, over and above the benefits accorded to the medical school and to the medical profession, the special admission program was implemented to serve the larger national interest of promoting an integrated society in which persons of all races are represented in all walks of life and at all income levels. . . . If any state interest can be said to be "compelling" for purposes of the Fourteenth Amendment, it is just such an interest in overcoming the isolation of minorities and bringing them into the mainstream of American society.

Any one of the numerous objectives served by the special admission program would appear sufficient, in itself, to justify the program's existence; surely, when viewed cumulatively, they remove any doubt as to the propriety of the medical school's consideration of race as one relevant factor in the admission decision.

In light of California's sizable minority population, and the current underrepresentation of minorities in the medical profession, the allocation of sixteen out of one hundred places to the special admission program can hardly be criticized as unreasonably generous. Moreover, only fully qualified applicants were admitted under the program and thus if there had not been a sufficient number of qualified disadvantaged minority applicants the medical school would not have accepted minority applicants simply to fill a quota. . . . In this respect, the sixteen places represented a "goal" rather than a "quota." . . .

Moreover, although the majority speculate that the broadening of the special admission program to disadvantaged applicants of all races will result in approximately the same amount of integration as the present program, that conclusion appears untenable on its face. Because all disadvantaged students need financial aid, the total number of such students a medical school can afford to admit is limited. As a consequence, inclusion of all disadvantaged students in the special admission program would inevitably decrease the number of minority students admitted under the program and thus curtail the achievement of all integration-related objectives. . . .

The majority's alternative suggestion that the integration of medical schools can be accomplished by increasing the size and number of medical schools is similarly unrealistic. The cost of medical educational facilities is enormous; absolutely nothing suggests that the necessary financial commitment for increased facilities will be forthcoming in the foreseeable future. It is a cruel hoax to deny minorities participation in the medical profession on the basis of such clearly fanciful speculation. . . .

To date, this court has always been at the forefront in protecting the rights of minorities to participate fully in integrated governmental institutions. . . . It is anomalous that the Fourteenth Amendment that served as the basis for the requirement that elementary and secondary schools could be *compelled* to integrate, should now be turned around to *forbid* graduate schools from voluntarily seeking that very objective.

I cannot join with the majority in concluding that the Constitution precludes the state through the Medical School of the University of California at Davis from pursuing of its own volition a program to provide for the effective integration of its student body.

Rehearing denied; TOBRINER, J., dissenting.

QUESTIONS FOR DISCUSSION

1. Does the special program for minority admission to medical school at the University of California at Davis discriminate against white people?
2. Did the court argue that race could not be used as a factor in allocating places for medical school admission?
3. If special programs such as the one at Davis are not legal, how can the proportion of racial minorities in professions such as medicine and law be increased?
4. Is the court decision a racist statement?
5. Is there a justification for establishing special programs, such as the one at

Davis, for other groups, such as war veterans and women? What should be the criteria for determining the eligibility of such groups? Who should decide?

SUGGESTED READINGS

Bunzel, John H. "*Bakke* v. *University of California.*" *Commentary*, March 1977, pp. 59–64.

Connolly, Paul H. "The Courts v. Self-Government." *National Review*, October 28, 1977, pp. 1225–1228.

Conrad, Thomas R. "Debate About Quota Systems: An Analysis." *American Journal of Political Science* 20(Fall 1976):135–149.

Haag, Ernest van den. "Reverse Discrimination: A Brief Against It." *National Review*, April 29, 1977, pp. 492–495.

Hook, Sidney, and Miro Todorovitch. "The Tyranny of Reverse Discrimination." *Change*, December/January 1975–1976, pp. 42–43.

Lindsey, Robert. "White/Caucasian—and Rejected: Medical School Admission Case of A. Bakke." *The New York Times Magazine*, April 3, 1977, pp. 42–47, 95.

Maguire, Daniel. "Quotas: Unequal but Fair." *Commonweal*, October 14, 1977, pp. 647–652.

"Meritocracy and Its Discontents." *The New Republic*, October 15, 1977. (A special issue devoted to the Bakke case and related matters.)

Is Enforced Busing of Students for the Purpose of Integration Unnecessary?

YES

IRVING KRISTOL
*The Busing Crusade**

Social psychologists have contributed relatively little to public enlightenment in our lifetime, and much to public confusion. But they have come up with one marvelous insight into the irrationalities of group behavior. It goes by the rather fancy name of "cognitive dissonance," and refers to the fact that people who believe strongly in a set

* Irving Kristol, "The Busing Crusade," *The Wall Street Journal*, June 17, 1976, p. 14. Reprinted with permission of The Wall Street Journal, © 1976 Dow Jones & Company, Inc. All Rights Reserved.

of ideas will tend to reaffirm those ideas most vigorously at the very moment when they are repudiated by reality.

The original and classic study of this phenomenon, by Leon Festinger, involved a sect of Midwestern millennialists who predicted the end of the world at a certain date. On that day, they assembled on a nearby hilltop and waited confidently for the hour of judgment to strike. The hour came, and passed, and nothing happened. So what did these true believers then do? They came down from the hill and redoubled their proselytizing efforts. Rather than confront ideological disillusionment, with its disturbing psychological implications, they insisted that it was someone's calculations that must have been in error, not their premises. The people who belonged to this sect did not look like fanatics, and certainly did not think of themselves as fanatics; nevertheless, fanaticism is a fair enough description of their mental condition.

It is a similar experience of "cognitive dissonance" and a similar kind of fanatical obstinacy that have given rise to the busing controversy of today. In purely rational terms, it is an absurd controversy. The absurdity derives from the fact that the proponents of busing seem, by now, pretty much to have forgotten the original premises of their argument. True, they will rise up in indignation against those who explicitly challenge those premises—but instead of actually defending them, they simply denounce the motives and character of the critics. It is as if the whole purpose of their crusade were now to get people to go up that hill—and never mind what would happen once they got there.

And, incredibly enough, the busing crusade has succeeded in making many influential converts at the very moment when one would expect it to be entirely discredited. Not among ordinary Americans, to be sure, whose common sense renders them largely immune. To be a recruit to *this* crusade, you really need to be a college graduate. It further helps if you are a "well-informed" person who works in the media. And you are most vulnerable to this folly if you are a judge, learned in the law and committed to intellectual sobriety. Once upon a time, the judiciary was regarded as a bulwark against the foolish passions of the populace. Today it is legitimate to wonder: who is going to protect the American people against the foolish passions of their judiciary?

THE BUSING PREMISES

What were the premises on the basis of which school busing was originally urged? There were three:

1. Legal segregation of the races, as embodied in the "Jim Crow" legislation of the South, was in violation of both the spirit and the letter of the Constitution. Also in violation of the Constitution were those cases of *de facto* [actually existing] segregation which were the result of deliberate official policy (e.g., school districting along racial lines).

2. The close and daily association of white and black schoolchildren would in and of itself engender greater interracial understanding and harmony.

3. Black students, once brought into closer contact with more highly motivated and better-prepared white students, would themselves become better students.

The first premise was indeed a strong one—in my opinion an incontestable one. The fact that the courts had tolerated official discrimination on racial grounds, despite the intent of the Thirteenth and Fourteenth Amendments, was a judicial scandal, and a reversal of this position was long overdue. But what, one may ask, has this to do with busing? Why couldn't the court simply strike down all such discriminatory laws and practices, and leave it at that?

The obvious explanation is that the courts did not trust the political authorities in the South to abide promptly by its decision. There were good enough grounds for such distrust, of course. But the demand for *prompt* reformation is, on its face, more than a little puzzling. Why should the courts have thought it possible that the consequences of a century-old policy could be quickly erased? Why were they so impatient? Why couldn't they allow the South to adjust gradually to a nonsegregated social order? After all, once those discriminatory laws and practices were struck down, it was certain that blacks would start crossing the previously prescribed boundaries. They might do so timidly at first, and in small numbers. But one would need a low opinion of black initiative and courage to believe that, with the law of the land now on their side, and the courts behind them, they would simply remain ghettoized.

One suspects that the judges of the Warren Court, like so many white liberals, found it hard to believe that blacks could cope with such problems without their paternalistic assistance. But in any case, the courts spared themselves the trouble of even thinking about this matter because, in the area of education at least, a simple and powerful "remedy" was at hand. This "remedy" was busing.

That busing could be envisaged as a "remedy" for official school segregation was made possible by the bland acceptance of premises (2) and (3). After all, the purpose of busing is not to punish white schoolchildren for the sins of their fathers and grandfathers (though there are prominent black spokesmen who seem to think just this). If the purpose of busing is "remedial," that is because busing will presumably make Americans less race conscious than segregation had permitted them to be, and would encourage black students to get a better education than segregation had allowed. One doesn't prescribe a "remedy" unless one is pretty sure it will have good effects. And these were the effects—racial harmony and superior black education—that busing was thought to cause.

That the compulsory mixing of the races, especially at a tender age, could and would have such effects was a doctrine preached by liberal social scientists for decades. They had theories to explain why it should happen and all sorts of experimental data that appeared to show it did happen. So persuasive have they been that the courts are now demanding busing in northern and western cities which never had any official segregatory policies. Segregation for whatever reason—even if voluntary or accidental—is now seen as an evil per se, not to be tolerated by a reinterpreted Constitution. Something called "integration" has now become the constitutionally prescribed goal. And by "integration" the courts now mean nothing more than a statistical racial ratio—*nothing* more. The assumption, of course, is that such a statistical goal, once attained, will automatically lead to friendlier interracial feelings and to superior educational achievement.

THEORIES IN RUINS

The various sociological and psychological theories which justified busing as a "remedy" for America's race problem are now in ruins. It is not only that more recent—and more honest and objective—scholarship has shown that these theories never were very credible in the first place. Even without such revisionist scholarship, there is experience and the evidence of one's senses to go by. Busing in most circumstances does *not* encourage interracial harmony, but instead is more likely to provoke racial hostility and violence. And busing does not improve *anyone's* educational achievements—if there were clear evidence that it did, you certainly would have heard of it by now.

Nor does busing even achieve that parody of "integration" represented by its superficial statistical goals. The more busing we have, the less "integrated," even in a purely statistical sense, are our schools. It is true that "white flight" is not merely the result of school busing—the movement to the suburbs has many other causes. But it is unquestionably one factor, and not a negligible one. A middle-class person in Manhattan (or in central Detroit or Cleveland) who wishes to send his children to a school that (a) is safe, and (b) actually teaches them something instead of simply maintaining order, *has* to move to the suburbs. As the proponents of busing are the first to insist, practically all the complaints of blacks about the quality of education in inner-city schools are valid. So why should white parents send their children to them?

Nevertheless, our doctrinaires persist in their crusade. As resistance grows—not only among whites, but among blacks too, the majority of whom are fed up with busing and are seeking other solutions—their determination grows in proportion. Now they want to start transporting schoolchildren into suburbs, out of suburbs—perhaps, soon, it will be cross-country. They'd rather march us up and down that hill forever than admit they were wrong.

The truly interesting questions are: What are the sources of this ideological fanaticism? How is it that people, who are perfectly sensible in other respects, succumb to it? We really don't need any more research on busing—we know that, though a truly integrated society is certainly our ideal, there is no point marching up *that* hill. We could indeed use new research on *alternatives* to busing—on more effective ways of achieving amicable race relations and better black education. But we need even more urgently new research on the peculiar social psychology of the busing crusade—this could give us some valuable insights into our contemporary distemper.

Is Enforced Busing of Students for the Purpose of Integration Unnecessary?

NO

NORMAN GOLDFARB
*Another Perspective on Busing**

Irving Kristol's Journal article "The Busing Crusade" (June 17) described those who press for school desegregation as suffering from "cognitive dissonance." This, said Mr. Kristol, "refers to the fact that

* Norman Goldfarb, "Another Perspective on Busing," *The Wall Street Journal*, August 23, 1976, p. 8. Reprinted with permission of The Wall Street Journal, © 1976 Dow Jones & Company, Inc. All Rights Reserved.

people who believe strongly in a set of ideas will tend to reaffirm those ideas most vigorously at the very moment when they are repudiated by reality."

The remainder of the article, written in the large brush strokes of conclusionary language, held that most of the premises of desegregationists have been proven false and that theories which justified busing "for a remedy for America's race problems are now in ruins." Finally, we were told that we need new research on the peculiar social psychology of the busing crusade to "give us some valuable insights into our contemporary distemper."

My city of Buffalo would make an ideal laboratory for such research, if Mr. Kristol is serious about the need for it. Currently the city's board of education, opposed to "forced" busing, is under court order to create a desegregation plan by October 15, which meets constitutional requirements.

However, Mr. Kristol's stereotype of those who actively pursue school desegregation is not applicable to the plaintiffs here. We are as diverse in our education, our occupations, and political and religious beliefs as we are in our individual motives for participating in this action. But there is one common bond: *the belief that purposeful segregation, the stamp of inferiority placed on blacks and other minorities by the white majority, must end, wherever it exists.*

That is the premise of our school desegregation suit. That is what these cases are all about. Those who believe, like Mr. Kristol, that the natural dynamism of events will correct purposeful segregation, are out of touch with reality. History teaches us that racial isolation does not yield to black initiative alone. While cities like Harrisburg, Pennsylvania, and Berkeley, California, have voluntarily desegregated their schools, facts in northern school cases reveal the ingenious means used by boards of education to create, enlarge, and perpetuate segregation.

A CENTURY-OLD STRUGGLE

Contrary to Mr. Kristol, courts have not ordered busing in northern and western cities unless unconstitutional segregation has been found. In Buffalo, the federal court decision climaxed a century-old struggle that intensified in the last decade. On October 11, 1867, Buffalo newspapers headlined "Ejection of Colored Children from Public Schools" after a Common Council edict led the school superintendent to eject two black children from a school they dared to attend after the passage of the Civil Rights Act of 1866.

We don't view busing as a remedy for America's race problems.

Does anyone? It is a useful device to end *forced* school segregation where, as in Buffalo, there has also been purposeful residential segregation. Guidelines for student transportation as to safety, distance and travel time, as laid down by the Supreme Court, are sensible.

One of the more accurate and realistic assessments of the meaning of busing was made by The Los Angeles Times, in an editorial after a survey by its reporters in late 1975. Its findings:

- In community terms, busing becomes accepted surprisingly quickly and rarely is the subject of long-standing controversy.
- In academic terms, busing has only a marginal impact in the long run, neither handicapping the achievement of majority children nor significantly improving the achievement of minority children.
- In terms of personal relations the results are ambiguous.
- Summing it up, busing doesn't have the deleterious effects that its critics assert, but neither is it a panacea for the problems, either educational or social, of blacks and Mexican-Americans.
- Busing will not always be as successful as it has been in Tampa. It will rarely be as controversial as it has been in Boston.
- The fundamental affirmation of the Supreme Court was that separate facilities cannot be equal. Busing has played only a small part in implementing that decision. But without it, thousands of children would still know only the inequality of separation thrust upon them because of their color.

Here in Buffalo, we don't believe that black students must sit next to white students to learn or that they will necessarily become more highly motivated or better students. We believe, like W. E. B. DuBois, that "other things being equal, the mixed school is the broader, more natural basis for the education of all youth. It gives wider contacts, it inspires greater self-confidence and suppresses the inferiority complex."

We don't believe that merely bringing black and white students together will correct the reasons for the learning disabilities of any child. We believe, however, that white students who go to school with black students from early on will realize that they are not superior simply because they are white. That, too, is education.

It is possible that an upgrading of the entire educational product will occur with desegregation because of the time and attention that must be given to the problem and because school boards and others sell desegregation by talking about quality integrated education. There must also be a huge effort to change the perception that many white principals and teachers have of black students. White parents will not permit the educational liabilities that existed in black schools, when there are no more white schools or black schools but just schools. Whether or not the quality of schools improves, desegregated schools will be *different*. The children involved will have a chance to discover their common humanity.

Mr. Kristol is correct on one point, that persistent desegregation efforts cause distemper. As activists from coast to coast unravel the sophisticated devices used by school boards to disguise purposeful segregation, more cities will join Buffalo, Omaha, Dayton, Denver, San Francisco, Minneapolis, Pontiac, Milwaukee, and others under court order. Distemper may grow but these cases are necessary steps in the historical process of achieving justice for America's minorities.

A NEED FOR AGILITY

The ultimate confrontation may not be between blacks and whites but between whites who believe in America's professed values and act on them and those who would leave matters as they are or would take actions leading to official apartheid. We do not believe the latter will happen but rather that solutions not yet thought of will be found. The solutions will include methods to arrest the decay of the cities which is the primary reason for white flight, not desegregation orders. However, for the needed thought to be given to those solutions and to be acted upon when found, advocates of change must be as agile, ingenious and as untiring as those who, by action or inaction, support an exclusionary society.

In the meantime, bonuses accrue where court orders have been issued. Voters recognize the emptiness of the promises of politicians who seek election on the basis of being against busing (substitute desegregation). Here, the county comptroller, a city court judge and several councilmen have won public office because of their efforts to keep the schools segregated.

Moreover, powerful conciliatory forces that otherwise might take a passive view of segregation have been set in motion. Recently, six hundred community leaders from fifty cities met in Washington. The topic was "Desegregation Without Turmoil." In Buffalo, a number of organizations, including businessmen, the clergy and citizens' groups, are intent on protecting the safety of the children and adherence to the law.

The day of the court's decision here, Mayor Stanley Makowski released the results of a city-commissioned survey. It indicated 75 percent of the people were for school integration. However, while 68.3 percent of the blacks favored busing, only 15.5 percent of the whites were in favor of busing. Assuming the whites didn't answer tongue-in-cheek, the next question here is how best to bring the views of 75 percent of the people to reality and meet constitutional requirements.

It cannot be done without the assignment of students to schools outside their neighborhoods, and the words of Chief Justice Warren Burger in the Swann case are applicable here. "All things being equal, with no history of discrimination, it might well be desirable to assign pupils to schools nearest their homes. But all things are not equal in a system that has been deliberately constructed and maintained to enforce racial segregation."

As awkward and painful as it is to apply a remedy, we must try. Otherwise, as the saying goes, we would leave the wounded in the hands of those who shot them down.

QUESTIONS FOR DISCUSSION

1. How successful has busing been as a means to promote integration?
2. What do Kristol and Goldfarb believe about the desirability of integration as a goal?
3. Does busing promote racial harmony?
4. What effect does busing have on the quality of education?
5. What alternatives to busing are available to promote integration? Have these been tried?

SUGGESTED READINGS

Cottle, Thomas J. *Busing*. Boston: Beacon Press, 1976.

Featherstone, Joseph. "Boston Desegregation." *The New Republic,* January 24, 1976, pp. 11–17.

Glazer, Nathan. "Is Busing Necessary?" *Commentary,* March 1972, pp. 39–52.

Graglia, Lino A. *Disaster by Decree: The Supreme Court Decisions on Race and the Schools.* Ithaca, N.Y.: Cornell University Press, 1976.

Kelley, Jonathan. "Politics of School Busing." *Public Opinion Quarterly* 38(Spring 1974):23–39.

Kirp, David L. "School Desegregation and the Limits of Legalism." *The Public Interest* 47(Spring 1977):101–128.

Rossell, Christine H. "School Desegregation and White Flight." *Political Science Quarterly* 90(Winter 1975/1976):675–695.

"The 'School Busing' Controversy in the Current Congress." *Congressional Digest,* April 1974, pp. 99–128.

Sowell, Thomas. "Black Conservative Dissents." *The New York Times Magazine,* August 8, 1976, pp. 14 ff.

Williams, Roger M. "What Louisville Has Taught Us about Busing." *Saturday Review,* April 30, 1977, pp. 6 ff.

PART TWO

Do Nongovernmental
Institutions
in America
Distort Democracy?

5.

Do the Mass Media Distort the News?

Democracy assumes that citizens will get accurate, undistorted information so that they can make intelligent choices. Since the mass media provide most of that information, they are essential to the democratic process.

The major political phenomena of the past two decades have also been media events. It is difficult to think of any important subjects of American political life during this period in which the media have not played prominent roles. Elections, impeachment, wars, riots, and acts of terrorism are only a few examples of these media events.

Television, particularly, has become an important feature of the election process. The televised presidential debates—Kennedy-Nixon in 1960 and Ford-Carter in 1972—generated enormous attention. Any factual error made during these debates could be devastating, as Mr. Ford realized after he commented that Poland was free from Soviet control. The trappings of the political campaign, moreover, are well suited to media manipulation. Slick television and newspaper advertisements were influential in winning votes. A favorable public image for a candidate can be shaped by a good media campaign.

So much of Watergate, too, was linked with media activity. Although Bob Woodward and Carl Bernstein, two reporters from *The Washington Post,* doggedly pursued the story that eventually led to the resignation of President Richard Nixon, it was televised congressional committee hearings that brought revelations of presidential wrongdoing right into our homes. Televised press conferences in which Richard Nixon was questioned by alert reporters gave visual evidence of the great strains that the President was experiencing and suggested that he was unable to carry out his duties.

Films from the battlefields in Vietnam carried into our living rooms the horrors of war. Reporters covering the war were given unprecedented freedom, and they were often critical of the way the government and the military were conducting the war.

Television gave wide coverage to such distressing aspects of the American involvement in Southeast Asia as the My Lai massacre (in which Vietnamese civilians were killed by United States soldiers) and the alarming prevalence of drug use.

The urban riots of the 1960s in such cities as Los Angeles, Detroit, and Newark were extensively covered on TV. When the electric power failed in the New York City area in the summer of 1977, television crews filmed the looters in the act of smashing store windows and carrying off furniture, television sets, and clothing.

Acts of terrorism also received prominent television coverage—the massacre of Israeli athletes at Munich in 1972, the frequent hijacking of planes by such radical groups as the Palestine Liberation Organization and the Japanese Red Army, and the kidnappings of industrialists in West Germany and Italy. Communication satellites in outer space permitted instant television reporting of these events.

Because of extensive TV coverage of depressing news from 1965 to 1974, such as the war in Vietnam, urban riots, campus disorder, terrorist acts, and Watergate, some writers criticized the television networks for presenting their version of reality, rather than the news itself. These authors suggested that television was portraying America in a negative light. Critics asked why television did not give adequate attention to Viet Cong atrocities rather than American misconduct in the war, to racial harmony rather than racial confrontation, to student moderates rather than to student extremists, and to the positive achievements of the Johnson and Nixon administrations in domestic and foreign policies rather than to the failures.

This chapter asks the question: "Do the mass media distort the news?" Political scientist Marvin Maurer contends that they do. According to Maurer, television news reporting in the United States is not neutral, but portrays American society in a negative way.

Maurer argues that television news has a greater impact and influence on audiences than newspapers because of the difference in format. Newspaper readers can skip those sections of the paper about which they have no interest and move instead to subjects that concern them. Television viewers, on the other hand, must watch an entire news program even if they are interested only in sports.

Television requires large audiences for the industry to make a profit. Maurer argues that to get these audiences, television must distort reality by entertaining or by becoming sensational. The result is that the picture of America is distorted and unflattering. Because the television media have considerable influence over the public, they are undermining traditional values and beliefs that are necessary for any established order to function.

In a speech delivered in London, Herbert S. Schlosser, then president of the National Broadcasting Company, defends television. He argues that TV media are not biased, and he suggests that complaints about news coverage come often from biased viewers, rather than from biased reporters. According to Schlosser, television is a looking glass that reflects the good and the bad. Television, consequently, is a conveyor of reality and is an essential instrument of democracy.

Do the Television Media Distort the News?

YES

MARVIN MAURER
*TV News and Public Opinion**

For over a decade now a mounting chorus of criticism has been aimed at the press and television for waging a one-sided assault on American social and political institutions. The mass media are accused of serving up a diet of negative, adversary-oriented news. One astute observer of Soviet-American ideological competition contends that our mass media depict the American people as "corrupt, dehumanized, brutalized, and racist."[1]

It is clear that the television media do not merely report the news. Even occasional efforts to intersperse the television news with favorable reports of American achievements and successes are insufficient to offset the strong diet of negative news. Television news, which is considered far more influential than print media, is not neutral. It is helping to undermine traditional values and beliefs necessary for any established order to function.

During the 1950s and 1960s political scientists conceded the adversary nature of television news programming but assumed it was just like other sources in that it was unable to alter basic beliefs and values.[2] Events of the past two decades, however, led to a different perspective as the grim combat in Vietnam, frightening urban ghetto riots, and national anguish over Watergate were all brought forth on the television screen. Peter Clark, who is president of the American Newspaper Publishers Association, was one among many TV critics who charged that television's "scandal-minded" approach was threatening the traditional values which include "national pride, respect for law and

---

* "TV News and Public Opinion" was written expressly for this volume by Marvin Maurer, Professor of Political Science, Monmouth College, New Jersey.

properly constituted authority, concern for one's family, and a substantial interest in material success."[3] This article explains why such an accusation against television is justified and why critics are correct in emphasizing that television rather than the newspaper is more likely to distort the news and create more powerful audience reaction.

NEWSPAPERS VERSUS TV

Television news has a greater impact on, and influence over, audiences than newspapers because of the difference in format. Print takes up "space" while television uses up "time." A newspaper reader may easily bypass all the political news and rush right on to the sports section, but not the television viewer. The latter, if a sports fan, would have to observe nineteen or so items—including commercials—offered in a thirty-minute news program before he has access to the sports report. The viewer, then, is a captive of the entire TV news program.

The format of television news requires the news program to emphasize sensational events.[4] Newspapers, too, report sensational news. With their more flexible format, however, they can afford to include background and historical data as well as news about average people and successful events. Readers are able to select items of interest to read, and unlike the television viewer reject material that is disagreeable or uninteresting.

While both television and newspapers devote their energies, talents, and resources to attract more and more viewers and readers respectively, they tackle their problem from different perspectives. Newspapers attempt to attract readers in terms of interest clusters whereby readers are encouraged to purchase a newspaper because it caters to their special interests, such as crossword puzzles or comic strips. Television news must capture and hold far larger and diverse audiences than the printed press to pay its way. An NBC executive lamented that "a newspaper . . . can easily afford to print an item of conceivable interest to only a small percentage of its readers. A television news program must be put together with the assumption that each item will be of some interest to everyone that watches."[5] As a result, television news departments have a formula for each item which in turn has consequences for the content of the news program.

FACTORS INFLUENCING THE NEWS

The fact that the television industry requires large audiences if it is to be profitable influences the character of television news programs. Television places great reliance on the Nielsen ratings to determine how large an audience watches a show at any time. Based on Nielsen's sampling of the nation's viewers, the networks know that the higher the audience rating, the more money can be charged to advertisers.[6] Thus, each news item has to have something in it for each viewer so that he or she will stay with the program. A news story must hold interest, or as an NBC executive explained to his staff: "Every news story should, without any sacrifice of probity or responsibility, display the attributes of fiction or drama."[7] Of course the networks claim they report the truth, but their concept of probity is not intended to pass a strict true or false test.

The television networks claim that their news programs provide a "mirror image of society."[8] According to television critic Edward Jay Epstein, a mirror image is television's version of events that occur in reality. Epstein offers the following example. In 1968, CBS News presented a film entitled *Hunger in America*. With pictures of an emaciated baby on the screen, the narrator told millions of viewers that "hunger is easy to recognize when it looks like this." He went on to say that this American baby died of starvation. A subsequent investigation revealed that the baby was "a three-month premature child . . . whose . . mother, a school teacher, had the premature birth after an automobile accident."[9]

CBS defended this report on the grounds that babies were dying of starvation at the time of the showing. Its staged version of reality was intended to produce a critical reaction toward this social problem. This example of *Hunger in America* shows that television's news formula seeks to avoid dullness in order to hold audience interest and at the same time it provides an image of its version of social and political reality.

The ever-increasing pace to secure higher audience ratings impels the networks to compromise standards of objectivity to the point where they will cooperate with extremist groups seeking publicity or even measure staff performance on criteria other than news reporting competency. For example, in January 1975, NBC presented a dramatic view of a grocery store exploding in Belfast. Obviously, television crews had been notified in advance of the action. Some network executives are aware of this latter problem. They are unable to come up with a solution because restraints on reporting violence and terror might hurt audience ratings and, in turn, the extremist groups would be tempted to escalate their terror to the point where the networks would have to provide coverage.

The need to attract large audiences is also influencing the character of professional journalism. Television news is now in the process of phasing out an older breed of commentators whose apprenticeship was in print journalism. Special rating teams hired by the networks claim that personality and style of the news commentator either attract or repel audiences. For example, *TV Guide* reporter David Chagall related how market-research teams recommended that newscasters be released from their assignments because they failed to induce perspiration in the test audience, signifying an incapability to arouse interest.[10] Thus, in order to attract audiences, television will increasingly become more a medium of entertainment than a source of news reporting.

In a recent speech television newsman David Brinkley argued that if news does not interest an audience, it should not be shown. Thus, he believed that the destruction of the most moderate of Arab states—Lebanon—should not be reported on television. He said, "Who really cares about it? Lebanese living in the United States . . . are a tiny fraction of 1 percent of our population." To Brinkley, then, news reporting "is a question of building our programs in order to have bigger audiences."[11] In a more critical vein, television news watchers John P. Roche and Edith Efron expressed concern that television has ignored the massive slaughters in Communist-controlled Cambodia partly because audiences are no longer interested in Indochina.

While the networks are among the staunchest defenders of free expression, as well as their own independence, they will compromise principles in order to enhance their audience ratings. In an astonishing article *The New York Times* described how ABC subordinated its news division's integrity to an outside influence. Soviet officials were permitted to censor and monitor ABC news stories about life in Russia. Some Soviet officials actually sat in ABC's New York offices reviewing its network reporting. *The Times* article contended that these startling concessions to the Russians were part of the network's effort to secure coverage rights for the 1980 Olympics.[12] ABC lost out to NBC; however, there is concern that NBC made similar concessions to the Soviet Union. In effect, we have a powerful news gathering and reporting institution that uses its resources to present versions of the news to suit its needs and priorities.

CONCLUSION

There is good cause to be concerned about the power and influence of television news. Its capabilities to provide news to almost every adult American is a fact that the Television Information Office is both quick and proud to report. Television news is indeed the main source of news for over two thirds of adult Americans. All segments of society—

including the most educated and affluent—believe in and rely on television news more than on any other news source.[13]

Television, then, is by no means a neutral reporting instrument. Michael Robinson's study of the impact of CBS's film, *The Selling of the Pentagon,* led him to conclude that television is able to alter once positively held views about American institutions and, perhaps, even more important, reduce the viewer's belief in his own ability to cope with and solve political problems. Robinson's data indicate that audiences experienced "a decrease in political self-esteem" and "a decline in political trust and confidence in the system." In turn, these "anti-institutional themes" reach the audience with one essential message: "None of our institutions respond, none of our political organizations succeed."[14] It is clear from this and other evidence that, as of now, there is no effective force capable of countering television's undermining of America's leaders and institutions.

Do the Television Media Distort the News?

NO

HERBERT S. SCHLOSSER
Broadcasters in a Free Society: Common Problems, Common Purpose*

. . . The American networks are regularly accused of news bias. We are told by some that television news is too liberal, and by others that it is too conservative. We hear that we emphasize the bad and ignore the good; that we don't deal with the real problems and issues; and that when we do, our reports are slanted. Self-styled media watchdog groups file a steady stream of complaints against us with any agency that will listen.

But we have found that charges of bias can usually be attributed to any news report that does not coincide with the complainer's own point of view. And, as David Brinkley has said, a biased opinion is simply one with which you do not agree.

* From a lecture by Herbert S. Schlosser, former President of the National Broadcasting Company, at the fifth of the tenth series of lunchtime lectures in the Concert Hall at Broadcasting House, London, February 12, 1976, pp. 10–12. Reprinted by permission.

We also run into the contention that a small, elite group controls a very powerful medium and is using it to brainwash the public. Our more sophisticated critics seem less concerned with that than they are with their view of us as the gatekeepers of public discussion, setting the agenda for public discourse independently of those who have been elected to govern the nation.

Both sets of critics fail to acknowledge the basic function of journalism in a free society. The editorial function may sometimes miss the mark, and its failings should be criticized. But the independent news judgments formed by professional journalists hold greater promise of contributing to an informed public than any official truth dictated by government.

Fortunately, opinion polls on my side of the Atlantic show that the public has confidence in the integrity of broadcast news and that this trust has increased steadily over the years. And when the public has been asked what medium of information it would choose to keep if it were allowed only one, television has received its overwhelming vote.

In all of these attacks on entertainment and news programming that I have been discussing, I believe there is an illusion common in both our countries [Great Britain and the United States] that the influence of broadcasting is somehow overwhelming. People think that television is doing something to them and they are unhappy about it. There is the feeling that television in some ill-defined way may be responsible for the lack of confidence in our societies today, and yet, at the same time, that it holds the promise of being saviour and panacea for us all.

But if we make it a scapegoat on which to lay our frustrations, and if we make the mistake of blaming television for society's various problems, we will only put off solutions by diverting attention from the real causes of these problems.

Some people, in both our countries, because they believe that television has a pervasive, and somehow negative influence—or because what they see can be upsetting or alarming—would like to fragment or diminish the broadcasting organizations.

But the free broadcasting system in each of our countries is a national resource and can be a countervailing force against the concentrated power of government and the pressure of organized special interest. I do not mean to present us as the last bastions against public or private tyranny. Obviously we are not. But we do represent a vital communications force and a means for informing the public of its fears, its hopes, its needs and its controversies. We try to manage it as best we know how. And if it were to be dispersed, the government and other self-serving interests—for whatever their purpose—could dominate the resulting fragments, to the damage of the public at large.

I believe we come nearer the truth about the influence of television if we regard it as a looking-glass that reflects the tastes, the attitudes, the events and the issues of our time—the good and the bad. It will reflect different things to different people. Yet when a whole nation can see a reflection of its diversity and its blemishes and its blessings, it can gain the experience and insight vital to the people of a democratic society.

As a channel for shared experiences and understanding, television in America accelerated the civil rights revolution, not by advocacy, but by showing people throughout the country what was happening to some of their fellow citizens.

The detailed television coverage of the events following the assassination of President Kennedy and the transition of government helped to unify and heal the nation.

Television changed the war in Vietnam from a remote abstraction to a horror in millions of living rooms, not by editorializing but by showing the population what was happening.

Television helped Americans to participate personally in the correction of government abuse by enabling them to witness the unfolding of the Watergate investigation; and to sit with the Congressional Committee deliberating the impeachment of their President.

And by showing the calm, orderly way in which President Ford assumed power, television helped restore the nation's confidence in its institutions.

In all these ways, and many more, television is a conveyor of reality and an instrument of democracy. And in our free societies broadcasters will be under pressure for recognition by those who feel they have a message for the nation. And often by those who may want to counter that message. We share a responsibility to be fair to all, but we must insist on our right of independent judgment. . . .

NOTES

1. Paul Hollander, *Soviet and American Society* (New York: Oxford University Press, 1973), p. 35.
2. Michael J. Robinson, "Public Affairs Television and the Growth of Political Malaise: The Case of 'The Selling of the Pentagon,'" *American Political Science Review* 70(June 1976):409–432.
3. Peter B. Clark, "The Opinion Machine: Intellectuals, the Mass Media and American Government," in *The Mass Media and Modern Democracy*, ed. Harry M. Clor (Skokie, Ill.: Rand McNally, 1974), p. 40.

4. Robinson, "Public Affairs Television," p. 428.
5. Edward Jay Epstein, *News from Nowhere* (New York: Random House, 1973), p. 40.
6. Ibid., pp. 83, 92.
7. Ibid., p. 4.
8. Ibid., p. 13.
9. Ibid., pp. 21–22.
10. David Chagall, "Only as Good as His Skin Tests," *TV Guide,* March 26, 1977, pp. 5–10.
11. David Brinkley, "A Question for Television Newsmen: Does Anyone Care?" *TV Guide,* March 19, 1975, pp. A5–A6.
12. Thomas Whiteside, "How ABC Buttered up the Russians—And Maybe Why?" *The New York Times,* November 23, 1975, sec. 2, p. 1.
13. The Roper Organization, *An Extended View of Public Attitudes Toward Television and Other Mass Media: 1959–1971* (New York: Television Information Office, 1971).
14. Robinson, "Public Affairs Television," pp. 410, 416, 419, 427, 429.

QUESTIONS FOR DISCUSSION

1. After tabulating a few evening television news reports, would you conclude that television news is biased? What is the basis for your conclusion?
2. What are some of the positive aspects of television news as a medium of information to Americans?
3. Do you believe that television news leaves listeners with a negative and hostile view toward American institutions or that it is a scapegoat for disagreeing groups that do not like to be criticized?
4. What advice or alternatives would you suggest to help viewers become less dependent on television news?
5. Does television news influence political behavior?

SUGGESTED READINGS

Altheide, David. *Creating Reality: How TV Distorts Events.* Beverly Hills, Calif.: Sage Publications, 1976.

Clor, Harry M., ed. *The Mass Media and Modern Democracy.* Skokie, Ill.: Rand McNally, 1974.

Epstein, Edward Jay. *News from Nowhere.* New York: Random House, 1973.

Friendly, Fred W. *The Good Guys, the Bad Guys and the First Amendment: Free Speech vs. Fairness in Broadcasting.* New York: Vintage, 1977.

Johnson, Nicholas. *How to Talk Back to Your Television Set.* New York: Bantam, 1970.

McLuhan, Marshall. *Understanding Media: The Extensions of Man.* New York: Signet, 1964.

Robinson, Michael J. "Public Affairs Television and the Growth of Political Malaise: The Case of 'The Selling of the Pentagon.'" *American Political Science Review* 70(June 1976):409–432.

———. "Television and American Politics: 1956–1976." *The Public Interest* 48(Summer 1977):3–39.

The Roper Organization. *An Extended View of Public Attitudes Toward Television and Other Mass Media: 1959–1971.* New York: Television Information Office, 1971.

6.

Do Interest Groups Strengthen Democracy?

In 1977, President Carter submitted an energy program to Congress. When the Senate proceeded to weaken the program, Carter sharply criticized the "oil lobby," accusing the oil industry of promoting a multibillion-dollar "rip-off" of the American people. In taking on a powerful economic interest group, Carter was continuing what has become a tradition for presidents in twentieth-century America. Theodore Roosevelt, Franklin Roosevelt, Harry Truman, and John Kennedy at one time or another battled the "special interests."

Presidents have not been the only ones to engage in this battle: progressives, populists, socialists, and liberals have all protested the undue and sometimes sinister influence of "special interests" or "pressure groups"—terms that clearly refer to the big corporations. By now most Americans have heard the charges that special interests are responsible for destroying the ecology, poisoning foods, polluting the atmosphere, encouraging nuclear proliferation, giving tax shelters to the wealthy, driving up medical costs, bribing legislators, creating a military-industrial complex, and blocking social reform.

Liberal and left-wing organizations, however, have not been the only groups to complain about the sinister influence of the special interests. Conservative and right-wing groups have also denounced the special interests, whom they associate with labor unions, civil rights supporters, liberals, and advocates of the welfare state. Their charges, too, have become familiar: special interests are responsible for welfare chiseling, inflation, school busing, economic decay, and government inefficiency.

Whether liberals or conservatives, many of the people who criticize the *special interests* argue that these special interests are in conflict with the *public interest*. By public interest, they refer to goals that benefit society in general, rather than a particular class, race, religion, or region. A political system is just, they contend, to the degree that laws reflect the interests of the entire community rather than one segment of it.

Other observers of interest groups contend, however, that there is no such thing as the public interest. When a group appeals to the public interest, they argue, it is really attempting to win broad support for its special interest policies rather than serve some objective community interest. When environmentalists delay the construction of an oil pipeline, for example, they may be furthering the goals of wildlife enthusiasts, but they are also harming the interests of pipeline workers who would have been employed in such a construction project.

An evaluation of the relationship between the special interests and the public interest requires an understanding of what is meant by interest groups (or pressure groups, as they are sometimes called). The traditional definition of an interest group is a collection of people who have common interests and who work together to achieve those interests. When a group becomes involved in the activities of government, it is known as a political interest group.

More than a century ago, Alexis de Tocqueville observed that Americans have a propensity to join associations. This observation has become as valid a description of the 1970s as it was of the 1830s. The United States has a large number of political interest groups—business, labor, professional, religious, and social reform.

Every area of big business makes its views known to political institutions. Oil lobbies, for example, monitor the activities of government in matters pertaining to taxes, environmental protection, leases, and imports. Business groups in other areas—such as munitions, shipping, steel, automobiles, and communications—watch government behavior dealing with subjects of interest to them.

Labor unions, too, are concerned with the activities of government at the national, state, and local levels. They sometimes ally themselves with the businesses they serve when the industries are threatened. For example, in 1977, steel unions joined with steel management to request that the United States impose quotas on steel imports from Japan when imports caused a reduction in domestic steel production.

Often, however, labor and business are in conflict. Unions are concerned with laws governing the right to strike, minimum wages, and other subjects that may affect the economic well-being of their membership.

Professional groups, too, find that government affects their livelihood. Doctors formed the American Medical Association, which is concerned with government activities in such areas as national health insurance, drug licensing, and the construction of medical schools. Medical school faculty and administrators, moreover, seek government grants, salary increases, and pension insurance.

Religious groups are concerned with government, also. They monitor government on such issues as marriage and divorce, adoption, Sunday closing laws, and education.

Social reform groups stake their claims on government, too. Women's rights associations seek to eliminate discrimination against women in employment and salaries. Civil rights organizations ask for expansion of economic and political rights for minorities. In addition, environmental groups urge government to protect the ecology.

Interest groups, then, appear in all sectors of American society. They engage in a variety of activities to influence government: talking to government officials, contributing to political campaigns, appealing to the general public, or organizing demonstrations. Some have even engaged in illegal activities, such as bribery and invasion of privacy.

INTEREST GROUPS AND THE PUBLIC INTEREST

It is clear that interest groups are active in American society. Dispute, however, centers on what the role of interest groups is and should be. A key question is: "Do interest groups serve the public interest?" One school of thought contends that interest groups make a vital contribution to democracy. They provide information to legislators, who can use these data to make laws. According to this school, interest groups are balanced out by opposing interest groups, a factor that allows the legislators to decide on their own without undue pressure from either side. Former Minnesota Senator Eugene McCarthy argues this position.

Another school of thought contends that each interest group pursuing its own goals does not lead to the harmony of all and the best laws. According to this view, interest groups are not equal—the economically strong interest groups are organized and are politically powerful, while the economically weak interest groups are ineffective. Interest groups, this school adds, have not served the public interest on many occasions in the past, such as in the United States participation in the war in Vietnam. South Dakota Senator George McGovern argues this position.

Do Interest Groups
Serve the Public Interest?

YES

EUGENE J. McCARTHY
A Senator Looks at the Lobbies*

The word "lobbying" has a derogatory ring. This is not surprising, for good or bad lobbying occurs in the processes of democracy at the point of rough transition where interests conflict and judicial processes fall

* From Eugene J. McCarthy, "A Senator Looks at the Lobbies," *The New York Times Magazine*, August 19, 1962, pp. 17ff. © 1962 by The New York Times Company. Reprinted by permission.

short. Lobbying is a test—sometimes a raw test—of the judgment and integrity of political officeholders, both elected and appointed.

Who are the lobbyists? What do they do in order to affect the course of government? How effective are they? Is lobbying a threat to democracy? Do government officials need more protection from lobbyists? What can or should be done about lobbying? It is important that these questions be asked and that an attempt be made to answer them.

This has been a most active year for lobbyists in Washington. They were drawn especially by the tax bill, the Trade Expansion Act, the medical insurance program and by the Sugar Act.

The activities of lobbyists on the Sugar Act, which involves foreign countries, have moved the Senate Foreign Relations Committee to make a special study of lobbying—or, as the committee described it, of "non-diplomatic activities of representatives of foreign governments or their agents in promoting the interests of those governments." Investigation or inquiry into the operation of lobbyists in other fields has been suggested by some members of Congress.

By statute, the lobbyist today is any person who solicits money or anything of value to be used principally to secure or influence the passage or defeat of any legislation by the Congress of the United States.

Lobbying has a long history. The word "lobby" appeared first in the English language about the middle of the sixteenth century. It was derived from the medieval Latin word *lobium,* a monastic walk or cloister.

Three hundred years later the word was in politics. It was used both to identify a hall or corridor in the British House of Commons and as a collective noun applied to all those who frequented these lobbies. It covered those who sought to influence men in office as well as newspaper men and others looking for news and gossip.

Today the word "lobbyist" is used both in its narrow legal sense and, more broadly, as a description of all attempts to influence not only the legislators but also any agency or officer of government. Registered lobbyists in Washington number approximately 1,100, but the number of persons and agencies involved in efforts to influence the government is much greater.

Some lobbyists represent big interests and well organized groups. The Chamber of Commerce and the National Association of Manufacturers have registered lobbyists along with the AFL-CIO [American Federation of Labor-Congress of Industrial Organizations]; so do the American Petroleum Institute, the Association of American Railroads, and nearly all major industrial and financial interests. The so-called little people and the unorganized or less organized also have lobbyists.

For example, the American Committee for Flags of Necessity, the Hualapai Tribe of Hualapai Reservation, and the Arthritis and Rheumatism Foundation are among those groups or organizations represented by lobbyists.

Some lobbyists are well paid; some get little more than expense money. Some operate directly on government officials, others primarily by indirection through appeals to constituents or voters. Some are professional, others amateur. Some lobbyists represent only one position or program, while others are available as freelancers on an issue-by-issue or client-by-client basis.

Some lobbyists are quite open—they seek their own gain, the protection of an economic advantage, or the elimination or reduction of advantages held by their competitors. These cry more often for equity than they do for justice. Others speak for the arts, for morality, for aid to the sick and for the oppressed among the family of man.

What do lobbyists do in order to affect government decisions?

The methods used by the lobbyists are almost as varied as their causes. Some appeal on a purely personal basis, as friend to friend. Some undoubtedly use monetary or material appeals, but there is little evidence of direct pay-off in lobbying activities affecting the Congress. In some fourteen years of membership in the Congress, I know of no case in which a member was moved to support or to oppose a position in response to any kind of direct financial or material reward. The indirect influence of campaign contributions is more difficult to assess but it is, I believe, more important.

The most common method of lobbying is that of simply appearing before a committee of Congress or speaking to individual members in an attempt to bring them to understand one's position or to influence them to support that position.

How effective are the lobbyists?

Some are wholly ineffective but take credit for what happens without, in fact, having in any way influenced events.

Among the regular lobbies, the postal employees' organizations are usually very active and, whenever postal pay legislation is before Congress, they are listed at or near the top in terms of total expenditures. In order to raise wages or to change working conditions significantly, the spokesmen for the postal workers of the country must influence either the Congress or the administration—or both—for government employee unions are not recognized and dealt with in the same way as other labor unions are by private employers. There is little doubt that the existence of this Washington lobby has influenced the Congress and successive administrations to raise salaries and to improve working conditions not only for postal employees, but for all government workers.

The major farm organizations in the country maintain regular lobbies in Washington. The American Farm Bureau Federation and the National Farmers Union usually take opposite sides on farm legislation. The apparent success of the two organizations parallels closely the success of the two major political parties. The Farmers Union position is favored when the Democrats are in power, and the Farm Bureau position when the Republicans are in power.

One of the most interesting and continuing lobbying efforts of recent years has been that in support of a bill which is known as H. R. 10. This bill proposes to change existing income tax laws to allow members of professions and other self-employed persons a limited income tax credit on money invested in private pension or retirement programs. [Such a change in tax laws was subsequently made and is known as the Keogh plan.] Starting almost from scratch, the supporters of this legislation have secured the approval of the House of Representatives and of the Senate Finance Committee. Victory in this case—if it comes—must be credited in great measure to the efforts of a lobby registered as the American Thrift Assembly, a kind of holding company or organizing lobby, which was supported in testimony by the U.S. Chamber of Commerce, the National Association of Manufacturers, the Farm Bureau, the American Medical Association and others.

In this session of Congress, lobbies have been most active in four major areas: taxes, trade and tariffs, medical aid for the aged, and extension of the Sugar Act. Undoubtedly the lobbyists did have or will have some effect on action in each of these areas.

Any significant change in tax laws attracts the attention of those who may be affected. The changes being considered this year were significant and controversial and the lobbying effort extensive.

Industries likely to be affected by trade and tariff policies are always well represented in Washington. Whenever an issue even remotely bearing upon trade is brought up for consideration, the representatives of these industries seek permission to testify. The hearings on the President's new tariff and trade program have attracted them in great numbers. Members of the House Ways and Means Committee and the Senate Finance Committee, which ordinarily hold trade and tariff hearings, are generally familiar with the testimony of these witnesses. They have been described as somewhat like professional soldiers who regularly go to battle, seldom win wars and suffer few casualties.

One of the most active Washington lobbies this year, and through the years, is that of the American Medical Association [AMA]—better known in Washington for what it is against than for what it is for. The spokesmen for the AMA have effectively opposed the inclusion of doctors in the Social Security retirement program. They were strongly opposed to amending the Social Security Law to provide for the payment of Social Security pensions to people who are permanently or totally disabled after they pass the age of fifty. And in the present session of Congress, the AMA lobby led the opposition to the establishment of a medical insurance program for the aged as a part of the Social Security program. [This program (Medicare) was subsequently enacted into law.] Action in this Congressional session has been a real test of the power of the AMA lobby.

Lobbying activities with reference to the Sugar Act revision this year involved lobbyists in greater numbers than ever in the past, and the lobbying activities were more intensive. At least twenty-two lobbyists testified before Congressional committees in behalf of the countries they represented. The list of lobbyists included former members of both the Eisenhower and Truman administrations, Washington lawyers, and public relations men. Their agreements with their principals varied from flat fees to contingency agreements, depending upon the action taken by Congress.

The massive lobbying activity this year arose from the fact that the administration recommended that the Cuban sugar quota of some three million tons, withdrawn from Cuba because of Castro, be purchased in the world market at something like 2.8 cents a pound rather than on a quota basis from designated countries at traditional premium prices. At the premium price the supplying country would receive approximately $54 a ton more than it would receive at world prices. The Administration's counter-proposal was an open, almost demanding invitation to every sugar producing country interested in getting a share of the premium market to seek representation. Most of them did.

We now come to the basic question: Is lobbying a threat to democracy?

The effects of lobbying can be good or bad, helpful or harmful to democracy, depending upon two things: the purposes or objectives of the lobbying effort, and the methods or devices by which the lobby seeks to accomplish its objectives.

There are some who take the extreme view that lobbies are by their very nature power blocs and therefore inconsistent with democratic government; that since lobbies represent special or limited interests, their objectives are of necessity not directed to the general welfare and, therefore, they should be abolished.

There are some who see nothing wrong with lobbies except when they represent economic interests.

There are some who hold that the dangers in lobbying arise from secrecy and behind-the-scenes operations and from the amount of money that may be spent by lobbyists.

There are regular demands that more publicity be given to lobbying activities, that lobbying be more closely regulated, and that the amount of money which can be spent by a lobbyist or lobbying groups be limited and fully reported.

Positively, the activity of lobbyists is often very helpful. Lobbyists can help maintain a balance between Congress and the Executive Branch of the Government. The Executive Branch has a prepared case, usually sustained by expert witnesses. The Congress can offer in opposition the knowledge and experience of its own members and that of the Committee staff or Congressional assistants. Often this is an unfair contest. The expert testimony of lobbyists or witnesses from outside may help to bring the contest closer to balance.

Congress, of course, does not depend entirely upon lobbyists for its information. It is the usual practice to call upon governmental experts and also on independent experts drawn from groups directly affected by the legislation under consideration or from related fields and from the academic profession.

For example, in special hearings on unemployment in 1959, invitations to testify were sent to these organizations: the National Association of Manufacturers, the U.S. Chamber of Commerce, the National Coal Policy Conference, the AFL-CIO, the United Mine Workers, the National Small Businessmen's Association, the Railway Labor Executives Association, and others. Representatives of the U.S. Departments of Labor, Commerce, and Defense were called. Leading labor economists were asked to submit papers, to testify, and to meet with the members of the committee. Hearings were also held in the field. These hearings were open to the testimony of anyone who wished to speak on the subject.

Apart from laws and regulations, there are some built-in protections against the power and influence of lobbyists. One safeguard is that usually there are organized lobbies on both sides of controversial issues: protectionists on the one hand versus freetraders on the other; the AFL-CIO opposed by the National Association of Manufacturers;

growers' associations against those seeking to improve working conditions of migratory farm workers; antivivisectionists against those who favor medical experimentation with animals.

Sometimes the opposition is not direct but involves competition for a larger share of a quota or a subsidy, or for greater participation in advantageous tax concessions.

Political party positions and programs, too, tend to eliminate large areas of political action from the influence of lobbyists. The political campaign in the United States is a rather severe testing. Most of the important national issues are raised during political campaigns, and most men who are elected to office have made firm commitments on most issues.

The President of the United States is called to account and judged by the people every four years; members of the United States Senate must run for reelection every six years, members of the House of Representatives every two years.

The activities of members of Congress are watched closely by colleagues, particularly by those of the opposite party. They are watched by newspaper men whose reputations in many cases are based upon their ability to ferret out and report any action and conduct unbecoming government officials.

In addition, of course, everyone who holds office must assume that there are at least two or three people—perhaps in his own party and certainly in the opposition party—who are quite willing to replace him and consequently are likely to give more than ordinary attention to his conduct in public office.

What can or should be done about lobbying?

Members of Congress cannot be fully protected from lobbyists by regulation. They cannot be expected to keep a check list of registered lobbyists or demand proof of registration or defense of nonregistration before responding to a request for conversation or for a conference. Yet, members of Congress and other government officials can be given some protection by law.

The present lobby registration act should be fully enforced, and financial reporting should be checked carefully. Fees contingent on successful lobbying should be outlawed. Care should be taken to remove from direct legislative determination those questions which should be settled by other branches of government: by the president, by special commissions, by departments and agencies of government or by international agreement.

Much of the agitation over the Sugar Act could have been prevented if the administration, acting directly or possibly in cooperation with the Organization of American States or the signatories to the International Sugar Agreement, had determined the way in which the Cuban sugar quota was to be allocated. There would have been some Congressional protest, since in a broad way Congress has determined sugar allocations since the Sugar Act was passed in 1934. But the protest would have been limited and the compromises so minor that extensive lobbying activities, brought on when the whole question of reallocation was left open by the administration, would have been discouraged.

Better salaries for government officials and sounder methods of financing campaigns would also lessen the likelihood of undue financial influence on public officials by lobbyists and others.

There is always the risk that public officials may be unduly subject to outside influence. But it is hard to imagine a meeting of a national legislature today that could or should be insulated from public pressure or demand. The practice of some primitive tribes, in which the wise men or elders withdrew from society periodically to consider laws and practices, is not likely to be revived.

The whole concept that lobbying opposes the majority, that it seeks to manipulate and subvert the majority will and the public interest, is unrealistic. Lobbyists seldom manufacture a problem. They call attention to an existing problem and try to guide the course of events. Action in Washington sometimes supports the judgment of J. B. S. Hardman, the philosopher and intellectual mentor of industrial trade unionism in America: "Majorities never rule, they merely give credentials to contending minorities."

Although lobbying does not usually involve a physical assembly—such as the 1932 veterans bonus march on Washington or current picketing of the White House—it does involve organization, a bringing together of citizens seeking a common objective. Thus, the act of lobbying is basically an exercise of the right to petition the government—a right set forth in the Constitution. Lobbying also involves, in a way, the exercise of the right of assembly.

In a democratic society there must be a point at which influences, both good and bad, are brought to bear upon government. The point at which these influences meet finally is in the elected and appointed officials of the country. They are supposed to be men skilled and experienced in politics and possessing the character to withstand improper pressures and improper demands.

Until a clear case can be made against the lobbyist, his voice should be heard in Washington. But his voice must be identified and, insofar as possible, restricted to that influence which is justified by the facts and the conclusions to be drawn from those facts.

| Do Interest Groups |
| Serve the Public Interest? |

NO

GEORGE McGOVERN
Pluralist Structures or Interest Groups?*

Pluralism, the "politics of interest," describes governmental decision making essentially as a competition among interest groups. The result of the competition—whether one side or another wins, or a compromise is reached—then defines the public interest.

The politics of interest is a flawed method for making national decisions and an incomplete description of how they actually are made. There is a public good which must be defined independently of political pressures or organized interests. Political leaders have an obligation to advance such qualities as morality and decency—to distinguish between right and wrong—regardless of how the interest groups balance those values.

Actually, in 1972 I tried at times to be a pluralist; but George Meany would not return my phone calls. And I do recognize the value of this competition and the role of interest groups. They help to move government by drawing attention to problems, shaping and proposing remedies, and providing one measure of the popular will. Or they help us avoid excuses and mistakes by subjecting our preferences to bargaining and debate, by demanding that different sides justify and negotiate their positions.

* George McGovern, "Pluralist Structures or Interest Groups?" Published by permission of Transaction Inc. from *Society*, vol. 14 #2. Copyright © 1977 by Transaction, Inc.

TRANSCENDENT ISSUES

But the issues which have been my focus in recent years seem to have transcended the bounds of the interest group model. Starting in 1963, our deepening intervention in Vietnam literally became an obsession for me. Yet at the beginning there were few interest groups weighing heavily on either side of that issue—and certainly there were none whose weight was registered effectively on staying out of the affairs of the Vietnamese people.

Later, the Democratic party reform effort was a direct challenge to the confederation of interest groups which had dominated the party since the New Deal. Of course parties are not interest groups. On the contrary, they are umbrellas under which we gather as many groups as we possibly can—even conflicting ones, if they can be kept in opposite corners of the same shelter—brought together quadrennially for the limited and common purpose of electing a president. So I saw the party reform movement as a service to the Democratic party. It opened the party to new concerns, new ideas, new people, even new groups. But by the same token, it was a threat to some important interest groups within the party.

These reforms, and the issue of Vietnam, are the two events which made my presidential candidacy possible—and necessary—in 1972. The conventional wisdom then was that I won the nomination in large part because, as chairman of the reform commission, I had written the rules of the game. That statement is not only untrue; it is irrelevant. There was nothing secretive about the rules. They were available in print, for the reading and planning use of all the candidates.

But it is true that without reform my bid for the nomination would have been far less feasible, and possibly hopeless. Without the new rules any candidacy might have been hopeless unless it was inspired or condoned by key labor leaders, the party regulars, and other constituencies of New Deal programs and old-line power arrangements. Certainly Eugene McCarthy and Robert Kennedy were vulnerable to their veto in 1968.

Except for the conflict with some AFL-CIO [American Federation of Labor-Congress of Industrial Organizations] leaders over the war, I had regarded myself as a good friend of organized labor and a far better choice for the working people of America than Nixon. But I was not one of their automatic votes in the Senate, and I offended them by opposing the Vietnam War. Beyond these differences, I did not believe that by pleasing only them the Democratic party could either secure the confidence of a majority of American voters or offer a sound direction for the country.

POPULIST RHETORIC

So I campaigned on the basis of a broader appeal. My announcement speech in January 1971 condemned "those who seek power by back-room deals or coalitions of self-interest." In December of that year I warned that we were "embarked on a dangerous trend toward control by a collection of elitists whose interests and inclinations dominate national policy irrespective of the public will, and often at the expense of the public good." In my acceptance speech I echoed a promise of Woodrow Wilson: "Let me inside the government, and I will tell you everything that is going on in there."

Of course populist rhetoric is standard political fare; even Republicans use it. But in 1972 there was a difference. The nomination campaign was an insurgency in the Democratic party. To a large extent it was made up of people new to the political process; its few veterans were primarily the novices of 1968. It was directed primarily against the war and the domination of special interests, especially corporate interests, in the Nixon White House. But my candidacy was also seen as a threat to certain Democratic party interests.

On grounds of ideology it is hard to understand why those interests did not coalesce once the nomination was won. Doubtless the obsession of the press with the [Senator Thomas] Eagleton affair confused all judgments. But there were other factors which had little to do with ideology, less to do with personality, and a lot to do with power. Some leading liberals, including the Executive Council of the AFL-CIO, correctly saw my campaign and my nomination as a disruption of traditional arrangements, signifying a diminution of their influence.

Among their miscalculations was the assumption that my campaign was a temporary diversion and that the back-room days would be back again in 1976. Actually, the campaign of 1972 was a reflection and a consolidation of forces already at work. It precipitated the struggle, but the struggle had to be waged sometime within the Democratic party. By 1972 the inadequacies of interest group politics and governance had become too much for the country to bear. The McGovern campaigners of 1972 were the minesweepers who cleared the way for the advancing Democratic forces of 1976.

OLD GUARD FAILURES

The war in Vietnam was the most obvious and most desperate failure of the old structure. Yet, among interest groups with real influence in Washington, this profound moral issue—this matter literally of life and death—was hardly even a part of the competition, even when as many as three fourths of the American people supported a program for withdrawal.

The noisy, sometimes offensive reaction to the oversight helped bring attention to other omissions as well. After the bold promises of the Great Society, the quest for racial justice had faltered at the higher threshold of economic opportunity. We also began at last to contemplate majority rights for women. The time had come when democracy had to become more than the domain of white males.

A separate alienation had been reflected in the [Governor George] Wallace campaign of 1968. It was founded in part on the notion of a white backlash against black aspirations; but there was far more to it. It, too, was a rejection of interest group politics. Some interest groups represented the rich; others represented the comparatively well off; others voiced the aspirations of the poor. But no one represented the people in between—who work hard to stand still, who earn too much to qualify for social welfare, and who in fact pay the bill while the rich shelter their income and wealth behind a convenient concessional tax code.

OLD AND NEW COALITIONS

In theory, at least, the tax and welfare proposals we developed in 1972 could have appealed to middle Americans, if those proposals had been better stated by proponents and less distorted by enemies. After the Wallace victory in Florida I rejected the thesis that Wallace voters were racists, and emphasized that "attention must be paid" to their legitimate concerns. And for a brief moment, beginning with the crucial Wisconsin primary, we did assemble a coalition of liberal professionals, youthful war protestors, minority and women's activists, small farmers, independent merchants, and disaffected workers. It was enough to win the Wisconsin primary and bring the nomination within reach. Indeed, I won ten primaries—including the two largest states, New York and California.

This coalition was fragile and highly vulnerable, as we learned in the fall. But if it were stylistically at odds with itself and some of the older interests, it was substantively consistent and still belongs together. On the surface the trends in 1976 might seem to dispute this thesis. The Democrats with the most specific, progressive, or populist programs were defeated in 1976. What happened?

Of course, there were a number of candidates splitting that potential vote. Further, such a coalition is obviously more difficult to form and to keep than coalitions of better organized and financed groups, which themselves are changing all the time. And many of the issues of the 1972 campaign (such as amnesty and tax reform), which were on the fringes of respectability then, are now accepted elements of our political dialogue on which virtually all the Democratic candidates took seemingly progressive stands.

But the most important development is that the reform process has been settled. Indeed, it was used again. This time it operated without deep divisions, even though it involved many of the same people, motivations, and potential antagonists.

In 1972 reform made the Democratic party accessible to an intensely motivated, issue-oriented group of people. In 1976 the party was again accessible to outsiders. With alienation reinforced by Watergate, a campaign which claimed to be for truth and against the mess in Washington—and by obvious implication against the tight structure through which decisions are made there—captured the Democratic nomination and the White House. A similar appeal nearly won the Republican nomination for Ronald Reagan against an incumbent president.

I wonder if we have really absorbed the meaning of this process. The performance of the old decision-making structure has been so distressing that the best politics last spring was to campaign against it. The most appealing candor was not the candor of specific programs, but the candor of "I don't know exactly what I would do, but I couldn't possibly do worse than they have." The Carter campaign was skillfully executed, without the fratricide of 1972. On the contrary, many of those activists who saw the insurgency as a threat in 1972 joined up enthusiastically in 1976.

In any event, the prospect of a Carter presidency is especially intriguing in the context of interest group politics. He is better positioned than any Democratic candidate since Roosevelt to see beyond the immediate demands of special interests to the longer-range needs of the country. I like that prospect. I like it not because of any fundamental disagreements with labor, with the Urban Coalition, or with any other part of the traditional Democratic constituency. Nor do I like it because I have any special understanding that he will necessarily set the same priorities or embrace the same positions that I would prefer. Rather, I like it because the old interest group governance is not enough, and because a less fettered president will have more freedom to lead the country.

INTEREST GROUP POWER

In theory, whenever needs or wants are felt strongly enough new groups will form to make their influence felt. But it is not that easy. Incumbency with interest groups, as with officeholders, is a powerful weapon. If some Americans are born joiners and organizers, others are not. If some groups are wise to the ways of Washington, others are not. If some groups communicate internally, others are isolated and cannot. And the consequence is the kind of trauma we experienced in the 1960s. It is the public opinion surveys telling us that most Americans feel that government represents someone other than them.

Interest group politics also impedes change. This belief is, of course, an ideological objection. To some Americans the conservative bias of interest group politics is one of its main virtues. But the content of this country—the economic structure, the accepted values, the scale of priorities—is still evolving, toward something better than we have now. Yet the solidly established and best endowed interest groups are really competing most vehemently for shares of the status quo. Along with people, interest group politics also tends to exclude fundamental issues from the competition. It especially excludes the future. This country, with the rest of the human family, faces long-term dangers which are poorly answered, if at all, by the demands of today.

The challenges of nuclear proliferation, of environmental pollution, of food shortages and population pressures, of international economic disorder, of resource depletion—all these issues relate far less to our present satisfaction than to our future safety. And the interest groups of ten, twenty, or fifty years from now are just not very well organized.

These are issues which demand a leadership that springs from moral and ideological considerations. They must be solved in the recognition that we can envision humane and honorable directions for the country only if we go beyond the bounds of process or pressure. Indeed, these issues require farsighted leaders with the will and the capacity to communicate with interest groups, to generate new groups, and to appeal to the country over the heads of them all. These issues also call for a strong central government and a strong president. I believe in that institution, even if I did not believe in a strong Richard Nixon, who disgraced the office, or in a strong Gerald Ford, which is a contradiction in terms.

STRONG LEADERSHIP

Certainly a strong presidency guided by moral and ideological convictions is a risky proposition. Perhaps it has fewer safeguards against the man on horseback capturing the people's imagination and trampling on basic rights. One attribute of pluralism is supposed to be that the concentrated attention and sharpened insights of interest group leaders modulate the swings of the public mood, thus limiting the audience and the appeal of demagoguery.

But we require aggressive leadership nonetheless, and I am not sure that it is riskier than the old order. The politics of interest did not, after all, detect the man on horseback who recently sneaked his horse through the back door of the Oval Office. He was not detected until he was galloping off with the Constitution.

The answer to that danger is not to restrict democracy; it is to keep the dust from settling too deeply again on the power of impeachment. So let us guarantee the rights of organization and free speech. Let us encourage their exercise and welcome the contributions to public policy which organized interests can make. But let us also recognize that these rights and powers are insufficient, either to fulfill democracy now or to sustain our democratic society in the future.

INCLUSIVE STRUCTURE

Our political structure should be more inclusive and should attend to the needs and wants of those people who are or will be left out of the pluralist equation. At the same time, we need inspired leadership to meet longer-term national goals. The latter suggests the denial of some present wants, even when I am proposing that we now add to the effective demands upon government. Is there a contradiction?

Some analysts believe that there is. It has been said that we suffer from an excess of democracy, from a cacophony of demands and an incapacity to negotiate clear national purposes upon which all can agree. The term is anomic democracy. It is described in a report to the Trilateral Commission as a condition in which "democratic politics becomes more an arena for the assertion of conflicting interests than a process for the building of common purposes." The authors of that study, *The Crisis of Democracy,* note that without common purpose we cannot have priorities, and without priorities executives, cabinets, parliaments, and bureaucrats have no basis for distinguishing among competing claims.

But the answer is not less democracy; that option is not even open. Rather, the need is for leadership which is willing to lift our vision, declare new national purposes, and clarify our choices. And such leadership, even in the denial of some interests, will earn and hold public support, and will stimulate the national confidence which is our greatest, most fundamental public need.

It really comes down to a matter of faith in the American people.

And despite my own disappointment at their hands four years ago, I believe that given the chance they will rally even to an uncomfortable cause when they can see that it will serve the good of us all.

"MORALITY ENLARGED"

All of us must speak in part from our own experience. My own personal involvement in politics began in the early 1950s. Since that time three great issues have dominated my political activity: the paranoid impact of McCarthyism in the 1950s; the civil rights revolution of the 1960s; and the American war in Indochina. All three of these issues challenged the basic morality and decency of American political leadership. All three of them were resolved by the ultimate triumph of moral principle over short-term political expediency.

As an American liberal, I accept the conclusion of the great British conservative Edmund Burke that "the principles of true politics are those of morality enlarged." That enlargement and application of morality is the chief obligation of politics and the most dependable hope for the American future.

QUESTIONS FOR DISCUSSION

1. How can you tell whether a lobby is powerful or weak?
2. Are lobbies essential to democracy?
3. Are there effective safeguards to the power and influence of strong lobbies?
4. How should the activities of lobbyists be regulated?
5. George McGovern observed in early 1977 that Jimmy Carter was "better positioned than any Democratic candidate since Roosevelt to see beyond the immediate demands of special interests to the longer-range needs of the country." To what extent do you believe that McGovern's observation was accurate in view of Mr. Carter's political behavior as president?

SUGGESTED READINGS

Congressional Quarterly Service. *The Washington Lobby,* 2nd ed. Washington, D.C.: Congressional Quarterly, 1974.

Deakin, James. *The Lobbyists.* Washington, D.C.: Public Affairs Press, 1966.

Holtzman, Abraham. *Interest Groups and Lobbying.* New York: Macmillan, 1966.

Lowi, Theodore J. *The End of Liberalism.* New York: Norton, 1969.

McConnell, Grant. *Private Power and American Democracy.* New York: Random House, 1966.

Milbrath, Lester W. *The Washington Lobbyists.* Skokie, Ill.: Rand McNally, 1963.

Salisbury, Robert, ed. *Interest Group Politics in America.* New York: Harper & Row, 1970.

Sinclair, John E. *Interest Groups in America.* Morristown, N.J.: General Learning Press, 1976.

Skolnick, Jerome H. *The Politics of Protest.* New York: Simon & Schuster, 1969.

Truman, David B. *The Governmental Process: Political Interests and Public Opinion,* 2nd ed. New York: Alfred A. Knopf, 1971.

7.

Has the Two-Party System Outlived Its Usefulness?

The late American humorist Will Rogers once quipped, "I am not a member of any organized political party; I am a Democrat." An examination of American political parties over the past few decades suggests that Rogers' comment about the Democrats applies to the Republicans as well.

At the national level Democrats have experienced serious internal conflicts. Eugene McCarthy challenged incumbent President Lyndon Johnson in the 1968 presidential primaries, and that challenge may have been a factor in Johnson's decision not to seek reelection. The 1968 Democratic party convention in Chicago, moreover, was characterized by violent confrontation between Chicago police and protesters against the war in Vietnam. This confrontation was a contributing factor in the defeat of Democratic presidential nominee Hubert Humphrey, because the television coverage of the clashes between police and protesters created an adverse impression of the entire proceedings. The confrontation, moreover, suggested to many Democrats that the party could not unite seemingly incompatible factions.

Divisiveness within the Democratic party may also be seen elsewhere. Even when both the presidency and Congress have been controlled by the Democrats, it seems that conflict rather than cooperation has often marked the relationship. In 1977, President Carter encountered strong opposition from within his own party in gathering support for his energy program. Democratic members of the House, moreover, objected strenuously to Carter's decision to cut the number of water-resource projects throughout the United States.

Republicans, too, have found themselves internally divided. Some Republicans demanded the resignation of former President Richard Nixon during the Watergate affair. The almost-successful challenge of Gerald Ford by fellow Republican Ronald Reagan (formerly governor of California) revealed serious party dissension over President Ford's policies and management of the presidency.

Both major parties, then, have shown a marked lack of party unity. This can be attributed in part to the fact that American political parties are decentralized; that is, the central party organization has little power over the state and local party units. Dissenting legislators belonging to the same party as the president cannot be disciplined for their uncooperativeness to the extent of denying them the renomination on their own party tickets. Legislative voting at the national level, consequently, is rarely conducted along strict party lines.

The separate election of president and members of Congress and the staggered election of senators (one third every two years) make it difficult to have a system of party government in which the elected members of a political party in the national government vote the same way on independent issues. This difficulty becomes more intense when one party controls the presidency and another party controls the legislature, and is compounded by our decentralized federal system of government.

Because American parties are weak institutions at the national level, much criticism has been directed against them. It has been charged that, because of a lack of strong ideological orientation within the two major political parties, their stances on important campaign issues are very similar, too similar to give American voters real choice at election time.

An examination of party platforms at national conventions shows the many similarities between the Democrats and the Republicans. Both accept the necessity of a strong defense and the need for basic welfare benefits to assure that every American has at least adequate housing, health care, and job opportunities. Each major party, moreover, has liberal and conservative wings. Each party's platform often appeals to the broadest constituency to allow its liberal and conservative wings some reason to support the national standard bearer. The platforms tend to avoid strong expressions of policy preference on many issues that might drive away support from a particular segment of American society.

Because of the lack of clarity in presenting the issues, the major parties are often criticized for not performing a function that they are supposed to do: inform the American people about the issues of a campaign. Some critics blame the two-party system for this condition and argue that it has outlived its usefulness. Only two parties, they contend, cannot possibly incorporate the viewpoints of the heterogeneous American society into their party philosophies. The parties tend, consequently, to move close to each other.

On occasion, however, the two major parties have been sharply differentiated. The presidential elections of 1964 and 1972, for example, revealed fundamental divergencies between the candidates of the two major parties. When Barry Goldwater ran in 1964, he charged that in the past, the Republican party had been a "me, too" party. Whatever the Democrats did, the Republicans said, "Me, too." There was a conservative majority, according to Goldwater and his partisans, which was submerged in the Democratic and Republican parties. The American people should have a "choice rather than an echo," according to this view. The defeat of Goldwater suggested that the theory of a conservative majority was wrong.

Also, the election of 1972 revealed wider differences than exist in most presidential contests. George McGovern's strong opposition to the war in Vietnam and his advocacy of stringent measures of social reform were in sharp contrast to the views of Richard Nixon. McGovern, like Goldwater, was decisively defeated.

Issues are strongly articulated in elections, but often these issues are presented by small parties. For the most part, the appearance of these parties in presidential elections is a constant element of American electoral politics. In the past, when the two parties moved too closely together, a third political party often was formed. One of the major parties might adopt the planks of the third party, thus contributing to the demise of the third party. Such was the case when in 1896, the Democratic party adopted the important policies advocated by the Populist party.

ARE THERE SIGNIFICANT DIFFERENCES
BETWEEN THE TWO MAJOR PARTIES?

The fact that the two major parties are coalitions of liberal and conservative elements has led some observers to say that the big parties offer no choice to the electorate. Political scientists Kenneth Prewitt and Sidney Verba contend that the parties are different in the following ways: they get their support from different social groups; the voters see differences between the parties; the campaign support given by groups varies; the political outlook differs; and also the party leaders support different legislation. Marxist author George Novack argues that the major parties are similar because the capitalists dominate both political parties. Elections in capitalist America are meaningless, he claims.

Are There Significant Differences Between the Democratic Party and the Republican Party?

YES

KENNETH PREWITT and SIDNEY VERBA
How Different Are the Two Major Parties? *

Does it make any difference who wins an election? When conservative Barry Goldwater won the Republican presidential nomination in 1964, he claimed that the voters finally had "a choice, not an echo." Goldwa-

* From pp. 158–163 in *Principles of American Government*, 2nd Edition, by Kenneth Prewitt and Sidney Verba. Copyright © 1977 by Kenneth Prewitt and Sidney Verba. Reprinted by permission of Harper & Row, Publishers, Inc.

ter argued that the two parties had become so alike in their political outlook that the voters had no real choice. Many people agree with this argument; they say a two-party system actually reduces choice because each party tries to get the support of a wide variety of groups. As a result each party tends toward the middle of the road, where most of the voters are supposed to be.

Others disagree. In a competitive party system, they say, the parties reflect the basic conflict between haves and have-nots, between rich and poor, businessmen and workers, producers and consumers.

Early American history showed this view to be correct. The first political parties were formed around conflicting economic interests. Under [Alexander] Hamilton's leadership the Federalist party protected the interests of business and trade, while the Jeffersonians were more favorable to the small farmer and the debtor class. Class differences between the parties may be found throughout American history and, some say, may be seen today in the Republicans and Democrats. . . . The Democrats get support from the poorer social classes and the Republicans get support from the richer social classes.

Which view is correct? Are the parties more or less the same in their political outlook, or do they reflect conflicting interests? Let's look at four kinds of evidence:

1. Whether the parties get their support from different social groups.
2. Whether the parties depend on different sources for campaign funds.
3. Whether the party leaders differ in their policy views.
4. Whether support for legislation differs between the parties.

THE PARTIES GET THEIR SUPPORT FROM DIFFERENT SOCIAL GROUPS

Different social groups support the two major parties. The differences go back to the coalition formed by President [Franklin D.] Roosevelt during the Great Depression. During this period the Republican party continued to favor conservative policies and thus kept the support of business interests and white Protestant voters. Meanwhile the Democrats introduced social-welfare programs such as social security and unemployment compensation and thus attracted the support of blacks, immigrant workers, and the poor.

The difference between the social groups supporting the Republicans and Democrats can still be seen today. In general Republicans tend to be of higher social status than Democrats. They tend to have better jobs, higher incomes, and more education than Democrats. However, the coalitions of the 1930s aren't as strong as they used to be.

Important changes are taking place. Workers still tend to identify with the Democratic party, but they're more willing to listen to Republican candidates. And at all social levels party ties are loosening. This is particularly true among younger voters.

Note, however, that other factors besides social class affect party identification. Regional, ethnic, and religious divisions cut across class lines. For example, a Catholic business executive is more likely than is a Protestant business executive to be a Democrat.

VOTERS SEE DIFFERENCES BETWEEN THE PARTIES

Voters see differences between the Republicans and the Democrats. They're likely to think of the Republicans as the party that favors business interests. Some voters like the Republicans for this reason: "I like to string along with big business and big money. Under the Republicans the country has prospered." Others vote against Republican candidates for the same reason: "Republican leaders are controlled by people with money—the Republican party is run by large corporations."

People have a very different picture of the Democratic party; they think of it as more likely to take care of the working class: "They try to improve working conditions—shorter hours—a higher wage rate—and are more interested in benefits for working people." Voters who are worried about inflation and welfare costs feel differently, however: "The Democrats are a giveaway party. Democrats always want to spend more than the government has. Business suffers when the Democrats are in power."

DIFFERENCES IN CAMPAIGN SUPPORT

Party differences may also be seen in the groups that give money to the major parties. A lot of Republican party money comes from wealthy individuals and businesses. On the other hand, a lot of Democratic party money comes from organized labor and liberal interest groups. For example, in 1968 national labor committees gave $7.1 million to political campaigns, an average of five or six cents per union member; nearly all of this went to Democratic candidates. The National Committee for an Effective Congress spent $400,000 in 1972 on House and Senate candidates; all but five were Democrats or independents.

DIFFERENCES IN POLITICAL OUTLOOK

Studies show that Democratic party leaders usually have a more liberal outlook than Republican party leaders. Democratic leaders favor social-welfare programs and are more willing to expand government social services. They are critical of big business and usually favor a more progressive income tax. By contrast, Republican leaders oppose many social-welfare programs and believe the government's role in this area should be limited. Republicans tend to fear the influence of labor unions and oppose increased business regulation.

A study of the political opinions of delegates to the presidential nominating conventions in 1956 found that the Democratic party "is marked by a strong belief in the power of collective action to promote social justice, equality, humanitarianism, and economic planning, while preserving freedom." The Republican party "is distinguished by faith in the wisdom of the natural competitive process and in the supreme virtue of individuals, 'character,' self-reliance, frugality, and independence from government."[1]

A survey ten years later had similar results.[2] Politically active Democrats were less willing than active Republicans to say the poor are responsible for helping themselves, and Democrats were more likely than Republicans to think the income gap between rich and poor is too wide.

PARTY LEADERS SUPPORT DIFFERENT LEGISLATION

Neither party can force its representatives in Congress to stay loyal to the party or to support the policies the party favors. As we have seen, the parties are loose, regionally based coalitions, not centrally directed organizations with cohesive programs. Although the president and congressional leaders can put pressure on party members, they can go only so far. Members of Congress are influenced less by their parties than by their financial backers and the interest groups that helped get them elected. So if we find that Democrats and Republicans vote differently in Congress, this must reflect differences in political outlook between the two parties.

Political scientists have studied how Democrats and Republicans vote in Congress and have reached these conclusions: (1) party members tend to vote the same way, and there are major policy differences between the two parties; (2) when members of Congress vote differently from other members of their parties, it's usually because of pressure from the voters back home or, more likely, from important interest groups in their home districts.

Differences between the two parties may be seen in *roll-call votes* or votes on various policies in the House of Representatives. [Robert A. Dahl in *Pluralist Democracy in the United States*] lists votes on a number of bills over the past twenty-five years . . . show[ing] a striking contrast between Republicans and Democrats.[3] On balance, the Republican party has opposed social-welfare programs and government regulation of the economy and has favored policies that stimulate free enterprise. The Democrats have tended to favor greater government involvement in the economy; they have tried to reduce income differences through tax reform; and they have favored social-welfare programs.

However, this description is not entirely accurate. Each party has sometimes protected conservative principles and sometimes called for reform. The first major attempt to regulate trusts was made by a Republican president, Theodore Roosevelt. And conservative southern Democrats have often blocked social-welfare legislation, particularly in the area of civil rights.

Still, various types of evidence show meaningful differences between the two major parties, differences based at least partly on conflicting class interests. The argument that Republicans and Democrats don't give the voter a choice doesn't hold up, nor does the argument that it makes no difference which party controls Congress.

POLITICAL PARTIES AND FOREIGN POLICY

In many foreign-policy issues political parties play a minor role. These are the nonpartisan issues of war and peace and national defense. Here both parties follow the lead of the President and his advisers. Since World War II foreign policy has been the responsibility of a small group of experts independent of serious party politics. This may be seen in a number of major foreign-policy decisions on issues like the Vietnam War, involvement in military alliances such as NATO [North Atlantic Treaty Organization], and the stationing of American military forces around the world. These policies aren't made by party leaders meeting to plan a bipartisan role for the United States in world affairs. They are made by the president, acting as leader of the nation rather than as head of his party, with the help of advisers from universities, major corporations, law firms, the State Department, and the Pentagon.

Are There Significant Differences Between the Democratic Party and the Republican Party?

NO

GEORGE NOVACK
*The Realities of American Democracy**

The American liberal abides by two articles of faith. One is the belief that he lives under a genuine democracy which, for all its imperfections, is still the freest and finest in the world. The other is the conviction that this form of government is here to stay and will never be superseded by a better. How do these propositions stand up to critical examination?

The United States unquestionably has all the attributes of a capitalist democracy—a Constitution, a Congress, political parties, regular elections, legal rights for its citizens enforced by the courts, freedom of publication, etc. In addition, the North Americans have deep-seated traditions of popular sovereignty which go back to the founding of the Republic. They have long been taught that the right to determine national policy belongs to the majority of the people, not to any plutocratic elite. They are quick to resent and resist flagrant abridgments of their rights.

What most Americans fail to see are the major contradictions in their political structure. Historically, as we have sought to show, democracy has been a form of rule accessible only to rich and privileged states which directly or indirectly exploit and oppress other peoples. Athens, the most celebrated democracy of antiquity, was a fiercely imperialist power. British democracy rested upon the plundering and subjugation of its dominions.

The prevalence of dictatorships in the colonial world is organically linked with the presence of democracies in the metropolitan countries. Democracy, like so many other things within the orbit of capitalism, is by and large a luxury reserved for the wealthiest countries who enjoy it at the expense of poorer peoples.

* From George Novack, *Democracy and Revolution* (New York: Pathfinder Press, 1971), pp. 190–196. Reprinted by permission of Pathfinder Press. Copyright © 1971.

The foreign relations of the United States since the end of the Second World War have conformed to this pattern. Washington has sought support from the most repressive forces in order to strengthen its international positions and curb or contain actual and potential anticapitalist revolutions. Its network of antidemocratic allies extends from Franco Spain and the NATO [North Atlantic Treaty Organization] dictatorship of the Greek colonels through South Africa to the military governments of Indonesia, Pakistan, and South Korea. Vietnam shows to what lengths the American imperialists are ready to go in propping up native hirelings and denying the right of self-determination to a small nation.

It has become widely recognized that the democratic principles professed by the partisans of "the free world" conflict with their military aggressions and complicity with autocracy abroad. It is not yet so clear that they are contravened by the realities of American life. The nominal equality of all citizens is at odds with the actual inequalities of American society; the owners of wealth wield far more power than the rest of the population; they constitute an oligarchy which exercises a social tyranny behind the facade of a representative democracy.

It is a law of civilization that political predominance inevitably falls into the hands of that class or combination of classes that commands the processes of production. Before the Civil War, the slaveholders were the decisive force in American politics because their cotton crop was the principal export of commercial United States. This gave enormous economic leverage and political weight to the representatives of the cotton barons in the national capital.

The regime of the southern states in the early nineteenth century showed how democratic forms can be combined with outright slavery. The democratic system since the Civil War has been rooted in a more subtle and disguised type of servitude. That is the exploitation of the wage workers by the capitalist proprietors of the economy, combined with the racial oppression of the bottom layers of the labor force.

The concentration of economic power in the mammoth corporations and financial institutions—and the political hegemony that goes with it—has accelerated decade by decade. According to a study by the Federal Trade Commission, the two hundred largest manufacturing corporations in 1968 controlled about two-thirds of all manufacturing assets—a proportion of total assets that was equal to the share held by the thousand largest corporations in 1941. This increase in power came at a time when the volume of industrial assets was growing very rapidly. A. A. Berle, the former State Department official, wrote in 1957: "In terms of power, without regard to asset positions, not only do 500 corporations control two thirds of the nonfarm economy, but within each of that 500 a still smaller group has the ultimate decision-making power. This is, I think, the highest concentration of economic power in recorded history.''

This power embraces the entire capitalist system. By 1960, United States foreign investments accounted for almost 60 percent of the world total. The gross value of American enterprises abroad is greater than the wealth of any country except the United States and the Soviet Union.

A number of economists and sociologists, such as C. Wright Mills, Paul Sweezy, and E. Digby Baltzell, have published studies of the anatomy of the U.S. ruling class in recent years. Their findings have been amplified by G. William Domhoff in *Who Rules America?* He estimated that in the early 1960s nearly one million persons belonged to the upper class, or 9.5 percent of the population. On the basis of the empirical evidence cited in his work, he concluded that this small minority controls the major banks and corporations and therewith the American economy; the presidency and the executive branch of the federal government; the federal judiciary; the military; the CIA and FBI; the regulatory agencies; the foundations; the elite universities; the largest of the communication media; and the important opinion-molding associations. This upper class, he concludes, owns a disproportionate amount of the country's wealth, receives a disproportionate amount of the country's income and contributes a disproportionate number of its members to the controlling institutions and key decision-making groups of the country.

If it could be said of England in 1832 that the members of the House of Commons were chosen by about two hundred landed families, it is no less true of the U.S. government today that its top echelons are directed and staffed by stewards of the two hundred largest corporations. Of the thirteen men who have been secretary of defense or secretary of war since 1932, eight have been listed in the *Social Register.* Of the last four tenants of this key cabinet post, two were formerly heads of the biggest auto manufacturers, General Motors and Ford, and their successors were closely associated with the largest military contractors.

The methods by which the possessors of wealth enforce their supremacy in deference to and defiance of the forms of democracy are devious and complex. They have been worked out over many decades of experimentation with the techniques of domination in a dollar democracy.

The main mechanism through which big business maintains control over the country and suzerainty over a large part of the planet is the two-party system. The Republican and Democratic parties are utterly committed defenders of the capitalist order, though their representatives may serve rival interest groups within it. The ruling class itself utilizes both political machines for its purposes, just as its counterpart in Canada relies on the Conservative and Liberal parties.

If the capitalist parties see two sides to every question, these are not the cause of the poor versus the rich. Their paramount concern is whether they are in or out of office. Though they do not have fundamental differences, the candidates of the two organizations joust avidly with one another, sparing no demagogy in appeals to the voters in order to win election. Once in office, they pursue the same bipartisan foreign policy and both take good care of the needs of the well-to-do.

Those who pay the piper call the tune in the shaping of government policy and the administration of its affairs. Campaigning is very expensive. Robert Kennedy spent two million dollars to win his New York senatorial seat in 1966. If they do not have inherited wealth like the Kennedys and Rockefellers, candidates must hold out their hats to the wealthy for finances. Lyndon B. Johnson set up a President's Club whose members paid $1000 apiece to receive communications—and presumably favors—from the White House.

The Committee for Economic Development reported in December 1968 that "according to the best available estimates at least $140 million was spent on all political campaigns in 1952, $155 million in 1956, $175 million in 1960 and $200 million in 1964. The preliminary figures for 1968 exceeded $250 million."

Most of this money came from the corporate rich. It enabled them to pick, promote, or drop candidates on all levels from the local districts to the highest executive posts and sway their decisions. In his book *My Brother Lyndon,* Sam Houston Johnson bluntly declared: "When a candidate has to raise many thousands from a single fat cat, can anyone seriously believe those big contributors are merely interested in good government? There isn't a single mayor, councilman, state legislator, governor, congressman, president or any other election official in this country who hasn't gotten a contribution from some fat cat expecting a government contract somewhere down the line."

The scandal of political fund-raising is only one aspect of the irremediable corruption at the core of bourgeois politics. Revelations of the venality of public officials in the municipalities, state administrations, and federal apparatus periodically break into the press—and but a small fraction of the cases are uncovered and publicized.

Politics is itself big business in the United States. It involves millions of jobs and appointments, the awarding of lucrative contracts, franchises, and concessions, the administration of justice, the incidence of taxation. The vast sums at stake make the political trough a cesspool of legal and illegal corruption.

That is only one side of the situation. The big business of politics is inextricably linked with the politics of big business. These two merge at the summit in the White House and its cabinet, Congress, and the Pentagon. The Defense Department, presided over by former presidents of General Motors and Ford during the Eisenhower, Kennedy, and Johnson administrations, is by far the largest spending agency in the country, with a budget of up to eighty billion dollars a year.

Since 1946 American taxpayers have contributed more than a trillion dollars to maintain the industrial-military complex. Each year the federal government spends more than seventy cents of every budget dollar on past, present, or prospective wars—and to sustain the profits of the Pentagon clients. The costs of the garrison state diminish the real wages of the workers through inflation and spiraling taxes and cut into all programs of public welfare.

Influence-peddling, behind-the-scenes pressures and interlocking directorates between the military and the contractors ensure that political figures comply with the requirements of the rich. The National Association of Manufacturers, the Committee for American Development, the Business Advisory Council, the National Advertising Council, the U.S. Chamber of Commerce, and similar associations, together with special representatives of the military contractors, assiduously contact the right officials in the right departments to do the right thing for the right company—and the upper class as a whole.

The poor have neither the time nor the money to participate in government sessions and keep track of what is going on. The corporations and financial houses not only retain lobbyists to look after their interests but hold legislators and judges in leash. Just as the railroads, lumber, and mining companies had senators on their payroll in the nineteenth century, so the oil and natural-gas tycoons, the utilities, the banks, insurance and mortgage companies, and arms makers have congressmen whom they have bankrolled for election at their beck and call.

This is more openly done in some countries than others. In England it is less direct than in Japan where the eight factions in the ruling Liberal-Democratic party can each count on receiving $30,000 a month from big business. This is called "rice money." Though the forms of collusion differ, the practice is general. Sherman Adams, Eisenhower's chief aide in the White House, was cashiered for taking favors from a New England manufacturer. He tells in his *Memoirs* that the president was reluctantly forced to fire him because some big contributors complained he had become a liability, injuring Republican chances in the next election.

The Democrats and Republicans resort to diverse devices to lessen the political rights of the masses. They restrict the franchise. Strict literacy tests, force, and fraud prevent numerous blacks and poor whites from voting in some southern states. Until 1970 in all but a few states, youth from eighteen to twenty-one, who are old enough to be drafted, were ineligible to vote. A sizable percentage of the lower classes do not register for fear they may lose income if called for jury duty or if they come to the attention of the tax collectors. A quarter or a half of the registrants may not cast ballots on election day, out of distrust or disgust with the choices offered them. Of the forty-seven million Americans who did not vote in the 1968 presidential election, nearly one half were disfranchised by strict residency laws, and many others had never bothered to register.

The basis of electoral representation for Congress and the state legislatures was grossly inequitable until recent Supreme Court "one-man, one-vote" decisions somewhat rectified the maldistribution. Rural areas were accorded parity with urban districts, though they may have had as few or fewer than one-tenth the inhabitants.

The most potent means of molding and manipulating public opinion is given to the ruling class through its grip upon the major media of communication—TV, radio, movies, the press, and educational facilities. In theory, a free press is available to all. In reality the view of life and versions of events suited to the powers-that-be are disseminated in millions of copies by the daily press, the newsweeklies, and the monthly magazines while nonconforming journals of anticapitalist opinion can reach only a few thousand readers for lack of financial resources and advertising.

Poverty snatches away from the dispossessed even those rights which capitalist democracy accords them on paper. Though they have the same formal rights, the rich and the poor do not get equal justice in the law courts, if only because of the delays and expense. Census Bureau studies have indicated that, at any given time, as many as one-half of those in many jails are there because they could not pay fines. And their skins were most likely to be black.

To uphold their political monopoly and prevent voters from having a distinct alternative to the capitalist candidates and programs, Republican and Democratic legislators make it exceedingly difficult, and in some states virtually impossible, for minority parties to get on the ballot. The 1969 New York City mayoralty race provided a typical act of exclusion. The incumbent mayor, having lost in the Republican primaries, ran under Liberal and an improvised Independent party designations. In order to secure two places on the top line of the voting machine instead of one, his henchmen successfully petitioned a subservient Board of Elections to declare invalid the petitions of the Socialist Workers and Socialist Labor parties, which would otherwise have occupied the mayor's chosen line on the machine. This cynical move helped return him to office.

Even if the electoral and governmental processes functioned more fairly, under monopolist domination the capacity to determine their own destinies would still be withheld from the American people. Democracy must have not only a political but an economic and social dimension. It must extend beyond the ballot box, which permits qualified voters to decide every so often which servitor of the status quo will take office, and beyond legislatures vassalized to the propertied interests. The most full-blooded capitalist democracy is no more than skin-deep, since it does not control the economic foundations of society or enable the masses to have a say in the most decisive areas of their lives.

NOTES

1. These findings are taken from a study of the delegates to the 1956 Presidential nominating conventions of both parties. These delegates come from every part of the country and from every level of party and government. For a full report see Herbert McClosky, Paul J. Hoffmann, and Rosemary O'Hara, "Issue Conflict and Consensus Among Party Leaders and Followers," *American Political Science Review,* June 1960, 420.
2. Sidney Verba and Norman H. Nie, *Participation in America: Political Democracy and Social Inequality* (New York: Harper & Row, 1972).
3. Robert A. Dahl, "Key Votes, 1945–1964," *Pluralist Democracy in the United States* (Skokie, Ill.: Rand McNally, 1967), pp. 238–242.

QUESTIONS FOR DISCUSSION

1. How would you compare the contention of Barry Goldwater, a conservative Republican, that the two major political parties offered the American people "an echo rather than a choice" with the views of George Novack, a Marxist?
2. If Gerald Ford had been elected president in November 1976, would he have pursued the same policies as President Carter?
3. Why do political parties play a minor role in foreign policy?
4. What structural changes in the American political system would have to be made in order to strengthen party unity at the national government level?
5. Would Novack's critique be weaker if public financing of all political campaigns were made compulsory?

SUGGESTED READINGS

Broder, David S. *The Party's Over: The Failure of Politics in America.* New York: Harper & Row, 1972.

Burns, James MacGregor. *The Deadlock of Democracy: Four Party Politics in America.* Englewood Cliffs, N.J.: Prentice-Hall, 1963.

Key, V. O., Jr. *The Responsible Electorate: Rationality in Presidential Voting, 1936–1960.* Cambridge: Belknap Press of Harvard University Press, 1966.

Mayhew, David R. *Party Loyalty Among Congressmen: The Difference Between Democrats and Republicans, 1947–1962.* Cambridge: Harvard University Press, 1966.

McClosky, Herbert, Paul J. Hoffmann, and Rosemary O'Hara. "Issue Conflict and Consensus Among Party Leaders and Followers." *The American Political Science Review* 54(June 1960):406–427.

Nagel, Stuart S. "Political Party Affiliation and Judges' Decisions." *The American Political Science Review* 55(December 1961):843–850.

Ranney, Austin, and Willmoore Kendall. *Democracy and the American Party System.* New York: Harcourt Brace Jovanovich, 1956.

Soule, John W., and James W. Clarke. "Issue Conflict and Consensus: A Comparative Study of Democratic and Republican Delegates to the 1968 National Conventions." *The Journal of Politics* 33(February 1971):72–91.

Truman, David B. *The Congressional Party: A Case Study.* New York: John Wiley & Sons, 1959.

Turner, Julius. *Party and Constituency: Pressures on Congress,* rev. ed., ed. Edward V. Schneier, Jr. Baltimore: Johns Hopkins Press, 1970.

8.

Does Voting
Reflect Popular Will?

Democracy requires citizens' participation in the political process, and voting is one form of that participation. Voting is supposed to be an expression of popular will. Voting, however, may distort popular will because of the voting turnout, the "weight" of each vote, and the "weight" of the information provided by different candidates in the election process.

One of the most important characteristics of the American electorate is nonvoting. Some people—foreigners, felons, and people under eighteen—are excluded by law from the vote. These exceptions, however, do not explain the fact that in presidential elections, as a rule, more than one third of the people who are legally able to vote do not vote. In off-year state and local elections, the proportion of nonvoters is higher.

Sometimes these nonvoters do not cast a ballot because of such obstacles as poor health or registration requirements. Many people do not vote, however, because they *choose* not to vote. This kind of political behavior may reflect a rational and conscious decision on the part of an individual not to favor a particular candidate. Often, however, socioeconomic factors, rather than an informed decision not to vote, play a prominent role in nonvoting behavior.

Studies of voting behavior reveal the socioeconomic features of the American electorate. Rich people tend to vote in larger proportions than poor people. The higher the level of education, the greater the participation in elections. Urban dwellers turn out to vote more often than do rural inhabitants. Higher voting participation is found among whites than among blacks, among men than among women, and among thirty-five to fifty-five-year-olds than among young or old people. So long as there is this disparity in participation, we can question whether the popular vote accurately reflects the popular will. Voting, some critics contend, represents the will of the active and affluent people rather than that of the poor and the uneducated. The laws that are enacted, consequently, are the laws of the active and affluent classes, according to this view.

In addition to voting participation, outcomes of elections can be distorted by the way in which the vote is "weighted." According to democratic theory, the principle of political equality should apply. This principle requires that each vote count the same. In practice, however, political devices have been instituted to work against this principle by giving some votes more weight than others. Two of these devices in the United States are malapportionment and the special institution Americans use to elect their president—the electoral college.

For years, representation in the United States House of Representatives and in both chambers of the state legislatures was malapportioned. Rural areas were over-represented because each district had equal power even if it was sparsely populated. In 1962, however, the Supreme Court held in *Baker* v. *Carr* that courts could intervene if state legislatures violated the Constitution by permitting the lower houses of state legislatures to become malapportioned. In 1964, the Court extended this ruling in *Wesberry* v. *Sanders* to include the United States House of Representatives. The court also ruled in 1964 in *Reynolds* v. *Sims* that both houses of state legislatures had to be apportioned on the basis of population.

The effect of these rulings was to strengthen the electoral power of the metropolitan and suburban areas. The principle of one person, one vote was finally realized in the state legislatures and in the House of Representatives.

Another factor that can distort the vote is the electoral college. The Framers of the Constitution created the electoral college because they wanted the president to be chosen by wise electors making independent judgments, rather than by the people themselves.

According to the electoral college system, the ordinary voter does not vote directly for the president but rather for a slate of presidential electors, which is made up of people chosen by the state party. The number of electors for each state is equal to the number of senators and representatives from that state. Heavily populated states have more electors than sparsely populated states because they have more representatives. These electors are not a group of independent people, as the Framers wanted. They have become, instead, representatives of the political parties and commit themselves to vote for their party's presidential candidate. The slate of electors that gets the largest number of popular votes gets *all* the electoral college votes for that state. To become president, a candidate must win a majority in the electoral college. If no one wins a majority, the House of Representatives make the choice from the three candidates with the largest number of electoral votes.

The electoral college system of electing a president has been subjected to criticism for over a century. A major criticism has been that it is possible to elect a president who has a majority vote in the electoral college but whose opponent has a majority of the popular vote. In 1876, for example, Samuel Tilden received more popular votes than Rutherford B. Hayes; yet, Hayes became president. Grover

Cleveland, moreover, experienced the same kind of loss to Benjamin Harrison in 1888.

Another criticism is that there is no legal requirement for electors to vote the way they have pledged. For example, in the presidential election of 1972, one elector committed to Richard Nixon voted instead for the Libertarian party candidate.

The effect of the electoral college system on the distribution of political power has been to give advantages to the heavily populated states, like New York, California, and Illinois because these states have large electoral votes. Presidential campaigners usually devote their attention to these more populous states because of the winner-take-all procedure. Indeed, support of the electoral college system comes from those groups in the big states whose power is strengthened by such a political device and from conservative politicians who would be penalized by electoral college reform.

In addition to distortion by malapportionment and the electoral college system, voting may not fairly reflect popular will if the information received by the public is one-sided. Specifically, if a candidate has enormous financial resources for campaigning, he or she can use those resources to gain an unfair advantage in an election. To remedy this inequity, a law authorizing public financing of *presidential* candidates in primaries and elections was enacted in 1974. Because of a case brought before the Supreme Court, some changes in the law were made. Public financing of the presidential primaries and election, however, was permitted for the first time in the 1976 election.

The law did not apply to elections to Congress. In 1977, President Carter endorsed legislation for public financing of congressional elections. Bills were introduced in the House and Senate. A filibuster that combined the talents of Republicans and southern conservative Democrats could not be broken, and no action was taken.

The system for financing congressional campaigns remains the same as it has been for years. Candidates must continue to raise funds from a variety of sources: personal wealth, private contributions, interest-group donations, party funding, and special events (such as fund-raising dinners).

This chapter contains debates about two of the issues affecting the relationship between voting and expression of the popular will: (1) Should the United States eliminate the electoral college and adopt a system of direct election of the president? (2) Should congressional campaigns be financed by government?

THE ELECTORAL COLLEGE

Every few years Congress discusses reform of the electoral college. Speeches are delivered, hearings conducted, and witnesses called. When the outcome of a presidential election is close, the clamor for ending the system becomes especially strong. In the presidential election of 1976, for example, a shift of 10,000 votes from Carter to Ford in Hawaii and Ohio would have elected Ford, although Ford trailed Carter by nearly 1.7 million votes nationally. Ford could then have won a majority in the electoral college, although Carter would have had a majority of the popular vote. Efforts to change the system in 1977 failed, however.

Four possible procedures for electing the president have been proposed: (1) retain the present system; (2) eliminate the procedure of allowing individual electors to vote for someone other than the person to whom they are pledged; (3) eliminate the electoral college and establish a system of direct election of the president; and (4) adopt a system in which candidates get the same proportion of the electoral vote as they receive in the popular vote on a state-by-state basis.

Democratic Senator Birch Bayh of Indiana introduced a bill in 1977 that would allow for direct election of the president. According to this bill, if no person received at least 40 percent of the vote, then a runoff election between the two leading candidates would be held. In the course of the Bayh committee hearings, political scientists Kenneth Kofmehl and Austin Ranney testified. Kenneth Kofmehl favors direct election of the president, and Austin Ranney makes a case against it.

Kofmehl argues that, compared to the present system, direct election would minimize the potential for fraud. The new electoral procedure would not weaken the two-party system since third parties have already appeared in the past thirty years for that purpose. The new system would make it impossible for a presidential candidate to win the popular vote but lose the election. Blacks, moreover, would not lose power since they have a larger turnout than whites in proportion to their numbers in many elections. Direct election would also strengthen the separation of powers in our system of government.

Ranney argues that the case against the electoral college has not been proven. Whenever there is no great need to change, there should not be change. Although favoring a system in which the will of the popular majority will be reflected in electoral victory, he indicates that the American people have accepted the electoral college system in the past, even when the presidential candidate with more popular votes lost the election. The chances of such an outcome occurring again are slim. The current system does not give undue influence to the ten biggest states because these states are not one-party states, but rather have competition between parties. Ranney asserts, moreover, that the new direct election system would probably weaken state and local parties.

CONGRESSIONAL ELECTIONS AND PUBLIC FINANCING

Since public financing of presidential elections became a reality, much attention has moved to the Congress. Common Cause, a public interest group, has noted that special-interest contributions have increased substantially in congressional campaigns. According to that organization, a total of $22.6 million was donated to congressional campaigners in the 1976 election, and this figure represented a $10 million increase over the amount spent in the 1972 election. Two thirds of the contributions in the 1976 campaign came from business and labor groups.

The bill to provide for public financing in senatorial election contests failed, as mentioned earlier. The two following selections are taken from the debate in 1977. Senator Dick Clark, a Democrat from Iowa, argues for the bill, and Senator John Tower, a Republican from Texas, argues against it.

Senator Clark contends that the bill is not an incumbent's bill since under the present system incumbents spend more money on campaigns than their challengers do. The bill would reduce the influence of the special interests. This influence has been increasing as may be seen from the higher interest-group contributions to congressional campaigns. If this bill is enacted, legislators will have more independence than they have at present.

Senator Tower argues that the bill would not transfer power from the special interests to the people, but rather from interest groups to bureaucrats. The bill would discourage participation of a citizen in a political campaign, and would lead to less campaigning on the grass-roots level. The bill would give advantages to the incumbent over the challenger, and to the smaller, more densely populated states over those states with a larger geographic area and widely dispersed population. The bill, moreover, would be costly to finance and would encourage bureaucratization.

Should We Abolish the Electoral College?

YES

KENNETH KOFMEHL
*A Case for Direct Election of the President**

. . . It is indeed a privilege to participate in your hearings on presidential election reform.

This undertaking, in my opinion, is even more important now than previously because the consequences of a misfire in the electoral college could be more damaging now than in times past and because there

* From testimony of Kenneth Kofmehl, U.S., Congress, Senate, Committee on the Judiciary, *The Electoral College and Direct Election,* Hearings on S.J. Res. 1, 8, and 18, 95th Cong., 1st sess., 1977, pp. 351–356.

appears to be less widespread public concern about this danger than in 1969 and 1970 when Congress last dealt with the problem.

In recent years, the resignations of a vice-president and president in disgrace, other revelations of corruption in high office, and growing public frustration with apparent unresponsiveness of government have seriously shaken faith in our public institutions.

As many have observed, a shift of less than 3,687 popular votes in Hawaii and 5,559 in Ohio would have given a majority of the electoral votes to Gerald Ford who had 1.7 million fewer popular votes than Jimmy Carter.

Had this occurred—especially as a result of a deliberate shopping for electoral votes which was at least contemplated according to testimony by Senator Dole before this subcommittee ten days ago—the legitimacy of our political system could very well have been irreparably damaged.

Despite this close call, the third such since 1960, caused in part by the efforts of minor party candidates to exploit the potentialities for mischief in the electoral college system, the general public does not seem nearly as aroused about the danger as eight years ago.

To some extent, this may have resulted from differential perceptions of the threat in 1968 and in 1976.

The possibility that George Wallace might throw the election into the House of Representatives or even determine which major party candidate won in 1968 stimulated a much greater outpouring of books, articles, and commentary in the mass media than the likelihood that Gene McCarthy might help deny election to the winner of the popular vote in 1976. . . .

Part of this indifference may derive from vigorous efforts made since 1969 to impugn direct popular election of the president, the only alternative to the system that would insure victory to the popular vote winner.

Some Ivy League intellectuals, such as the late Alexander Bickel, who wish to preserve what they believe to be the purported advantage for big states in our present electoral system, have published numerous books and articles in liberal journals of opinion like the *New Republic* and *Commentary*. Sympathetic newspaper columnists and editorial writers have echoed their views. For example, yesterday *The New York Times* contained a very misleading editorial on electoral college reform.

There are numerous fallacies in the principal arguments advanced by participants in this endeavor.

Frequently, they have indulged in transparent projection, attributing defects of the electoral college system to the direct popular election process.

An excellent example of this is their contention that direct election would encourage voting fraud and necessitate time-consuming and costly recounts.

Quite the contrary, as you pointed out earlier today, the temptation and likelihood of success for such fraud is much greater under the present system where stealing but a few thousand votes in a state or two could suffice to throw a large enough bloc of electoral votes to determine the outcome. . . .

Under direct popular election, votes would still be tabulated and reported on a state-by-state basis. Hence, any accusations of fraudulent behavior in particular counties could just as readily be checked by localized recounts as now.

An even more flagrant example of such projection is their argument that the electoral college is a bulwark of our two-party system and that instituting a direct popular vote for president would encourage its disintegration.

Examination of presidential elections since World War II indicates that is not true.

Starting with the splinter parties of Strom Thurmond [States Rights party] and Henry Wallace [Progressive party] in the 1948 campaign and continuing with slates of unpledged electors in 1960, George Wallace's [American] party in 1968, and Gene McCarthy's independent presidential candidacy in 1976, there has been a succession of serious efforts to throw the election into the House or to cause the outcome of the major party contests to be different than they otherwise would have been.

The electoral college system invites such fragmentation, because a rather small minor party that is geographically concentrated, can harvest a significant number of electoral votes.

In 1948 with but 2.4 percent of the popular vote, Strom Thurmond won thirty-nine electoral votes. A shift of less than 9,000 votes in California and 19,000 in Illinois would have denied either major party candidate a majority of the electoral votes.

In 1968 with 13.5 percent of the popular vote, George Wallace garnered forty-five electoral votes and received another one from a faithless elector.

If there had been a total change of less than 42,000 votes in Alaska, New Jersey, and Missouri, Nixon would not have had a majority in the electoral college.

In neither of these elections was the minor party popular vote combined large enough to deny both major party candidates a 40 percent plurality no matter how close the race between them.

In 1976, Gene McCarthy would have had to receive over three

times the 751,728 votes he got—which was less than 1 percent of the total—all at Carter's expense, to be able to reverse the popular vote decision.

Yet by taking a total of only 23,182 more votes in Ohio and Wisconsin from Carter, McCarthy could have insured Ford a majority of the electoral votes.

Under direct popular election of the president, the factor many political scientists believe is primarily responsible for maintaining our two-party system would remain in full force: election of the chief executive and members of Congress by plurality votes from single-member districts.

Moreover, this is reinforced by the Federal Campaign Reform Act which favors the two major parties in its provisions for public financing of elections, State laws that prohibit dual nominations, the organization of Congress by the two major parties, and numerous other considerations.

A plausible argument advanced by opponents of direct popular election is that the electoral college system affords vital protection for disadvantaged minorities.

In fact, there was substantial validity in it as applied to one such minority—blacks—until a few years ago.

When blacks were extensively disenfranchised in southern states, there was justification for the extra voting power enjoyed by blacks located in large pivotal nonsouthern states as a necessary compensation. . . .

Now, however, successful implementation of the civil rights laws of 1960 and 1964 and the Voting Rights Act of 1965 has dramatically altered the situation.

. . . of those who were registered to vote in the south, a slightly higher proportion of blacks than whites reported that they had voted in 1968.

Southern blacks maintained this level of turnout in the November 1972 election. . . .

The potency of black votes in southern states was resoundingly demonstrated in the 1976 presidential election. Hence, this argument no longer applies with much force to blacks.

Solicitude for minority interests should be adequately achieved by the dynamics of building majorities. In most cases, there is no preexisting majority, but one has to be aggregated.

On any issue, opposing sides try to attract a sufficient number of minority groupings to constitute a majority. In this endeavor, special attention is devoted to cohesive minorities whatever their composition—ethnic, religious, or other. . . .

I would like to accentuate the positive and shift from rebutting criticisms to stressing virtues of this reform.

Its adoption should impart new vitality to our entire political system.

For many years, there has been concern about the large percentage of chronic nonvoters in the U.S. electorate. It is much higher than in other Western democracies.

A contributing factor has been a sense of futility among members of the opposition in states dominated by one party.

At present, their votes for a presidential candidate are discarded at an intermediate stage in calculating the electoral votes.

With the advent of direct popular election, votes wherever cast would count in the totals.

Besides helping overcome individual voter apathy, this should stimulate each major party to extend its efforts into the strongholds of the other. The resultant spread of competitiveness between the major parties into all parts of the country should significantly strengthen our two-party system.

Direct election of the president would undergird the vital separation-of-powers feature of our political system, which parenthetically includes federalism.

According to James Madison in *The Federalist Papers,* separation of powers involves not only setting up separate branches of government but also having them responsive to different constituencies. That is, the people voting in different combinations.

Direct popular election accords closely with this principle. The president would be elected, as many now believe he is, from a nationwide constituency; senators on a statewide basis; and representatives from districts.

In this connection, at the Constitutional Convention in 1787, James Madison, James Wilson, Gouverneur Morris, and several other prominent founding fathers expressed the view that direct election of the president by the people would be the best method. It did not prevail then, primarily because of conditions that have long since ceased to exist.

For these reasons, which are only a few of the more salient that could be cited, I strongly urge this committee to report out favorably Senate Joint Resolution 1, proposing an amendment to the Constitution to provide for the direct popular election of the president and vice-president of the United States.

In my opinion, it is the best of the proposals currently under consideration and deserves approval in its present form.

Thank you.

Should We Abolish the Electoral College?

NO

AUSTIN RANNEY
*A Case Against Direct Election of the President**

Mr. Ranney: Senator Chafee expressed some regret a little earlier that everybody or almost everybody that came before the committee seemed to be strongly in favor of the idea and that the committee could perhaps learn from someone who was strongly against it.

I am afraid that I fall in neither of those categories. As you are well aware, there is an old verdict in Scottish jurisprudence of neither guilty nor innocent, but "not proved."

I really feel that fits the arguments that I have been hearing about this issue not only this time, but for some time past. On both sides we have a case that consists largely of speculation. It is reasoned speculation, to be sure. But, quite frankly, it is difficult for me to see why so many people can be so passionately in favor of this amendment on the ground that it will do many good things; or that others of equal eminence and patriotism can be so passionately against it.

So I am going to present my views on this rather from the standpoint of a skeptic. I guess I would start with the idea, once very eloquently phrased by John F. Kennedy, about social change in general. I think it applies particularly to constitutional amendment.

He said, "If it is not necessary to change, it is necessary not to change." If that seems reasonable, at least as applied to a constitutional amendment, then it takes me back to my old days as a high school debater.

We are told that the affirmative side of the proposition has, as its first burden, establishing a need. That is, they have to prove out that a real, substantial evil exists. Then they have to prove that their particular proposition will eradicate that evil. Then they have to prove that, in the course of eradicating that evil, it is not likely to bring with it other evils as great as or greater than the evil it seeks to eradicate.

* From testimony of Austin Ranney, U.S., Congress, Senate, Committee on the Judiciary, *The Electoral College and Direct Election,* Hearings on S.J. Res. 1, 8, and 18, 95th Cong., 1st sess., 1977, pp. 261–269.

That may or may not be a good way to look at problems like this, but I am used to it. So, if you will forgive me, that is the way I am going to look at this one.

First of all, what is the need that the proposal that we have before us is supposed to eliminate?

I think that the guts of it is that it will make impossible the election to the presidency of a candidate who receives less popular votes than one of his opponents. Unquestionably, it would do that.

So, the question is this: How bad is that evil?

. . . Nobody argues that it would be a good thing that somebody who has fewer popular votes should be elected. However, let it be said that the three previous times in our history that this has happened, we did not have a revolution. People did not refuse to recognize the legitimacy and authority of the president. The president was elected according to the due constitutional process. They might have thought that the process was not so good, but there were no drastic results.

Nevertheless, I would agree with everybody who has spoken here today that, other things being equal, I would prefer that that never happen in the United States. Sort of on first principles, quite aside from any actual social damage that it might do, it offends me to think that a person who got fewer votes would win over a person who got more votes.

So the next question becomes this: How imminent a danger is this?

. . . I think the chances of its ever happening again are very slim. I do not say that they are nonexistent. I say that they are very slim. Let me try to tell you why I think they are very slim.

It was possible in 1888 because of the very different structure of national presidential politics at that time. If you look at the arithmetic of Grover Cleveland and Benjamin Harrison's election, you will discover that Cleveland won very big in a relatively small number of mostly southern states in the days when the solid South was really solid for any Democratic candidate. Harrison won very narrowly but in a fairly substantial number of larger, more populous northern states.

If that were still the basic arithmetic, it might still work that way. However, in this century, there are no automatic one-party states. There is no state, not even Massachusetts—although it may come closest to it—that is automatic and in the bag for the candidate of one party or the other.

Moreover, if we remind ourselves of the arithmetic of the electoral college, we discover that in just 10 states with the largest number of electoral votes—California, New York, Pennsylvania, Illinois, Texas, Ohio, Massachusetts, Michigan, Florida, and New Jersey—

they have a combined total of 259 electoral votes. As you know, only 270 are needed to elect a president.

What about these states? Well, in the first place, they are all competitive states. Not one of them is a cinch for either the Republican or Democratic candidate.

Second, the currents of public opinion that seem to influence the outcome of the election nationally also affect them, too. Consequently, most of them vote for the winner. Take all of the presidential elections since 1932 in these 10 states. There were 120 total possibilities for them to vote, and those States have, taken as a group, voted 101 times—84 percent of the time—for the winner.

In only one election, the election of 1968, have as many as five—or half the states—voted for a loser. Even in 1968, they were split evenly. In every other election, they have gone anywhere from 6 States to all 10 of them for the winner.

. . . The currents of opinion, the decision of voters that make some voters shift to one candidate where they might ordinarily have voted for the other candidate, or for some voters to vote where they might ordinarily not vote at all—the same currents that we could detect nationally would also be found in these states. . . .

Until you have a time in which a substantial number of these states deviate from the way things are going nationally, it seems to me that the probabilities of a minority president being elected are very slim. I repeat that I do not say that it is impossible. I only say that it is unlikely.

Mr. Ackerson: If I may interrupt on that very point, you mentioned that risk being very slim before. This committee has had presented to it at a number of times various studies based upon computerized tests of voting patterns over periods of time which have reached the conclusion—at least one of the studies reached the conclusion—that in a close election there is a fifty-fifty chance that the second-place finisher in the popular vote will be the first-place finisher in the electoral vote.

That is not a slim percentage. Do you disagree with that conclusion?

Mr. Ranney: I do not want to sound antiscience, but I would have to see a good deal about the basis of those computer predictions; what kind of areas, what kind of data. You know the old saying about computers: garbage in, garbage out. If the data are absolutely impeccable and correct, then perhaps a fifty-fifty chance is correct.

Mr. Ackerson: I think these were statistical studies, but I agree it is difficult to analyze without study.

Mr. Ranney: History indicates that it has not happened yet. The greatest likelihood of its happening seems to me to have been in 1960. It was by far the closest election this century.

I remember election night of 1976. I was telling people that there cannot have been a presidential election since the nineteenth century where you had as many states being carried by such a small margin as was the case here.

I checked those figures. I soon discovered that that was not true. In 1960 there were a substantially larger number of states that were carried by an eyelash. John Kennedy, as you know, got a plurality of less than 200,000 votes out of many, many millions cast. Even so, he carried states enough to win, although with small margins.

Let me say just once more, I am not saying that it could never happen. Obviously, it could. I am saying that it has not happened for eighty-eight years and is not likely to happen again. . . .

In a very real sense, the Congress of the United States, and if both Houses pass this with the necessary two thirds, ultimately the legislatures of the states are going to have to weigh the probabilities of that bad thing happening against the probabilities that other, different—but equally and perhaps worse—things might happen as a result of adopting the direct election amendment. . . .

Well, it seems to me that one very likely consequence that I would give a very high probability to is an even further weakening of the state and local parties; particularly state parties, but local parties as well.

One of the things that keeps them going—as well as they do keep going, which is a little worse all the time, as television and public funding take over, and as the various rules remove their role even in the selection of presidential candidates—if, on top of depriving them of most of the role that they used to play in the selection of presidential candidates, you now deprive them of any kind of a significant role in campaigning for the presidency as well, then it seems to me that you would weaken them. In some instances, it would all but make them disappear. . . .

Mr. Ackerson: Mr. Ranney, I believe you were in the room when Professor Uslaner testified a little while ago. He concluded that any proliferation or splintering or weakening of the parties, as I understand his testimony, is very unlikely under a direct election plan.

Mr. Ranney: It is slightly a different issue. I am addressing myself to the weakening of the state parties, which I have heard no one say anything about yet.

Mr. Ackerson: With respect to the national parties, I think he was testifying—

Mr. Ranney: The weakening of the parties is different from the splintering of the parties. We could have a two-party system into the indefinite future. Yet, those parties could be very weak and meaning-less.

In fact, I would argue that, although we have a two-party system for the election right now, those parties—at least as far as the nomination of the presidential candidate is concerned—have all but disappeared. They hardly mean a thing. They are neutral arenas within which the candidate forces now battle for the nominations.

So the splintering of the parties is a rather different issue from the weakening of the parties.

However, since you raise the question, let me make a few comments on it.

I am rather struck by the fact that I have not heard today, nor have I heard very much in all discussions of this issue—and I hope you will look into it with some subsequent witnesses on this question—there is no discussion of the one major nation in the world which now elects its president substantially the way we would elect our president if the Bayh amendment were adopted. That is, of course, the French system for electing their president.

Their rule is this. If no candidate receives an absolute majority on the first vote, there is a runoff election. It is very instructive to observe what has happened in French elections during that time. I think there is no question of the fact that, although there are many other factors that enter into the French system that are leading toward an abandonment of the old, very fragmented, fractionalized, multiparty system of the third and fourth Republics, one of the things that has worked quite significantly against that is the French system of elections. There is a very significant reason for this.

A large number of candidates are encouraged to run. I think there were seven candidates in the most recent French presidential election. They hope to have some say about who will be the two finalists. They hope to be able to take votes away from so and so and/or to bargain with one of the first two finishers, with quid pro quos for throwing their support to one or the other of the people who are going to be in the finals.

It is also interesting to note that in the last French election, the leaders at the end of the first go-around included Mr. Mitterand. He lost in the final election to Mr. D'Estaing in part because of some deals that Mr. D'Estaing had made with some of the candidates and their parties that had run third and fourth and fifth and sixth in the first round.

It may well be—it is interesting to note that, at least the French public opinion polls that were taken at that time showed, that if you ask people to express their first and second and third preferences, Mr.

Mitterand had a larger collection of first and second preferences than Mr. D'Estaing did.

In fact, if we are going to go toward this kind of an election, we should be particularly worried about getting the president who represents the most preferences or most people—which is a different thing from who gets the most votes when you can only vote for one person or not.

Perhaps the committee and the Senate ought to consider the possibility of introducing the principle of the preferential vote, at least on the first ballot.

Mr. Ackerson: Ordinal voting?

Mr. Ranney: Yes. So, if there are six or seven candidates on the ballot, you just do not mark X for one; you mark them in order: one, two, three, four. You discard the low man; there are various ways of doing it.

Mr. Ackerson: That suggestion has been made and has been given some consideration. As I recall, the major objection to that suggestion is the confusion that voters are thought to face in that kind of situation where they are asked to order a number of candidates.

It would be a striking and new kind of voting pattern for them. Does that cause you any kind of pause in connection with this suggestion?

Mr. Ranney: I think the electorate could catch on. After all, they do it in the Republic of Ireland. If the Irish can do it, we certainly can do it. So that would not worry me.

I am not sure that that would be a good idea. All I am saying is that it does seem to be a logical extension of many of the arguments that I have heard about this morning and afternoon in favor of this particular amendment. . . .

I want to say something about my extreme skepticism about how the amendment would likely affect the nature of campaigning. We have heard people say that the candidates would go where the votes are.

It is not at all clear that they would. Would a candidate go to a rally in Pittsburgh instead of a rally at Indianapolis because more people live in Pittsburgh and because the state lines do not exist?

It is my guess that he would go wherever he would get maximum television coverage. It might be that a visit to Indianapolis, Fargo, or Grand Forks would be more television-newsworthy than would be Pittsburgh.

I do not think that there is any great evidence that the candidate showing up in the flesh in a particular town has any great significance as long as the other kinds of campaigning, particularly television ads, are going on.

As long as we are guessing, I would think that it is a more reasonable guess that, under this amendment, now that the states no longer mean a thing, it would be more likely to have national advertising relatively undifferentiated as to the states. There would be many more national telecasts and national-based ads.

There would be much less emphasis upon the candidate getting out and showing himself in the particular places. I do not know whether that would be a good thing or a bad thing. But the assumption that the candidate would suddenly be making lots of appearances in the great metropolitan centers because there are a lot of votes there and never showing up at the lesser places, seems to me to be a guess that does not seem to be terribly plausible.

If I may summarize and then try to answer any further questions you might have, I say this. I am simply skeptical about the whole thing.

It seems to me that the evil the amendment seeks to prevent is unlikely to happen. What you are dealing with here, therefore, is not a very pressing problem.

It is not as pressing a problem as, for example, the problem of presidential succession, Senator Bayh's previous amendment. That had some consequences that some of us were not terribly happy about.

There seems to me to be a real possibility—I cannot say certainly any more than the proponents of the amendment can say certainly that we are going to have a minority president—there seems to me a certainty that several things would happen to our political parties, to our mode of campaigning, to the kinds of candidates that might enter in the whole process.

So I wind up remaining to be convinced that the imminence and the size of the evil that this amendment addresses itself to are such that we ought to go ahead and risk the evils that might ensue, whatever those probabilities might be.

QUESTIONS FOR DISCUSSION

1. What effect would direct election of the president have upon the two-party system?
2. Would black people benefit from direct election of the president?
3. If a person were elected president with a minority of the popular vote but a majority of the electoral college vote, what effect would this development have on popular support for the president?
4. Which system—electoral college or direct election—is more in accord with political democracy?

5. What effect would a system of direct election of the president have on political campaigning strategy by the presidential candidates?

SUGGESTED READINGS

"A Bad Idea Whose Time Has Come." *New Republic*, May 7, 1977, pp. 5–8.

Bickel, Alexander M. *Reform and Continuity: The Electoral College, the Convention, and the Party System.* New York: Harper & Row, 1971.

Longley, Lawrence D., and Alan G. Braun. *The Politics of Electoral College Reform.* New Haven, Conn.: Yale University Press, 1972.

Matthews, Donald R., ed. *Perspectives on Presidential Selection.* Washington, D.C.: The Brookings Institution, 1973.

Peirce, Neal R. *The People's President: The Electoral College in American History and the Direct Vote Alternative.* New York: Simon & Schuster, 1968.

Polsby, Nelson W., and Aaron B. Wildavsky. *Presidential Elections*, 3rd ed. New York: Charles Scribner's Sons, 1971.

"The Question of Changing the U.S. Electoral System." *Congressional Digest*, August/September 1974.

Sayre, Wallace S., and Judith H. Parris. *Voting for President.* Washington, D.C.: The Brookings Institution, 1970.

U.S. Congress. Senate. Committee on the Judiciary. *The Electoral College and Direct Election.* Hearings on S.J. Res. 1, 8, and 18, 95th Cong., 1st sess., 1977.

Should Congressional Elections Receive Public Financing?

YES

DICK CLARK
*Congressional Campaigns Should Be Publicly Financed**

. . . Mr. President, for the fourth time in the last five years we are embarking today on yet another effort to reform our campaign finance law. Four times in five years. These campaign bills, in fact, are becom-

* From testimony of Dick Clark, U.S., Congress, Senate, 95th Cong., 1st sess., July 25, 1977, *Congressional Record*, 123, S12705–06.

ing very much like appropriations measures: we take them up annually. Each year we have made progress—public disclosure of contributions and expenditures, limitations on contributions, creation of an independent election commission, and more. Above all we have dramatically revamped the process of electing the president of the United States.

There have been several senators here today who have indicated that they think that action was unwise, to go to public financing of presidential elections. I think before the debate is completed it will be clear, and I think it is already clear to the vast majority of the American people, that we do not want to go back to the system of financing campaigns that we saw in the previous presidential election in 1972.

But each year we keep coming back to campaign finance reform because the problems that plague our own congressional elections just do not seem to go away, and public confidence in Congress and in the process by which it is chosen I think continues to decline. That decline will continue, and we will have to keep coming back year after year, unless we realize that we can no longer tinker with an antiquated system of total private financing of congressional elections. Like an old tire with too many miles and too many patches, it simply cannot be repaired. It must be replaced, and the bill that we debate here this week, S.926, is the replacement that is needed.

S.926 will provide for a mixed system of public and private financing of Senate general elections. S.926 is not nearly as ambitious as the bill that this body passed in 1974. S.926 does not apply to elections for the House of Representative, for example; the sponsors believe it would be more appropriate for the House to fashion its own campaign reform bill. S.926 does not apply to primary elections; while we have always supported public financing in primaries, it is our belief that the new system should be proven in the general elections before being extended to primaries.

Unlike the 1974 bill and the existing presidential system, S.926 would not eliminate private contributions from general election campaigns. There seems to be some misconception in the earlier debate that individuals are somehow limited by this legislation. They are in no way affected in terms of private contributions in S.926. Indeed, by using the matching concept that worked so well in last year's presidential primaries, S.926 will significantly increase both the value and the impact of small contributions from individual citizens.

But while the proposed framework for public financing may have changed since the 1974 campaign reform legislation, the reasons for adopting it clearly have not.

Contrary to what the senators from New Mexico and Tennessee

argued a few moments ago, about the bill being an incumbent's bill, let us look at the facts. Under the present system incumbents continue to spend twice as much on their campaigns as challengers—that is what the record shows—ever since we have been keeping records on public disclosure since 1972. And special interest groups continue to contribute more than three times as much money to incumbents as to challengers. And not surprisingly incumbents under the present system continue to get reelected more than 95 percent of the time.

In one important respect, however, things have changed since 1974, and they have changed for the worse: Because of public financing special interests were largely removed from last year's presidential campaign. But having been shut out of the race for the White House, the private dollar managed to find a new home in Congress.

Let me just cite three or four statistics. In only two years from 1974 to 1976 the increase in special interest giving was astronomical. Business, professional, and agricultural group contributions went from $4.8 million in 1974 to $11.6 million in 1976, more than double in that one election. Business groups alone increased their contributions from $2.5 million in 1974 to $7.1 million in 1976, nearly tripling in only 2 years. Labor contributions, already high in 1974 at $6.3 million, exceeded $8.2 million in 1976.

All told, special interest giving by the various PAC's [political action committees]—labor, business, farm, et cetera—increased by more than 80 percent in only one election, in two years, from $12.5 million in 1974 to $22.6 million in 1976.

There is every reason to believe that that trend will continue and by next year congressional elections promise to be virtually flooded with special interest money.

It has been argued that we should have continued private and special interest money in the presidential races in some of the earlier debate here today. But I think that one of the things we should cover in this weeklong debate is exactly what kind of special interest money went into the 1972 presidential race, the 1968 races, and the 1964 races, to show indeed how much money, and what kind of money particularly, went into these races.

Under the present system of total private financing, candidates have little choice but to accept special interest dollars. Few candidates even among well established incumbents can raise sufficient funds from individual citizens to finance a competitive race, and I think the records will show that quite clearly in the disclosures that have occurred since 1972.

While large private contributions may not directly buy a Senator's vote they certainly buy access and influence. As Senator Russell Long put it so well, it is "monetary bread cast upon the water to be returned 1,000-fold."

Each of us know, I believe, that we lose at least a small piece of independence with special interest dollars that are accepted. It is not a question of corruption. Of course not. It is a question of influence and access. I personally believe that it is naive to hold that millions of dollars of special interest campaign funds go into campaigns for no purpose of influence, whether that be labor money, medical money, or other kinds of special interest money.

I just do not believe that all of these people get together, group their money, and put it into elections for no particular purpose, without any intent of influence, and without it ever having any impact on anyone's decision. I find that difficult to believe.

And that is what one must believe, it seems to me, if you hold that the special interest contributions, and the level of those contributions, are indeed a wise occurrence. . . .

But under the Constitution we cannot simply prohibit special interest contributions. That became clear I think in Buckley against Valeo. We could, of course, reduce the contributions limits, but without providing an alternative source of funds we would only be further locking present incumbents into place.

I must say that if one argues that the special interest money, as was argued here earlier today, really has no impact, there is nothing about it that really influences one, then it seems to me that you cannot at the same time argue that disclosure is a good idea. Why do we need disclosure if there is absolutely no effect on any member in terms of accepting special interest contributions?

I think we need another way to finance elections, a system that will enhance the power of the individual citizen, that will encourage small private contributions, that will restore competition in the political process. That system, funded by the voluntary $1 tax checkoff and small contributions from individual citizens, is exactly what is involved in S.926.

It has been said earlier in the debate that this will limit participation in the political process. That is not the case; it in no way affects any individual's contributions.

Mr. President, over the next several days the opponents of this bill will use every conceivable argument in pleading their case—and that is fair enough; it is a natural thing. But I urge our colleagues to keep track of their arguments very carefully, and not to be surprised to find these opponents on both sides of several issues.

Let me cite a few arguments that have been made here today.

It has been said that public financing is too costly, that it is a raid on the Treasury, and that it is bad by its very nature; and then we see the amendment offered to double the cost of public financing by covering primary elections. Even though public financing is a very bad idea from that point of view, it is argued that it ought to be extended beyond general elections to include primary elections.

It does not seem to me that we can have it both ways. If it is bad, if it is undesirable to have public money, why would anyone want to extend it to primary elections?

It may be said that the spending limits are too low. . . .

It may be said that the spending limits may be used to protect incumbents. I do not think that argument has been used on the floor yet today, but it no doubt will be: that it is just too low, and protects incumbents.

Then it seems to me that they have said, on the other hand, that in fact the limits are too high, because it involves putting too much money into the political process.

They will say that the bill does nothing to cut special interest money, and then will offer a substitute bill, as I understand it, to provide tax credits, which does nothing to cut special interest money. And while arguing that special interest money is in no way controlled in S.926, it has been argued that special interest money in no way affects members of Congress in any case.

It has been said that the bill does not give enough money to minor parties; and then it has been said that it is a raid on the Treasury.

It has been said that the two-party system must be maintained, and that this bill will undermine the two-party system; but at the same time it is said that we need to better finance third and fourth parties to challenge those two parties.

I think we will hear these arguments and more, and I think when one gets all done and looks at all the arguments, one thing is clear: It is a plea to preserve the status quo—that is what is at issue—where incumbents dominate and special interests foot the bill. And while I disagree with the distinguished minority leader (Mr. Baker) on the merits of public financing, I believe the distinguished minority leader was absolutely correct earlier today on two occasions, and last week, when he said that if this bill should pass, "it will change, in a very basic way, the nature of the political system."

Mr. President, I think it is high time for such a change. . . .

Should Congressional Elections Receive Public Financing?

NO

JOHN TOWER
*The Case Against Public Financing of Congressional Campaigns**

Mr. President, the notion that passage of public financing legislation will eliminate the influence of special interest groups on federal elections is a false one. As the editors of the *Wall Street Journal* recently pointed out, the results of the last electoral "reform" was not a transfer of power from "the interests" to "the people," but was a transfer of power from individuals with one kind of political resource to individuals with another.

The Supreme Court ruled in the *Buckley* case that although Congress may limit the amount of money a person or organization can give directly to a campaign, it cannot limit truly independent expenditures respecting candidates or issues. Thus an organization such as a labor union or action group might spend large sums of money to oppose a particular candidate whose ability to reply is constrained by the expenditure ceiling he must observe as a condition of accepting public funds. Consequently, the influence of the special interests has not been eliminated but has been strengthened. . . .

Not to be overlooked is the enhancement of the biggest pressure group of them all—the federal bureaucracy. The conduct and possibly the outcome of senatorial elections will be lodged in the hands of unelected bureaucrats in the Federal Election Commission.

DISCOURAGEMENT OF CITIZEN PARTICIPATION IN POLITICS

If enacted into law, S.926 would discourage all but minimal participation of a citizen in senatorial campaigns. As a start, the taxpayer may not designate the candidate or party which will receive his checkoff. Instead, the bureaucrats at the Federal Election Commission make that determination. Thus, an independent's tax money may well be added to the coffers of Republican and Democratic candidates.

* From testimony of John Tower, U.S., Congress, Senate, 95th Cong., 1st sess., August 1, 1977, *Congressional Record*, 123, S13182–87.

Nor is there any real incentive to make meaningful personal contributions. The amount of tax deductions and credits is severely limited.

In a similar vein, volunteerism is discouraged. Experience with the Federal Election Campaign Act demonstrates that because of the intricacies of that law, with its incumbent regulations and interpretations, only the most experienced lawyers, accountants and professional campaign managers dare manage a federal election campaign. Some technical error can trigger a federal criminal prosecution or civil liability. Gone are the days of the citizen armies that nominated and elected Dwight D. Eisenhower to the office of presidency. The additional restrictions on the action of senatorial campaigns will further discourage volunteer management.

Citizens who wish to support or run as third party or independent candidates are discouraged from doing so. Under the bill, independents and third-party candidates are given short shrift. A minor or third-party candidate must raise privately 10 percent of the total expenditures a candidate would make in the general election or $100,000—whichever is smaller—to qualify. For most, this is an impossible task.

DECREASING THE TIES OF A SENATOR
TO HIS CONSTITUENTS

If we are to learn anything from the 1976 presidential election we find that the combination of limited funds and the need for strict accounting forced candidates to rely heavily on television and radio. In large- and medium-size states this would simply mean that the candidates could not travel in the state to meet and talk with the people.

In addition, the curtailment of grass-roots contributions, as S.926 would do, would tend to have the effect of insulating the candidate from taking stands on controversial issues. In the past a candidate was compelled to spell out where he stands on many issues to raise significant funds. But under S.926 when he receives public funding, he may be reticent to deal with matters of substance.

ABRIDGMENT OF THE CONSTITUTIONAL RIGHT OF
POLITICAL EXPRESSION AND EQUALITY OF TREATMENT

The American Bar Association's special committee on election reform cautioned that the expenditure limitation in S.926 presents substantial legal questions regarding the curtailment of first amendment rights of free speech and expression. The Bar Association report suggests that the more desirable way of limiting the influence of money in the electoral process with the minimum of interference with the first amendment rights is through full disclosure of private contributions which are limited to reasonable amounts.

Equally disturbing is the inequality. . . .

Incumbents and major party candidates are favored over independents and challengers.

Smaller, more densely populated states are favored over those states with a larger geographic area and widely dispersed population. The formula does not take into account the problems of travel and multimedia markets, which may differ considerably from state to state.

Prof. Roy A. Schotland, of Georgetown University, questions the fundamental soundness of expenditure limits and raises questions about the equity of the ceilings. In a recent study, he points out that if the limits prescribed in the new proposal had been in effect in 1972 and 1974, twenty-nine of seventy-three candidates in the smaller States would have broken the law while only eight of fifty-one candidates in the larger states would have exceeded their limits.

ENHANCEMENT OF THE ADVANTAGES OF INCUMBENCY

If enacted into law, S.926 will help to keep in office the persons who are already there. It will exclude fresh talent and new ideas. The expenditure ceilings in the bill will have the effect of freezing the status quo; it discriminates against new candidates who may need to spend larger amounts of money merely to achieve name recognition.

It is therefore repugnant to the spirit of the Constitution in advancing the establishment of the first state political party in our history as a nation. This upsets every historic tradition of limited government by compelling the American taxpayer to finance opinions and candidates of the "established party" which he or she may abhor.

ENLARGEMENT OF THE REGULATORY AND TAX BURDEN

The cost estimates for this bill are seriously underestimated. Its proponents claim that, if the bill is passed, the presidential election campaign fund will still have a surplus in December 1980, in the neighborhood of $50 million. However, if House campaigns are added to the bill—as they must be to make it work—the fund's deficit may be as high as $19 million. Where will this deficit funding come from? The Treasury? The public will not get the complete bill for S.926 until it is too late to refuse payment.

Persons who refuse to check off the campaign financing option on their tax returns will be forced to pay for congressional campaigns anyway. Their taxes will have to pay the tremendous administrative costs of implementing this legislation.

The bill will only increase bureaucratic redtape and candidate confusion. Anticipating passage of the bill, the Federal Election Commission has already requested an additional appropriation of nearly $1,800,000 for expenses to handle the administration of public financing for the 1978 Senate elections. Further, since the bill contains conflicting reporting requirements, the FEC will have to issue a considerable amount of new regulations. Finally, candidates will need to incur greater costs for attorneys and accountants in order to be sure that they are in compliance with the law.

In conclusion, Mr. President, I urge that we not take precipitous action in this matter. The only other major change in the election of senators—the Seventeenth Amendment providing for direct popular vote—was before Congress for some 80 years before it passed in June 1911. In contrast, the Rules Committee had a scant three days of hearing on S.926.

QUESTIONS FOR DISCUSSION

1. What kinds of campaign expenses would be covered by S.926?
2. How would the political behavior of senators change if S.926 becomes law?
3. How would public financing of senatorial election campaigns affect the two-party system?
4. What effect would the bill have on illegal contributions?
5. What effect would the bill have on campaign techniques?

SUGGESTED READINGS

Adamany, David W. *Campaign Finance in America.* North Scituate, Mass.: Duxbury Press, 1972.

_____. "Money, Politics, and Democracy: A Review Essay." *American Political Science Review* 71(March 1977):289–304.

_____, and George E. Agree. *Political Money: A Strategy for Campaign Financing in America.* Baltimore, Md.: Johns Hopkins University Press, 1975.

Alexander, Herbert E., ed. *Campaign Money: Reform and Reality in the States.* New York: The Free Press, 1976.

_____. *Financing Politics: Money, Elections, and Political Reform.* Washington, D.C.: Congressional Quarterly, 1976.

Bode, Ken. "Money for Campaigns." *New Republic,* February 19, 1977, pp. 8, 10–11.

Glantz, Stanton A., Alan I. Abromowitz, and Michael P. Burkhart. "Election Outcomes: Whose Money Matters?" *Journal of Politics* 38(November 1976):1033–1038.

"The Question of Federal Financing of Congressional Election Campaigns: Pro & Con." *Congressional Digest,* March 1977.

Udall, Morris K., and Lowell P. Weicker, Jr. "Use Tax Dollars to Elect Congress?" *U.S. News & World Report,* April 25, 1977, pp. 63–64.

PART THREE

Are
Policy Makers
Too Influential?

9.

Is the American Presidency Too Powerful?

Political Scientist James MacGregor Burns wrote in 1965: "The presidency today is at the peak of its prestige. Journalists describe it as the toughest job on earth, the presiding office of the free world, the linchpin of Western alliance, America's greatest contribution to the art of self-government."* At that time, he had ample evidence for the claim of presidential eminence. The United States was then at a record high point in prosperity. Lyndon Johnson had won a landslide election for the presidency the year before and was a popular figure. Civil rights laws were being enacted, and the President's role in promoting human freedom was acclaimed. Johnson's Great Society—with its welfare programs and generous government spending—would, proponents argued, end poverty, eliminate slums, and create if not a heaven on earth, then at least the best material society the world had ever known. In foreign policy, the United States was leader of the "Free World," and the President was its spokesman. Congress, moreover, looked to him for leadership both in domestic and foreign policy. It is true that the United States was becoming heavily involved in the war in Vietnam, but the big antiwar movement was not to appear for a few years. Besides, Lyndon Johnson argued, the nation could have both guns and butter, and the war in Southeast Asia would end quickly if the United States persevered.

Much has changed since 1965. Riots in the urban ghettos shattered the illusion that civil rights programs would appease poor blacks. Vietnam tore the nation apart as hundreds of thousands of Americans fought in a war without apparent end. Prosperity gave way to inflation and unemployment brought on by high government spending, commodity price increases, and an energy crisis. Rev-

* James MacGregor Burns, *Presidential Government: The Crucible of Leadership* (Boston: Houghton Mifflin, 1966), p. 313.

elations of government wrong-doing—police surveillance of dissenters, illegal entries into private homes, and unwarranted income tax audits of dissenters and activists—led to challenges of the authority of political institutions. The repercussions of the Watergate break-in, particularly, symbolized that challenge. If, as the Watergate affair implied, government officials did not feel that the law applied to them, then it seemed to many critics of the system that the law need not apply to "just plain folks" as well.

The presidency as an institution was an important part of the system under attack. To be sure, individual presidents and the power of the institution have always been targets for critics from the day that George Washington took office. By the 1970s, however, the institution had grown enormously. Now the stakes involved in the power any president exercises are greater than ever.

The office of the president has grown because of developments in several key arenas, the most notable of which are foreign policy, national security, demands for public services, the character of Congress, and the media.

In foreign policy, the United States has abandoned its pre-World War II policy of isolationism and has adopted a policy of internationalism. Particularly up to the early 1950s, many countries of the world looked to leadership by the United States—and specifically the president as chief diplomat—to protect their security or to furnish aid.

The nature of war has changed, and with the changes the burden of responsibility the president bears for national security has increased. In the age of high-speed missiles and hydrogen bombs, the United States can no longer rely on having time to mobilize its vast resources for war. The president would have less than fifteen minutes notice in the event of a nuclear attack by the Soviet Union.

Big government (and the services it provides) has been accepted as necessary to improve the plight of the weak and the poor. The president is chief administrator of hundreds of agencies dealing with such areas as child welfare, health, housing, and food. As government services have become more plentiful and diverse, public demand for them has increased.

Although Congress has not been a rubber stamp for the president, it has often preferred to give him discretionary powers. Congress has been too cumbersome in structure, with its many committees, to provide the same kind of leadership offered by the president, a factor that has enhanced the position of the president.

The media have added to the strength of the president. The president is always news. Television, radio, newspapers, and magazines all feature stories about the chief executive, thus providing a direct line to the electorate that earlier presidents would have envied.

Because of the growth of presidential power, many questions are asked about that power. Two important questions, however, are as follows: (1) Are strong presidents desirable in the American political system? (2) Was the Nixon presidency an aberration?

ARE STRONG PRESIDENTS DESIRABLE?

The equation of a strong president with a good president is a modern liberal idea. Classical liberals of the nineteenth century did not believe in strong government. Government can solve problems and the president can play a major role in moving government to solve these problems, according to many twentieth-century liberals and others who believe in strong government.

Theodore Sorensen, a former adviser to President Kennedy, argues that events require a president to act since Congress often refuses to exercise its authority. For example, Congress could easily have thwarted the will of the president during the Vietnam war by cutting off military appropriations but chose not to do so. Congress, moreover, could have held an executive witness in contempt for improperly invoking executive privilege in the Nixon administration but failed to do that as well.

In the clamor to associate the power of the presidency with the abuses of power by President Nixon, the supporters of congressional power overstate their case, according to Sorensen. Congress will not be less hawkish, less resistant to the military-industrial complex, and less vulnerable to the special interests than a strong president. A strong president is responsive to the national interest and long-term needs. A strong president would clean out corruption, impound funds for useless defense items, promote trade, and encourage human rights abroad.

In opposition, political scientist Nelson W. Polsby asserts that most presidents aspire to be considered great presidents—an honor usually bestowed by historians, political scientists, and other opinion makers. The surest way for presidents to achieve "greatness" in the rating game is to demonstrate strong, even dominant, leadership. In their quest for greatness, however, strong presidents create too many expectations and can sacrifice the needs of the nation because they are eager to demonstrate their strength and decisiveness.

THE NIXON PRESIDENCY—AN ABERRATION?

Democratic government requires that all people obey the law; democracy could not survive in a society in which the supremacy of law was not widely respected. The Nixon presidency—culminating in the Watergate affair—was characterized by violation of the laws at the presidential level.

Although much information is now publicly available for an understanding of the activities of the Nixon administration, debate continues about the significance of this low point in American presidential history. British journalist Peter Jenkins explains that Watergate may best be understood by studying one man, Richard Nixon, rather than the institution of the presidency. Jenkins charges that Nixon was morally unfit to occupy his high office. The historical record suggests questions about Nixon's mental health. His behavior in the Cambodian intervention in 1970 and in the handling of the Watergate affair is cited as evidence for mental instability.

Jenkins portrays Nixon as a man not only "devoid of moral sense" but also lacking common sense. He is described as possessing a second-rate mind and a vulgar intelligence, as preoccupied with appearance rather than substance, and with power rather than policy. Nixon, according to Jenkins, was "not corrupted by power; he corrupted power."

Writer Nick Thimmesch contends that Nixon's behavior in office was not significantly different from that of his predecessors. Presidents from Franklin Roosevelt to Lyndon Johnson are guilty of some of the more serious charges made against Nixon: obtaining confidential federal income tax records and causing tax audits to be conducted in a discriminatory manner; and using illegal wiretaps and ordering surveillance on citizens "for purposes unrelated to national security, the enforcement of laws, or any other lawful function of his office." According to Thimmesch, Nixon's presidency was not aberrational.

Are Strong Presidents Desirable in the American Political System?

YES

THEODORE SORENSEN
The Case for a Strong Presidency*

. . . I am here to say a good word for the presidency—not the president, but the presidency. (An easy way to remember that is that it ends in "y" which is one of three magic letters. No one can be nominated for president in this country unless his name ends in "y," "n," or "r." Sorensen's Law, keep it in mind. It will be true in 1976 just as it has been true in every election since World War II.) I am for a strong presidency, and I make no bones about it. I also happen to be for a strong Congress and a strong judiciary. That's what I think the Founding Fathers intended—to have all three branches of the government strong.

* Pp. 27–33 in "The Case of a Strong Presidency" by Theodore C. Sorensen from *Has the President Too Much Power?* edited by Charles Roberts. Copyright © 1974 by the Washington Journalism Center. Reprinted by permission of Harper & Row, Publishers, Inc.

I am also for a strong press, which is, if not a fourth branch of government, certainly a center of power in this country. While I agree with all the editorials all of you write from time to time deploring the attacks upon the press in its battle with the presidency, I happen to believe that the power of the press still exceeds that of the presidency and the Congress combined. Oscar Wilde was right when he said, "In America the president reigns for four years, but journalism reigns forever."

I also happen to believe, as we talk about powerful institutions, in two strong political parties; and I think many of the problems we face these days result not from too much power in the presidency, but from the decline of political parties as instruments of authority in this country. But there is no doubt in my mind that Congress already has enormous power, if it only had the guts to use it. If it could organize itself in twentieth-century fashion, if it could steel itself to speak with some will and authority, then I think the Congress could easily be the equal of the presidency without tearing down the presidency or bringing it down to the present level of the Congress.

But instead Congress prefers to avoid these questions. It apparently prefers to talk about some future problem instead of the present problem. We are now about to have saddled upon us the war powers bill, which is Congress's answer to the illegal exercise of presidential authority in the war-making area. I happen to think it has been illegally exercised, and Congress could have cut off appropriations at any time. Instead, it labors and brings forth the Javits bill, which says nothing about Indochina. In fact it exempts Indochina but states that on future occasion if the president illegally takes this country into war, after he has done so for a certain period he must ask Congress—at the time when the war is at the height of its popularity—to extend his authority to carry on this illegal war.

The same is true with executive privilege. There isn't the slightest doubt in my mind that executive privilege has been improperly and illegally invoked by the Nixon Administration on more than one occasion. But the response to that among the Senate Democrats was to work up an elaborate set of rules and procedures as to what should be done when executive privilege is invoked. All Congress has to do is once hold an executive witness in contempt for improperly invoking executive privilege, and it will be illegally invoked a lot less in the future. As I have already pointed out, the same is true of presidential misconduct. Instead of amending the Constitution to have a single six-year term or provide for new elections in mid-term, one impeachment might have the healthiest possible effect on presidential misconduct in the future.

The powers of the Congress are enormous. President Kennedy

once said to me he never realized until he reached the White House how powerful the Congress can be. Congress could cut off the president with one part-time secretary if it does not like the way he is operating his staff, for example. That power of the purse has never been utilized to its fullest. Nor has the power of Congress to legislate—not structural changes in the presidency, but changes in the method of selecting our presidents—or the power of Congress to investigate, and to educate, and to pass on nominations. These are all powers that could be used skillfully in a way to bring presidents to their knees if that is the wish of the Congress, or at least to end their excesses. But Congress does not wish to do so. It prefers to complain that it has no power and that the president is constantly usurping powers.

But whether Congress uses these powers or not, I am unwilling to dismantle or debilitate the presidency to stop the president of the United States, whoever he may be, from the power to do good or evil in order to turn the leadership of this country in national affairs over to the Congress. That was tried during much of the nineteenth century, unsuccessfully, in my opinion, and it certainly did not give us the kind of leadership and the progressive results we have had in the twentieth century.

Here again the fact that the pressure comes from those liberals and scholars who say that their own objectives are progressive or humanitarian puzzles me. Why does anyone think that the Congress over the long run is going to be less hawkish than the president when it comes to questions of war and peace? History tells us exactly the opposite. Even Lyndon Johnson was more restrained in his approach to Indochina than Congress, in my opinion, would have been in the early years if it had been making the decisions on whether to bomb Hanoi, bomb the dikes, and invade the north.

Why does anyone think that Congress is going to be more resistant to the military-industrial complex than is the president? If there is still a complex, it is composed not only of the manufacturers, but the local governments, the local unions, the local chambers of commerce, and all the others who are much more effective in getting congressmen and senators to load up the defense budget than they are in pressuring the presidency or even the armed services. Why does anyone think that the Congress is going to be more liberal than the presidency on questions of civil rights and civil liberties? The Congress over the long run is inclined to be much more responsive to the winds of prejudice and popular pressure back home and much more responsive to the white majority.

I could go on. Why do we think the Congress is going to pay less attention to the special interests, less attention to local pressures, more attention to the unorganized, the handicapped, the weak and unrepresented individuals in this country? That simply has not been borne out by history. Congress is by nature more responsive to local pressures and to short-term needs that are likely to be reflected in the next election. The president is more likely over the long run to think more of the national interest, to think more of long-range interests, to think of his place in history, to be less accessible to lobbyists, to pay less attention to organized mail campaigns. The presidency is much more able to speak with one voice than the Congress, much more able to move the bureaucracy, much more able to carry out policy than the legislative branch.

But, when I talk about a strong presidency, let me also make clear what I do *not* have in mind. To be a strong president, one does not need a monopoly of power. It was never intended that the president should govern autonomously in this country, that he should not share power with the Congress, the courts, and other institutions. A strong president does not need to concentrate all executive power in the White House instead of giving his departments and agencies some leeway. He does not need a huge, servile staff shielding him from all criticism and adverse information, agreeing with his every word and gesture, and all of them claiming to speak for the president when they call up to give their various orders to the agencies.

I believe that those in the White House should be truly personal advisers and assistants to the president. If not, if they are going to have little empires of their own, then they ought to be confirmed by the Senate and they ought to be subject to testimony before the Congress. But there is no need to have little empires in the White House. Also, there ought to be limits on the extent to which the White House can interfere politically with the executive departments and agencies, particularly the independent agencies, the investigative agencies, and the Internal Revenue Service.

To be a strong president does not require excessive secrecy or seclusion. Isolation is a problem with every president, but we have never seen it to the degree that we have in the last two [Johnson and Nixon]. We have never in history had a definition of executive privilege comparable to that which Mr. Kleindienst [Nixon's attorney general] handed down—one that could prevent testimony from any individual employed by the executive branch, that applied to past presidential aides as well as present aides for all time, that covered criminal activity as well as presidential policy, and that apparently covered even impeachable offenses. That doctrine, if there were anything to it, would make the remedy of impeachment nearly useless.

A strong presidency does not require a president who holds himself to be above the law, who defies the requests of grand juries and the orders of courts, and who engages in wiretapping and burglary, or engages in secret bombings and then falsifies the official records of the executive branch. That is not what I mean by a strong president. For that matter, it's not necessary for a strong president to have a lavish empire of several homes, countless helicopters, yachts, jets, limousines, brightly uniformed guards, and all the rest. A certain amount of that is necessary for presidential security, travel, and convenience—and because Americans do exalt their presidency to some extent. But it has nothing to do with the strength of the presidency.

And, finally, a strong president doesn't prove his strength by using his muscle against the press or against little black children or against hungry old people or against others who are in no position to defend themselves. No, a strong president ought to be strong because of the strength of his ideas, because of the strength of his character and leadership, because of the strength of the people whom he attracts to his team to help him run the government.

Would I want a strong president today? Absolutely. I think a strong president today could clean out corruption in this government from top to bottom. The incumbent would have if he were really a strong president. I think a strong president today could fill some of these important posts that have gone vacant for an incredibly long period of time because the incumbent is unable to attract top people to serve in this administration.

A strong president would impound funds (and if impoundment is held illegal, he would find some other way of doing it) that are being appropriated for useless defense items, including the Senate's recent change in the military pension system that is going to saddle us with billions and billions of dollars of cost in the future. A strong president would be impounding that—not funds for hospitals and school lunches.

A strong president would have allocated heating oil in this country a long time ago with a workable system to make sure that nobody goes cold this winter. He would have gotten tough with the oil industry in the same way that Jack Kennedy got tough with the steel industry, to make sure that the independents survive, that competition survives in that industry, and that prices remain reasonable.

A strong president today would pull together the government to speak with one voice on questions of trade and on the combined question of trade with the Soviet Union and human rights inside the Soviet Union, instead of simply allowing any businessman to make any deal he wants, regardless of whether the Soviets pursue a policy we like or dislike.

Part of the problem is the fact that the American people when they talk of a strong presidency expect too much. They hold the president responsible for the fall of every sparrow, so it's not surprising that many presidents try to take on too much, try to control too much. If our expectations and demands could be more life-size, perhaps the presidency, as Senator Mondale [now vice-president] has said, could be more life-size.

My own opinion is that, in the long run, all of these issues are going to be settled not by questions of power, not by amendments to the Constitution, not even by legal solutions—although as a lawyer I am reluctant to admit there isn't a legal solution to everything. But, by the old-fashioned process known as comity—not comedy, we have enough comedians, but comity—c-o-m-i-t-y, respect and reciprocity between the branches of government. That is what the Founding Fathers intended when they drew up the Constitution. It's very clear any one of the three branches of government, if it so wished, could totally harass and restrict the others. If he wanted to, the president could veto everything the Congress passes. He could eke out with an eyedropper the funds for those programs that are passed over his veto by the Congress. He could refuse to fill judicial vacancies. The Congress in turn could harass every presidential aide, block every presidential request. The courts in turn could do the same.

The possibility for crisis is always going to be present under our Constitution. But if each branch will recognize that it is not always going to have its own way, that it must work with the other branches, that government in this country is necessarily a partnership among them, then I think the danger of a real crisis or confrontation can be avoided, and we will survive even this president and this present mess and go on to the glories of which we are capable.

Are Strong Presidents Desirable in the American Political System?

NO

NELSON W. POLSBY
*Against Presidential Greatness**

Until election day is past, candidates for president campaign among their fellow citizens with the simple end in view of being elected. Once they are inaugurated, however, presidents frequently yearn for an even

* From Nelson W. Polsby, "Against Presidential Greatness," *Commentary*, January 1977, pp. 61–64.
Reprinted from *Commentary* by permission; copyright © 1977 by the American Jewish Committee.

higher office—a niche in the pantheon of "great" presidents. Membership in this exclusive society is, on the whole, not to be achieved through sheer popularity. Was there ever a more popular president than Dwight D. Eisenhower? Yet we all "know" he was not a "great" president, nor even a "near great" one.

How do we know this? Essentially I think the answer is: we know it because historians tell us so. In each generation, or possibly over a shorter span, a consensus arises among the authors of political and historical texts about how well various presidents met the alleged needs of their times. These opinions are in turn the distillate of writings of journalists and other leading opinion makers who were contemporaries of the various presidents, filtered through the ideological predispositions of the current batch of history writers.

This means that running for great president is a chancy business, since the admissions committee is small and self-conscious, somewhat shifty-eyed, and possibly even harder to please than, let us say, the wonderful folks who guard the lily-white portals of the Chevy Chase Club. Some presidents are smart enough to take out a little insurance. Surely that was one extremely good reason for John Kennedy to invite Arthur Schlesinger, Jr., to join his White House staff and to encourage him to keep notes. Schlesinger's father, also a distinguished historian, was after all the author of two well-publicized surveys of historians—in 1949 and 1962—that ranked presidents for overall greatness.

Lyndon Johnson and, evidently, Richard Nixon, pursued somewhat different strategies. Apparently neither found a court historian wholly to his liking—though after an unsatisfactory experience with Eric Goldman, perhaps Johnson found Doris Kearns more tractable and useful for somewhat similar purposes. Both recent presidents caused their administrations to engage in what might be called over-documentation of their official activities. Johnson hauled tons of stuff down to his museum in Texas where a staff composed "his" memoirs at leisure. One assumes the Nixon tapes, had they remained undiscovered, would have been employed to some such similar end.

In general, authorized ex-presidential memoirs are pretty awful to read, and nobody takes them seriously as history. At best they can be self-revelatory, and hence grist for the analyst's mill, but they are mostly stale, dull, self-serving documents. By common repute the best ex-presidential memoir ever written was that of Ulysses S. Grant. It was about his Civil War service, not his presidency, and so it is probably too much to expect that it would have saved Grant's presidency from the adverse judgment of "history."

We must conclude that writing memoirs may be a respectable way to fatten the exchequer of an ex-president, but that it is of negligible value in running for great president. Hiring, or charming, a court historian is a somewhat better investment, and especially if, by calculation or misfortune, the court historian's account appears after the death of the president in question. Reflective readers may find it slightly loony that presidents would want to control what people think of them after they have died, but the desire to leave an admiring posterity is surely not all that unusual among Americans. Moreover, among those Americans who land in the White House one can frequently discern an above-average desire to control the rest of the world, future generations, if possible, included.

What is it that historians like to see on the record when they make their ratings? It is impossible to speak with assurance for all future generations of historians. Fads and cross-currents make it difficult even to read the contemporary scene in a perfectly straightforward way. Nevertheless, over the near term, I think it is fair to say that the predominant sentiments of historians about presidents have been shaped by the experience of the New Deal, a longish episode in which presidential leadership was generally perceived to have saved the country not merely in the sense of restoring a modicum of prosperity to the economy, but more fundamentally rescuing the political system from profound malaise and instability.

The evidence that the New Deal actually did either of these things is, as a matter of fact, rather thin. But I shall not argue that attentiveness to evidence is a strong point of the gatekeepers of presidential greatness. They do, however, appear very much to admire presidents who adopt an activist, aggrandizing, constitutional posture toward presidential power. As the senior Schlesinger wrote: "Mediocre presidents believed in negative government, in self-subordination to the legislative power." My view is that this reflects a New Deal-tutored preference for a particular sort of political structure rather than a statement of constitutional principles about which there can be no two opinions.

William Howard Taft, later a notably activist chief justice, put the classic case for the passive presidency when he wrote:

> The true view of the executive function is, as I conceive it, that the president can exercise no power which cannot be fairly and reasonably traced to some specific grant of power or justly implied and included within such express grant as proper and necessary to its exercise. Such specific grant must be either in the federal Constitution or in an act of Congress passed in pursuance thereof. There is no undefined residuum of power which he can exercise because it seems to him to be in the public interest.

Poor Taft! That sort of argument got him low marks for presidential greatness, and especially since he evidently acted on his beliefs.

Says James David Barber, author of the recent study of *The Presidential Character*, ". . . he was from the start a genial, agreeable, friendly, compliant person, much in need of affection."

Whereas the senior Arthur Schlesinger's 1962 survey rated Taft an "average" sixteenth, between McKinley and Van Buren on the all-time hit parade, Theodore Roosevelt, Taft's friend and patron, comes in a "near great" seventh, just below Andrew Jackson on the list. Roosevelt's theory of the presidency undoubtedly helped him in the sweepstakes. He said:

> I declined to adopt the view that what was imperatively necessary for the nation could not be done by the president unless he could find some specific authorization to do it. My belief was that it was not only his right but his duty to do anything that the needs of the nation demanded unless such action was forbidden by the Constitution or by the laws. Under this interpretation of executive power I did and caused to be done many things not previously done by the president and the heads of the departments. I did not usurp power, but I did greatly broaden the use of executive power. In other words, I acted for the public welfare, I acted for the common well-being of all our people, whenever and in whatever manner was necessary, unless prevented by direct constitutional or legislative prohibition.

The beginnings of this conflict in constitutional interpretation and practice have been traced back to the founding of the Republic. In those early years, Leonard White found:

> The Federalists emphasized the necessity for power in government and for energy in the executive branch. The Republicans emphasized the liberties of the citizen and the primacy of representative assemblies. The latter accused their opponents of sympathy to monarchy and hostility to republican institutions. . . . Hamilton . . . insisted on the necessity for executive leadership of an otherwise drifting legislature; Jefferson thought the people's representatives would readily find their way if left alone to educate each other by free discussion and compromise. . . . By 1792 Jefferson thought the executive power had swallowed up the legislative branch; in 1798 Hamilton thought the legislative branch had so curtailed executive power that an able man could find no useful place in the government.

In the present era there is no real conflict at the theoretical level. The last sitting president even half-heartedly to argue against a self-aggrandizing presidency was Eisenhower. To be sure, a few voices—notably Eugene McCarthy's—could be heard proposing structural limitations on presidential powers in the dark days of Vietnam, but the resonance of his argument has faded quickly.

Even the remarkable shenanigans of the Nixon years seem only slightly to have diminished the enthusiasm of opinion leaders for strong

presidents. Theodore Sorensen has gone so far as to advance the com-
forting view that we have nothing to fear from a strong president because Nixon was not in fact a strong president. In the light of such
ingenuity one can only conclude that even today the mantle of presidential greatness is available only to those presidents who subscribe to
a constitutional theory affording the widest scope for presidential
action.

Does the historical record suggest any other helpful hints to the aspir-
ing presidential great? Indeed it does. Crises are good for presidential
reputations. Over the short run, as countless public-opinion surveys
have shown, a small crisis in foreign affairs followed by a small show of
presidential decisiveness is always good for a boost in the president's
ratings. These ratings, moreover, are evidently indifferent to the effi-
cacy of the presidential decision; triumph or fiasco, it makes little
short-run difference.

    Presidential greatness, however, is not decided over the short run.
Yet the things that mass publics like today are frequently attractive to
historians when painted on a larger canvas. Our three "greatest" pres-
idents were reputedly Washington, Lincoln, and Franklin Roosevelt.
The service of all three is intimately associated with three incidents in
American history when the entire polity was engaged in total war.

    Total war—that is, war engaging some major fraction of the gross
national product in its prosecution—creates vastly different conditions
of psychological mobilization than the nagging, running sores of limited
wars, which, in time, invariably become extremely unpopular. Lyndon
Johnson was one president who showed awareness of the irony implicit
in the popularity risks of restricting, as well as pursuing, a limited war.

    To those scrupulous souls who shrink from manufacturing a war
of total mobilization in the service of their future reputations, is there
anything left to be said? Surely lessons can be drawn equally from our
least successful as well as our most successful presidents. Harding,
Grant, and, one surmises, Nixon, lurk somewhere near the bottom of
the heap. The smell of very large-scale scandal (not the small potatoes
of the Truman era) attaches to the administration of each.

    Assuming, for the sake of argument, that presidents want to run
an administration untainted by scandal, can they do it? Considering the
scale of operations of the United States government, the general absence of corruption in the conduct of its business is an admirable
achievement. One doubts that if some illegal and greedy scheme were
discovered somewhere in the vast labyrinth of the executive bureaucracies, the president would be held strictly to account. One doubts it
unless one of three conditions obtains: the president, once apprised of

the scandal, failed to act promptly to set things right, or, second, trusted friends and close associates of the president were involved, or, worse yet, the president himself were involved.

Only Richard Nixon, it will be observed, with his well-known penchant for presidential firsts, hits the jackpot on this list of no-no's. Neither Harding nor Grant escaped blame for the criminal acts of others close to them, but both are commonly held to have been themselves free of wrongdoing.

A final arena in which presidents achieve greatness is in the legislative record. Normally, what is required is a flurry of action, like FDR's hundred days, or Woodrow Wilson's first term. A kindly fate can sweep a new president into office along with a heavy congressional majority of his own party. With a little more luck there can be a feeling abroad in the land that something must be done. Whereupon, for a little while at least, the president and Congress together do something. Great strides in the enactment of public policy are commonly made in this fashion. And it is now settled custom that the president gets the long-run credit.

Thus many of the factors that go into presidential greatness appear to boil down to being in the right place at the right time. Much of the rest consists of having others put the right construction on ambiguous acts. Understandably, quite a lot of White House effort consequently goes into cultivating favorable notice for the incumbent. And here, at this point, a worm begins to emerge from the apple. The scenery, cosmetics, and sound effects that go into good public relations, unless strongly resisted, can begin to overwhelm more substantive concerns. The aspiration to presidential greatness, which under ideal circumstances can provide an incentive for good presidential behavior, under less than ideal circumstances leads to a great variety of difficulties. For fear of being found out and downgraded, there is the temptation to deny failure, to refuse to readjust course when a program or a proposal doesn't work out. There is the temptation to hoard credit rather than share it with the agencies that actually do the work and produce the results. There is the temptation to export responsibility away from the White House for the honest shortfalls of programs, thus transmitting to the government at large an expectation that loyalty upward will be rewarded with disloyalty down. There is the temptation to offer false hopes and to proclaim spurious accomplishments to the public at large.

As [British writer] Henry Fairlie and others point out, a presidency that inflates expectations can rarely deliver. Worse yet, such a presidency gives up a precious opportunity to perform essential tasks of civic education, to help ordinary people see both the limitations and the possibilities of democratic government. George Reedy [former press secretary of President Lyndon Johnson] and others have observed that a presidency made of overblown rhetoric and excessive pretension can lose touch with the realities of politics, can waste its resources on trivialities, can fail, consequently, to grasp opportunities to govern well.

This, such as it is, is the case against the pursuit of presidential greatness. It is a case based upon a hope that there can be something approximating a restoration of democratic manners in the presidency. There are, however, good reasons to suppose that such a restoration will be hard to accomplish.

Part of the problem is structural. The complex demands of modern governmental decision making require that presidents receive plenty of help. They need advice, information, criticism, feedback. They also need people to take care of the endless round of chores that fall to a president's lot: press secretaries, congressional liaison, managers of paper work and the traffic of visitors. Presidents also need to be able to trust the help they are getting, to be able to feel that what is being said and done in their behalf does genuinely place presidential interests first. From these requirements comes the need for an entourage of people whose careers in the limelight are solely the product of presidential favor. And from this entourage invariably comes what I suppose could be called the First Circle of presidential Moonies.

These are the people who "sleep a little better at night," as Jack Valenti so memorably said, because the charisma of their chief powers the machinery of government. During the day, we can be sure, they wear sunglasses to keep from being dazzled by "that special grace" (as members of John Kennedy's entourage frequently put it). . . .

The needs of White House staff to bask in reflected glory, plus risk-aversion in the face of the work habits of the mass media, are a potent combination tending to sustain a president's interest in president worship. Moreover, the mystique of the presidency can be useful politically, vesting the visit in the rose garden, the invitation to breakfast, even a beseeching telephone call to Capitol Hill, with an added value that can spell the difference between political victory and defeat. And of course a president may simply grow fond of being coddled.

Added to these are the powerful factors in the world and in the American political system that have brought the president to the forefront: the increased importance of foreign affairs in the life of the nation, an area in which the president has no serious constitutional rival; the creation and proliferation of federal bureaucracies, all of them subject to presidential influence and supervision; the growth of the mass media with their focus upon the personalities at the center of our national politics, and the decline of political parties as a countervailing force. No wonder the entire political system seems president-preoccupied.

Against this formidable array of forces a plea for modesty of presidential aims, for prudence and moderation in the choice of instruments, for a scaling-down of promises and claims of achievement, seems unlikely to attract widespread agreement, least of all from presidents and their entourages bent on making their mark on history.

QUESTIONS FOR DISCUSSION

1. Are strong presidents less vulnerable to interest-group pressures than Congress?
2. How can we be assured that strong presidents will act the way Theodore Sorensen says they will?
3. If you accept Polsby's criticism of the criteria used to evaluate great presidents, how would you rank past American presidents?
4. Does Congress need additional legal power to prevent a president from becoming too strong?
5. Is there any evidence about Jimmy Carter's political behavior in office that reveals his approach to "presidential greatness?"

SUGGESTED READINGS

Bailey, Thomas A. *Presidential Greatness*. New York: Appleton-Century-Crofts, 1966.

Burns, James M. *Presidential Government*. Boston: Houghton Mifflin, 1973.

Cronin, Thomas E., and Rexford G. Tugwell. *The Presidency Reappraised*, 2nd ed. New York: Praeger, 1977.

Dunn, Charles W., ed. *The Future of the American Presidency*. Morristown, N.J.: General Learning Press, 1975.

Fairlie, Henry. *The Kennedy Promise: The Politics of Expectation*. New York: Doubleday, 1973.

Goldsmith, William. *The Growth of Presidential Power*. 3 vols. New York: Bowker, 1974.

Mansfield, Harvey, ed. *Congress Against the President*. New York: Praeger, 1975.

Mueller, John E. *War, Presidents and Public Opinion*. New York: John Wiley & Sons, 1973.

Schlesinger, Arthur M., Jr. *The Imperial Presidency*. New York: Popular Library, 1973.

Weaver, Paul H. "Liberals and the Presidency." *Commentary*, October 1975, pp. 48–53.

Was the Nixon Presidency an Aberration?

YES

PETER JENKINS
Portrait of a Presidency*

"How could it have happened? Who is to blame?" Richard Nixon asked these questions rhetorically on 30 April 1973 when, flanked by the bust of Abraham Lincoln and the American flag, he addressed the people for the first time on the subject of Watergate. "I want to talk to you tonight from my heart on a subject of deep concern to every American," he began. He had been appalled to hear of the Watergate break-in on 17 June 1972; he had ordered a full investigation and had been assured repeatedly by men in whom he had faith that no members of his Administration were involved; not until 21 March 1973 had he had reason to doubt these assurances, and as a result of information given to him on that day he had assumed responsibility personally for conducting intensive new inquiries; he was determined to get to the bottom of the matter and to bring out the truth, no matter who was involved. He accepted responsibility but not blame; it would be cowardly to blame his subordinates he said, thereby imputing that they were to blame. And with that he declared: "I must now turn my attention once again to the larger duties of this office."

A year later to the day the President released a 1,200-page transcript, edited in the White House, of tape-recorded meetings and telephone conversations covering chiefly the six weeks preceding that first public defence of himself on television. Whether or not they are taken to establish his guilt of criminal offences, specifically obstructions of

* From Peter Jenkins, "Portrait of a Presidency," *New Statesman*, May 17, 1974, pp. 688–692. Reprinted from the *New Statesman*, London, by permission. © The Statesman & Nation Publishing Company Ltd., 1974.

justice, the transcripts utterly condemn his presidency. They present an intimate portrait of a man morally unfit to occupy his high office. They question the previous judgment of most critics and admirers alike that Richard Nixon, whatever his deficiencies, is a man of quick mind and firm grasp, a consummate politician. The questions he asked himself about Watergate—"How could it have happened? Who is to blame?"—must now be asked about his presidency. How did such a man come to occupy the White House? . . .

"OPERATION CANDOR"

. . . We are obliged to consider seriously, the more so in the light of the new evidence of the tapes, whether the root explanation is that the White House in 1968 became occupied by a psychopath, possibly a schizophrenic. Several of the transcripts reveal "P" [the President] playing twin roles, one moment Richard Nixon (Mr. Hyde) and another the President of the United States (Dr. Jekyll). According to reports from Washington, the tapes themselves reveal the contrast of tone and voice in which he acts out this split personality. Washington has long been rife with rumor concerning the President's mental health, some of it well-authenticated from within the Administration. Certainly his observable behavior has often, to say the least, been strange, although paranoia and manic-depression, too easily mistaken for schizophrenia (a rare complaint), are conditions frequently to be found in the wielders of great power.*

In the streets of Paris after Pompidou's funeral, the President appeared seriously disturbed—"This is a great day for France." He revealed a morbid concern for his health in a speech in the Rose Garden to members of the White House staff last summer on his discharge from the hospital where he was treated for what was officially diagnosed as viral-pneumonia. He pledged himself to disobey the advice of his doctors to ease up a bit.

> I just want you to know what my answer to them was and what my answer to you is. No one in this great office at this time in the world's history can slow down. This office requires a president who will work right up to the hilt all the time. That is what I have been doing. That is what I am going to continue to do. . . . I know many will say "But then you will risk your health." Well, the health of the man is not nearly as important as the health of the nation and the health of the world.

* See Hugh L'Etang's *The Pathology of Leadership*, Heinemann, 1969, on Churchill's cyclothymia, pp. 156-7; he called his severe depressions 'Black Dog'.

There was the famous incident at the height of the Cambodia crisis when he escaped from the White House at night and is reported to have addressed his valet, Manolo Sanches, from the podium of the deserted House of Representatives. A White House aide at that time tells of how he ranted and raged, ordering the invasion of Cambodia as a retribution against the Congress for turning down his latest nomination to the Supreme Court. For me the most striking insight into the President's mentality came last year during his short-lived and inevitably doomed "Operation Candor." In Memphis, Tennessee, he met behind closed doors with Republican governors who were desperate for reassurance that it was his intention to have out the truth. "Mr. President, are there any more bombshells in the wings?" he was asked. He replied that there was none within his knowledge, and this assurance was reported at a press conference.

The next day, back in Washington, Judge [John] Sirica was informed that eighteen minutes of a crucial tape recording was mysteriously obliterated by an electronic buzz. Later testimony in the court allowed no doubt that the President was aware of this, and aware that it would have to be revealed to the court, when he gave the governors the assurance they asked in Memphis. This was not the behavior of a politician. A politician, surely, would have said to them: "I know this is going to look bad for me, but I want you to know about it now and to know that it was an accident—we don't even know for sure how it happened—and that no one in the White House deliberately erased that tape." A politician would have tried to defuse the bombshell in the wings. Nixon instead behaved like a child denying that a vase has been broken while the pieces are lying on the floor in the next room, bound to be discovered. Either he had become utterly reckless, no longer concerned with the remaining shreds of his credibility, or unable to connect with reality. He was beyond the reach of conventional political analysis.

How are we to explain the tapes, not their contents but their very existence? They are the central mystery of the man and his presidency. Richard Nixon will go down as the first president of the United States, indeed so far as we know the first leader in the history of the world, to have bugged himself. It seemed highly probable that he would in the end be hanged by his own tapes from that truly sensational moment on 16 July last year when Alexander Butterfield, an obscure former White House administrator, was brought forward as a surprise witness before the Ervin committee to reveal the existence of listening devices in the White House. The system, which he said was highly sensitive and would pick up any sounds of conversation in the President's offices, including the lowest tones, was automatically activated by voice and the president retained no manual control over its operation.* Here was an astonishing case of man abdicating sovereignty to machine. . . .

Other presidents had made use of tape recordings but none so far as we know had so violated their own privacy. Asked by an interviewer about the meaning for him of Quakerism, the religion in which he was brought up, Nixon first mentioned "the stress on privacy." That Nixon may have wanted to get the goods on his colleagues, friend and foe alike ("Nobody is a friend of ours. Let's face it," he said to John Dean) does not explain why by his choice of system he should entrap himself. All he needed was a button under his desk, as LBJ had. Nor does the official explanation as given by Butterfield to the Ervin Committee wash. ("There was no doubt in my mind they were installed to record things for posterity, for the Nixon library. The President was very conscious of that kind of thing.") Were the tapes to be deposited in the Nixon library with their expletives undeleted? Was posterity to be shown a Nixon totally different from the image so assiduously projected to the public in his life time?

GUARDED WITH FAMILY

The contemporary Nixon insists on coats and ties being worn in the presence of the President. "I hope to restore respect to the presidency at all levels of my conduct," he told an interviewer. "I believe in keeping my own counsel," he told another, Stewart Alsop. "It's something like wearing clothing—if you let down your hair you feel too naked. I remember when I'd just started law practice, I had a divorce case to handle and this good-looking girl, beautiful really, began talking to me about her intimate marriage problems." Alsop: "And you were embarrassed?" Nixon: "Embarrassed? I turned fifteen colors of the rainbow. I suppose I came from a family not too modern, really." According to Gary Wills, whose *Nixon Agonistes* (Signet 1970) is outstandingly the best book on the subject, "Nixon, so ill at ease among strangers, remains guarded with intimates, with his very family— hiding grievances from his brother under strict decorum, writing his mother in tones of a geriatric manual." Was posterity then to be given the real Nixon, the unexpurgated version?

Whatever his intentions concerning the tapes, his assumption presumably was that they would remain firmly within his control, preferably and probably their existence even unknown. Yet this was risky. Haldeman knew; Haldeman's man [Larry] Higby knew, and he was no

* Although he retained no mechanical control over the system, he could, of course, at any time order its suspension. We now have reason to believe he sometimes did. . . .

more than an office boy; Butterfield knew; the Secret Service knew. The risk became greater as the Watergate scandal began to break open yet the reels continued to turn. . . .

The existence of the tapes, the way in which they were made, poses an unanswered question concerning the President's mentality, indeed his rationality. Their contents, even as edited for publication by the White House, censored and quite possibly doctored, fly in the face of the received view of the President's political abilities. Not only do they reveal a man devoid of moral sense but also one severely lacking in common sense. Columnists Rowland Evans and Robert Novak, while underlining his limitations, wrote in their book, *Nixon in the White House* (Random House 1971) that "his steel-trap mind could comprehend difficult concepts and memorize great quantities of facts." The transcripts provide no evidence of such capacity, rather the reverse: the President rambles indecisively; he has difficulty marshalling the facts; he reveals elementary ignorance of the American legal system, all the more remarkable in a professional lawyer.

We feel ourselves in the presence of a thoroughly second-rate mind, a crude and vulgar intelligence, a man with no command of language, a man wholly concerned with appearance rather than substance—with "how it will play," with what he calls "PR" [public relations]. From this authentic encounter with the private Nixon it is hard any longer to imagine the public Nixon, or the official Nixon, the foreign policy president with his encyclopedic knowledge and expert's grasp of foreign affairs, the ideological conservative, the student of the scholar-president Woodrow Wilson. Yet that same Nixon, until Watergate, had won wide respect if not as a man or for his purposes at least for his abilities. . . . Beleaguered American liberals especially were mesmerized by him. Economist Robert Lekachman could write: "President Nixon has constructed the most coherent conservative program in recent memory," and "the President's politics are as astute as his code message to the majority is clear." Michael Harrington, the socialist, was one of many who regarded Nixon not as "some kind of moral monster" but as a "conservative ideologue." But what if, after all, he is a psychopath?

THE BORN LOSER

His entire presidency, the rise and fall of Richard Nixon, and Watergate too, its genesis and its meaning, begin to focus if we examine him not as a success but as a failure. He had failed, although narrowly, in his bid for the presidency in 1960; he had failed, humiliatingly, in his run for the governorship of California in 1962; and in 1968 when a donkey could have beaten a Democrat, Richard Nixon, born a loser, nearly managed to snatch defeat from the jaws of victory. It should have been impossible that year to have come near to losing. Nixon had going for him Johnson's withdrawal, Rockefeller's haverings, Bobby Kennedy's assassination, Humphrey's catastrophe at the Chicago convention. . . . The Democrats were in disarray, liberals on the run, old ideologies and old alignments were crumbling: a great vacuum opened up in American politics and there was Richard Nixon, the only available body to fill it.

MEN WITHOUT IDEOLOGY

He never for a moment forgot during his first term that he was the "43-percent president." He lacked legitimacy, felt himself to be a usurper in Washington, that enemy city still in the hands of "HODs" (held-over Democrats). His entire first term was a campaign for re-election, and not even for reelection, as he seemed to see it, but for election, for a victory that he could count according to his own strange standard, by which anything short of total victory is defeat. It is not easy to discern in his first term any other purpose. His 1968 campaign was without theme, lacking in serious policy content. It was run by men without ideology. There was not even a "plan" to end the war, although he claimed there was. His strategy for winning rested on the assumption that the Democrats would lose. His early successful campaigns in California, all of them unscrupulous and dirty, had been conducted according to the principle that negative attacks on the incumbent are what win elections. He attributed his defeat in 1960 to the fact that he was on the inside, on the receiving end of Kennedy's oppositional assault. In 1968 he was back where he belonged and liked to be—on the negative side of the question.

When the campaign found a slogan it was by accident. He spotted a child in the crowd with a placard which said "Bring Us Together." He had this made the theme for his victory statement but it was mere rhetoric and had no philosophical foundations in the Administration's policy intentions. John Mitchell early on told reporters: "Watch what we do instead of what we say," and it was good advice because the Administration in its perennial search for some conceptual framework for itself said things which bore little relation to its actions or intentions. The only strand of coherence was in its determination to retain power. This meant, first and foremost, holding together the conservative forces which had produced the hairsbreadth victory in 1968. The strategy for 1972, put simply, was 1968 plus Wallace. That made Mitchell's "Southern strategy" the keystone throughout. Everything else was subordinate, appearance, "PR."

Changes in policy were simply new "game plans." Policy towards Vietnam was conducted on the assumption that anything which looked like a defeat would alienate the 1968 constituency. "Vietnamisation," which turned out to be a popular policy, was at first conducted covertly for fear that it would alienate the Right. In 1970, announcing the Cambodian invasion, Nixon declared: "I would rather be a one-term president than a two-term president at the cost of seeing America become a second-rate power and see this nation accept the first defeat in its proud 190-year history." But in 1971, following the disastrous mid-term campaign, at the time of the Laotian operation and with things going badly all round, it was decided that Nixon should present himself in 1972 as the peace candidate.

It was the same story on the home front. Patrick Moynihan interested him in Disraeli, so for a time "reform" became the catchword of the Administration. But the programs for reform lacked coherence. Moynihan's plan for guaranteed family incomes to replace the welfare mess conflicted with the Southern strategy so a work requirement was added in and the plan eventually collapsed under the weight of its own contradictions, abandoned in the end by a president who had never been committed to it except as a "game plan." In 1971, with the economy in trouble, the President was widely supposed to have undergone a "Keynesian conversion." It is most unlikely that he did, simply that he saw the prospect looming of being the first president since Hoover to seek and fail to achieve a second term. "My strong point, if I have a strong point," Nixon told an interviewer, "is performance. I always produce more than I promise." But the performance of his Administration was mostly poor for all its military staff structures and systems-analysis jargon. It was not until 1972, with the visits to Peking and Moscow, that anything began to go right for the Nixon Administration.

The fear, the real fear, of losing in 1972 goes a long way towards explaining Watergate, by which we mean not simply the break-in at the Democratic National Committee headquarters but all the other abuses of power, bribery, corruption, sabotage and espionage which went on. Because by the time of the actual Watergate break-in in June 1972 Nixon had his reelection virtually sewn up, and because with McGovern for an opponent he won by a landslide of the votes cast, it is easily forgotten just how vulnerable he was—or felt—at the early formative stages of the affair. In mid-1971, a White House aide told Haynes Johnson of *The Washington Post*: "The President was walking into a one-term presidency on almost every issue." The opinion polls showed Ed Muskie, the hero of the mid-term campaign, running ahead of Nixon, with Kennedy and Humphrey running him neck and neck. By May, Muskie was beating Nixon 48 percent to 39 percent! . . .

THE POWER MACHINE

The narrow win in 1968, the grave uncertainty concerning 1972, had another consequence, Nixon never felt that he possessed adequate power, or adequate power that he could use openly. His conversation with Dean on 15 September 1972, by which time his reelection was certain, is revealing:

P: We are all in it together. This is a war. We take a few shots and it will be over. We will give them a few shots and it will be over. Don't worry. I wouldn't want to be on the other side right now. Would you?

D [Dean]: Along that line, one of the things I've tried to do, I have begun to keep notes on a lot of people who are emerging as less than our friends because this will be over some day and we shouldn't forget the way some of them have treated us.

P: I want the most comprehensive notes on all of those who tried to do us in. They didn't have to do it. If we had a very close election and they were playing the other side, I would understand this. No— they were doing this quite deliberately and they are asking for it and they are going to get it. We have not used the power in this first four years as you know. We have never used it. We have not used the Bureau [FBI] and we have not used the Justice Department, but things are going to change now. And they are either going to do it right or go.

There is no suggestion here that self-restraint had held them back. The suggestion rather is that there were things they didn't dare do, or things they couldn't do through insufficient control of the power machine. For example, J. Edgar Hoover had vetoed a plan approved by the President in July 1970 which would have authorized breaking and entering and other illegal acts by the intelligence-gathering and law-enforcement agencies. In consequence a covert parallel apparatus began to be constructed in the White House—in December of 1970 an Intelligence Evaluation Committee to collect domestic intelligence (about which little is still known) and in June 1971 the Plumbers Unit, which we may assume was not idle between the [Daniel] Ellsberg burglary in September of that year and the Watergate operations in the early summer of 1972. And we should remember that the one decisive act of his second administration before it became crippled by Watergate was the brutal terror bombing of the North Vietnam cities in December 1972.

The decision-making structure of the Nixon Administration reflected the same concern with the lack of effective power. The White House staff grew from 250 to 510. Foreign policy was conducted from the basement of the White House and Henry Kissinger's National Security Council apparatus effectively replaced the State Department. The State Department was "bureaucracy," a bad word in the vocabulary of Nixonism. The budget was similarly drawn into the White House. In order to narrow the basis of decision making (and also to spare the President human contact, which he found so uncongenial) overlordships were created in each major area of government. The wires led back to the White House, where the President could deal with one man per subject. Haldeman and Erlichman exercised a power far greater than any responsible cabinet officer with the exception of Mitchell, and Connally during his occupancy of the Treasury.

CONCENTRATED POWER

The cabinet fell into disuse. In 1972 it met only eleven times. In that year there were only five bipartisan meetings with the congressional leadership, only eleven with the Republican leadership. There was nothing new in presidential impoundment of funds voted by Congress but the Nixon Administration's use of that power was novel and ominous. For impoundment was used to remove from the Congress the power of the purse, as a means of denying the Congress its power to determine national priorities and refusing to implement policies which the Congress had legislated. It was the same story with the party. The election campaign was run from the White House through the front organization which came to be known as CREEP (the Committee to Reelect the President). In 1972 Nixon did not run as a Republican candidate but simply as Richard Nixon. As in the mid-term elections, reactionary Democrats in the South were helped in their campaign against Republican candidates; other Republicans received precious little help from the President and none of the vast sums of money accumulated at CREEP.

Within the White House, too, power was concentrated in fewer and fewer hands. A former White House aide Richard Whalen, one who got out in good time, has described how Haldeman and Erlichman "regarded governing as little more than an extension of campaigning. Campaign politics, regardless of party and candidate, is inherently conspiratorial. Because the only purpose and binding force of the enterprise is victory, almost any means towards that all-important end can be justified with a modest amount of rationalization." . . .

The men around Nixon were men without constituency, without commitment; not one of them had ever run for sheriff. They were men from advertising agencies, real-estate men, salesmen and image-manipulators, in Whalen's words, "buttoned-down scurrying aides" who "had the mission of protecting the President from disorder. . . ." Haldeman, who had seen Nixon break down in his 1962 California campaign, had the special task of preventing this from happening again. Haldeman and Erlichman controlled the flow of information to him, were intermediaries to his decisions and orders. Erlichman once told a cabinet officer that the President had no philosophy, only did what was feasible and tactically rewarding. "There is no ideology, no central commitment, no fixed body of thought," said another White House aide proudly. Whalen quotes another as saying, "Haldeman and Erlichman shield the President by monopolizing him. One of them is present at every meeting—he sees no one alone. He has made himself their captive. Sometimes the 'Germans' don't carry out Nixon's orders, or they let papers sit on their desks for a while because they are certain he won't find out. How *can* he find out? All the channels flow back to Haldeman." When the President on 30 April 1972, the night of their resignation, described Haldeman and Erlichman as "two of the finest public servants it has been my privilege to know" he meant it. The transcripts show that he could hardly contemplate life without them.

SPLIT PERSONALITY

Nixon was not corrupted by power, he corrupted power. A powerful presidency doesn't have to produce a crook any more than a strong man has to be a thug. Richard Nixon was not inevitable. Watergate was not decreed by the Vietnam war nor the civil war at home: Hubert Humphrey could have been elected president in 1968 and very nearly was. Nixon very nearly won in 1960, probably did if the votes had been counted honestly in Chicago, and then there was no war, no social disorders; but he would still have been Nixon. McCarthyism rose and fell under Truman, militarism and obsessive concern with national security grew under Eisenhower; but there were no Watergates.

Nixon's presidency is the projection of his personality, his probably split personality. A charlatan and opportunist, lacking any firm commitment or ideological belief, he made do with the traditional, fundamentalist values of his middle American background which he expounded in public. The force of his destructive personality is evil but happily his exercise of power has been inept and lacking in direction, mistaking appearance for substance, concerned more with petty vendetta than with wide-scale repression. As Haldemen lamented: "We are so [adjective deleted] square that we got caught at everything." A PR man does not have the makings of an effective tyrant. He is a thoroughly nasty piece of work who brought disgrace upon his exalted office and his country and who killed a lot of people in Asia. Watergate was entirely characteristic of his presidency—dishonest, disgraceful, inept. "How could it have happened? Who is to blame?" It happened because the Americans elected Richard M. Nixon to be president of the United States, an unfortunate choice. But how were they to know they were electing a psychopath? "Who is to blame?" Nixon is to blame—Nixon's the one.

Was the Nixon Presidency an Aberration?

NO

NICK THIMMESCH
*The Abuse of Richard Nixon**

Back in those miserable months of 1973 and 1974, many defenders of President Nixon thought he was being unfairly vilified by the press and by Congress. These apologists did not excuse Nixon's abuses of presidential power, but they thought that his predecessors had likewise abused the power of their office, and that it was unfair to single out Nixon for condemnation. Nor did they try to justify the Watergate cover-up, but they thought it unfair that only Nixon's Administration was so closely scrutinized. Who knows whether previous presidents would have also tried to obstruct justice, if they had been subject to such a blistering investigation?

This argument that Nixon's Administration was no different than

---

* From Nick Thimmesch, "The Abuse of Richard Nixon," *The Alternative,* April 1976, pp. 5–8. Copyright 1977 *The Alternative: An American Spectator,* Bloomington, Indiana 47401. Reprinted by permission.

his predecessors' became thinner and thinner as his case weakened and his misrepresentations swelled. By the time on August 9, 1974, when the helicopter took him away, tears and all, to exile in San Clemente, almost everyone was convinced of his singular perfidy—so that even now the pundits rave hysterically whenever his name is mentioned.

In the meantime, however, the [Senator] Church committee investigation of intelligence activities has revealed a wealth of material about previous administrations which may put Nixon's in some perspective. We learn, for example, that President Franklin D. Roosevelt ordered FBI [Federal Bureau of Investigation] Director J. Edgar Hoover to snoop on hundreds of Americans who had sent FDR telegrams "all more or less in opposition to national defense" or that approved Charles Lindbergh's criticism of Roosevelt. A few years later, Hoover was sending "personal and confidential" letters to President Truman which contained tidbits of political intelligence—reports of Communist influence in a senator's speech, advance word that a scandal was brewing which would be "very embarrassing to the Democratic administration," and confidential reports on which publications were going to break stories exposing organized crime and corrupt politicians. The Eisenhower Administration also willingly received confidential advisories from the FBI on the role of Communists in the civil rights movement and derogatory raw files on individuals charging the federal government with racial discrimination.

We learn that Presidents Kennedy and Johnson did not halt these questionable practices by the FBI, and actually were happy to make use of them. Kennedy had the FBI pursue steel company executives and newsmen alike during the steel crisis of 1962. Attorney General Robert F. Kennedy, despite repeated denials, had all manner of foes and suspects, including newsmen, wiretapped. He is also finally revealed to be responsible for the wiretapping and bugging of Martin Luther King, Jr. And no other president leaned on the FBI to investigate citizens suspected of being his "enemies" as Lyndon Johnson did. Members of Senator Barry Goldwater's staff, a witness in the Bobby Baker case, government bureaucrats, people attending the 1964 Democratic convention, Mrs. Anna Chennault, Spiro Agnew, Vietnam war protesters—all fell under federal surveillance because of Johnson's feelings of fear and vengeance.

None of these presidents ever faced the remotest possibility of impeachment. Most of them were secure with majorities of their own party in Congress, and they all presided in times when Washington was not in the mood to disembowel itself—as was the case during Nixon's Administration. These presidents were also smart enough not to install constant tape-recording systems in the Oval Office, nor, above all, to squander their political power ineptly. If Richard Nixon is guilty of anything at all, it is that he threw away the overwhelming support given him by the American people in 1972.

Now that we know some more about previous administrations, however, wouldn't it be interesting to measure them by the charges drawn up by the House Judiciary Committee against President Nixon? The charges in Article I about obstruction of justice, and in Article III about contempt of Congress, refer mainly to the Watergate break-in and cover-up, and are therefore unique to the Nixon Administration. But what about the charges in Article II dealing with the abuse of presidential power?

Consider Section 1, for example, wherein it was charged that Nixon personally and through his subordinates endeavored "to obtain from the Internal Revenue Service in violation of the constitutional rights of citizens confidential information contained in income tax returns . . ." and to cause tax audits and investigations "in a discriminatory manner."

It was charged that: (1) [presidential aide] H. R. (Bob) Haldeman, invoking the President's authority, arranged to get from the IRS [Internal Revenue Service] the report of its investigation of Governor George Wallace and his brother, Gerald. Adverse material from that report was leaked to columnist Jack Anderson. (2) [Presidential aide] John Ehrlichman secured from the IRS the tax returns of Lawrence O'Brien, Democratic national chairman. While the returns showed large amounts of income, Ehrlichman's attempt to link this income with Howard Hughes apparently failed. (3) [White House Counsel] John Dean asked the IRS to develop information on some 575 members of Senator George McGovern's campaign staff. But IRS Director Johnnie Walters refused to comply with the Dean request, and the matter was dropped.

Now, nasty as all this business is, it is hardly new in Washington, as Clark Mollenhoff, the journalist who became Nixon's ombudsman, can well testify. Presidents have alternately used the IRS to "get" political enemies, as well as to do favors for friends. As Mollenhoff points out in *Game Plan for Disaster*, there is "no way in which access to tax returns can be used to harass an honest man, but an unscrupulous taxing agency can grant favored treatment" to political friends when protected by IRS secrecy. And it is clear that the transgressions of the Nixon Administration on this score were small compared with those of previous administrations.

The Truman Administration was rife with IRS scandals. In 1952, 174 IRS officials were fired, and nearly all were subject to criminal charges. A former IRS Commissioner, Joseph D. Nunan, Jr., was indicted and convicted. Assistant Commissioner Daniel L. Bolich was indicted on personal tax fraud, and indicted again as a key figure in the tax-fix ring run by Henry Grunewald in Washington. President Truman's appointments secretary, Matthew Connelly, was convicted with T. Lamar Caudle on charges of defrauding the government by accepting oil royalties in return for helping a St. Louis man escape prosecution on tax fraud.

Republican administrations made sure that prominent Democrats who let their taxes slip got plenty of heat from the IRS. When the Democrats were in, they did the same to name-Republicans. For example, Iowa's Governor William Beardsley was indicted and convicted on an income tax charge after a prominent Iowa Democrat urged the action on the Democratic administration of Harry Truman.

When Robert F. Kennedy was attorney general, he had the IRS send income tax materials and returns on many labor racketeers, and some of this information was leaked to the press. President Johnson secured the returns of countless individuals, and often sent copies of those returns to his crony, Abe Fortas, or to the Fortas law firm, for perusal. So by comparison, Nixon was hardly in the same league with his predecessors.

Or consider the second general charge in Article II—that President Nixon had misused the FBI, the Secret Service, and "other executive personnel" by unconstitutionally directing them to use wiretapping and other forms of surveillance on citizens "for purposes unrelated to national security, the enforcement of laws, or any other lawful function of his office."

As evidence for this charge, it was stated, first, that between 1969 and 1971 Nixon, with Henry Kissinger attending to the details, had seventeen persons wiretapped, including journalists and White House staffers, ostensibly to determine who was leaking information to the press about national security matters. The taps were regarded as legal at the time, were authorized by Attorney General John Mitchell, and put into place under the direction of FBI Director Hoover, with reports on the tapped conversations going to Kissinger. Critics claim that Nixon and Kissinger instituted the taps to check the loyalty of staffers, and that there was no substantive need for them.

Second, it was stated that Tom Charles Huston, acting on presidential order, drafted a plan of interagency surveillance, surreptitious entries, and mail covers, and got tentative approval from Nixon. But Mitchell and Hoover opposed this decision, and Nixon withdrew his approval five days later.

Finally, it was stated that Nixon allowed the now infamous "Plumbers" unit to be established. Though a federal judge declared that Nixon had no prior knowledge of the Plumbers' burglary of the office of Daniel Ellsberg's psychiatrist, the burglary was authorized by members of the president's staff.

Now if wiretapping, creating a short-lived "Huston Plan" [a comprehensive plan by the Nixon Administration to spy on American citizens], and breaking into a private citizen's office are considered impeachable offenses, what do we know about any similar activity taking place in previous administrations?

According to information developed by the Church committee, Attorney General Robert F. Kennedy authorized wiretaps in 1962 on *New York Times* reporter Hanson Baldwin and his secretary, which lasted about one month. FBI records showed that Kennedy authorized wiretaps on a reporter for *Newsweek* magazine in 1961 as part of an investigation of a leak of classified information. Still other FBI materials show that Kennedy authorized wiretaps on at least six other American citizens, including three officials from his own executive branch, a Congressional staff member, and two registered lobbying agents for foreign interests.

All these Kennedy taps were justified as in the interest of "national security." Why Baldwin, his secretary, and the *Newsweek* reporter were wiretapped was never explained. But the Kennedys loved to punish and reward the press, and Baldwin and the *Newsweek* reporter were strong critics of the man John F. Kennedy named as his Secretary of Defense, Robert S. McNamara. As of this writing, the Senate Intelligence Committee has not determined the true intent of the other six taps. It has been suggested, however, that their purpose was to influence Representative Harold Cooley (D. N.C.), then chairman of the House Agriculture Committee, to come round to the Kennedys' wishes on a pending sugar bill.

Another way the Kennedys abused power was in their attempts to get even with people who had crossed them. For example, when Victor Lasky's unflattering portrait, *JFK: The Man and the Myth,* rose to number one on the best-seller list, Lasky found himself under investigation by the Justice Department. Though Robert Kennedy denied that he authorized any probing of Lasky, he admitted, after insistent questioning by the late Senator Kenneth Keating, that an "overzealous" official had undertaken such an investigation without Kennedy's approval. Lasky maintains that he was actually "followed" during this period, and thought it somewhat humorous that the "overzealous" official was a former Senate committee investigator who specialized in wiretapping. This official attempted to learn whether Lasky was connected with subversive activities. Subsequently, Lasky was charged by several Democratic state chairmen as being an ex-Communist, and

National Chairman John Bailey described him as a "Birchite," though neither description fits. Thus, the executive wing of government, under the Kennedys, used its power in an attempt to defame one of its critics (a felony in itself, according to 18 U.S. Code 1503).

Kennedy rough stuff often came down on the press as well. California Republican Congressman Bob Wilson, in a speech in the House, described how a publisher was wined and dined at the White House and then sent to see Attorney General Kennedy at the Justice Department. There followed a discussion of a possible antitrust violation involving the publisher's paper. Soon, the publisher issued an order that columnists and newsmen on the paper were to let up in their criticism of the New Frontier.

There was no more flagrant abuse of power in the Kennedy Administration, however, than the establishment of a "Get [Teamster's Union leader Jimmy] Hoffa Squad" which Robert Kennedy built into the Justice Department with the full knowledge of his brother, the President.

On an organizational chart at Justice, the labor and racketeering unit is a subdivision of the Organized Crime Section of the Criminal Division, and that's where the Hoffa investigation belonged. But Robert Kennedy's hatred of Jimmy Hoffa was obsessive, and in his Justice Department, Hoffa belonged to him. Walter Sheridan, the former FBI man who showed unblinking loyalty to Kennedy, headed the special squad out to get Hoffa. This unit was autonomous, arrogant, ruthless, powerful, never lacking for funds, and probably illegal. Sheridan ordered all manner of federal manpower into action, including FBI men and a team of twenty lawyers. It was the power and money of the federal government brought to force against a single citizen, though admittedly a seamy one.

As Charles Shaffer, an eager member of the squad, said: "Some people say Kennedy was out to get Hoffa. Well, let me tell you, they are 100 percent right. And Bobby couldn't wait. He asked me when was the earliest I could start. I said two calendar months. He said be here Monday."

The pursuit was relentless. "I knew where he was twenty-four hours a day," Sheridan bragged. A book by Esther and Robert James told how Hoffa was convinced he was followed by FBI agents constantly, had his phone tapped, his mail opened, and electronic listening devices beamed at him from half a mile away, which were aided by invisible powder that agents rubbed on his clothing. FBI agents, Hoffa claimed, were disguised as bellhops, desk clerks, maids, and doormen in the hotel where the Teamsters held their convention. The IRS combed the tax returns of Teamster officials and the firms they had contracts with. FBI men stole Teamster records and then accused Teamster leaders of destroying them.

Hoffa was finally "gotten" when a Teamster, in league with the "squad," spied on Hoffa and produced evidence that Hoffa was trying to bribe a juror. Kennedy was so delighted that he threw a party for the "Get Hoffa Squad" in Georgetown. His loyalists presented him with a leather wallet embossed with the very words the jury foreman uttered when he announced the verdict against Hoffa.

Let us turn now to the Johnson Administration, which, according to William C. Sullivan, onetime assistant to J. Edgar Hoover, used the FBI for political purposes more than any other administration. (Roosevelt's was second on his list.) One of the worst activities of the FBI is to institute a "name check," meaning to collect raw material about a given person, much of it misinformation supplied by his enemies. Now the "name check" that the Nixon White House ran on CBS correspondent Daniel Schorr has been written about *ad nauseam*. But it wasn't until the Church committee was forced to do a little digging that it learned that President Johnson ordered "name checks" on at least seven journalists, including NBC's David Brinkley, Peter Arnett of the Associated Press, and Joseph Kraft, the syndicated columnist.

In 1964, when Johnson's top aide, Walter Jenkins, was arrested in a homosexual situation in the men's room of a YMCA near the White House, Johnson had Bill Moyers ask the FBI to run "name checks" on all persons employed in Senator Barry Goldwater's office. J. Edgar Hoover had told Johnson, according to Moyers, that two employees of the Republican National Committee, former Goldwater staffers, might have tried to entrap Jenkins. The suspicions of Hoover and Johnson were unfounded.

Johnson also had the FBI do "name checks" on dozens of people who sent telegrams to the White House in 1965 critical of U.S. Vietnam policy. According to Church committee material, names of other critics of Johnson were also sent to the FBI to be checked and reported on.

Johnsonian power, activated by political anger, came to bear on the Bobby Baker case in 1967. The FBI, in 1965, refused a request from the Criminal Division of the Justice Department to wiretap a witness in the Baker investigation. So the Criminal Division had the Bureau of Narcotics in the Treasury Department do the job. According to Marvin Watson, a White House aide, Johnson became quite "exercised" when he learned about this in 1967, and ordered the FBI to conduct a "run down" on the man who headed the Criminal Division in 1965, as well as four officials in the Treasury Department, and specifically, to determine whether any of these people had associations with Robert F. Kennedy.

And Johnson, like President Nixon, was happy to receive political information on U.S. senators which the FBI had picked up as a "bonus" in its electronic surveillance of foreign intelligence targets for national security purposes. Again, a perverse use of national security.

The records also show that on October 30, 1968, Johnson asked the FBI to conduct "physical surveillance" of Mrs. Anna Chennault, widow of the famous leader of the "Flying Tigers," who became a prominent Republican activist. Thus Mrs. Chennault was spied on in New York City and Washington, according to FBI man Sullivan, "for the purpose of developing political information which could be used against Mr. Nixon" in the presidential campaign.

Similarly, Johnson ordered the FBI to check telephone toll call records in Albuquerque, New Mexico, to determine if vice-presidential candidate Spiro Agnew had phoned Mrs. Chennault or the South Vietnamese embassy on November 2, 1968, when he was campaigning in Albuquerque. Johnson was told by the FBI that there were no such records. The FBI subsequently reported that Johnson was interested in the activities of Mrs. Chennault and Agnew because he was "apparently suspicious that the South Vietnamese were trying to sabotage his peace negotiations in the hope that Nixon would win the election and then take a harder line towards North Viet Nam."

In a "Top Secret" statement which the Senate Watergate Committee had, but never pursued, FBI man Sullivan described how Johnson had the FBI set up a "special squad at the [1964] convention to be of assistance to him in various ways." The alibi was that this "security squad" would "guard against militants, etc." Sullivan commented: "Nothing of this scope had ever been done before or since, to my memory. Included in the assistance rendered was the development of political information useful to President Johnson." In short, LBJ ordered a spy-squad to work for his personal political purposes which included snooping on the Mississippi Freedom Democratic Party and Martin Luther King.

Now, remember John Doar, who, as special counsel to the House Judiciary Committee, carefully and soberly considered the sins of Richard Nixon? No one questioned Doar's thoughtful approach to the awesome chore of collecting the evidence and making a case for impeachment charges. But then no one knew about the "Doar Plan," which has just been revealed in the last few months.

On September 27, 1967, John Doar, as Assistant Attorney General for Civil Rights, sent a twelve-page confidential memo to Attorney General Ramsay Clark on the problem of troublemakers in urban areas. At the time, the Republic was afflicted with endless racial disorders in the cities. President Johnson wanted something done about it quickly, and Attorney General Clark had the word.

Doar recommended that a "single intelligence unit" be established to analyze the enormous output of the FBI "about certain persons and groups who make the urban ghetto their base of operation." But Doar also wanted other agencies of government to be used in keeping track of urban troublemakers.

"This is a sensitive area," he wrote, "but the poverty programs, the Labor Department programs and the Neighborhood Legal Services, all have access to facts which a unit in the Department might find helpful. At the very least the intelligence unit should know where the poverty programs are operating, where the Neighborhood Legal Services are located, who is staffed there so that if there were a need in a particular area, the unit would know where to go to get additional factual material.

"Other investigative agencies of the federal government might also furnish intelligence information, for example, the intelligence unit of Internal Revenue Service. I found that in Detroit this unit, under the direction of John Olszewski, had by far the best knowledge of the Negro areas in Detroit. According to Olszewski, the Alcohol, Tax and Tobacco Unit has the best intelligence on the geography of ghetto areas. The Narcotics Bureau is another possibility, and finally, my experience in Detroit suggests that the Post Office Department might be helpful. Perhaps utilization of other agencies' intelligence potential is too big and difficult a task, but I raise it for your consideration."

No one has charged that anything is illegal in this memorandum, but the potential for abuse is clear. Doar, however, has never even been called to testify about it. Nor was Ramsay Clark ever questioned about "Operation Garden Plot," the Army operation he approved that spied on civilian troublemakers in major cities. When the excesses of "Garden Plot" were publicized, it was the military, not Clark or Defense Secretary Clark Clifford or Lyndon Johnson, father of these schemes, who caught the hell.

Will we ever know the whole story of the Bobby Baker case, how this remarkable wheeler-dealer used his White House connections, and whether President Johnson could have been dragged through it the way Nixon was through Watergate? Too bad that in this time of telling all, Senator Everett Jordan isn't alive to tell why he didn't push the full investigation of the case through the Rules Committee which he headed. According to Clark Mollenhoff, such an investigation would have reached right into the Oval Office of LBJ. But Johnson held sway over Jordan, and the Democrats outvoted the the Republicans, 42–33, to back him and stop the inquiry.

Or will we ever know the full story of the Kennedy Administration? Some are convinced that there is a "Protect Kennedy Organization" at work in Washington, and that it numbers prominent senators, journalists, lawyers, and activists who cannot bring themselves to the notion that all was not well in Camelot.

True or not, we did see a parade of men who served in high posts in the Kennedy Administration—Robert S. McNamara, Richard Goodwin, Theodore Sorensen, Roswell Gilpatric, McGeorge Bundy, and John McCone—testify that they never heard President Kennedy or Robert Kennedy issue direct orders to assassinate Fidel Castro or even to indulge in serious discussion of such a plot. Additionally, Senator Edward Kennedy announced that it was inconceivable that his late brother, the President, would ever authorize an assassination of a foreign leader. *The Washington Post* ran an article wherein Richard Goodwin described a situation where he was alone with Kennedy and the President told him he would never get involved in any assassination scheme. From New York, other Kennedy men announced that Robert F. Kennedy never would have allowed anything like that either.

But President Kennedy and Robert F. Kennedy did authorize "Operation Mongoose," a secret war against Castro, which was an attempt to overthrow his regime. That program involved Roswell Gilpatric and Goodwin, and at one point, pushed a scheme to disable Cuban sugar workers with chemical spray. Church's investigators did not press their case too hard on this one.

Nor did they give more than casual attention to the strange case of Judith Campbell (Exner), who alternated her favors between President Kennedy and Sam Giancana, a mobster murdered before he could testify about his alleged role in the assassination plot of Cuban Premier Fidel Castro. Whatever the peccadilloes of President Kennedy, there is good reason to question his judgment, in terms of national security, in getting involved with a woman who not only was intimately linked with a Mafia figure, but one who was dealing with the CIA [Central Intelligence Agency] on a plan to assassinate Castro. Impeachable? If Nixon had been so involved, no question but a Democratic Congress would have impeached him for it.

Senator Barry Goldwater, who is sometimes weak on specifics, claims Senator Church protected the Kennedys. Said Goldwater: "The first few witnesses on assassinations all put their finger on the Kennedy White House. It was obvious that Church was trying to cover up for the Kennedys."

"He had witnesses called back, trying to get them to change their testimony. He brought in Maxwell Taylor, McGeorge Bundy, and Richard Goodwin, who had no real knowledge of the assassination plots, and just kept saying that they couldn't imagine Jack Kennedy doing anything like that. All these statements came from the PKO

('Protect Kennedy Organization') and sounded like they came out of the same typewriter.''

There did seem to be a disproportionate number of people with Kennedy connections in the CIA investigation. Senator Church asked John Doar (Kennedy man) for advice on which legal talent to hire. Doar referred him to Burke Marshall (Kennedy man), a member of the screening committee for the Kennedy Library, and Marshall was hired as a consultant.

Then Marshall, former counsel to IBM [International Business Machines], recommended that Church hire F. A. O. Schwartz, a partner in Cravath, Swaine and Moore, the law firm representing IBM, and general counsel to the committee. Katzenbach and Gilpatric (Kennedy men) are partners in that firm, and both were called in to testify.

Church also hired Robert S. McNamara's former son-in-law, Barry Carter, to serve as deputy chief of the military intelligence investigation; and Peter Fenn, son of Dan Fenn, onetime assistant to President Kennedy, and presently Director of the Kennedy Library. Wouldn't you know, one of young Fenn's assignments was to check into the files on Robert F. Kennedy at the Kennedy Library. Maybe it's ethical, but it's all too cozy.

The recent revelations about the Kennedy and Johnson White Houses show only the tip of the iceberg: Who knows what else went on during their administrations? What other people were wiretapped, followed by FBI agents, investigated on a "name check" basis? What cover-ups were arranged, what monies disbursed at the Justice Department, what threats made on the telephone, what civil servants fired or transferred? What documents were and are being destroyed? What is hidden away at the Kennedy Library? Did Nixon really outdo his predecessors in the abuse of power?

No absolution of Nixon is given here. The man certainly abused the powers of his office, and his abuses were reprehensible. But my point is that Adam and Eve did not meet at the Watergate. Richard Nixon's White House may have been like Milton's "Palace of Pandemonium," and Washington at the time could be thought of as "the burning lake of Hell," but the Fall of Man did not occur in his administration. It preceded it by eons.

QUESTIONS FOR DISCUSSION

1. Was the Nixon presidency aberrational?
2. Are there differences between the abuses of presidential power by Richard

Nixon and the abuses of presidential power by his five predecessors in the highest office?

3. What can be done to prevent the abuse of presidential power?

4. Why were most of the abuses of presidential power from Franklin Roosevelt to Lyndon Johnson not brought to public attention until the time of the Watergate affair?

5. Does the domestic and foreign-policy record of the Nixon presidency support the charges by Jenkins that Nixon possessed a second-rate mind and lacked common sense?

SUGGESTED READINGS

Barber, James David. *The Presidential Character: Predicting Performance in the White House,* rev. ed. Englewood Cliffs, N.J.: Prentice-Hall, 1977.

Bernstein, Carl, and Bob Woodward. *All the President's Men.* New York: Simon & Schuster, 1974.

Corwin, Edward S. *The President: Office and Powers,* 4th ed. New York: New York University Press, 1957.

Cronin, Thomas E., and Rexford G. Tugwell. *The Presidency Reappraised,* 2nd ed. New York: Praeger, 1977.

Fairlie, Henry. *The Kennedy Promise: The Politics of Expectation.* Garden City, N.Y.: Doubleday, 1973.

Kearns, Doris. *Lyndon B. Johnson and the American Dream.* New York: Harper & Row, 1976.

Lukas, J. Anthony. *Nightmare—The Underside of the Nixon Years.* New York: Viking, 1976.

Mansfield, Harvey, ed. *Congress Against the President.* New York: Praeger, 1975.

McConnell, Grant. *The Modern Presidency,* 2nd ed. New York: St. Martin's Press, 1976.

Safire, William J. *Before the Fall: An Inside View of the Pre-Watergate White House.* Garden City, N.Y.: Doubleday, 1975.

Wills, Gary. *Nixon Agonistes.* Boston: Houghton Mifflin, 1970.

10.

Is the Bureaucracy Acting in a Responsible Manner?

When the Constitution was ratified in the eighteenth century, only a few hundred people were employed by government at the national level. Today, however, there are about 2,500,000 civilian federal employees. Millions of other public employees serve the armed forces and the agencies of state and local governments. About one out of every six employed people in the United States works for government either at the national, state, or local level.

Government has grown remarkably in this century because of its increased activities in a number of areas. The most important, however, are foreign policy, economics, and welfare. In terms of foreign policy, the small country that achieved independence from the British in 1783 has become a superpower in the twentieth century. This fact has spurred the growth of the bureaucracy.

In the 1790s, the United States did not need a strong defense establishment that could mobilize its men and divert its limited economic resources in the event of war. A large ocean and the balance of power in Europe offered some protection from foreign invasion. So long as military technology remained simple and so long as Europe was divided politically, the United States needed only a small regular army for defense. A militia could be used to supplement the army if necessary, but principal reliance was placed upon the navy. Throughout the first century of the American Republic, moreover, even that navy did not require enormous expenditures of money.

Today, however, the United States plays a role of leadership in the conduct of foreign policy throughout the world. Vast ocean space can no longer protect the country from attack. The United States, moreover, is the only country strong enough to challenge the military might of the Soviet Union.

To meet the challenges of the post-World War II period, the United States has adopted a policy of internationalism, avoiding the isolationism of its past history. Today millions of people are employed by the federal government to manage its foreign policy needs.

These needs have required the services of large numbers of people in the armed forces. Government, moreover, has been engaged in dispensing foreign aid, gathering intelligence information, assisting individuals and groups abroad, and helping to promote the needs of a global economy.

In addition to the growth of foreign-policy activities, economic factors are responsible for government expansion. Business and labor groups have demanded government participation in various sectors of the economy. These demands have been translated into bigger government.

Business has asked for government assistance to build highways, improve railroads, construct dams, widen waterways, and administer tariffs. Business, too, has requested government support for research in energy, transportation, and military technology.

In addition to business, labor has sought government involvement in the economy. It has asked for government inspection involving safety at work sites, government supervision of minimum wage laws, and government employment for those who cannot find jobs in the market economy. Labor has asked for government protection of unions against the strong power of business.

Foreign policy and domestic economic pressures, then, have increased the size of the bureaucracy. The emergence of the welfare state, too, has contributed to government growth. Individuals and groups have demanded government help to provide for health care, social security, housing, and education. All of these goals require programs that are administered by government.

That government has grown is widely acknowledged. What is controversial, however, is whether such growth is necessary and how accountable the bureaucrats are (or should be) to duly elected officials. This chapter asks two questions dealing with these matters: (1) Is more government intervention the best way to solve economic and political problems? (2) Should the Central Intelligence Agency (CIA) be more closely monitored by Congress?

IS BIG GOVERNMENT GOOD GOVERNMENT?

Ever since the administration of Franklin Roosevelt and the birth of his New Deal programs, the idea that big government is good government has found considerable support among liberals. The traditional liberal view in nineteenth-century America was one that feared big government. With the coming of the Great Depression, however, the liberal philosophy has changed to belief in government as a force for good. This feeling was reflected in such presidential programs as Roosevelt's New Deal, Truman's Fair Deal, and Johnson's Great Society. A basic assumption underlying these political philosophies was that it is desirable to establish government programs to promote the good life. According to this assumption, many of the evils of society, consequently, could be eliminated by government programs.

In accordance with this philosophy, government programs were established, and agencies were created or enlarged. For example, the government built housing to eradicate slums, constructed dormitories to house college students, provided subsidies to talented young people to promote the arts, and instituted antipoverty programs to end want. All of these measures were enacted in part because of the belief that government could remedy social evils.

Although these liberal programs have been criticized from the time that they were adopted in the 1930s, criticism used to come mostly from conservatives who oppose the principle of government interventionism to remedy social evils. Criticism has continued from these conservatives, but now also comes from people who used to accept the need for big government. These new critics have been dubbed "the new conservatives" because on many issues they oppose government programs as being ineffective and counterproductive. Thus, the criticism against government spending to remedy social ills now comes from many sources.

In a discussion dealing with the need for government intervention to meet the needs of the future, socialist Michael Harrington argues that socialism is the answer. Although people who call themselves socialists differ about the meaning of the term *socialism,* Harrington identifies it with the coupling of public ownership of the main economic institutions of a country with the political institution of democracy. According to Harrington, global problems of economic productivity, welfare reform, and environmental protection can no longer be solved by private decision making. The future will be collective and social. Public ownership and political democracy will assure that the future will be planned to serve the greatest public needs. Public ownership, consequently, means bigger government.

Representative Sam Steiger, Republican from Arizona, contends that intervention by an ever-growing government bureaucracy is detrimental to progress. He argues that government bureaucracy is too big, unwieldy, inefficient, and wasteful. It is, moreover, counterproductive to the purposes for which it was created. Steiger notes that even liberals are reassessing the desirability of using government to solve social problems.

THE CIA AND ACCOUNTABILITY

Another major issue concerning the bureaucracy is accountability. Particularly in the American political system of separation of powers, the chain of command of the bureaucracy is not always clear. The Constitution provides for both congressional and executive control over the bureaucracy. In practice, however, this separation of authority has resulted in a problem of accountability because the president and the Congress often disagree about policy.

Accountability has been a major problem in the conduct of foreign policy and the maintenance of national security. Foreign policy requires secrecy, and the president, intelligence officials, and diplomatic and military personnel often try to limit the information available even to elected officials, lest national secrets become known to hostile governments.

Because of the sensitive nature of its work, the CIA has been criticized for avoiding accountability. The investigations of the CIA conducted in 1975 revealed improper activities by that agency. For example, it became clear from these investigations that CIA officials were involved in Watergate operations. Many other CIA activities, moreover, were unknown to most members of Congress until they were uncovered by these investigations. Some legislators professed indignation about revelations that the CIA was involved in undermining governments abroad and in planning assassinations. Calls for reform of the agency, consequently, became louder.

Some members of Congress have recommended closer congressional supervision to control intelligence agencies. Democratic Senator Frank Church of Idaho conducted extensive investigations of these agencies. He argues that a permanent Senate oversight intelligence committee should be established. The reason for the intelligence abuses of the past may be attributed in part to a dereliction of congressional responsibility. The present arrangement of dispersing congressional supervision throughout several committees will not work because intelligence activities are far ranging. The new oversight committee, he feels, can be trusted to keep national security secrets confidential. The independence of the committee, moreover, would be assured by the requirement that committee members will be rotated after serving six years. The staff, too, will serve limited terms.

Conservative Republican Senator Barry Goldwater argues that too much congressional intervention in foreign policy is bad for national security. The proposed bill would be inadequate because national security secrets would not be kept confidential. The proposed committee system, he asserts, is an assault on the seniority system because it requires rotation of committee members. Such a procedure, moreover, would inhibit the development of expertise.

Is More Government Intervention the Best Way to Solve Economic and Political Problems?

YES

MICHAEL HARRINGTON
*A Hope**

Either Western man is going to choose a new society—or a new society will choose, and abolish, him.

It is clear that the contemporary revolution will continue to re-shape the human environment in the most radical way. If anything, time will speed up even more, for the cybernated technology of today proceeds by geometric leaps and bounds rather than by arithmetic progression. Short of an atomic holocaust, which would simply write an end to the whole process, there is no reason to think that it will slow down. And . . . the consequences of this development are not merely material and scientific. They invade the spirit, the psychology, politics, and every other aspect of life.

In this context, America has for some time been engaged in the wrong argument. It has been debating as to whether or not the future should be collective and social, and ignoring the fact that the present is already becoming so. The real issue is not whether, but how, this future will arrive—unwittingly or consciously chosen.

If the new society imposes itself upon a people who do not notice a revolution, the moment will constitute the decadence of the Western ideal.

The West has marked itself off from other cultures precisely by its confidence in the future. The religious form of this faith is most iden-tified with St. Augustine, who, breaking with the cyclic theories in which time was a great wheel turning around itself, asserted the pil-grimage of history toward the City of God. The secular version of the same hope dates at least from the Renaissance and culminates in the capitalist and socialist visions of progress. It was this Faustian rest-

---

lessness that drove the Western powers to remake the world during the last several centuries.

Along with this futurism there was the affirmation of the power of reason. The importance of this commitment cannot be evaded by recourse to a fashionable irrationalism. Of course, the absolute, unquestioned faith in reason has been disproved; yes, there were excesses of the Enlightenment [a philosophical movement of the eighteenth century characterized by belief in the power of human reason] tradition like [French philosopher Auguste] Comte. But it was the theoretical and practical intelligence which lifted Western man out of the mire and made him, for a while, lord of the earth. Now, if reason has turned out tragically, so has the West. And if men cannot control the products of their own brain, there will be no place to hide, for mystics or for anyone else. Without rational human direction, the accidental revolution is not moving toward a rebirth of poetry but toward an inhuman collectivism.

In short, if the new society is blundered into, then all of the decadences described in this book will come roughly true. [nineteenth-century French poet and critic Charles] Baudelaire will have been right, for the vast, uncomprehended social structure will have little place for beauty. [Nineteenth-century German philosopher Friedrich] Nietzsche will have been right, and the dream that men can order their own destiny will have come to naught. Max Weber [a German sociologist] will have been right, for the age of bureaucratic, antispiritual rule will come to pass. [Psychoanalyst Sigmund] Freud will have been right, for the growth in technological competence will be repressive of man's deep, instinctual life. And so on and so on.

And yet, there is the possibility that the West will freely choose a new society.

No option which can be taken will solve all human problems. The most happy outcome could even be, as Norman Mailer [a twentieth-century American writer] has suggested, only that suffering will be raised from the level of fate to that of tragedy. For when there are no longer plagues, famines, and natural catastrophes to blame death and evil on, the essential finitude of men could become all the more stark and stripped of its accidental qualities. And, contrary to [German socialist Karl] Marx, in a society where men die from death because they have been born, there could be a religious renaissance as well as a heroic atheism.

The claim put here is minimal. The free choice of the future will not abrogate the human condition. But it will provide the context in which autonomous human beings can grow in depth and understanding, which is all the West has really ever asked.

In order to choose the new society rather than being chosen by it, the West must make this accidental century conscious and truly democratic. And this goal I would call socialism.

There are many arguments against using the word "socialism." Most Americans do not understand it. Communism uses the term as a rhetorical mask for a bureaucratic minority that imposes its private desires upon a social technology. Worse yet, the Communists have attempted to identify socialism with totalitarianism. In the emergent nations, the word "socialism" is used to describe the socialization of poverty for the purposes of accumulating capital. These societies, as the great socialist theorists would have predicted, are far distant from the ideal of the free development of the individual which is of the socialist essence. And even in Western Europe where the Social Democratic parties have maintained the democratic content of socialism, they have often equated their vision with a welfare state more than with a new civilization.

Despite all these semantic and historic drawbacks, the term must be used. With the exception of the United States, socialism is what the most democratic forces in the West call their dream. And even more basically, the nineteenth-century socialists, for all their failures of prediction, were the first to anticipate the present plight and to attempt to resolve it. They were right when they said that the way in which men produce their worldly goods is becoming more and more social. They were right in asserting that this complex, interdependent technology could not be contained within a system of private decision making. And if there is to be a humane outcome to the contemporary Western adventure, they will have to be made right in their faith that the people can freely and democratically take control of their own lives and society.

And this last idea is the heart of the socialist hope. . . . From the very beginning, the socialists knew that modern technology could not be made just by dividing it up into tiny parcels of individual ownership. It is of the very nature of that technology to be concentrated and collective. Therefore, the socialists assigned a new and radical meaning to democracy. The people's title to the social means of production would be guaranteed, they said, not through stock certificates, but through votes. The basic economic decisions would be made democratically.

In this context, the nationalization of industry is a technique of socialism, not its definition. It is one extremely important way of abolishing the political and social power that results from concentrated private ownership. It also facilitates directing economic resources to the satisfaction of human needs. When the people "own" the state through political democracy, then public corporations are truly theirs, and nationalization is an instrument of freedom. But there are other ways to forward the democratization of economic and social power. Fiscal and monetary policy, a cooperative sector, and taxes are among them.

In these terms, the one set and undeviating aspect of socialism is its commitment to making the democratic and free choice of the citizens the principle of social and economic life. All other issues—the extent of nationalization, the mode of planning, and the like—have to be empirically tested and measured in the light of how they serve that end. For certainly the old popular definition of socialism as the simple and wholesale nationalization of the economy has not survived the experience of this century, and particularly the Communist experience. At the same time, it has become abundantly clear that the commanding heights of the economy—where decisions affect more of life than most laws of congresses and parliaments—cannot be left to private motives.

. . . I am suggesting that the only way the accidental revolution can become socially conscious of itself is through a profound economic and social deepening of democracy. This I call socialism.

Is More Government Intervention the Best Way to Solve Economic and Political Problems?

NO

SAM STEIGER
*Bureaucracy: Paternalism on the Potomac**

There are very few absolute truths, so existing ones are well known. It may be presumptuous of me, therefore, to share with you the following as an absolute but it is.

When individuals are confronted with a problem they cannot solve, or when they seek to attain a goal that is beyond reach, and they allow government to assume the mission, two results occur: (1) the

* From Marjorie Holt, ed., *The Case Against the Reckless Congress* (Ottawa, Ill.: Green Hill Publishers, 1976), pp. 79–86. Reprinted with permission from *The Case Against the Reckless Congress*, Marjorie Holt, ed., $1.95. © Green Hill Publishers, Inc., Box 738, Ottawa, Illinois 61350.

government structure formed to accomplish the task spends more time on justification of the structure than on the task; (2) the longer the structure exists, the less effort is spent on the mission and the more effort is expended in the care and feeding of the structure.

I call this Steiger's Law. It's true of entities other than government; government, however, is the most visible and viable sinner. The federal government is clearly the greatest, most unswerving devotee of these truths.

. . . it must be recognized that the federal government, as designed by the Framers of the Constitution, has developed into a complex of myriad and independent structures that by no stretch of the imagination resemble the Republic's original design.

The federal government, particularly in the past two decades, has managed to evolve into this series of structures not through any schemes or plans but as a reaction to another absolute truth. This truth states that where there is a vacuum of power, someone or something will always fill it.

I shall attempt to trace the causes of the present situation, which has led us to this total capture by our own structure.

From colonial times through the first third of this century the tasks of our government were limited, concerned only with the means of survival. As the nation grew, affluence and a growing sophistication developed. This sophistication saw merchandising of candidates, with aspirants for federal offices selling the notion of federal services in areas that previously had not been viewed as federal responsibility. The sheer volume of this largesse from Washington so engulfed us that we were unaware of the enormity and consequences of our willingness to be seduced.

We are now in the second generation of Americans who see nothing incongruous about federal involvement in the qualitative judgments of individuals. Secure in their receipt of food, shelter, and clothing they not only demand federal succor but choose to substitute federal judgment for their own. In the course of this evolution Congress ceased to function in even the limited capacity decreed by the Constitution and thus became the best example of Steiger's Law. That is, Congress is so totally involved in maintaining its own structure that it has abandoned its constitutional mission.

After many years of indifference and malfeasance, we are now beginning to hear this theme of too much bureaucracy from some strange quarters—liberal Democrats. For example, a famous senator from a large eastern state recently declared, "There is a very serious kind of rethinking of the best way to meet the human needs of our society. Over the past few years, many have come to see that one of the greatest dangers of government is bureaucracy."

Was this Senator James Buckley, conservative Republican of New York? No. It was Senator Edward Kennedy, liberal Democrat of Massachusetts.

Another prominent senator recently told his colleages, "The liberals have to reevaluate their posture. Each program looks good, but you put 100 of them together and the results are more negative than positive. The federal bureaucracy is just an impossible monstrosity, you can't manage it, there's no way to do it."

Was this Senator Barry Goldwater of Arizona? No. It was Senator Gaylord Nelson, liberal Democrat of Wisconsin.

A New England governor has just announced, "The liberal Democrats are going to have to admit that they've made some huge mistakes creating this maze of federal programs that just breeds inefficiency and frustration. It's a disgrace. Some of the federal programs I've worked with as mayor and governor border on criminality. You put $1,000 in one end and the people don't get six cents out the other end."

Was this Republican Governor Meldrin Thompson of New Hampshire? No, it was Democratic Governor Philip Noel of Rhode Island.

In the last year, similar statements have been made by Senator Edmund Muskie, the Democrat's vice-presidential standard bearer in 1968; by newly elected governors Jerry Brown of California, Michael Dukakis of Massachusetts, and Hugh Carey of New York; and by George McGovern's former campaign manager, Senator Gary Hart of Colorado, among many others.

The reason for this relatively new concern among leading "liberal" Democrats is the plain and simple fact that the bureaucracy has grown so large, so unwieldy, so inefficient, so wasteful, so counterproductive—in many cases, so disastrous—in recent years that even the most confirmed believer in the power of government to do good is downright alarmed.

In December 1975, *Newsweek,* which had previously not been known as a die-hard opponent of government economic planning and social programs, devoted a major cover story to the increasing problems caused by "Big Government." The cover was a cartoon of a bloated Uncle Sam.

As the authors of this article pointed out, "With a combined federal, state and local workforce of 14.6 million people and a total expenditure of $523.2 billion, government on all levels now accounts for 37 percent of the gross national product . . . as against 12 percent in 1929." The largest increase in the bureaucracy, they add, has been the "astronomical [growth of] federally funded social programs and the state and local governments that must administer them." . . .

The sprawl of the bureaucrats in the past 15 years is almost impossible to comprehend. In that time period 236 new federal bureaus, departments, or agencies have been organized, while only 21 have been phased out of existence. There are no less than 1,250 federal advisory boards, committees, commissions and councils, most of which meet infrequently and do little work but serve as easy sources of patronage. They do, however, cost the taxpayer at least $75 million a year.

It is almost impossible to terminate any bureaucracy once it is set up. For instance, as UPI [United Press International] reporter Don Lambro points out in his valuable book *The Federal Rathole,* we are still supporting two commissions set up to protect us against the World War II Nazis! Other commissions have such titles as "The Interdepartmental Screw Thread Committee" and the "Panel on Review of Sunburn Treatment."

It is inevitable in such a situation that a tremendous amount of wasteful and needlessly confusing duplication should exist. The advocates of the often proposed new Agency for Consumer Protection (it could not be called the CPA because those initials are already taken!) had to be continually reminded that no less than fifty federal agencies and bureaus are already engaged in consumer protection.

Seven separate federal programs provide funds for out-patient health centers; eleven separate programs provide funding for child care; fourteen independent units of the vast Department of Health, Education, and Welfare administer as many separate programs for education of the handicapped. No less than twenty-five different services, bureaus, or offices of a dozen different departments finance research on water pollution.

At the same time that the Surgeon General's Office is requiring every cigarette packet to warn that they are "dangerous" to our health the Department of Agriculture finances a study of Oriental tobacco for "improving the quality of American cigarettes."

With all this confusion and duplication it is little wonder that more and more experts in the fields involved are concluding that the widespread federal social programs (which account for most of the increased bureaucracy) are simply not doing the job for which they were intended. That is, they are not really helping the needy in any effective way. What these programs do very well is provide highly paid jobs for more and more bureaucrats and lackeys. When Daniel Moynihan, a liberal Democrat from New York, . . . examined the poverty program, he concluded that most of the money went for salaries of highly paid professional social workers and administrators and that the poor saw relatively little of the huge sums spent. It is no accident that the two richest counties per capita in the United States are the Washington, D.C. "bedroom" counties of Montgomery, Maryland, and Fairfax,

Virginia, which are heavily populated by high salaried government officials.

Although the bureaucracy in large part can accomplish little good, it can and does effect much harm to many citizens. Thousands of small businesses, which provide jobs for hundreds of thousands of citizens, are being literally forced out of business by the growing costs of government paperwork. So bureaucracy provides jobs for bureaucrats but at the same time destroys countless jobs in the private sector.

For example, there is a single Labor Department form, called EBS-1. It requires a thirty-one-page detailed report from all employers offering pension plans for their employees. To fill out the form correctly, the estimated cost is about $700 per employee. Now large business can absorb this cost by passing it on to the consumer—that's all of us—but many small businesses simply cannot afford to hire that many high-priced lawyers and accountants. So they choose not to make pension plans available to employees.

The total cost of paperwork generated by big government is estimated to go as high as $40 billion a year—about $800 a year for the average American family. If that amount were added to salaries, the families could doubtless spend that money in far more economically productive ways. Almost 5,300 different forms are employed by the federal government today. *Ten billion sheets of paper* flow through federal offices annually. This quantity of forms would fill up four million cubic feet of space.

Congress cannot evade—indeed it must accept—much of the blame for this state of affairs. At least one hyperactive representative has introduced an average of two bills a day during the 1975 session. As of July 1975 more than 8,000 bills had already been introduced in the House for this Ninety-fourth Congress. This does not count 502 resolutions, 476 joint resolutions, and 291 concurrent resolutions.

We find ourselves on a treadmill—as soon as anyone sees anything wrong anywhere, he wants to pass a law; very often a law is passed, followed by hundreds of regulations issued by the various concerned bureaucracies (many duplicating, some even contradictory). Then the new laws and regulations create new problems so a cry goes up for yet more laws! And so the process continues.

The *Federal Register* is a U.S. government daily publication listing all the latest rules and regulations promulgated by the thousands of federal agencies in order to implement their interpretations of the laws of Congress.

During the 1960s the total *Registers* for one year came to about 15,000 pages. As late as 1970 an annual collection still came to only about 20,000 pages, in small type. Yet in four years time, this massive compilation had grown to more than 46,000 pages of rules and regulations, including more than 20,000 regulations of all conceivable shapes and sizes. In 1975, we may expect well over 50,000 pages, including more than 25,000 separate regulations.

As Congressman Edward Hutchinson of Michigan recently phrased it,

> We are heading toward a society in which the individual is allowed increasingly less control over his or her daily life. Important decisions on how best to do business, how to grow crops, how to shop at the supermarket, how to travel, how to educate one's children, in short how to live, are being usurped by the government which sees no limits to its powers.

In the last year, a majority of Congress has unfortunately taken several more steps to strengthen this dangerous trend. The House approved, by a vote of 288–119, . . . a bill to "de-Hatch" federal employees and allow them to engage in active partisan politics (a practice long barred by the Hatch Act). This bill (HR 8617) was opposed by me and many of my good friends and colleagues, but on this issue we did not prevail and the civil service will now become increasingly politicized and politicized, moreover, toward the left.

I also opposed HR 2559, passed by one vote . . . on July 30, 1975. This bill (Executive Level Pay Raises) gave members of Congress (as well as senior civil servants) automatic cost-of-living raises every October 1; besides obviously contributing to the inflationary spiral, this bill insures that Congressmen will be exempt from the ravages of inflation and will be spared the responsibility of voting themselves future salary adjustments. As Representative E. G. Shuster, Republican of Pennsylvania, put it, "The American people would be better off if Congress got a pay decrease when the cost of living went up and a pay increase when the cost of living went down."

By including itself in a growing bureaucracy, now automatically costing us more every year, Congress has done itself and the people a great disservice. One of the few checks on the expanding bureaucracy has thus been weakened.

. . . We have a difficult task before us—to reduce a trend of forty years—but with the will, we can do it. We will have to do it, if democratic government is to survive.

The siren call, "Let the Feds do it for you," absolutely must be resisted and rejected.

QUESTIONS FOR DISCUSSION

1. Is the free-enterprise system necessary for political democracy to be achieved?
2. Do you agree with Harrington that the future will be collective and social?
3. Do you agree with Steiger that "although the bureaucracy in large part can accomplish little good, it can and does effect much harm to many citizens"?
4. Is paperwork a consequence of government bureaucracy, or of any bureaucracy, whether public or private?
5. How do you account for the vast growth of government bureaucracy in the past half century?

SUGGESTED READINGS

Adams, James Ring. "Why New York Went Broke." *Commentary*, May 1976, pp. 31–37.

Drucker, Peter. *The Age of Discontinuity: Guidelines to Our Changing Society.* New York: Harper & Row, 1969.

Friedman, Milton. *There's No Such Thing as a Free Lunch.* LaSalle, Ill.: Open Court, 1975.

Goldwater, Barry. *The Coming Breakpoint.* New York: Macmillan, 1976.

Harrington, Michael. *Socialism.* New York: Saturday Review Press, 1972.

Howe, Irving, ed. *Essential Works of Socialism.* New York: Bantam, 1971.

Parkinson, C. Northcote. *Parkinson's Law and Other Studies in Administration.* Boston: Houghton Mifflin, 1957.

Rourke, Francis E. *Bureaucracy, Politics, and Public Policy.* Boston: Little, Brown, 1969.

Thompson, Victor A. *Bureaucracy and the Modern World.* Morristown, N.J.: General Learning Press, 1976.

Wildavsky, Aaron. *The Politics of the Budgetary Process,* 2nd ed. Boston: Little, Brown, 1974.

Wilson, James Q. "The Rise of the Bureaucratic State." *The Public Interest* 41(Fall 1975):77–103.

Should the Central Intelligence Agency (CIA) Be More Closely Monitored by Congress?

YES

FRANK CHURCH
*The CIA Needs Stronger Congressional Supervision**

First of all, let me say, Mr. Chairman, I am very much pleased and gratified by the testimony of the majority leader, who foresaw the need for a permanent Senate oversight intelligence committee years ago.

If ever his foresight was substantiated, it was in the course of the investigations of the Senate Select Committee in recent months.

We have conducted the first serious investigation of the FBI [Federal Bureau of Investigation] since its inception more than a half century ago.

We have conducted the first serious investigation of the CIA since it was established more than thirty years ago.

The abuses that we found must be viewed in part as the result of the dereliction of congressional responsibility. I cannot believe that if the Congress had been watching these agencies in which we entrust so much power and permit to operate in so much secrecy, that these abuses would have or could have occurred.

It is not my purpose this morning to review in detail the findings of our investigation. I think that most of you are aware that in the case of the CIA we not only discovered twenty years of illegal mail openings involving individual American citizens, [but also] the interceptions of 100,000 cables sent to or from individual citizens.

We found an extensive involvement in conspiracies to murder certain foreign leaders extending over a period of years. We also found that the agency had engaged in spying activities directed against American citizens, although this was expressly contrary to the provisions of the law of 1947 that created the CIA.

In the case of the FBI we found the beginnings of a secret police

---

* From U.S., Congress, Senate, Committee on Government Operations, *Oversight of U.S. Government Intelligence Functions*, Hearings on S. 317, S. 189, S. Con. Res. 4, S. 2893, and S. 2865, 94th Cong., 2nd sess., 1976, pp. 27–30.

in this country, elaborate plans laid out for the purpose of harassing thousands of citizens whose only offense was that of disagreeing with the policies of the government, which the Constitution and the laws of this country guarantee them the right to do.

We found vendettas conducted against the leaders of the civil rights movement carried to almost unbelievable extremes.

In the case of the Internal Revenue Service, we found tax investigations commenced against citizens concerning whom no tax delinquency was even suspected, for the purpose of harassment.

We found, in that agency which I would regard as having more intelligence information on more American citizens than all the other governmental agencies combined, which they get on the fifteenth of April every year, a habit having formed by which that agency transfers these confidential tax returns to other agencies of the government, having nothing to do with tax matters, again, for purposes of harassment.

These abuses, Mr. Chairman, have to be prevented in the future. For that reason, the final two months of the committee's work will be devoted to a series of recommendations having to do with the correction in the existing laws that will give us some safeguard against the repetition of these abuses in future years.

The first recommendation that the committee will make has to do with the subject before you today, that is, the establishment of a permanent oversight committee.

Why is it needed?

The obvious answer is that it is needed because the present arrangements will not work, they have not worked. The intelligence activity of the federal government is far-ranging. It involves agencies that were mentioned by the majority leader, not only the CIA, but the DIA [Defense Intelligence Agency], the NSA [National Security Agency], certain other national intelligence components of the Defense Department, and the counterintelligence and counterespionage functions of the FBI.

Jurisdiction is divided now between any number of committees of the Congress, the Finance Committee, the Foreign Relations Committee, the Armed Services Committee, and it is not possible therefore—the judiciary committee—for an adequate surveillance of that entire intelligence community to be exercised under current conditions.

Furthermore, our experience over the past months enables me to confidently tell you that the work cannot be done on a piecemeal basis or by a subcommittee of another standing committee which is primarily engaged in a different basic responsibility. It will require a well-staffed committee directing all of its attention to the intelligence community.

Again, by experience, it will require a very large part of the time of the senators who serve.

So for these reasons, a permanent oversight committee is necessary, and I would like to make three observations having to do with three principles that I think need to be embodied in any legislation that your committee may recommend. Some of them have already been mentioned; I will not prolong the discussion of those that have.

The first principle relates to the power that will be given this permanent oversight committee, and I believe that it cannot possibly do its work unless it has the right to pass upon the authorization legislation. In other words, it must be a legislative committee in that respect.

It must have that power in the normal way over those agencies that deal primarily with national intelligence, those would be the CIA, DIA, NSA, the defense programs which deal with sophisticated technological collection systems and the counterintelligence functions of the FBI. All of these are what are called national intelligence.

Now, the investigating power of the committee should extend beyond these particular agencies to look into other intelligence operations in other departments that may be subject to abuse concerning which charge may be raised from time to time. So that the first principle, then, if this committee is to have the tools to do its work, would be the jurisdiction to pass on annual authorizations for those agencies that are primarily involved in strategic or national intelligence.

The second principle that I would endorse is the principle of rotating membership, both for the members of the committee and for the staff. That rotating membership, I think, should be patterned after the Senate itself: six years with one third of the committee coming on fresh every two years in which manner two thirds would remain experienced, but at the same time we would minimize the risk of having the committee co-opted by the very agencies that it seeks to supervise.

If that is true of the members of the committee, it is equally applicable to the staff.

The third principle has to do with the question of how we are going to resolve the problem of dealing with secrecy under the framework of the Constitution.

Everybody recognizes that the existing condition is chaotic and we would hope that with the creation of an oversight committee, procedures could be regularized for dealing with legitimate secrets.

I might say, in that regard, that it was possible for the select committee to work out arrangements with the executive branch for obtaining all of the information we required in conducting our investigation. We were very careful to provide maximum security so that no item of a sensitive national security character has leaked, to our knowledge, from the committee, during the whole course of its investigation.

I think that such a permanent oversight committee could be made relatively leakproof. I cite to you evidence of this record of the Joint Committee on Atomic Energy through the years.

However, leaks, as we all know, are not confined to the congressional branch. We have had the experience of many leaks from the executive agencies, often planted and planned, for the purposes of the administration. That has been a practice that all administrations have engaged in in the past, and we ought not to overlook the fact that the principal problem faced by the CIA at the moment in connection with leaks has to do with neither the executive or the legislative branches but with former agents of the CIA itself. It has to do with the [former CIA agent] Philip Agee syndrome which agents once having worked for the CIA and having become familiar with the other personnel and their assignments leave the agency and turn against it, and then publish the identification of these former employees and blow their cover.

That has been a principal source of difficulty. . . . We in the select committee took the precaution at the outset of our investigation to reach an understanding with the CIA whereby we asked for no names currently assigned abroad, we asked for no sources abroad of intelligence information because we did not think that the identification of intelligence sources or the names of employees assigned abroad were necessary for our work, and we did not even want to take the risk of the possibility of inadvertent exposure.

I believe, despite the confusion on this question, that once the facts are laid before you, it will be seen that there are ways of protecting legitimate secrets that can be resolved by a permanent oversight committee. Gentlemen, the question of secrecy and the right of the Congress to deal with classified information are basically questions that must be resolved if we are to preserve our constitutional form of government. That establishes the Congress as a separate but equal and independent branch.

I would hope that we would never accept the principle that it is exclusively the right of the executive branch to determine what a national secret is, and exclusively the prerogative of the executive branch to decide what may be revealed, and what they can conceal, because once we do that, the ball game is over.

To grant the executive such prerogative would, in my judgment, undermine any reasonable opportunity for a permanent oversight committee to expose wrongdoing, to expose the abuse of power, to correct inefficiencies, to expose illegal action contrary to the intent of the Congress and contrary to the well-being of this Republic.

Should the Central Intelligence Agency (CIA) Be More Closely Monitored by Congress?

NO

BARRY GOLDWATER
Too Much Congressional Intervention in Foreign Policy Is Dangerous*

In the last few years, the Congress has attempted to exert greater influence on the nature and conduct of our foreign policy.

What are the results?

Two good allies, Greece and Turkey, have been alienated.

Jewish immigration from Russia has been reduced.

The hands of our president have been tied in the day-to-day conduct of foreign policy.

U.S. intelligence is demoralized and its effectiveness greatly diminished.

Our allies seriously question America's reliability, if not our collective sanity.

Our adversaries take comfort in watching us tear ourselves apart.

Mr. Chairman, I have here page one of *The Washington Post* of January 7, 1976. Three headlines paint a picture of American foreign policy today.

The left-hand column is entitled, "CIA Giving $6 Million to Italian Centrists."

In the middle, below the picture, "CIA Agent Welch Buried" with the subtitle, "Ford, Kissinger Among Mourners at Arlington."

On the right, the headline reads, "Two Soviet Ships Head for Angola."

Taken together the headlines describe an impotent giant—our nation.

Disclosure of covert aid to Italy is the direct result of the Hughes Amendment to the Foreign Aid Bill adopted by the Senate on October 2, 1974.

---

* From U.S., Congress, Senate, Committee on Government Operations, *Oversight of U.S. Government Intelligence Functions*, Hearings on S. 317, S. 189, S. Con. Res. 4, S. 2893, and S. 2865, 94th Cong., 2nd sess., 1976, pp. 346–348.

This means approximately 50 senators and over 120 congressmen may receive highly sensitive information on a covert action. It also means public disclosure is almost inevitable.

Worst of all, it gives a personal veto to any member who disagrees with a covert action—with the veto coming in the form of subrosa release to *The Washington Post* or *The New York Times*.

Mr. Chairman, I shall oppose any general legislation dealing with the intelligence community which fails to provide for:

One, a repeal or severe modification of the Hughes Amendment.

Two, criminal sanctions against any member of the intelligence community who releases classified information having voluntarily entered into a secrecy agreement.

And three, a flat prohibition against any intelligence agency revealing the name or identity of any foreign agent employed by the United States to the Congress or any of its committees or members.

S. 2893 fails to deal with these vital matters.

Specifically, I am opposed to S. 2893 known as the "Intelligence Oversight Act of 1976" for the following reasons:

1. The Senate needs one more standing committee about as much as the nation needs more inflation. We are merely adding another layer on the cake.

2. Members of this proposed "B" Committee would be appointed by the Majority Leader and the Minority Leader. This is contrary to Senate practice where appointments to standing committees are the prerogatives of the Senate Steering Committee on the Democratic side and the Committee on Committees of the Senate Republican Conference.

3. Limiting the tenure of Senators to six years on the proposed committee is an assault on the seniority system and inhibits the development of expertise.

4. At variance with the practice of other standing committees, the proposed committee would have a chairman and a vice-chairman. Also, unlike other standing committees, the chairman would be appointed by the proposed committee instead of the entire Senate. The vice-chairman, a member of the minority party, would have the authority to act for the chairman in his absence. This is contrary to Senate precedent where the ranking majority member acts for the chairman in his absence, or whoever is senior on the majority side. I believe the majority party should control the standing committee.

5. No single committee of the Senate should be given legislative jurisdiction over all the intelligence activities of the U.S. government. Because the senators are already spread very thin in their commit-

tee assignments, the provision allowing senators to serve on the proposed committee in addition to all others is merely going to compound the problem.

Moreover, the best Senate staffs have at least a few persons of long service thereby providing continuity and reducing the possibility of legislative error.

The proposed new committee would have ultimate authority to disclose any intelligence secrets by majority vote. No matter how strongly a senator may feel about a foreign policy issue to overturn a policy through the disclosure of secrets can only lead to peril for the nation. Such a provision may raise constitutional questions—questions I shall leave to those versed in constitutional law.

S. 2893 requires the intelligence agencies of the government to give prior notice on the intention to carry out "certain kinds of intelligence activities" before they are initiated. While prior notice is required in some nonsensitive departments and agencies, I believe that intelligence by its very nature must be given special treatment. Prior notice could place the lives of agents in grave peril. And, even if their lives were not in peril, prior disclosure to committees of the Congress would tend to dampen their ardor. . . .

If the Congress wants more oversight, the existing committees can and should be required to perform. I believe they will be responsive.

QUESTIONS FOR DISCUSSION

1. Can a permanent congressional oversight committee of intelligence activities be trusted to keep national security secrets confidential?
2. The plan designed by Senator Church would require rotating membership for the new oversight committee members and staff. What are the strengths and weaknesses of this plan in serving as an instrument for overseeing intelligence agencies?
3. Should Congress have a stronger role in intelligence activities than it has had in the past?
4. Who is more responsible for making classified national security information public—the president or Congress?
5. Would national security be jeopardized or strengthened with the formation of such an oversight committee?

SUGGESTED READINGS

Agee, Philip. *Inside the Company: CIA Diary*. New York: Penguin Books, 1975.

Barnet, Richard J. "Dirty Tricks and the Intelligence Underworld." *Society* 12(March/April 1975):52–57.

Borosage, Robert. "Secrecy vs. the Constitution." *Society* 12(March/April 1975):71–75.

_____, and John D. Marks, eds. *The CIA File*. New York: Grossman, 1976.

Cline, Ray S. *Secrets, Spies and Scholars*. Washington, D.C.: Acropolis Books, 1976.

Halperin, Morton H., et al. *The Lawless State: The Crimes of the U.S. Intelligence Agencies*. New York: Penguin Books, 1976.

Harrington, Michael J. "Capitol Hill Outsmarted: Congress Boots the CIA Probes." *The Nation*, May 22, 1976, pp. 615–618.

Marchetti, Victor, and John D. Marks. *The CIA and the Cult of Intelligence*. New York: Alfred A. Knopf, 1974.

Rositzke, Harry. *CIA's Secret Operations*. New York: Reader's Digest Press, 1977.

Ross, Thomas B., and David Wise. *The Invisible Government*. New York: Vintage, 1974.

U.S. Congress. Senate. Committee on Government Operations. *Oversight of U.S. Government Intelligence Functions*. Hearings on S. 317, S. 189, S. Con. Res. 4, S. 2893, and S. 2865. 94th Cong., 2nd sess., 1976.

11.

Is Congress Ineffective?

When Woodrow Wilson studied power relationships within the federal government in the late nineteenth century, he entitled his book *Congressional Government,* in which he described the powers of the Congress as the dominant ones of the time.

Had Wilson been alive and engaging in similar research activities in 1970, however, he probably would not consider that title an accurate description of power relationships, for by 1970 congressional power was declining. Foreign and domestic policy considerations, the outlook of members of Congress, and the structure of Congress itself contributed to this decline. Many of these factors continue to diminish congressional power today, although Congress is now beginning to reassert its constitutional prerogatives with vigor.

Foreign policy has become a vital factor in the erosion of congressional power. A look at the Constitution alone, rather than the record of actual events, suggests that Congress does have enormous power in the conduct of foreign relations. Congress has the power to declare war, provide for an army and a navy, enact laws, authorize appropriations, and organize the administration of government. The Senate, moreover, has special powers for approving treaties and confirming appointments.

In fact, however, congressional power in foreign policy has become more apparent than real. The power of Congress to declare war has often been bypassed by the president's power as commander in chief. For example, presidents sent American troops into Korea in 1950 and into Vietnam in 1965 without declarations of war. American participation in these areas were wars if the loss of lives, rather than a legal technicality, is the criterion of judgment.

Senate power over treaties, moreover, has declined as the president has used executive agreements that do not require senatorial approval. Franklin Roosevelt, for example, exchanged fifty destroyers in return for the lease of certain sites for naval bases in the British West Atlantic without congressional authorization.

In domestic policy, too, Congress has at various times given powers to the president that allow considerable discretion. For example, presidents have been permitted, within limits, to raise or to lower tariff rates, to reorganize agencies of government (subject to veto by Congress), and even to institute price and wage controls in peacetime.

Congressional power over the budget—so vital to any domestic program— has also been declining during this century. Although Congress has played an important role in formulating the budget, the predominant influence has been exercised by the president and the bureaucracy. For example, the president has been able to impound funds appropriated by Congress. Even when impoundment was not an issue, the president retained budgetary power. The process of budget making is a time-consuming one, and until recently, Congress had to work relatively quickly to consider the president's budget, an advantage that has strengthened presidential power.

In 1974, Congress instituted reforms through which it restricted the president's ability to impound funds. It also adopted spending ceilings. The 1974 law stipulated that in the event these ceilings are breached, Congress must impose taxes or a higher national debt limit. The Congressional Budget Office was established to assist the legislature in achieving its objectives. In spite of the law, however, the president continues to play the major role in deciding government spending.

Congress, then, has willingly and unwillingly given up power to the president and to executive agencies. Many members of Congress have given up power voluntarily because they believed that the president, rather than the Congress, *should* have authority in certain areas. One of these areas has been national security. Attempts by Republican Senator John Bricker of Ohio in the 1950s to limit the treaty-making power of the president, for example, were turned down by the Congress.

Congressional power has also declined because of the slowness of congressional operating procedure. The many committees that a bill must go through before it becomes a law make the legislative process cumbersome. To be sure, Congress may act swiftly during an emergency, as the rapid enactment of laws during the first hundred days of Franklin Roosevelt's first administration attests, but that kind of activity is the exception rather than the rule. Bills must face the substantive committees in both houses of Congress. Hearings must be conducted, and delays are numerous. However, some problems—such as military crises, strikes in major industries, and sharp disruptions of the economy—often require prompt response. Congress is not structured for that kind of response.

The power of Congress is diminishing, and the beneficiaries of this decline in power have been the president and the bureaucracies. Congress has made efforts in the 1970s to reestablish its power and has succeeded in many cases. Congressional investigations of former President Richard Nixon's involvement in the Watergate coverup resulted in Nixon's resignation. In foreign policy, Congress has imposed severe constraints on the president's power, such as the thwarting of the Ford Administration's attempts to have the United States pursue a more activist foreign policy in Angola's civil war. Congress, moreover, has altered considerably or changed many of President Carter's domestic proposals in such areas as energy, taxes, breeder reactors, and water resources.

This chapter considers two examples of a redistribution of power designed to benefit Congress—one concerning the government agencies in every field of activity and the other dealing specifically with the power of the Congress in the conduct of foreign policy. These questions are (1) will sunset laws give Congress more power to control the bureaucracy?; and (2) should Congress have stronger powers in the conduct of foreign policy?

SUNSET LAWS

Congress has sought ways to control the growth of the bureaucracy. It has observed the tendency of government organizations to expand their activities, budgets, and the number of employees. At times members of Congress have felt helpless to control this growth.

Sunset laws have been recommended to limit the size of the bureaucracy. A bill was introduced in the Senate in 1977 to institute this reform. Under the sunset laws each agency of government would have to ask Congress every five years to consider whether or not that agency should continue. If Congress decided that the agency should not continue, the "sun" would "set" on the agency, and it would be disbanded.

Political analyst Peter DeLeon argues that sunset laws would strengthen Congress in overseeing government agencies and programs. DeLeon contends that sunset laws are necessary and that Congress is capable of coping with the enormous problems of five-year evaluations.

Political scientist Ron Randall argues against the sunset proposals. He contends that the task of evaluating every government agency from a zero base would be impossible to perform. He cites the many devices that state agencies have used to circumvent the purpose of the sunset laws. He adds that these laws would be detrimental to social welfare programs.

CONGRESS AND FOREIGN POLICY

In the late 1960s, when the war in Vietnam appeared endless, Congress directed more and more criticism against presidential conduct of the war. In committee hearings, in the chambers of both houses, and in speeches throughout the country, legislators contended that their traditional powers in the conduct of foreign policy had been undermined by presidents.

In 1970, Congress used its appropriation powers to limit the president's conduct of the war. Congress specifically forbade the use of funds for financing the sending of ground troops into Cambodia. In 1973, it worked to constrain the president's powers even further through its approval of the War Powers Act, which required that the president consult with Congress in every possible instance before committing troops in combat or in undeclared war. In the event that the president does commit troops without a declaration of war, he must submit a report to Congress within forty-eight hours. The president must withdraw those forces when Congress so directs or within sixty days unless during that period Congress declares war, extends the time limit, or cannot meet because of physical attack from a hostile country.

From the debate in the Senate over the War Powers Bill, liberal Republican Senator Jacob Javits argues that the bill is necessary to curtail executive power to make war and to restore Congress' constitutional powers. The bill would prevent future Vietnams. Without such a law, he states, Congress would be forced to rely on its appropriations powers to exercise a role in this policy area. The bill, moreover, is necessary because proponents of presidential power seem to be asserting that the president can do anything he wishes without sharing war-making power with Congress.

Conservative Republican Senator Barry Goldwater argues that the War Powers Bill would confound our allies and enemies and weaken our defense alliances. Specifically, he states that the bill would leave the United States standing helpless in the face of an all-out attack against a friendly nation such as Israel. It would, moreover, even block humanitarian assistance, such as the 1964 Congo rescue mission in which the United States military saved many non-Americans from rebel atrocities. The bill would give Congress too much power. The Founding Fathers established a limit to congressional power by indicating in the Constitution that Congress has the power to declare war, not to make war. He argues that Congress has other means to influence presidential war-making actions without this law.

Will Sunset Laws Give Congress More Power to Control the Bureaucracy?

YES

PETER DeLEON
*Sunset Laws Are Necessary**

Mr. Chairman and distinguished members of the subcommittee, it is a privilege to testify before you on S.2, the Sunset Act of 1977. Before beginning, let me take a second to note that the views I express are my own; they are not necessarily shared by The Rand Corporation or its research sponsors.

The Sunset Act of 1977 is a valuable continuation of the Congressional Budget Act of 1974 by which Congress became an active (as opposed to reactive) participant in the budgetary process. Whereas the Congressional Budget Act encouraged Congress to recognize and act upon the overall budget, the Sunset Act permits Congress to evaluate the individual programmatic components of the budget.

. . . S. 2 commits the Congress to a systematic evaluation of virtually all governmental programs, but, at the same time, does not concretize the procedures or specify impossible schedules. The standing committees are given a specific mandate but one with sufficient flexibility to permit them to adopt their evaluations and schedules to match the particular idiosyncrasies of the programs within their purview and the priorities they consider appropriate.

POLICY TERMINATION AND SUNSET LEGISLATION

Before turning to the problems I see confronting sunset legislation in general and S. 2 in particular, let me briefly suggest why the concept of policy termination is a worthwhile objective, and how sunset legislation represents a very tangible means for implementing policy termination. There is little reason to expect that any program or agency, no matter

* From U.S., Congress, Senate, Committee on Government Affairs, Hearings, before the Subcommittee on Intergovernmental Relations to Require Authorizations on New Budget Authority for Government Programs at Least Every Five Years, to Provide Review of Government Programs Every Five Years, and for Other Purposes (Sunset Act of 1977), 95th Cong., 2nd sess., 1977, pp. 368–371.

how well designed and operated, should live in perpetuity. Programs are governmental responses to particular societal problems. These problems and the societies in which they exist almost certainly change significantly with the passage of time. It is only natural to expect, then, that the problems' attendant policies and programs should change in equally significant ways and, as they become ineffective or antiquated, perhaps even die. Yet there is much evidence that policy termination, especially as manifested in terms of public organizations or agencies, is the great exception rather than the rule. [Political scientist] Herbert Kaufman suggests in his recent Brookings Institution study that if government organizations are not immortal, they certainly have a higher probability for long life than most of man's other creations; only 6 percent of the governmental agencies in his sample of over 400 have been terminated since 1923. Similar longevity records are less common in private industry because of the forces of the economic marketplace.

The Sunset Act of 1977 is not designed to rectify this condition. Its principal sponsor has testified that "very few of the agencies that are going to be considered for termination will be eliminated." Furthermore, organizations, policies, and programs are not identical. Still, what S. 2 does do is undisputably important. It mandates congressional oversight by requiring the committees of Congress to review and evaluate on a systematic basis their own legislative acts; it requires Congress to define in operational terms a program's objectives and evaluation and measures; it permits Congress to correct or redress possible deficiencies that this review process might uncover; and it gives Congress the evidence necessary to terminate a program should that option prove attractive (as it might in cases where various programs are consolidated). These oversight roles, in essence, will encourage the Congress to meet policy problems by adjusting programs whose magnitude, effect, and uncertainties are relatively well known rather than leaving Congress with little option other than drafting new legislation which would be replete with much greater uncertainties.

It is clear to me and, judging from the number of cosponsors of S. 2, many members of the U.S. Senate that sunset legislation is not only a good idea, but an idea whose time has come. The continuing proliferation of the number of agencies and programs, the growing ascendancy of the "uncontrollable" part of the yearly federal budget (close to 77 percent in fiscal year 1977), the fact that the nation can no longer afford whatever programs it might wish, and the increasing concern of its citizens that their government is too big, bureaucratic, and unsympathetic to their needs combine to explain why the Sunset Act of 1977 is particularly responsive to the needs of the time. Its titles encourage statements of program objectives and evaluation criteria because of their requirements for comprehensive review. The evaluation cycle should reveal program overlaps and duplications and, in so doing, force program tradeoffs within functional areas as well as promote greater efficiency. Last, but hardly least, the sunset review procedures will provide Congress with evidence on why programs fall short of their objectives, thereby providing more pre ise guidelines for the drafting of future legislation.

GENERAL OBSERVATIONS

In examining the problems voiced regarding sunset legislation, I would like to consider briefly some of the issues raised last year in the hearings before the Committee on Government Operations and the Committee on Rules and Administration on the Government Economy and Reform Act of 1976. The witnesses repeatedly posed four critical questions: Is sunset necessary? Would the increased work load be unmanageable? Are the standing authorization committees the appropriate review bodies? And are the required evaluation criteria and techniques available?

Is Sunset Necessary?

Some have argued that the fundamental processes of sunset legislation—the systematic review, evaluation, and potential elimination of programs and agencies—are already well established in the government. The restrictions of the federal budget and the efforts of the executive branch to hold the budget down serves as a surrogate market mechanism (or sort of budgetary Darwinism) to winnow out duplicate or ineffective programs. Therefore, they contend, specific sunset legislation is unnecessary and to legislate it would only add another set of tasks that would divert agencies from carrying out their responsibilities. Although this argument is logically appealing, it is sadly inaccurate. Although few dispute the sincerity of the executive branch in its efforts to keep federal spending as low as possible and that this commitment *should* eliminate ineffective or redundant programs, as noted above the evidence does not support the hypothesis. The incremental approach to budgeting appears to dominate the executive budget and rigorous evaluation across large functional areas is rarely attempted, let alone accomplished. Even more important, however, this argument implies that Congress need not concern itself with systematic program evaluation and possible termination because the market mechanisms controlled by the executive branch of the government will weed out the inefficient programs almost automatically. Thus, not only is the argument inaccurate but, in a government characterized by checks and balances, Congress should not surrender such powers as this proposition implies.

Is It "Doable"?

There is little doubt that the Sunset Act would require a significant increase in the amount of work on Congress' part. Therefore, the question "Is it doable?" was repeatedly voiced in the hearings. I cannot pretend to resolve the issue here; indeed, I will return to it presently when I propose some suggestions for possibly increasing the feasibility of implementing the Sunset Act. I wish to make two points here. First, many of the same pessimistic arguments were raised regarding the projected work loads that were to be imposed by the Congressional Budget Act of 1974. Yet few will argue today that the new demands are not being met, or furthermore, that the monetary and personnel costs of that Act are not commensurate with the returns. Second, one needs to ask if there is any alternative? It is not clear to me (for reasons raised above) that Congress can afford to permit "things as usual" to continue. Significant opportunity costs are surely attached to thorough and virtually universal programmatic reviews but it is problematic if the necessary investment in additional staffs and responsibilities could be better spent elsewhere. I contend that one's time is better invested systematically evaluating an effective body of programs linked to precise objectives rather than formulating new laws based on crucial uncertainties. Older legislation should not be permitted to proceed relatively unattended.

Sunset Reviews by Authorizing Committees

Some have raised the question as to whether the standing committees are the appropriate review bodies. This school of thought asserts that because of the committee's understandable reluctance to recognize the shortcomings of its earlier authorizations, the committee that wrote the initial authorization for a program should not be asked to review its effectiveness. This argument is carried further by some who suggest that the standing committee, by its very nature, has close—almost intimate—ties with the implementing agency and the program recipients and that these might unfairly influence or bias its review deliberations. This potential conflict of interest has so worried Common Cause that John Gardner has suggested in earlier testimony that committee members be rotated so as to ensure the relative objectivity of the evaluation committees. While I can appreciate these concerns, I find them somewhat overstated. They neglect the sizeable advantages of having the authorizing committee evaluate the programs. Not only does the continuity of the committee and its membership guarantee a large amount of pertinent expertise, it also suggests an organizational memory. That is, the members of the authorizing committee can recall the original rationale behind the bill and its objectives with greater clarity than a new committee might. At the same time, it would be more capable of noting divergencies from the bill's original intentions and changes in the relevant environments. Even if one were to discount these advantages, the alternatives would render S. 2 virtually infeasible. A single oversight committee could not possibly review all the programs of the federal government. The Common Cause suggestion of rotating committee membership would require such a major congressional reorganization that S. 2 would surely be lost in the shuffle. It is preferable, I submit, to operate within the current system than to press for such a sweeping alteration.

Can We Evaluate?

Finally, many witnesses testified that the difficulties inherent in evaluating government programs were so pervasive and intense as to render the critical evaluation component of sunset legislation unmanageable. Former Director of OMB [Office of Management and Budget] James Lynn, the Comptroller General from the General Accounting Office, then Secretary of Commerce Elliot Richardson, and John Gardner of Common Cause all broached this specific concern. Dr. Alice Rivlin, Director of the Congressional Budget Office, spoke for many when she said that "evaluation is an evolving art. In our highly complex and interdependent society, it is not always possible to determine what the situation would be if a certain program were terminated." One DHEW [Department of Health, Education, and Welfare] witness was even more pessimistically to the point; after cataloging the problems in evaluating his department's programs, he concluded that "we are almost pre-Copernican in our understanding of the social science methodology in this area." Indeed, often times it is not even clear what are the objectives an act is designed to achieve.

I scarcely intend to downgrade these accurate and appropriate warnings. However, I must ask, is the counsel of despair a real alternative? I immediately recognize and grant that the problem of evaluating a large and variegated number of programs is extremely difficult. S. 2 implicitly realizes this by not mandating any single evaluative mechanism upon the standing committees, thus permitting them to choose their own devices and tailor them to their particular programs. The basic question, however, remains: can the government afford to create and operate programs it has little hope of evaluating? The answer is obviously no. To succumb to the evaluation problem is a virtual admission of legislative or executive irresponsibility. To postpone sunset legislation because we do not currently possess the requisite tools is to ignore the complex, pressing problems that face the nation today. Better confront them directly now than to wait for that vaguely promised date when social scientists make good their assurances on evaluation methodologies and social indicators.

Will Sunset Laws Give Congress More Power to Control the Bureaucracy?

NO

RON RANDALL
*What's Wrong with Sunset Laws**

A national sunset law may be closer than most of us think. Senator Edmund Muskie (D., Maine) has reintroduced it, President Carter endorsed it when he was a candidate. In both houses of Congress, fallen liberals hasten to co-sponsor it. Conservatives have rallied to an idea that takes all the work out of being a conservative.

On January 10, Senator Muskie introduced the "Sunset Act of 1977" (S. 2)—substantially the same bill he sponsored last year. That bill died in the last session, but not before it went through several days of hearings, picked up considerable bipartisan support in the Senate and House, where a companion bill was sponsored by James J. Blanchard (D., Mich.) and Norman Y. Mineta (D., Calif.) and a bipartisan host of co-sponsors, and generated endorsements from a wide range of

---

* From Ron Randall, "'Zero-Base' Budgeting: What's Wrong with Sunset Laws," *The Nation*, March 19, 1977, pp. 331–334. © copyright 1977, The Nation Associates.

individuals and groups. The bill is tailor-made for President Carter. As a Georgia state Senator, he recalls in *Why Not the Best?*, he was "appalled to discover that we spent all of our time assessing proposals to finance new programs only. Once a program had been in operation for a year, there was little likelihood that it would ever be closely examined again. It would just grow inexorably like a fungus . . . ." The National Chamber of Commerce will be eager to help President Carter stamp out federal fungi; it pledged itself last year "to commit substantial effort to passage of [this] sunset bill."

Sunset legislation is yet another of the panaceas that congressmen espouse as the burden of continuous reelection campaigns outweighs their crucial oversight role on programs previously authorized and funded. Sunset has a beguiling appeal—after a certain period of time, a program automatically terminates unless explicitly renewed by legislative process. "Outraged by the waste" in many of the special programs he has sponsored or supported during the past decade, Muskie introduced the original bill with the best of intentions, and "not as a suggestion that we abandon our commitment to solving the nation's problems." But conservatives support the bill with precisely that end in view—all of the social welfare legislation passed over heavy and time-consuming opposition would be periodically resubjected to this ordeal. . . .

One cause for worry is the impossibility of the task. Existing institutions cannot perform evaluations of all government programs at this rigorous level. The other worry is that attempting a sunset review would create a severe bias against social welfare programs.

First, the task is nearly impossible. Although no one knows for sure how many federal government programs exist, most counts of domestic programs run well over 1,000. With a five-year review schedule, more than 200 sunset reviews would be conducted annually by the House and Senate committees. William A. Morrill, HEW [Health, Education, and Welfare] assistant secretary for planning and evaluation, uses the conservative figure of $1 million as the cost for a zero-base evaluation of each HEW program—or $370 million over five years for standing committees in one house to evaluate all 370 HEW programs; more than double the current HEW funding for evaluations. One hesitates to estimate the staff increases each standing committee would require for this level of evaluation.

The bill does mandate help for the committee from other government units. The Comptroller General would automatically furnish the appropriate committees with results of prior audits and reviews of the various programs coming up for consideration. More onerously, each standing committee may request "information, analyses and reports" for the reviews from the General Accounting Office (GAO), the Congressional Budget Office (CBO) and the Congressional Research Service. Finally, the bill instructs all agencies—whether or not involved in a program under sunset review—to provide the standing committee with such "information and assistance as the committee may request."

The Office of Management and Budget [OMB] alone is spared under the amended bill. Perhaps that is because former OMB Director James T. Lynn told the Muskie subcommittee that the staggering workload required of OMB in the original version of the bill "would—necessarily—give way to 'pro forma' examination." CBO Director Alice Rivlin cautioned that "the zero-base budgeting idea is useful if it is not taken too literally." However, the amended version of the bill does take the idea literally—and throws much of the burden in her lap. Comptroller General Elmer B. Staats has a long list of reservations about specific provisions in the original bill and general reservations about undertaking the zero-base or sunset review process "across the board without some prior experience." The testimony last year to the subcommittee involved a parade of experts politely stating that such reviews of all government programs are impossible.

The committee amending the bill paid slight attention to such testimony. The sunset review schedule was stretched from four to five years. The committee decided that the original bill's reviews by OMB were duplicative, and eliminated them. Other amendments grant standing committees more discretion to define what comprises sunset reviews if this serves the committees' purpose, and reduces the number of steps in the review process.

Where would this leave the standing committees if they were compelled to carry out a sunset review every five years of the programs under their jurisdiction? For some, it would mean a resort to loopholes. One loophole allows that the sunset "review shall be undertaken in the scope and the detail the committee having jurisdiction deems appropriate." Thus the standing committee will have final say about the nature of sunset reviews. The sophistication of the review, the diligence with which it is conducted, and the extent to which it is truly zero-base will depend on the committee's enthusiasm for the program and its relationship to the agency running the program. It is unlikely, for instance, that Senator Muskie will persuade the other members of the Senate's Public Works Committee to conduct through reviews of its pork-barrel programs.

Coordinated analysis of related programs is crucial to meaningful zero-base or sunset reviews. The bill attempts to address this issue by ordering the Comptroller General to classify "each program in only one functional and only one subfunctional category" to facilitate comparison with related federal efforts. Although an awesome task for the GAO, that skirts the critical issue of a decentralized and irrational system of committee jurisdictions, where a Food Stamp program is assigned to the Agriculture Committee and public assistance goes to a House Ways and Means Committee and a Senate Finance Committee. Comprehensive review of related programs can never be accomplished as long as related programs go to different committees which all jealously guard their turf. The answer is a major overhaul of the committee system. The recent reorganization of the Senate, a watered-down version of the recommendations of the study panel headed by Senator Adlai Stevenson (D., Ill.), which reduced the number of committees from thirty-one to twenty-five, is only a first step toward the major overhaul required for the coordinated analysis in the sunset bill. Senator Muskie understands the importance of committee reform. He has said:

> I think the committee jurisdiction problem is a very serious one . . . . As far as I am concerned I would be willing to throw all my committee assignments into the pot . . . and come up with a rational way of reorganizing our responsibilities so that we can do it more efficiently, and clearly.

No one is following Muskie's lead and he continues as chairman of the Senate Budget Committee.

The second major concern about sunset legislation is that the attempt to conduct zero-base reviews for all programs will produce results severely biased against social welfare.

The report accompanying last year's bill asserts that "one of the major strengths in [the bill], as amended, lies in the absolute neutrality of the proposed process." But as Senator Muskie and the subcommittee staff know, governmental arrangements and procedures are rarely neutral. Under the present legislative structure, any form of sunset law will, at the expense of social welfare programs, help defense programs and all manner of bricks and mortar, construction and other pork-barrel programs that require capital outlays. Past experience with the process of evaluation supports this assertion. That experience is twofold—a long history of evaluation for programs involving defense and public works (weapons systems, dams, highways, etc.) and a short history for social welfare programs.

For decades, evaluations of expected costs and benefits have been used to justify construction of dams and highways, dredging harbors, etc. When committee members are disposed to authorize a construction project, they find an analyst who will show that the benefits exceed the costs—not a difficult task—since every cost-benefit analysis is full of assumptions, the slight manipulation of which can greatly alter the ratio of costs to benefits.

Mr. Carter, when governor of Georgia, discovered how easily a cost-benefit analysis could be manipulated in the hands of the U.S. Army Corps of Engineers. He describes in *Why Not the Best?* the analysis produced by the Corps for a dam proposed on the Flint River fifty miles southeast of Atlanta: "Exaggerated claims for benefits were combined with shrunken costs estimated to justify the project." Congressmen, confronted with experts disputing the assumptions of an analysis, know their constituents will be deaf to that battle, but grateful for the jobs, increased recreation, elimination of floods, or whatever else the project is said to provide.

Social welfare does not provide the specifics of cost versus benefit that enable defense and public works programs to retain their momentum. The experience of the past decade is that evaluation of social welfare programs is incredibly difficult. Objectives are stated imprecisely, often they cannot be quantified. Because many of them have multiple objectives, it is impossible to do a complete evaluation. And since objectives frequently overlap, the effects of one program cannot be isolated from all the others. Even John Gardner, testifying for last year's sunset bill, admitted that the technique of evaluation is in an early stage. Curiously, for a man who was in the thick of social welfare programs while HEW Secretary, this becomes an opportunity to learn rather than a pitfall for his former programs: ". . . our learning curve is going to be steep in the early years of this program. We are going to know much more about evaluation and review after the first year than we did when we started." However, there may not be as many social welfare programs to practice on in the second round. Sadly, program opponents have seized upon expensive but incomplete social welfare evaluations to prove that the Great Society/social welfare programs of the past decade have not worked.

As if evaluation bias against social welfare programs were not enough cause for concern about a sunset law, other provisions compound the advantages for capital outlay projects. Drafters of last year's version of the bill recognize that "a program authorizing the construction of a dam or missile system clearly cannot be evaluated in the same way as a program intended to alleviate poverty or restore urban neighborhoods," and by so doing they unwittingly make evaluation of many construction projects moot. The bill exempts from sunset reviews many government construction programs authorized in the year before the scheduled review; thus it promises to produce a quinquennial pork-barrel feast that will make the annual congressional scramble for appropriations pale by comparison. To be sure, it would make no sense to cut off money from a government program in mid-construction, but a bill geared toward "absolute neutrality" should make a similar concession for social welfare programs. It does not.

Another possible source of bias is the filibuster, which in the past has been used much more frequently to stop progressive social welfare/civil rights legislation than to trim defense or public works programs. Senator Muskie is obviously worried about the potentially damaging consequence of the filibuster. His most recent version of sunset includes what he calls a "one-year grace period for programs which terminate unintentionally, rather than by design," because of a Senate filibuster or scheduling problems in the Senate or the House. In the long run, however, the filibuster or threat of one will take its toll. Every five years (prolonged into the sixth with an extension resolution), sunset will exact exorbitant political payoffs to anti-social welfare Senators in order to renew America's already inadequate commitment to social welfare.

Political power is a closely related question. Constituencies favoring construction projects are powerful, and Congress will likely bend before that power during the sunset review. Constituencies for social welfare are generally weak, and at present, when the public is looking for ways to ease high taxes, programs designed to attack societal problems are less popular than ever. In this climate, the sunset review will hit the social welfare programs particularly hard, freeing funds for the waiting hands of various construction lobbies, or promising tax relief to the biggest constituency of all.

Senator Muskie frets about "regular public opinion polls telling us that the American people have lost faith in their government" and uses the tired litany about failed social welfare programs to justify a sunset law:

> We have spent billions on health care, and enacted hundreds of health-oriented programs, yet we still have not cracked the fundamental problem—providing high-quality care at a price people can afford.
>
> We have spent billions on education, only to find that our high school graduates are not learning even the basic reading and writing skills.
>
> And we have spent billions on the problems of our cities, yet the root cause of those problems . . . still remains.

Instead of offering the easy answer of zero-base reviews, which will inaugurate an unworkable process and result in serious distortion of current national government priorities, Congress would much better serve the country by facing the real issues—cumbersome committee organization, unhealthy relationships among certain committees, agencies and clientele, and negligent congressional oversight of executive branch programs. Last year's bill had a sunset provision of its own, which terminated the zero-base procedure unless renewed at the end of 1982. Like its predecessor, the Planning Programming Budgeting System, sunset almost certainly would have been allowed to die in 1982. Curiously, that provision is not in this year's version. But a great waste of money and energy and a great distortion of priorities can be avoided by not allowing the sun ever to rise on the 1977 sunset bill.

QUESTIONS FOR DISCUSSION

1. Would sunset laws cut federal spending?
2. What alternatives to sunset laws could achieve the same results of cutting unnecessary government expenditures?
3. Is the present system of congressional oversight inadequate to deal with the growth of government spending?
4. Is the sunset law proposal a liberal or conservative device?
5. What effect would the sunset laws have on welfare programs?

SUGGESTED READINGS

Arlen, J. Large. "Are Sunset Laws the Answer?" *Wall Street Journal,* July 9, 1976, p. 12.

Behn, Robert D. "The False Dawn of the Sunset Laws." *The Public Interest* 49(Fall 1977):103–118.

Delfico, Joseph F. "Proposed Sunset and Zero-Base Legislation." *GAO* [General Accounting Office] *Review* 11(Winter 1977):34–40.

Gardner, Judy. "Doubts over 'Sunset' Bill Fail to Deter Backers of Concept." *Congressional Quarterly Weekly Report,* November 27, 1976, pp. 3255–3258.

Havemann, Joel, and Richard E. Cohen. "Taking Up the Tools to Tame the Bureaucracy: Zero-Base Budgeting and Sunset Legislation." *National Journal,* April 2, 1977 pp. 514–520.

Leone, Richard C. "Sunset Proposal: How to Ride Herd on the Budget." *The Nation,* May 22, 1976, pp. 625–627.

Pyhrr, Peter A. "Zero-Base Approach to Government Budgeting." *Public Administration Review* 37(January 1977):1–8.

Scheiring, M. J. "Zero-Base Budgeting in New Jersey." *State Government* 49(Summer 1976):174–179.

U.S. Congress. Senate. Committee on Government Operations. *Government Economy and Spending Reform Act of 1976.* Hearings before a Subcommittee on Intergovernmental Relations on S. 2925, 94th Cong., 2nd sess., 1976.

U.S. Congress. Senate. Committee on Rules and Administration. *Government Economy and Spending Reform Act of 1976.* Hearing on S. 2925, 94th Cong., 2nd sess., 1976.

Should Congress Have Stronger Powers in the Conduct of Foreign Policy?

YES

JACOB JAVITS
The Case for the War Powers Bill*

Mr. President, on behalf of myself, Senators [John] Stennis, Democrat, of Mississippi, [Thomas] Eagleton, Democrat, of Missouri, [Lloyd] Bentsen, Democrat, of Texas, [Robert] Taft, Republican, of Ohio, and fifty-three additional cosponsors who have joined with us, I introduce the War Powers Act—a measure which, in our judgment, establishes practical and well-considered procedures to assure a proper role for the Congress according to the Constitution with respect to committing the nation to war. The legislation introduced today is identical to the bill passed by the Senate on April 13, 1972, by a vote of sixty-eight to sixteen. It is particularly significant that both the majority leader and the minority leader have joined in cosponsoring this bill, I am also very pleased to note that among its sponsors is the deputy leader of the Democratic side, Senator Robert C. Byrd of West Virginia. . . .

* From U.S., Congress, Senate, Senator Jacob Javits speaking for the War Powers Bill, 93rd Cong., 1st sess., January 18, 1973, *Congressional Record* 119:1394–1395.

. . . [the War Powers Act] is a bill to end the practice of presidential war and thus to prevent future Vietnams. It is an effort to learn from the lessons of the last tragic decade of war which has cost our nation so heavily in blood, treasure, and morale. The War Powers Act would assure that any future decision to commit the United States to any warmaking must be shared in by the Congress to be lawful.

No legislation can guarantee national wisdom, but the fundamental premise of the Constitution, with its deliberate system of checks and balances and separation of powers, is that important decisions must be national decisions, shared in by the people's representatives in Congress as well as the president. By enumerating the war powers of Congress so explicit and extensively in Article I, Section 8, the Framers of the Constitution took special care to assure the Congress of a concurring role in any measures that would commit the nation to war. Modern practice, culminating in the Vietnam war and the result of a long history of executive action employing the warmaking power which weaves in and out of our national history, has upset the balance of the Constitution in this respect.

The central core of the War Powers Act is contained in Sections 3 and 5 of the bill. Section 3 consists of four clauses which define the conditions of circumstances under which, in the absence of a congressional declaration of war, the armed forces of the United States "may be introduced in hostilities, or in situations where imminent involvement in hostilities is clearly indicated by the circumstances."

The first three categories are codifications of the emergency powers of the president, as intended by the Founding Fathers and as confirmed by subsequent historical practice and judicial precedent. Thus, subsections (1), (2), and (3) of section 3 delineate by statute the implied power of the president in his concurrent role as commander in chief.

Subsection (4) of section 3 is perhaps the most significant; while subsections (1), (2), and (3) codify emergency powers which are inherent in the independent constitutional authority of the president as commander in chief, subsection (4) deals with the delegation by the Congress of additional authorities which would accrue to the president as a result of statutory action by the Congress, and which he does not, or would not, possess in the absence of such statutory action. Thus, subsection (4) regulates and defines the undertaking of a "national commitment."

Section 5 provides that actions taken under the provisions of section 3 "shall not be sustained beyond thirty days from the date of the introduction of such armed forces in hostilities or in any such situation unless—"the continued use of such armed forces in hostilities or in such situation has been authorized in specific legislation enacted for that purpose by the Congress and pursuant to the provisions thereof."

Section 5 resolves the modern dilemma of reconciling the need of speedy and emergency action by the president in this age of instantaneous communications and of intercontinental ballistic missiles with the urgent necessity for Congress to exercise its constitutional mandate and duty with respect to the great questions of war and peace. . . .

ICBM

Our experience . . . has demonstrated how much harder it is to get out of an undeclared war than it is to get into one. In dealing with this situation, Congress has been forced back onto relying solely on its power over appropriations. We have seen how difficult and unsatisfactory it is for Congress to try to get a meaningful hold on the Vietnam war through the funds cutoff route.

Yet there are a group of pundits, historians, and commentators who would have us fly directly in the fact of this tortuous experience and confine ourselves to the funds cutoff route. Those who would so advise us are either too timid or too conservative to try institutional reform. They would have us face the presidential war power so often used as a fine tuned, subtle, and decisive instrument with a clumsy, blunt, and obsolescent tool. The fund cutoff remedy is there now and will be there when the war powers bill becomes law. It can then be an excellent sanction, but it is not a substitute.

The obvious lesson for Congress is to devise ways to bring to bear its extensive, policy powers respecting war at the outset, so that it is not left to fumble later in an after-the-fact attempt to use its appropriations power. This is what the War Powers Act seeks to do.

If James Madison had pressed his point on September 7, 1787, during the debate in the Constitutional Convention, we might not be faced with our current agonizing dilemma. Madison proposed then that two-thirds of the Senate be authorized to make treaties of peace without the concurrence of the president. . . .

However, Madison withdrew his proposal without putting it to a vote.

It is not clear whether Madison was speaking seriously or facetiously. It is clear, however, that presidents have tended to see their role, as commander in chief conducting a war, as the decisive power of the presidency. President Nixon articulated this view very precisely . . . :

> Each of us in his way tries to leave [the presidency] with as much respect and with as much strength in the world as he possibly can—that is his responsibility—and to do it the best way that he possibly can. . . . But

if the United States at this time leaves Vietnam and allows a Communist
takeover, the office of president of the United States will lose respect and
I am not going to let that happen.

The effort embodied in the War Powers Act is the fulcrum, in my
judgment, of the broader attempt of the Congress to redress the
dangerous constitutional imbalance which has developed in the relationship between the president and the Congress. Unless Congress suc-
ceeds in reasserting its war powers I do not think it can succeed in
reasserting its powers of the purse which have grown so weak in comparison with the executive branch.

The publicists and the lawyers of the presidency have been busy
for years now in advancing a new constitutional doctrine. According to
this novel doctrine the president has inherent powers, in his role as
commander in chief, to override any other powers conferred anywhere
else in the Constitution.

We have reached a point where proponents of the presidency
seem to be claiming that the power of the commander in chief is what
he himself defines it to be in any given circumstance. This is the challenge that must be met by the Congress. If this challenge is not met
successfully by the Congress, I do not see how it can prevent the
further erosion of its powers and jeopardize freedom itself.

Most senators are already familiar with the War Powers Act. It
was the subject of extensive, and indeed historic, hearings before the
Foreign Relations Committee in 1971. . . . The bill was subjected to
further intense scrutiny in a major Senate debate which lasted from
March 29 to April 13, 1972, when the Senate voted sixty-eight to sixteen to adopt the legislation. . . .

The sponsors of the War Powers Act are hopeful that this year the
bill will be considered on its merits in the House of Representatives,
where it has not yet received full committee hearings or been accorded
a debate and a vote on the floor of the House. In 1972, the House of
Representatives passed a bill principally sponsored by Representative
Zablocki seeking advance notice from the president and requiring a full
report in instances involving the use of the armed forces in hostilities
without specific prior authorization by the Congress. This bill essentially accepted the notice provisions of the War Powers Act, but went
no further. In the ensuing conference between the Senate and House,
the conferees could find no common ground, as the House measure
completely eliminated the Senate principle of joint control by the president and the Congress of the warmaking power. In this endeavor,
above all others, the House and the Senate should be partners in a

common cause to protect the viability of the Congress as a coequal branch of Government under our constitutional system.

Mr. President, I do take heart from the fact that the new bill introduced this year by Representative Zablocki contains some significant new elements bringing it closer to the Senate bill. For one thing, it provides for further consideration of the president's actions by Congress.

For another thing, it seeks to specify and define the emergency situations in which the president is empowered to use the armed forces without a declaration of war. I am encouraged by these new provisions in the Zablocki bill. They give evidence that the House of Representatives, and the leaders on this vital issue in that chamber, have not frozen their thinking on war powers. I look forward to a further convergence of views.

Mr. President, the Congress itself is on trial in the eyes of the people and the War Powers Act is a decisive test. The issue addressed by the War Powers Act is a fundamental constitutional issue. It rejects the premise that the issue of "presidential war" can be handled by making distinctions between "good" presidents and "bad" presidents. We could never arrive at an agreed criteria for making such judgments and there is no way such distinctions could be applied to presidential wars on an ad hoc [for one special purpose only] basis.

The need is for legislation which will assume congressional involvement at the outset of all wars. Our constitutional system requires a confidence that the Congress will act as responsibly as any president in the national interest. Even more significantly, it assumes that the national interest can best be defined and acted upon when both the president and the Congress are required to come to an understanding as to what is the national interest.

The War Powers Act embodies practical and well-conceived procedures to implement the constitutional war powers of Congress in a manner which fully meets the requirements of national security in the modern world.

Should Congress Have Stronger Powers in the Conduct of Foreign Policy?

NO

BARRY GOLDWATER
*The Case Against the War Powers Bill**

In 1951, a current favorite of the New Left, Dr. Henry Steele Commager, rebuked congressional critics of President Truman's undeclared war in Korea by writing in the *Time* magazine that the constitutional issue "is so hackneyed a theme that even politicians might reasonably be expected to be familiar with it." Professor Commager lectured that questions involving executive power have come up time and again in the past and time and again both history and the courts have returned clear answers in support of executive decisions to commit troops outside the nation.

In 1961, following the Korean war, the buildup of over 400,000 U.S. ground forces in Europe, and the Lebanon occupation, another contemporary paragon of peace, Senator William J. Fulbright delivered a lecture at Cornell University in which he argued "that for the existing requirements of American foreign policy we have hobbled the presidency by too niggardly a grant of power." Referring to what he called the dynamic forces of the twentieth century—communism, fascism, and aggressive nationalism—Senator Fulbright warned that "[it] is highly unlikely that we can successfully execute a long-range program for the taming, or containing, of today's aggressive and revolutionary forces by continuing to leave vast and vital decision-making powers in the hands of a decentralized, independent-minded, and largely parochial-minded body of legislators."

What has happened in the interval to cause these foreign policy internationalists, together with so many of their liberal brethren, to spin 180 degrees the other way toward the very choices which they had formally labeled as being held only by "unregenerate isolationists"? The answer, in my opinion, is simply that they, as many Americans, have become so mesmerized by events in Vietnam that they believe it is possible to legislate against the past.

* From U.S., Congress, Senate, Senator Barry Goldwater's statement against the War Powers Bill, 93rd Cong., 1st sess., January 29, 1973, *Congressional Record* 119:2387.

Forgetting the experience of a post-World War I Congress which thought it had enacted neutrality laws so wise and virtuous that we could never again be drawn into a major conflict, and unmindful that such restrictions left this nation unprepared to help avert the world catastrophe that later erupted, the new isolationists would bind the president in a chain of restrictions that would surely confound our allies and enemies alike, weaken the defense alliances that keep foreign disturbances away from our own shores, and hamper our national ability to defend future vital interests. What is more, the specific legislation used to these ends is so rigidly drafted it would leave the United States standing by helpless in the face of an all-out attack against valuable friendly nations, such as Israel, where we have no significant forces already stationed, and would even block humanitarian assistance, such as the 1964 Congo rescue mission in which the U.S. military saved almost 2,000 non-Americans from rebel atrocities.

Contrary to disclaimers by its sponsors, the War Powers Bill severely restricts the freedom of the executive to respond in all emergencies. Unless there is an actual attack, or threat of attack which is both "direct and imminent," against the United States, its citizens, or the armed forces, U.S. troops cannot be deployed into troubled areas [without . . .] specific statutory authority. In reality, however, U.S. security interests stretch far beyond these immediate emergencies to ones in which the harmful consequences will not develop until months or perhaps years later. One example is a Soviet move to close off the Strait of Molacca from free world commerce.

Even in the emergencies where the bill allows presidential reaction, it provides a limit of thirty days on such conduct absent additional congressional approval. The bill also creates a legislative process by which Congress can shut off any such emergency conduct prior to thirty days. Thus, the bill grants Congress a veto over military activity even in those areas where it is conceded the president possesses a constitutional power to act.

The bill thereby defines the boundaries of the constitutional allotment of the war powers between Congress and the president, something the Founding Fathers never attempted to do. For the declaration of war clause does not confer upon Congress the sole power whereby the country can be engaged in war. In fact, the Constitutional Convention purposefully narrowed the authority of Congress by substituting "declare" for "make" in that clause. This was done in an age when the declaration was already in disuse, there having been thirty-eight wars in the Western World from 1700 to 1787, and only one of which was preceded by a declaration of war. And so, even by the eighteenth century, the declaration had come to mean no more than a formal

notice to a nation's own people and to the outside world that an existing state of war was officially acknowledged. At least this is how it is
defined in the sole standard dictionary of the English language then
published, and it is how the Constitution has been interpreted during
the succeeding 183 years of practice.

It may come as a surprise, but there have been over 200 foreign
military hostilities in the history of our Republic and only five of them
were declared. These engagements have ranged from minor rescue
operations to deployments of thousands of ground forces into battle,
such as the 14,000 U.S. troops who fought in Russia after World War I.
These incidents attest to a consistent practice under which American
presidents have always responded to foreign threats with whatever
force they believed was necessary and technologically available at the
particular moment. Whether these restrictive measures were prudent
or not is a separate issue from the constitutional question; but who is to
say that President Kennedy was unwise in seeking the removal of
missiles from Cuba that were being aimed at 80 million Americans, as
one notable example?

The truth is, there are circumstances in which any president must
have flexibility of action in order to meet a present crisis which might
develop into an unalterable threat against our national security in the
future, as well as to cope with a crisis which obviously represents a
direct and immediate danger. Advocates of war powers restrictions
miss the point that inaction in a time of true emergency might bring
forth far more bloodshed in the future than if forceful steps were taken
promptly.

To those who contend this concept will lead to extended involve-
ments, such as another Vietnam, I answer that this reveals a blitheful
ignorance of recent history. Congress passed over twenty-four statutes
supporting the Vietnam war with both money and authority, a fact that
has been judicially confirmed.

Nor do I accept the excuse that politicians could not have voted
otherwise. If the executive can exert an open or subtle appeal for
support of American troops in the field, the ranks of Congress are not
shy of those who pander the equally compelling promise of a swift and
easy peace and an end to pitiful crowds of starving refugees whom they
blame upon U.S. policies.

The power of the purse, with its related control over the size of
the military services and kinds and amounts of defense systems, combined with the treaty power and an oft-overlooked discretion with respect to the delegation of vast powers over the allocation, production,
and trade of strategic materials and of other powers for directing the
national economy to war-oriented purposes, constitute an impressive

base from which Congress can alter or influence the course of American involvement in the foreign sphere. These are the means by which the Founders meant for Congress to share in important decisions on matters of foreign military policy, and Congress cannot alter this arrangement by any legislative device short of a constitutional amendment.

QUESTIONS FOR DISCUSSION

1. What are the war-making powers enumerated in the Constitution for Congress and the president?
2. Is Congress not likely to give the president authority to continue military activity after the president's initial time limit for sending armed forces into combat abroad has been reached?
3. Regardless of the War Powers Act, what political constraints does the president face in getting the United States involved in another Vietnam-type war?
4. According to Senator Goldwater, liberals have switched their views from supporting a strong president in the conduct of foreign relations to supporting a strong Congress. Why has this change occurred? Do you suppose that there has been a reversal of the conservative position from supporting a strong congressional role in foreign policy to supporting a strong presidential role?
5. Had there been a War Powers Act on the books in 1963, would the United States have become involved in the war in Vietnam?

SUGGESTED READINGS

Goldsmith, William. *The Growth of Presidential Power.* 3 vols. New York: Bowker, 1974.

Halberstam, David. *The Best and the Brightest.* New York: Random House, 1972.

Hoopes, Townsend. *The Limits of Intervention.* New York: David McKay, 1969.

Johnson, Lyndon B. *The Vantage Point.* New York: Holt, Rinehart and Winston, 1971.

Mansfield, Harvey, ed. *Congress Against the President.* New York: Praeger, 1975.

Mueller, John E. *War, Presidents and Public Opinion.* New York: John Wiley & Sons, 1973.

Novak, Michael. "The Presidency and Professor Schlesinger." *Commentary*, February 1974, pp. 74–78.

Polsby, Nelson W. *Congress and the Presidency*, 3rd ed. Englewood Cliffs, N.J.: Prentice-Hall, 1975.

Schlesinger, Arthur M., Jr. *The Imperial Presidency*. New York: Popular Library, 1973.

Weaver, Paul H. "Liberals and the Presidency." *Commentary*, October 1975, pp. 48–53.

12.

Does Judicial Review Strengthen Democracy?

Of the three major institutions of the federal government—president, Congress, and Supreme Court—the last is the least democratic. Although democracy requires periodic elections, the members of the Supreme Court are appointed, never run for office in popular elections, and once on the court, usually remain there for life or until they retire. Presidents, senators, and representatives may envy this luxury of not having to run for public office.

The Supreme Court's power of judicial review is—at least on the surface—another undemocratic feature of this arm of government. Judicial review is the power of the Supreme Court to examine state and federal laws and the acts of state and federal public officials to determine whether or not they are in conflict with the Constitution. If these laws and acts are in conflict, then the Court may declare them invalid. The fact that a majority of nine unelected members of the Court may declare null and void the laws enacted by the representatives of the majority of the people seems to be a limitation on the principle of majority rule. The argument is often made, however, that the specific content of court decisions has strengthened, rather than weakened, democracy.

Judicial review is a component of the American political genius. In contrast, the British system of government permits the courts to interpret the laws but not to declare any act of Parliament invalid. Judicial review is not specifically mentioned in the Constitution. Debate surrounds the question of whether or not the Framers intended the Supreme Court to have this power over the laws of the federal government. There is general agreement, however, that the Framers understood that judicial review is applicable to acts of state legislatures in conflict with the Constitution. The Supreme Court first declared an act of Congress unconstitutional in *Marbury* v. *Madison* (1803). In this case the Supreme Court found the Judiciary

Act of 1789 to be in conflict with Article III of the Constitution. Today, the Supreme Court's authority to declare a statute unconstitutional is unchallenged.

Over the past century the Supreme Court has exercised its power of judicial review in a variety of cases. Those who have benefited from the Court's decisions have hailed the wisdom of the Court. The "losers" have often called for limiting the jurisdiction of the Court, amending the Constitution, enlarging the size of the Court, or impeaching the Chief Justice.

Court decisions have not supported one group of people exclusively. In the early part of the twentieth century, for example, court decisions were more favorable to property owners, states' rights advocates, and segregationists. Since the days of the Warren Court (named for former Chief Justice Earl Warren) in the mid-1950s, however, courts have been more favorable to groups demanding greater extension of civil rights and civil liberties. The changing character of court decisions is a reflection of such factors as the composition of the court, legal precedents, and the political environment. One factor that has received much attention, however, is the philosophical outlook of the judges.

Two principal philosophical outlooks have marked the role of the judge: judicial activism and judicial restraint. Judicial activists contend that judges should exercise great freedom in declaring statutes unconstitutional. They argue that taking sides politically is inevitable and that there are no neutral principles of law constraining court members. Judges, they add, should use their power to achieve goals they consider important.

Those who favor judicial restraint contend that judges should avoid substituting their own policy preferences for those of duly elected public officials. The task of the judges, according to this view, is to apply the law, not to assert biases in favor of social reform.

Nonlawyers are often unconcerned with these different philosophies and tend to be more interested in the actual outcomes of Supreme Court decisions than in the attitudes governing the judges in making their decisions. To the layman, moreover, it is often easier to evaluate the decisions of the Supreme Court in liberal-conservative terms than to look at the reasons behind the decisions. These perceptions have led many people to believe that judges have changed their position from liberal to conservative (or vice versa) when in fact the judges have not changed their philosophical outlook.

The case of Felix Frankfurter may be used as an example. Frankfurter was an advocate of judicial restraint. When he was appointed to the Supreme Court during Franklin Roosevelt's second Administration, the Supreme Court was declaring New Deal legislation unconstitutional. Frankfurter was able to side with the liberal Congress over the conservative Court because of his belief in the limited role of the Court.

When in the 1950s Congress was passing conservative laws, Frankfurter often sided with the conservative legislature in upholding laws even when he regarded those laws as undesirable. Frankfurter then was considered a conservative by many people. In fact, Frankfurter did not change. He remainded consistent in his legal philosophy of what the role of the courts should be.

In practice these two philosophies of the role of the Supreme Court are rarely held in absolute form. More often than not, Supreme Court justices and legal scholars support activism in some cases and restraint in others.

This chapter deals with the subject of judicial philosophy. Specifically, the question is asked: Should the courts pursue a philosophy of judicial restraint?

Particularly in the days of the Warren Court, the Court increased the frequency with which it invalidated statutes on constitutional grounds. Landmark cases struck down segregation statutes, malapportionment practices, and the legality of some police tactics. In recent years, however, the (Warren E.) Burger Court has moved away somewhat from the judicial activism of the Warren Court.

Legal scholar Wallace Mendelson presents the doctrine of restraint as advocated by Justice Felix Frankfurter. Mendelson asserts the view that the proper source of authority for making laws in a democracy is the elected legislature, not the appointed Court.

J. Skelly Wright, a judge of the United States Court of Appeals for the District of Columbia Circuit, defends the activist position as represented by the Warren Court. The Court, he argues, should be activist in order to keep the community true to its own fundamental principles when legislatures become overzealous and weaken fundamental tenets of the system. The Court must protect unpopular minorities not only from governmental persecution but from governmental neglect as well. According to Wright, the Warren Court acted within the proper framework of the activist position.

Should the Courts Pursue
a Philosophy of Judicial Restraint?

YES

WALLACE MENDELSON
*The Orthodox, or Anti-Activist View—Mr. Justice Frankfurter**

Judicial review has been a storm center in American history because it involves political choice without commensurate political responsibility. Oliver Wendell Holmes said:

> . . . I think it most important to remember whenever a doubtful case arises with certain analogies on one side and other analogies on the other, that what really is before us is a conflict between two social desires, each of which seeks to extend its dominion over the case, and which cannot both have their way . . . . Where there is doubt, the simple tool of logic does not suffice, and even if it is disguised and unconscious, the judges are called on to exercise the sovereign prerogative of choice.[1]

The "great generalities" of the Due Process and the Commerce clauses, for example, can be judicially interpreted in the light of laissez-faire [no government interference] or the opposite. Either way, the people have no direct recourse, for federal judges are not answerable at the polls. As though recognizing this tension between judicial review and popular government, the Supreme Court has long since developed a series of self-restraining principles. Justice Louis Brandeis expressed their essence when he said, "The most important thing we do is not doing."[2] What he meant, of course, is that the more the Court restrains itself, the greater are the freedom and responsibility of the people to govern themselves. He did not suggest that judicial review should be abandoned; after all, it is an established part of our constitutional system. But he recognized that standards for judgment are often vague; that the judiciary has very limited capacity to find and assess all of the data necessary for an informed judgment on the broad social issues behind the immediate claims of litigants; that judicial intervention in such matters is necessarily sporadic, indeed largely haphazard;

* From Wallace Mendelson, ed., "The Orthodox, or Anti-Activist View—Mr. Justice Frankfurter," in *The Supreme Court: Law and Discretion.* Copyright © 1967 The Bobbs-Merrill Company, Inc., pp. 6–14.

that judges have no unique immunity from error; and that error in upholding a statute can be corrected by the people far more readily than error raised to the status of a constitutional limitation. And so it is that Brandeis—like Justice Felix Frankfurter—was "forever disposing of issues by assigning [i.e., leaving] their disposition to some other [more politically responsible] sphere of competence."[3] For ultra-activists this, of course, is nothing less than abdication of judicial duty.

Perhaps the most basic of the Court's self-restraining principles is avoidance of unnecessary constitutional commitments. After all, there is fatal "finality" in a decision on the meaning of the Constitution. The only legal way the people can change it is the cumbersome, minority-controlled process of formal amendment. And so, as Mr. Justice Brandeis summarized the ancient tradition:

> "Considerations of propriety, as well as long-established practice, demand that we refrain from passing upon the constitutionality of an act of Congress unless obliged to do so in the proper performance of our judicial function, when the question is raised by a party whose interests entitle him to raise it." *Blair* v. *United States,* 250 U.S. 273, 279. . . .

The Court has frequently called attention to the "great gravity and delicacy" of its function in passing upon the validity of an act of Congress, and has restricted exercise of this function by rigid insistence that the jurisdiction of federal courts is limited to actual cases and controversies and that they have no power to give advisory opinions. On this ground it has in recent years ordered the dismissal of several suits challenging the constitutionality of important acts of Congress. . . .

The Court developed, for its own governance in the cases confessedly within its jurisdiction, a series of rules under which it has avoided passing upon a large part of all the constitutional questions pressed upon it for decision. They are:

1. The Court will not pass upon the constitutionality of legislation in a friendly, nonadversary, proceeding, declining because to decide such questions "is legitimate only in the last resort, and as a necessity in the determination of real, earnest, and vital controversy between individuals. It never was the thought that, by means of a friendly suit, a party beaten in the legislature could transfer to the courts an inquiry as to the constitutionality of the legislative act. . . ."

2. The Court will not "anticipate a question of constitutional law in advance of the necessity of deciding it . . . . It is not the habit of the court to decide questions of a constitutional nature unless absolutely necessary to a decision of the case. . . . "

3. The Court will not "formulate a rule of constitutional law broader than is required by the precise facts to which it is to be applied . . . . "

4. The Court will not pass upon a constitutional question although properly presented by the record, if there is also present some other ground upon which the case may be disposed of. This rule has found most varied application. Thus, if a case can be decided on either of two grounds, one involving a constitutional question, the other a question of statutory construction or general law, the Court will decide only the latter . . . . Appeals from the highest court of a state challenging its decision of a question under the federal Constitution are frequently dismissed because the judgment can be sustained on an independent state ground . . . .

5. The Court will not pass upon the validity of a statute upon complaint of one who fails to show that he is injured by its operation . . . . Among the many applications of this rule, none is more striking than the denial of the right to challenge to one who lacks a personal or property right. Thus, the challenge by a public official interested only in the performance of his official duty will not be entertained . . . . In *Fairchild* v. *Hughes*, 258 U.S. 126, the Court affirmed the dismissal of a suit brought by a citizen who sought to have the Nineteenth Amendment declared unconstitutional. In *Massachusetts* v. *Mellon*, 262 U.S. 447, the challenge of the federal Maternity Act was not entertained although made by the commonwealth on behalf of all its citizens.

6. The Court will not pass upon the constitutionality of a statute at the instance of one who has availed himself of its benefits . . . .

7. "When the validity of an act of Congress is drawn in question, and even if a serious doubt of constitutionality is raised, it is a cardinal principle that this Court will first ascertain whether a construction of the statute is fairly possible by which the question may be avoided. . . . "[4]

A related principle finds expression in the doctrine of political questions. It holds that courts should avoid involvement in matters traditionally left to legislative policy making; in matters as to which there are no adequate constitutional standards to guide judicial judgment; or in matters as to which there are no adequate modes of judicial relief. In *Coleman* v. *Miller*,[5] for example, the Court was asked to decide whether a proposed constitutional amendment had expired simply because it had not been ratified by three fourths of the states in a "reasonable" period of time. Refusing decision, the Court said:

> . . . Where are to be found the criteria for such a judicial determina-
> tion? None are to be found in the Constitution or statute . . . . When a
> proposed amendment springs from a conception of economic needs, it
> would be necessary, in determining whether a reasonable time had
> elapsed since its submission, to consider [among other things] the eco-
> nomic conditions prevailing in the country, whether these had so far
> changed since the submission as to make the proposal no longer respon-
> sive to the conception which inspired it or whether conditions were such
> as to intensify the feeling of need and the appropriateness of the pro-
> posed remedial action. In short, the question of a reasonable
> time . . . would involve . . . appraisal of a great variety of relevant
> conditions, political, social, and economic which can hardly be said to be
> within the appropriate range of evidence receivable in a court of jus-
> tice . . . . On the other hand, these conditions are appropriate for the
> consideration of the political departments of the government.

Another principle of judicial restraint recognizes, as Chief Justice
John Marshall said, that "the question, whether a law be void for
repugnancy to the Constitution, is, at all times, a question of much
delicacy, which ought seldom, if ever, to be decided in the affirmative
in a doubtful case."[6] As Mr. Justice [Bushrod] Washington put it a few
years later:

> . . . the [constitutional] question which I have been examining is in-
> volved in difficulty and doubt. But if I could rest my opinion in favor of
> the constitutionality of the law . . . on no other ground than this
> doubt . . . that alone would . . . be a satisfactory vindication of it. It
> is but a decent respect due to the wisdom, the integrity, and the pa-
> triotism of the legislative body, by which any law is passed, to presume in
> favor of its validity, until its violation of the Constitution is proved be-
> yond all reasonable doubt. This has always been the language of this
> Court . . . and I know it expresses the honest sentiments of each and
> every member of the bench.[7]

In this view, a legislative act may be held invalid only when the
Court is prepared to say that no reasonable mind could uphold the
legislative view. For doubt entails choice, and in a democracy, choice
is the province of the people. This rule of doubt is related to the
common-law guide—the reasonable man. Who is this creature? Like
jury and legislature, he symbolizes all of us. He is an "external standard," an American Everyman, whereby the troubled judge seeks to
guard against his own personal bias in favor of the "views and feelings
that may fairly be deemed representative of the community as a continuing society."[8]

Behind all these self-denying ordinances of the orthodox tradition
lies a common principle: Government by the judiciary is a poor substi-

tute for government by the people. With this and its supporting doctrines, there has been all but universal agreement, on and off the bench.
Thus it may be fairly called the orthodox view, though in practice it is
not equally respected by all judges. The anti-activist is perhaps a bit
more concerned, and a bit more successful, than others in distinguishing between "law" and his own heart's desire. In this no one can hope
to be completely successful, yet we know as a matter of experience that
some men—on or off the bench—achieve much more objectivity than
others. Mr. Justice Frankfurter's opinion in the second *Flag Salute*
case[9] is no doubt the classic modern expression of the anti-activist
approach.

When Professor Frankfurter left Harvard for the bench in 1939, he
was generally considered a liberal—in some quarters even a radical.
More recently, he has been accused of conservatism. Yet it seems clear
that his basic outlook did not change. In private life he was one of the
great liberals of our day. But it is crucial in his philosophy that a judge's
private convictions are one thing, his duty on the bench quite another.
This was the teaching of Holmes. By failing to heed it, the proprietar-
ians among the "Nine Old Men" [members of the Supreme Court
during the early years of the New Deal] destroyed the old Court—just
as the libertarians might have destroyed the new one, if they had had
enough votes to do so. As both professor and judge, with respect to
both liberty and property, Felix Frankfurter was skeptical of government by the judiciary. The judge's job, as he understood it, is to decide
"cases" and "controversies," not to create a brave new world—for
the legislative function has been given to others:

> . . . As society becomes more and more complicated and individual
> experience correspondingly narrower, tolerance and humility in passing
> judgment on the experience and beliefs expressed by those entrusted
> with the duty of legislating emerge as the decisive factors in . . .
> adjudication.

He found strange indeed the neo-activist conception of democracy
which holds that the people may be trusted with relatively unimportant
things but not with those deemed crucial; i.e., with economic problems
but not with those of civil liberty.

It is not that the Justice loved liberty less, but rather that he loved
democracy—*in all its aspects*—more. The difficulty is that both individual freedom and majority rule are indispensable in the democratic
dream. Yet neither can fully prevail without destroying the other. To
reconcile them is the basic problem of free government. Chief Justice
[Harlan F.] Stone put it briefly:

. . . There must be reasonable accommodation between the competing demands of freedom of speech and religion on the one hand, and other interests of society which have some claims upon legislative protection. To maintain the balance between them is essential to the well-ordered functioning of government under a constitution. Neither is absolute, and neither can constitutionally be made the implement for the destruction of the other. That is where the judicial function comes in.

Mr. Justice Frankfurter could not believe or pretend that reconciliation is achieved via word play with clichés like "liberty of contract" or "freedom of speech." The single-value, conditioned reflex gave him no respite from the painful process of judgment. For he knew, with Holmes, that his own "certitude was not the test of certainty"—that when legislatures disagreed with him they might be right. It followed that judicial intrusion upon the extrajudicial processes of government was permissible only in accordance with that ancient tradition of restraint which all American judges have professed—when their particular "preferred place" values were not at stake.

Obviously Mr. Justice Frankfurter found the crux of the democratic process not so much in its immediate legislative product as in the educative and tension-relieving role of the process itself. A generation ago he wrote:

. . . In a democracy, politics is a process of popular education—the task of adjusting the conflicting interests of diverse groups, . . . and bending the hostility and suspicion and ignorance engendered by group interests . . . toward mutual understanding.

To frustrate these pragmatic political accommodations by judicial absolutes is to frustrate our chief device for maintaining peace among men who are deeply divided—sometimes even in their conceptions of right and wrong. Moreover, "holding democracy in judicial tutelage is not the most promising way to foster disciplined responsibility in a free people."

It is ironical that Mr. Justice Frankfurter is now condemned by some for the very quality that won him a seat on the bench—respect for the political processes. It is even more ironical that, for essentially the same approach that earned the conservative Holmes a liberal reputation, the liberal Frankfurter is now deemed by some a conservative. What has changed, of course, is the relative liberalism of Court and legislatures. But in Felix Frankfurter's view the people's representatives are due equal deference, be they liberal or conservative. He saw as an abiding democratic principle what some find merely a gambit in the great game of power politics.

One need not insist that the Justice never fell short of his own goal. But surely his defections were few, and it may be that he left more choices to the people than has any other great modern judge (except, perhaps, Learned Hand). If this is abdication—as some insist when their "preferred place" values are at stake—it is abdication in favor of "the exhilarating adventure of a free people determining its own destiny."

Plainly Felix Frankfurter was always uneasy with judicial supremacy—whether with respect to personal interests called property, or those called liberty. Of course, the people may go wrong (whatever that means ultimately). Yet, in his view, "to fail and learn by failure is one of the sacred rights of a democracy."

Here, no doubt, is the heart of the matter. Behind all the subtle complexity of his jurisprudence lay a patient confidence in the people. He completely rejected what Professor Berman calls the "underlying assumptions" of Soviet law—that "the citizen is not a mature, independent adult . . . but an immature, dependent child or youth . . . ." And so, from first to last, Felix Frankfurter was wary of judicial efforts to impose Justice on the people—to force upon them "better" government than they were able at the moment to give themselves. It was his deepest conviction that no five men, or nine, are wise enough or good enough to wield such power over an entire nation. [Philosopher] Morris R. Cohen put it bluntly: If judges are to govern, they ought to be elected.

Should the Courts Pursue a Philosophy of Judicial Restraint?

NO

J. SKELLY WRIGHT
The Role of the Supreme Court in a Democratic Society—Judicial Activism or Restraint? *

One of the [Earl] Warren Court's severest critics tells us that during the Chief Justice's tenure the Supreme Court has "wrought more fundamental changes in the political and legal structure of the United States

* From J. Skelly Wright, "The Role of the Supreme Court in a Democratic Society—Judicial Activism or Restraint?" *Cornell Law Review* 54(November 1968):1–3, 12–15. © copyright 1968 by Cornell University.

than during any similar span of time since the [John] Marshall Court had the unique opportunity to express itself on a [clean slate]."[10] This has distressed those who counsel judicial restraint.

Remembering that certain past Supreme Courts, particularly those of the twenties and early thirties, also tried to play an active role in shaping our society, the apostles of restraint warn that even though we may approve the results that the Warren Court has decreed, we still must chastise the Court for assuming an activist role.[11] For even if the changes are desirable, they say the Court is not the proper institution to initiate them. Rather, the sorts of judgments the Court has made are the province of the legislatures; and, of course, the Court must not legislate. After all, it was the illicit role of a super legislature that the Nine Old Men [members of the Supreme Court during the early years of the New Deal] are said to have assumed.

These critics are particularly upset because, just as many of the ill-fated "activist" decisions of the past were decided by recourse to the open-ended concept of substantive due process, so many of the Warren Court's path-breaking decisions have been rendered pursuant to the equally open-ended concepts of equal protection and procedural due process. It is into these generalized constitutional commands that the justices are most likely to read their own personal predilections and thus render ad hoc justice. Consequently, both the old Court and the Warren Court are criticized for much the same reasons.

There is, however, an obvious difference between the two Courts. The Nine Old Men were trying to halt a revolution in the role of government as a social instrument, while the Warren Court is obviously furthering that effort. Its most significant pronouncements have decreed change in the status quo, not its preservation. Rather than invalidate legislative efforts at social progress, its decisions have ordered alteration of widespread and long accepted practices, including many which had not been legislatively sanctioned in the first place. In Professor [A. A.] Berle's phrase, the Warren Court has functioned as a "revolutionary committee."[12]

Simply to say, however, that the Warren Court has frequently ordered change while the old Court tried to halt it does not itself establish that the one has done a good job and the other a bad one. Nor does it establish that either Court should have acted at all. It is my contention that the Warren Court has not simply decreed the right results, but also that it was right to have decreed them. Its active role in shaping our society has been a necessary and proper one. It is, then, necessary to distinguish its performance from that of certain "activist" Courts of the past whose performances were certainly injudicious. . . .

JUDICIAL REVIEW IN A DEMOCRACY

. . . there can of course be no doubt that ours is essentially a society where the exercise of power draws its legitimacy from the consent of the people. Moreover, the sort of society we are going to have is to be determined by the people. Our faith is not simply in our ability to choose wise rulers, but in our ability to rule ourselves wisely. Learned Hand was not alone when he said that he would find it irksome to be ruled by a bevy of platonic guardians even if he knew how to choose them.[13]

The Court, then, is not to function as a nine-man bevy, reviewing legislation from the same, but presumably more enlightened, perspective as the legislature. When the majority, speaking through the legislature, has decided that the legislation is desirable, it is not for the Court to strike it down simply because it thinks otherwise. Yet whenever the Court strikes down legislation, it says to the majority that it may not have its own way. If the Court is to refrain from doing this simply because the justices find the status quo preferable, when and on what basis is it to strike down legislation? What are the Court's institutional characteristics that enable it to bring to the appraisal of legislation a new and different perspective unavailable to the legislature? How can the Court presume to say to the present majority that it cannot have its own way because its wishes are contrary to its own fundamental principles?

But just as an individual may be untrue to himself, so may society be untrue to itself. The Court's reviewing function, then, can be seen as an attempt to keep the community true to its own fundamental principles. Maintaining these "enduring general values" of the community is a task for which the Court's structure makes it peculiarly well suited. Professor [Alexander] Bickel suggests that judges have, or should have, the leisure, the training, and the insulation to follow the ways of the scholar in pursuing the ends of government. This is crucial to sorting out the enduring values of a society. And it is not something that institutions can do well on occasion, while operating for the most part with a different set of gears.[14]

Moreover, in considering questions of principle, courts are presented with the reality of their application. Statutes deal typically with abstract or sometimes dimly foreseen problems. Courts are concerned with the flesh and blood of an actual case. This tends to modify, perhaps to lengthen, everyone's view. It also provides an extremely salutary proving ground for all abstractions; it is conducive, in a phrase of Holmes, to thinking things, not words, and thus to the evolution of principle by a process that tests as it creates.[15] "Their insulation and the marvelous mystery of time give courts the capacity to appeal to men's better natures, to call forth their aspirations, which may have been forgotten in the moment's hue and cry."[16] This is what Justice Stone called the opportunity for "the sober second thought."[17] Charles Black put it more concisely when he termed judicial review "the people's institutionalized means of self-control."[18]

This conception of judicial review, casting the Court as the guardian of enduring principle and as a check on overzealous legislatures, depicts the Court as an essentially conservative rather than creative force in our society—hardly the "revolutionary committee" Professor Berle has called the Warren Court. The political and social realities of the twentieth century, however, have required government to essay an affirmative role in its service to its citizens. The Court, as part of government, must participate in that affirmative role.

This, of course, does not minimize the importance of protecting fundamental individual rights from governmental invasion. The original Bill of Rights was essentially negative, putting beyond the reach of government the world of the spirit and raising procedural barriers to governmental intrusion. The definition of these barriers in opinions such as Brandeis's dissent in *Olmstead* [*Olmstead* v. *United States,* 227 U.S., 438, 471 (1928) (dissenting opinion)] or his concurrence in *Whitney,* [*Whitney* v. *California,* 274 U.S., 357, 372 (1927) (concurring opinion)] which have since carried the day, has been crucially important in charting the direction in which our society has moved. But today, as [Harvard law professor] Archibald Cox put it:

> [T]he political theory which acknowledges the duty of government to provide jobs, social security, medical care, and housing extends to the field of human rights and imposes an obligation to promote liberty, equality, and dignity. For a decade and a half, recognition of this duty [of the Court] has been the most creative force in constitutional law.[19]

The more traditional rationales of judicial review do not quite fit when the Court's role is so utterly different. Yet the specter of the Court ruling the people persists and is, if anything, even more ominous where the Court is telling the government what it must do, not simply what it cannot do. What, then, is the Court's legitimate role in delineating constitutional duties? Again, the legitimacy of the Court's decrees must be derived from the community itself. Just as society may not be true to its enduring principles, so may it not be fully aware of its emerging ones. And just as the Court should maintain the one set of principles, so should it support and encourage the adoption of others.

The law need not, as Learned Hand suggested, "be content to lag behind the best inspiration of its time until it feels behind it the weight of such general acceptance as will give sanction to its pretension to unquestioned dictation.''[20] Rather, the Court must foster the best inspiration of the time and help it win general acceptance.

Nevertheless, inspiration is "best," not simply because the individual Justices think so, but because it accords with the ideals of the community itself. Today the most important of those ideals is political equality, and the Warren Court is correct in perceiving it as the dominant theme of American political development. The accuracy of this perception gives the Court's equal protection pronouncements their legitimacy.

It was the inaccuracy of the old Court's perception of community ideals that made its performance so bad. For what the Nine Old Men tried to put beyond the reach of government, both state and federal, was "the momentous issue of the welfare state itself"[21]—an issue so political that it cannot and should not be determined by a court.[22] It is certainly not an issue about which there is a consensus in the community, moral or otherwise. It is in fact *the* issue around which politics in this country has generally been divided. "Principles" bearing on the issue, though fervently believed by those professing them, are utterly conflicting. Unlike the ideal of political equality, they represent the creeds of particular political parties, but are not the enduring principles of our society itself. The issue of the welfare state must, and will, be "determined by 'dominant opinion' with or without judicial approval.''[23] Yet this was just the issue which the old Court told the people they could not determine for themselves by trying to place the minimum wage, the federal income tax, and government price control beyond the majority's reach.

To some critics, the Warren Court's implementation of political equality has also seemed a novel and illegitimate judicial theme.[24] Equality, however, is not a novel ideal at all. It is only that the range of its required application is becoming broader and more evident as the community becomes aware of the extent to which the world of the poor and of the Negro differs from that in which the bulk of the public lives. The apparent novelty of the Court's recent equal protection decisions stems "from the Court's partial recognition, reflecting a new awareness on the part of the public, that the freedom embodied in constitutional guarantees as they have historically been limited is, for the economically and socially disadvantaged, no freedom at all.''[25]

In this context, and in the era of positive government, it is incumbent on the Court to protect unpopular minorities not simply from governmental persecution, but from governmental neglect as well. For just as there are certain groups in society that have proved politically advantageous to oppress, so there are others whose interests are consistently bypassed by the political process in the rush toward the great society. This explains the necessity for affirmative decrees.

Because the Warren Court, unlike the old Court, has affirmatively applied the true principles and ideals of our community to protect those whose interests go unprotected elsewhere, it has acted properly. . . .

NOTES

1. Oliver Wendell Holmes, *Collected Legal Papers* (New York: Harcourt Brace Jovanovich, 1920), p. 239. Generally, easy cases are settled in the lower courts; those reaching the Supreme Court do so almost inevitably because they are, as Holmes put it, doubtful.

2. See Alexander M. Bickel, *The Unpublished Opinions of Mr. Justice Brandeis* (Cambridge, Mass.: The Belknap Press of Harvard University Press, 1957), chap. 1.

3. Louis L. Jaffe, "The Judicial Universe of Mr. Justice Frankfurter," *Harvard Law Review*, 62(1949):359.

4. Concurring opinion in *Ashwander* v. *TVA*, 297 U.S. 288 (1936).

5. 307 U.S. 433 (1939).

6. *Fletcher* v. *Peck*, 6 Cranch 87 (1810). To what extent Marshall practiced this principle of judicial restraint is another matter.

7. *Ogden* v. *Saunders*, 12 Wheaton 213 (1827).

8. See Benjamin N. Cardozo, *The Nature of the Judicial Process* (New Haven, Conn.: Yale University Press, 1921), pp. 88–90.

9. *West Virginia State Board of Education* v. *Barnette*.

10. Philip B. Kurland, "The Supreme Court 1963 Term, Foreword: Equal in Origin and Equal in Title to the Legislative and Executive Branches of Government," *Harvard Law Review* 78(1964):143.

11. See Paul A. Freund, "New Vistas in Constitutional Law," *University of Pennsylvania Law Review* 112(1964):631; Paul A. Freund, "The Supreme Court Under Attack," *University of Pittsburgh Law Review* 25(1963):1.

12. A. A. Berle, *The Three Faces of Power* (New York: Harcourt Brace Jovanovich, 1967), p. vii.

13. Learned Hand, *The Bill of Rights* (Cambridge, Mass.: Harvard University Press, 1958), pp. 73–74.

14. Alexander M. Bickel, *The Least Dangerous Branch: The Supreme Court at the Bar of Politics* (Indianapolis, Ind.: Bobbs-Merrill, 1962), pp. 25–26.

15. Ibid.

16. Ibid., p. 26.

17. Harlan F. Stone, "The Common Law in the United States," *Harvard Law Review* 50(1936):4, 25.

18. Charles S. Black, *The People and the Court: Judicial Review in a Democracy* (New York: Macmillan, 1960), p. 107.

19. Archibald Cox, "The Supreme Court 1965 Term, Foreword: Constitutional Adjudication and the Promotion of Human Rights," *Harvard Law Review* 80(1966):93.

20. Learned Hand, "The Contribution of an Independent Judiciary to Civilization," in *The Spirit of Liberty,* ed. Irving Dillard (New York: Alfred A. Knopf, 1952), pp. 15–16.

21. Robert G. McCloskey, "Economic Due Process and the Supreme Court: An Exhumation and a Reburial," *Supreme Court Review* (1962):51.

22. Maurice Finkelstein, "Judicial Self-limitation," *Harvard Law Review* 37(1924):338, 345.

23. McCloskey, "Economic Due Process and the Supreme Court," p. 51.

24. Kurland, "The Supreme Court 1963 Term," p. 144.

25. Jan G. Deutsch, "Neutrality, Legitimacy, and the Supreme Court: Some Intersections Between Law and Political Science," *Stanford Law Review* 20(1968):226.

QUESTIONS FOR DISCUSSION

1. Is judicial restraint a conservative or a liberal doctrine?
2. Can you reconcile judicial activism with political democracy?
3. In what way is the judicial activism of the Nine Old Men different from that of the Warren Court? Do you believe that the difference justifies the activism of the Warren Court?
4. What are the kinds of subjects that the Supreme Court has avoided dealing with in the past?
5. Does the philosophy of judicial activism benefit particular groups of people? If so, which groups? Why?

SUGGESTED READINGS

Berle, Adolf A. *The Three Faces of Power.* New York: Harcourt Brace Jovanovich, 1967.

Bickel, Alexander M. *The Supreme Court and the Idea of Progress.* New York: Harper & Row, 1970.

Black, Charles L., Jr. *The People and the Court.* New York: Macmillan, 1960.

Carr, Robert K. *The Supreme Court and Judicial Review.* New York: Holt, Rinehart and Winston, 1942.

Glazer, Nathan. "Towards an Imperial Judiciary?" *The Public Interest* 41(Fall 1975):104–123.

Hand, Learned. *The Bill of Rights*. New York: Atheneum Press, 1965.

Horowitz, Donald L. "Are the Courts Going Too Far?" *Commentary*, January 1977, pp. 37–44.

Jackson, Robert A. *The Struggle for Judicial Supremacy*. New York: Vintage, 1960.

Rodell, Fred. *Nine Men*. New York: Random House, 1955.

Shapiro, Martin. *Freedom of Speech: The Supreme Court and Judicial Review*. Englewood Cliffs, N.J.: Prentice-Hall, 1966.

PART FOUR

Whither
Public Policy?

13.

Can the Federal Government Resolve America's Domestic Problems?

From the time of ancient Greece to the present, political philosophers have debated what should be the proper relationship between government and people. Some have favored powerful government, while others have argued for weak government. The record of domestic policy in the United States since the New Deal suggests that it is difficult for any major ideological group to be consistent on this subject. Twentieth-century liberals, for example, are often associated with a belief in a positive or strong government. Although nineteenth-century liberals advocated a policy of *laissez-faire* (to leave alone), which called for only limited government intervention in society, modern liberals contend that strong government is necessary to undo the social injustices of a capitalist system.

Modern liberals, however, are not likely to be consistent on the government-people relationship. They are, for example, likely to be opposed to big government when that government means large police forces and invasions of privacy by the government. They also tend to be suspicious of one of big government's major components—the armed forces.

Modern conservatives, in contrast, are associated with a belief in weak government. Conservatives criticize the ever-growing bureaucracy, governmental red tape, and welfare programs. Often, however, conservatives favor government involvement in society to promote police power or to provide for national security.

Because of the changing character of American society, a sharp liberal-conservative dichotomy on the government-citizen relationship has not evolved. Instead, conservatives and liberals are selective about the kinds of government programs they advocate. Liberals and conservatives may even find themselves on the same side of a domestic issue. Welfare reform was introduced by the "conservative" Nixon Administration, but had the support of many liberals, for example. The Nixon Administration's abolition of the draft, moreover, found favor among liberals and conservatives.

Although the liberal-conservative dichotomy about the role of the state has become less apparent in society, the problems concerning both liberals and conservatives remain matters of importance to those interested in the well-being of the American polity. This chapter deals with some of the economic, social, environmental, and legal problems and presents strongly held views on these subjects. Specifically, three questions are asked: (1) Are massive government subsidies the answer to America's urban problems? (2) Should the government regulate the sale and ownership of guns? (3) Should the government restrict the development of nuclear power?

URBAN PROBLEMS

Particularly since the presidency of Lyndon Johnson, the problems of the cities have received national attention. Riots in the ghettos of New York, Newark, Detroit, and Los Angeles have called attention to the problems of slum housing, inadequate education, limited job opportunities, broken families, juvenile delinquency, and crimes of violence.

The near bankruptcy of New York City has spotlighted the financial problems of the cities. Since middle-class families are abandoning the cities and moving to the suburbs, moreover, the economic strength of the cities is declining.

Federal government programs have been established to deal with urban problems of health, housing, education, and crime. In spite of these programs, however, cities continue to deteriorate. One solution for the problems of the cities is offered by Paul R. Porter, a former head of a Marshall Plan mission to Greece. He recommends a Universal Local Income Tax, which, with proper safeguards, would provide the means to rebuild the cities. Under this tax the federal government would remit to each local community a uniform percentage of the federal income tax paid by its residents, to be shared among overlapping local governments as each state government may decide. This tax would avoid the red tape and waste from the current federal income tax system through which federal funds are disbursed from federal to local government agencies.

Political scientist Norton E. Long, however, has reservations about government's ability to solve urban problems. Specifically, he is critical of the advocates of a Marshall Plan for the cities. The Marshall Plan supplied massive doses of economic aid to the countries of Western Europe after World War II. Western Europe used that aid successfully to recover from the ravages of war. Long contends, however, that the conditions that made the Marshall Plan a success are not applicable to American cities today; consequently, a Marshall Plan for the cities would not work.

GUN CONTROL

Every time a prominent figure is assassinated in the United States, there is a public outcry for gun control. Congressional bills are introduced and hearings are conducted. Yet, meaningful gun control legislation is minimal. Some people contend that this failure to enact effective legislation to regulate the sale and ownership of guns is caused by the influence of the powerful National Rifle Association, an interest group with strong commitments from its members.

Supporters argue that gun control would reduce thousands of shootings of Americans every year. Opponents contend that criminals will get guns whether or not we have gun control and that the Second Amendment to the Constitution gives citizens the right to bear arms. The case for gun control is made here by Democratic Senator Edward Kennedy of Massachusetts and the case against by Robert J. Kukla, a writer who has done specialized research on this subject.

NUCLEAR POWER

Environmental protection has become an important national issue. No longer are industries free to pollute the atmosphere and rivers; instead, they are required to install pollution-control devices. Local, state, and national authorities conduct inspections to assure compliance with the laws.

Environmental protection has been applied to many areas of the economy, including mining, industrial production, and fishing. One subject that has aroused considerable controversy is nuclear energy. The United States faces an energy crisis and is importing more oil now than it did in 1973, the year of the Yom Kippur war. Like other countries, it has tried to become more self-sufficient in energy so that it will not have to depend on foreign imports of energy resources.

Nuclear power has become a vital energy resource for the future. The issue of nuclear safety has caused environmentalists and others to campaign actively for alternative sources of energy. In the following selections, Democratic Senator Mike Gravel of Alaska argues in favor of restricting nuclear power development, and Democratic Representative Mike McCormack of Washington takes the opposing view.

Gravel argues that nuclear power reactors produce deadly radioactive wastes. These wastes may escape into the environment, causing cancer and genetic change. By sharing technology for producing nuclear energy to many countries around the world, the United States is promoting nuclear weapons capability abroad. According to Gravel, the United States will become increasingly dependent upon foreign suppliers because it will not be self-sufficient in uranium.

McCormack contends, in opposition, that the United States must rely on nuclear energy. Many alternative methods of producing energy are still in the experimental stage. Nuclear energy is safe, clean, cheap, and reliable. He argues that to curtail development of nuclear energy, moreover, would be to increase unemployment.

Are Government Subsidies
the Answer
to America's Urban Crisis?

YES

PAUL R. PORTER
*Is Recovery Really Possible?**

A TESTING OF OURSELVES

If American cities do not recover, it will not be because the physical effort is too much for us. Relatively, the task calls for less material effort than was shown by any one of a dozen devastated cities of Europe in their rebound from the war. Or by the rebuilding of Hiroshima. At home we have the example of the postwar surge in housing construction; in 1970 every third home had been built in the preceding twenty years.

The nature of the political adaptation should not be beyond us. A new expansion of governmental powers is not needed; there would, instead, be a reduction. The enabling laws which would be required are few and almost prosaic compared to the legislation that was the under-pinning of the New Deal. The idea is no bolder than the Marshall Plan.

If we muff the beckoning chance to restore our cities to health, it will be because of ourselves—something in our present view of things or in our spirit that sets us widely apart from the generations of Americans who came before us. I do not believe that we are that different, but nonetheless we ought to look behind some indications that we may be.

The confident vision of America we had thirty years ago has un-deniably become dimmer and without another to take its place we are

* From *The Recovery of American Cities*, pp. 191–204, by Paul R. Porter. © 1976, Sun River Press. By permission of the publisher, The Two Continents Publishing Group, New York, $8.95.

uncertain about goals. If . . . the reality has outrun the "scholarly apparatus," it has outrun the rest of us as well, but it is not because the world around us has become too complex for us to understand. Rather, we are held back by mood and habit. . . .

Of central importance in our prevailing mood is an unresolved confusion about the potential of self-reliance in an urban society. The confusion has grown worse as we have become more urban. It has produced, as we have seen, a strange convergence of some conservatives and some liberals in support of proposals which undervalue self-reliance—a government dole, for example, in preference to an adequate minimum wage. Others are untroubled by policies which deliberately deny self-reliance to some workers as a way to control inflation. Perhaps the greatest damage to the practice of self-reliance arises from the casualness with which we now reach for a subsidy to close a gap between costs and income. A clear understanding of subsidies (and of payments which are *not* subsidies) is fundamental to the recovery of cities.

THE TENDENCY OF SUBSIDIES TO BECOME PERMANENT

The Joint Economic Committee of the Congress, worried by the trend toward even more subsidies, has had its staff make estimates of the mounting costs to taxpayers. A recent staff study estimated that private-sector subsidies rose by 50 percent between the fiscal years 1970 and 1975. While some of the reasoning is in error—the study, for example, accepts uncritically the fallacy of a homeowners' subsidy—correction of the error does not change the finding that an enormous jump occurred in just five years.

People who carry the tattered banners of conservative and liberal usually disagree about the subsidies that they want, but both groups have contributed heavily to the spread of the practice. Commonly, the political concern about subsidies is simply the question of who will benefit. Affluent suburban commuters may grow indignant about a subsidy to ranchers which raises the price of beef but feel no embarrassment in telling their congressman that an operating subsidy for mass transit is one of the most important issues before the nation.

There is an essential place for subsidies in our economy. Cities will need help for another twenty years or so and there are other subsidies—the delivery of mail comes to mind—which are not hard to justify. The many kinds of subsidies and the conditions under which they may be justified are complex questions which are largely outside our specific interest, but so far as cities are concerned a simple statement suffices. The purpose of the subsidy should be to cure a condition and not to perpetuate it. Yet, once a subsidy is established, there is a danger that it may become unshakably permanent.

I believe I can make my point with an anecdote. When I was head of the Marshall Plan mission to Greece a quarter of a century ago, a Greek organization asked me to support its plea to the Greek government for a cost-of-living adjustment in pensions received by its members. The organization called itself the Society of Descendants of the Former Water Carriers of Piraeus and so intriguing was its name that I inquired about its history, which was this. Until about the turn of the century households in Piraeus, the port of Athens, were supplied with water by men who delivered it from door to door in buckets. Then a modern water system was installed, and the water carriers became technologically unemployed. With commendable humaneness, the government gave them termination pay in weekly installments.

Jobs, however, were scarce, and after several renewals the termination pay was formally converted into lifetime pensions. But then a problem of justice arose which might have been the inspiration for Professor John Rawls and others who hold that justice requires, not equality of opportunity, but equality of results. The ages and health of the former water carriers varied, and some died sooner than others. The heirs of some complained that families of the deceased, already at a disadvantage, were deprived of pensions paid to the fortunate living. The Greek Parliament's member from Piraeus quickly grasped the unfairness of the situation and persuaded his colleagues to amend the special pension law to provide that rights to the pension would be inherited for his own lifetime by the beneficiary's eldest son, who by custom was expected to help other members of the family. With frequent adjustments for inflation, this was the status a half century later of pensions that began modestly as termination pay.

Mayors of large American cities, upon taking the oath of office, automatically become honorary members of the Society of Descendants of the Former Water Carriers of Piraeus. They would be derelict of duty if they did not use their membership card to press for improvements in the permanent pension that without deliberate intent we have established for our cities.

Yet, even within a tolerance for an excessive reliance on subsidies, I believe most people will recoil from the idea of a *permanent* subsidy for cities. A prudent assessment must begin with the obvious fact that their political influence is falling as their share of the national population shrinks. Added to this is the fact that they are losing the sympathy of friends upon whom they are increasingly dependent.

The New York City financial crisis had uncommon aspects: It was universally agreed, for example, that in the past the city had been improvident in its borrowing, and there was no doubt a basis for the belief of many New Yorkers that elsewhere in the nation many people were not upset to see the nation's biggest city receive a comeuppance. But other cities, even without a financial crisis, are also likely to encounter growing impatience with their need for help. Contributing to that impatience is the continued plea for more money without a corresponding assurance that the need for help is temporary. It will be good politics for mayors to generate confidence in the recovery of cities; bad politics to act as if the idea were imposed upon them. A part of a mayor's job is to lead parades. . . .

ENDING THE FEDERAL GUARDIANSHIP

Because the proposal . . . about federal payments to cities is a drastic departure from present practice, let us go over it once more in order to avoid any possible confusion. Federal grants to cities are now of three kinds: categorical grants, block grants (a consolidation of some former categorical grants), and revenue sharing. A categorical grant may be used only for a specified purpose. A block grant allows for discretionary use among several purposes, while no restriction is placed on the use of funds from revenue sharing. Obviously, the latter is popular with local governments. "The best thing since ice cream," Mayor Moon Landrieu of New Orleans has said of it.

I propose a distinction of an entirely different kind. I start with the fact that a large part (though not necessarily all) of the money which a local government receives from the federal government has merely made a round trip. Only a short time earlier it was paid to the federal government as income taxes by people who live in the community to which it is returned.

This has been going on for over forty years and all that time we have thought that the earth was flat, so to speak. The flat-earth view holds that money which the federal government takes from a local community and returns to it is *federal* money. But let us think of the earth as round. The round-earth view holds that money collected from and returned to the same community is actually *local* revenue which has been fitted into the federal individual income tax as a convenient way of collecting it.

The fit is a poor one since the amount that comes back is irregular, uncertain, and subject to negotiation with a half dozen federal agencies. Nonetheless, in the round-earth view, it is still local money. To obtain a good fit, eliminating the losses and frustrations which now occur in the local revenue's homeward journey, I propose that the federal government remit to each local community a uniform percentage of the federal individual income tax paid by its residents, to be shared among overlapping local governments as each state government may decide (and subject to an upper limit to be described later).

In adjusting our perception to a round-earth view, it helps, as was said earlier, to think of the returned revenues of local origin as an implicit local income tax. As a future policy formalized in legislation, a better name will be the Universal Local Income Tax. Think of it not as an additional tax, which it is not, but as a spin-off that, as a convenience to taxpayers, rides piggyback on the income tax which the federal government collects for national purposes. In practice, the individual income tax would have two parts—one for local, one for national purposes—and both would be collected together.

This tax spun off for exclusively local use would be set at a level that would be all the "federal payment" most local governments would need. But several hundred, including (by my estimate) all large cities, must have outside help and would therefore receive, in addition, a subsidy based on each city's need (which would diminish and disappear as the city recovers).

This is the substitute that I propose for the present system of federal grants. It would bring a revolution in federal-local relationships. Financial independence would be restored promptly to all local governments that could meet their costs from conventional revenues plus the Universal Local Income Tax. For those that must also have a subsidy, the restoration would take place progressively.

Local governments should like the idea because the remitted local income tax would be larger than revenue sharing and would have the same unrestricted use. It should appeal to people who are attracted to the graduated income tax and would like all states to have one because of its progressive nature. Indeed, one can foresee proposals being offered to make the federally collected local income tax higher, in order to replace regressive sales taxes and possibly to reduce the burden of the property tax on residences.

However, some who may favor the idea of a local income tax in principle will balk at it if local governments are free to use the revenues in accordance with the apparent wishes of their electorate. They hold that local governments will not do the right things unless important parts of their budgets are under the control of federal agencies, which exercise that control by making or not making categorical grants and by agency guidelines that govern the use of a grant.

There are clearly many people who believe that without a powerful and pervasive federal guardianship, local governments may fail to perform certain functions which in themselves may or may not be wise ones. Can they be depended upon to keep the air clean, enforce suitable health standards, provide manpower training for unemployed youth, build a subway, combat crime, or house the poor? These individuals feel intensely about one or more such purposes and are prepared to sacrifice a great deal of home rule to achieve them.

Their concerns deserve to be treated with respect and sympathy. We can do so by first considering if the low esteem for local government implicit in their thinking is justified, and then by looking at the comparative merits of home rule and the federal guardianship in particular cases.

The case for freeing local governments from financial dependency does not rest upon a supposed return to a Golden Age. Local government has never had one. Towns and small cities in which a personal relationship between voters and officials is possible generally have the kind of local government that is acceptable to a majority of the citizens who vote. In many communities the number who could vote was restricted until recently by a shameful denial of voting rights to blacks, but that practice has been largely overcome. A big increase in the number of black local officials is evidence of the change.

The historical record of local government in big cities is generally not a cause for national pride, although there are exceptions. Among them, the record of honest and efficient administration, initiative, fiscal responsibility, and genuine rapport between city hall and neighborhoods which prevailed in Milwaukee during the twenty years that Dan Hoan was mayor probably has not been excelled anywhere. But for a long period misrule and scandal were as common as good administration, and in the early years of this century there was some merit in the reluctance of state legislatures to grant cities the larger degree of home rule that reformers sought. (There was also much corruption in many state legislatures.)

If there was never a Golden Age, there has been, however, a great improvement in the quality of big city government in recent decades. Instances of corruption are not unknown, but on this nasty issue the statistical record of contemporary mayors compares favorably with that of governors, congressmen, and judges. Nor is honesty the main measure of improvement. Professionalism in administration has blossomed in the years the condition of cities has worsened (there is no evident relationship between one event and the other). Moreover, in at least the ten cities which were studied for this book, a real sensitivity for the concerns of all citizens is unmistakably evident at city halls. On the record of the last several decades most local governments may be expected to use their recovered powers honestly, fairly, and competently. This deserves to be said despite some financial mismanagement (which is not confined to local governments).

In weighing the merits of the guardianship it should be recognized that the federal government has played a valuable role in spurring local governments to a broader view of their responsibilities. Categorical grants, on their plus side, have been useful in pinpointing some neglected areas of public service. But with these things having been largely accomplished, it is time to ask: How much of the guardianship is still needed?

The purposes that the guardianship is expected to serve are a miscellaneous lot. There is one set, including such goals as clean air and reduction of crime, which, although they do not affect all citizens equally, are nonetheless broadly based. Because they are purposes of general concern, they should be financed by conventional revenues and the Universal Local Income Tax.

Financial assistance to mass transit, if local electorates wish it to be subsidized at all, should be switched from categorical grants to the Universal Local Income Tax. The magnitude of sums involved is a special reason to bring decisions under home rule. Under the Mass Transportation Act of 1974, the federal government may pay 80 percent of the new capital costs of mass transit and 50 percent of the operating costs. If the same amount of money represented by these potential grants were available to a local government without being earmarked (that is, as a part of the Universal Local Income Tax), more important uses for it might be found. This is precisely why decisions on its use should rest exclusively with officials directly responsible to local voters. When such large sums must either be used for an earmarked purpose or lost altogether, local officals may be tempted to spend more on new facilities than is needed and to be lax about operating costs.

The strongest case for a partial supervision of local governments through financial assistance by the federal government exists with respect to the needs of the poor. Welfare, housing, and the preparation of people for self-reliance are the purposes that meet this test. They are also purposes which are intimately related to the recovery of cities. Where the sums they require are relatively modest, local governments should bear the cost with the assistance, of course, of the Universal Local Income Tax. But in those big cities and other communities where the needs of the poor are large enough to require external aid, it would be appropriate to include the financing of these needs, or most of it, within the transitional subsidy.

We come, then, to this principle: Purposes of general interest now financed through categorical or block grants and not specifically germane to the recovery of cities should be financed through the Universal

Local Income Tax and through conventional local revenues in such sums as each local government deems fit. The federal guardianship for these purposes would be discontinued in all communities. Costs of government which are caused by poverty, if relatively large, would be financed by subsidies paid to a small proportion of local governments according to their need. While subsidies continue, a federal control over their amount and use would be maintained.

There is another aspect of categorical grants which thus far has not been considered. In the case of many of them, their potential withholding by the federal government is a means to ensure the protection of rights of minorities. The same protection, however, can be given less awkwardly by agencies of the federal government specifically qualified for the administration of justice. . . .

HOLDING CITIES ACCOUNTABLE FOR THEIR RECOVERY

Some degree of federal guardianship for cities that require a subsidy is inevitable while the subsidy lasts. Despite the spread of subsidies in recent years to a much broader range of public services and private activities than we have known before, it is unthinkable that the Congress will vote aid to cities without requiring some federal supervision of its use. Where subsidies are needed, our course should lie between too much federal control and not enough, and in setting this course our concern should be the purpose of the guardianship.

From time to time someone proposes a "Marshall Plan for cities." The proposal is always highly generalized without any suggestion of how it might operate. The intent seems to be a call for more money for cities, which misses the two valid points in the analogy. Because the recurrent proposal reflects a misunderstanding, I trust that I may be forgiven for drawing upon my experience in the Marshall Plan. Besides directing the operation in Greece, I was at other times assistant administrator for program and resident supervisor of all operations in Europe. In the course of my study of American cities I have come to the firm conclusion that if the money that they receive from the federal government were more wisely spent, they would soon need less of it—which brings us to the valid points in the Marshall Plan analogy.

The purpose of the Marshall Plan was the earliest feasible recovery of the nations that needed our help. Upon recovery aid ended. The second thing in the Marshall Plan experience that is relevant today is the relationship that prevailed between the American government and the governments of the nations that were aided. American aid was contingent upon the development by the European nations of effective recovery programs and upon demonstrable progress, but detailed intervention of the kind that characterizes categorical grants was avoided. For this reason, a large American bureaucracy was also avoided. I estimated once that, apart from persons engaged in technical assistance, one quarter of the agency's working hours were devoted to preparing information for the Congress. I cite this, not to suggest that the information which the Congress requested was excessive, which it was not, but as evidence that we had a lean agency.

In contrast to the Marshall Plan experience, the federal relationship with local governments lacks a central purpose other than permanent aid, severely cramps local initiative, and multiplies employment in the federal supervisory agencies far beyond true need. It is difficult to discover a benefit from the HUD [Department of Housing and Urban Development] budget for research and policy development that is equal to the construction costs of 2,800 homes at $25,000 each.

Cities should be held accountable for making demonstrable progress toward recovery. To be accountable they need freedom to develop and pursue individualized programs adapted to conditions as diverse as those of New York City and Kenosha or Dallas and St. Louis. The Universal Local Income Tax would free them from federal supervision of local affairs that are not specifically related to recovery, and in the recovery effort itself there should be a large measure of discretion about how to achieve agreed targets.

But with respect to the matter that counts—satisfactory progress toward making the city again competitive with its suburbs as a place of residence and toward relocating able-bodied poor people for better opportunity—the federal government should be a hard taskmaster. It should insist upon difficult targets, and if the local effort is poor, the federal government should be prepared as a last resort to cut the amount of aid until corrective action is taken. Once the federal government has established broad public confidence in its own role, not many local officials will wish to risk a public explanation of why federal aid was cut. . . .

The recovery of cities is possible because the requirements of recovery are rather ordinary. Some day the great decaying patches in inner cities, which people leave as soon as they can afford something better, must be cleared and rebuilt. Rebuild, then, as homes for people who work nearby, and do it now. When factories leave cities, help people who need factory work to follow the departing jobs. The evolutionary trend in metropolises toward decentralization of residence, trade, and employment is not in itself an obstacle to the recovery of cities. The trend means more spaciousness for living, more moderate land costs, and the potential of shorter journeys to work. Stop interfer-

ring, and rejoice. Cities must have help, but give it to them in ways that
will cause the need for it to fade away.

These are the policies of recovery and if they soon seem prosaic,
so much the better.

Are Government Subsidies
the Answer
to America's Urban Crisis?

NO

NORTON E. LONG
*A Marshall Plan for Cities?**

The nation's mayors, meeting in Chicago, have sent their plea for aid to
the President-elect. Unfortunately, although they indicated what they
would like the nation to do to help the cities, they appear to have
remained silent concerning what the cities are prepared to do to help
themselves. A review of our foreign-aid experience may help to clarify
some of the problems of mounting a program of domestic municipal aid
on a comparable scale. For example, a Marshall Plan for cities has
frequently been advocated. . . . However, the idea has been little
more than a catchy slogan to symbolize big federal dollars and contrast
our willingness to aid in the recovery of Europe with our grudging
support of our own cities. Consideration of the Marshall Plan and the
reasons for its success and the failures of our programs elsewhere than
in Europe has much to offer those seriously concerned with structuring
a federal aid program with any real promise of achieving for our cities
what the Marshall Plan did for the nations of Europe.

Since a major proposal of the mayors was to establish an urban-
development bank similar to the World Bank, one might have hoped
that they had at long last come to recognize the necessity of restoring
the viability of the local economies of the cities. If there is one thing our
foreign-aid experience should have taught us, it is that we can only help
those who are ready, willing, and able to help themselves. Failing this,

---

* From Norton E. Long, "A Marshall Plan for Cities?" *The Public Interest* 46(Winter 1977):48–58. ©
1977 by National Affairs, Inc.

what results is a welfare program that merely postpones the day of reckoning and deepens dependency. The first point about the Marshall Plan, usually completely disregarded by advocates of a similar plan for our cities, is that it was designed to restore the war-ravaged economies of European nations. It was a program of investment to replace entire industries, not just a program of income redistribution and maintenance to restore and sustain a standard of public and private consumption. It was only concerned with maintaining consumption until its major investments revived the economies of the European nations and restored them to self-sufficiency. No comparable plan for restoring the local economies of our cities to self-sufficiency has been envisaged, let alone formulated. Indeed, there is little or no understanding of cities as entities with local economies that must produce as well as distribute, and redistribute the wealth that permits public and private consumption. We must conceptualize these local economies and ask why some have become inadequate to meet the demands and genuine needs of private and public consumption.

A second point that is highly relevant to a federal program for cities is that the individual countries under the Marshall Plan were responsible for making the integrated plans for the recovery of their economies. These plans were not dreamed up in Washington, though the United States government had some voice as the banker for the program. It is impossible for Washington to make plans that meet the individual requirements of thousands of more or less unique local economies. The narrow interests of the Washington bureaucracies, their state and local counterparts, and the forces that they represent could scarcely, if ever, cooperate in the formulation of an economic plan for a city, or subordinate their concerns in the unlikely event that such a plan were adopted. And given the realities of the other pressures at work, the interests of suppliers, unions, and other producers would overshadow those of the local inhabitants.

Our experience with plans and planning has been depressing, for the most part. To a large degree, planning requirements in federal legislation have produced expensive busy work, clearance problems, and empty ritual. For example, some serious purposes were at least originally entertained in the proposal requirements of the Model Cities program, but the cities lacked the capability to formulate appropriate proposals. The resultant widespread use of consulting firms thus negated the very reasonable assumption made by the Department of Housing and Urban Development (HUD) that a city whose staff could not formulate a proposal could not be expected to carry it out. Despite the seeming wisdom of HUD's position it proved practically impossible to maintain. But this lesson appears to have been lost on those who need most to profit from it.

The federal government cannot depend on the cities to make competent plans for the revival of local economies. Their failure to use revenue-sharing funds in a serious way to begin restoring local economies indicates what might well be the fate of larger funds. Only recently has serious work in urban economics begun. Conventional municipal finance has remained innocently unaware of the relationship between fiscal solvency and the state of the local economy. Cities haven't even started to keep ledgers acknowledging that, like countries, they must pay for their imports with exports, and what they cannot pay for they must either produce themselves or do without. City expenditures are treated as pure "merit consumption," and not as investments of scarce resources that, to some important degree, must generate a return if they are to be sustained.

The federal government must help cities develop adequate conceptualizations of their local economies to facilitate competent plans for improving them through appropriate investments and other measures. Washington must also assist in the training and supply of competent staffs to do this economic analysis. In addition, it must exert continuous pressure, without masterminding, to insure that resources are not dissipated, but employed in ways that hold genuine promise of aiding fiscal recovery. The cities should be assisted and pressed to plan for their economic recovery; at the same time, they should accept and demand the responsibility of coordinating the appropriate federal programs—in health, housing, education, manpower, law enforcement, and the rest—in a concerted effort to improve the local economies.

Only when federal policy descends to the concrete context of the local community can we measure both its intended and unintended effects. The local communities are the socioeconomic cells of the larger body politic. Only when these cells are healthy can the nation be healthy; a nation of sick cities is a sick nation. We therefore have to regard them as functioning social organizations, a view largely ignored by macroeconomics and census data alike. Because cities and local communities do essential sociological and economic work, we must come to grips with them both as testing grounds for policy and as building blocks of a sound national political economy.

THE PROBLEMS OF RESTORATION

The experience of the Marshall Plan should also indicate the differences as well as the similarities of the economic problems involved. The economies of many of our cities have been ravaged, but not by war; and while our cities have experienced quite palpable physical devastation, for the most part it has not resulted from shelling by an organized enemy. Most important, as we discovered when we extended foreign aid to the underdeveloped countries, the economies of the European nations were already going concerns that only needed tiding over to restore them to health. Unfortunately, this was not the case with the underdeveloped countries, nor to an important degree is it true of troubled cities.

Although crime, vandalism, and riots are far from unimportant, physical devastation accounts for only some of the problems besetting city economies. The relatively straightforward task of physically rebuilding Europe under the Marshall Plan was quite different and far simpler than the task of restoring our cities. The contemporary analogue of the wartime destruction of the European economies is the disinvestment in industrial and residential areas that manifests itself in empty, blighted, gutted, and abandoned factories, office buildings, warehouses, lofts, houses, and apartments. The reasons for this disinvestment have to be faced if the process is to be halted and reversed. The single most important explanation is profitability. For many reasons, the costs in many cities have become far out of line with those prevailing elsewhere. Hence the search for profit entails disinvestment in existing industry, as well as the failure to attract new investment. The mayors will find that federal low-interest loans will not by themselves produce any fundamental change, and will in fact simply mask the problems they are designed to cure. . . .

THE WAGES OF SOCIAL DISINVESTMENT

There are important social and psychological consequences for the individuals and communities afflicted with these employment problems. As [psychoanalyst Sigmund] Freud pointed out, the job is the most important factor integrating the human personality. Where it provides little or no respect for oneself or others, the effect is debilitating, especially where there are no other institutions adequately performing the same function. The loss of meaningful participation in the mainstream economy has resulted in neighborhood decay, social disorganization, crime, vandalism, blight, and housing abandonment—all the phenomena of crisis associated with the ghetto. A seemingly cancerous process leads to the rapid destruction of sound housing and stores in neighborhoods populated by those trapped on welfare or in the secondary labor market. Their incomes are inadequate to maintain their properties. The constant moves to evade paying the rent not only force properties into rapid obsolescence, but also undermine neighborhood attachments and social control, and result in a turnover of school populations that signals educational failure. . . .

Constitution Plaza in Hartford and Pruitt-Igoe in St. Louis symbolize the failure of the brick-and-mortar approach to urban problems. HUD and the cities have been far more interested in physical rather than social structures, in physical rather than social capital. But gleaming central business districts surrounded by festering, crime-ridden, spreading slums, plagued by drug addiction and unemployment, bear witness to the truth that cities do not live by brick alone. A committee of the National Academies of Science and Engineering was asked to recommend a program of urban behavioral research to HUD. Even the engineers were emphatic that our knowledge of technology far exceeded our understanding of the social conditions necessary for its application. Despite all this Operation Breakthrough was the major HUD effort.

CITIES WITHOUT CITIZENS

To understand this persistent and seemingly perverse concentration on bricks and mortar, it must be realized that the unions, construction industry, real-estate industry, banks, insurance companies, architects, planners, federal bureaucrats, politicians, and media all have something to gain, even from building uneconomic monuments. We have not yet learned to put together an equally powerful coalition to strengthen social structures, whose building materials rarely provide remotely comparable profits or other rewards. But once again, our foreign-aid experience is instructive. Outside of Europe, foreign aid frequently led to elite enrichment, black markets, military hardware, inflation, and misdirection of resources. Many of our federal domestic-aid programs have had similarly sorry results. In effect, we have created systems of perverse incentives that stimulate investments as tax gimmicks rather than producing jobs, that co-opt indigenous leaders and foster neighborhood disintegration. We have bred municipal inflation and undermined productive local economies—in the name of benevolent intentions toward cities, the poor, and the minorities.

The federal government has generated harmfully unrealistic expectations without recognizing its incapacity to fulfill them. In the judgment of [political economist] Anthony Downs, the Johnson housing goals, which were never formally abandoned, would have required a national effort in housing comparable to waging World War II—an effort that, if made, would have had disastrous effects on other social needs. As another example of unrealistic expectations, the Department of Labor was recently quoted as asserting that "the typical family of four requires $15,500 a year to maintain a moderate standard of living." The Department of Labor did not say how untypical such an income was, or what level of GNP [Gross National Product] the nation would need to permit the typical family to have that income. The impression leaps to many an impressionable mind that wages under $15,500 should be regarded as untypical, and hence substandard. As another example, labor leaders in St. Louis were aghast when they learned that top companies in the city were paying only $9,000 a year—with the city fathers and the media, they have been busily putting the axe to three fourths of the city's jobs as substandard. But neither they nor the federal government has ever bothered to find out the actual distribution of wages. Nor are they in the least concerned with what the businesses they have been driving out can afford to pay in wages yet remain competitive. . . .

Unfortunately, the values that only the affluent can afford dominate our thinking about what should be done by those whose circumstances make such values an insupportable and even disastrous luxury. The poor cannot afford to emulate the rich. Idleness may be attractive for the jet set, but it can become a nightmare for the poor. The rich can afford individualism, privacy, and the indulgence of an anarchical libertarianism in their personal lives, since they are securely supported by a corporate order. The poor must help themselves; they cannot afford the luxury of either purchased privacy or purchased security. Despite the claim that the police and the legal order will provide security for the poor and the working class, we know this to be a liberal myth. Neighborhoods police themselves. The liberal who does not blink at the use of union muscle to produce a closed shop decries as fascistic any attempt to produce a closed and physically secure neighborhood. Organizations are good for unions and corporations, but a powerful territorial organization is anathema to police and civil libertarian alike. Our dominant liberal ideology denies the necessity of social control and acts to denigrate and undermine it where it exists. In practice this is to preach social disorganization in the guise of defending liberty and individualism, and to recommend flight as the only realistic remedy—for those who can afford to flee. But society dissolves without a normative structure with motivated, committed citizens.

For some time we have supposed that we could operate cities without citizens by treating legally franchised, casual voters as if they were a functional equivalent. We are beginning to learn that the normative order on which our cities depended in the past was not the product of their formal governments but of the many informal governments of their ethnic neighborhoods. . . . These neighborhoods—cooperative social organizations founded on a normative order, social control, and trustworthy leaders—are the social capital truly analogous to Europe's war-ravaged industries. The halting and reversal of the processes leading to their destruction, and the provision where possible of viable substitutes, are what an effective federal aid program for cities should be about. Such a plan would have as a major goal changing the present federally sponsored system of perverse incentives that contributes so much to the cities' woes. William Skinner, the eminent Stanford anthropologist, has shown how the overseas Chinese maintained their informal governments and their family structures under the most hostile environments for thousands of years. It is only now, with the corrosive influence of American cities, that the Chinese family is breaking up.

THE ROAD TO THE "RESERVATION"

After this bleak picture of decay and disintegration, people want to ask for a solution. There are no easy answers, but there are indications of the form a solution will have to take, in neighborhoods and institutions that are resisting and even overcoming social disorganization, and re-creating local social structures. This is the kind of capital a Marshall Plan for cities will have to help build and, just as importantly, prevent from being subverted and destroyed. In St. Louis, the famed Italian Hill and the St. Ambrose Church—recognized even in the Soviet Union—offer an excellent example of . . . a "defended neighborhood." The Hill is a working class neighborhood of 30,000 to 40,000 residents in tiny houses on small lots; almost anywhere else it would have become a slum. After visiting the other attractions of St. Louis—the Arch, Busch Stadium, and Pruitt-Igoe—visiting foreign officials were brought to the Hill to see one healthy, hopeful part of the city. Here, in an old, low-income neighborhood, the houses are well kept up, the streets are clean, people help each other, the kids are well brought up, the streets are safe, and housing values are stable and rising. This is an example of the kind of social capital an urban Marshall Plan would seek to create, if possible, and maintain. But when these foreign visitors asked at a neighborhood party what the city, state, and federal governments had done for the Hill, the answer was, "Not a god-damned thing." There was a short addendum: "Yes, the federal government, the city, and the state drove a super highway right through the neighborhood and we had to fight like hell to get [Transportation Secretary John] Volpe to build a bridge to keep the neighborhood together."

The Hill is often dismissed because it is both Italian and Catholic, two factors that supposedly make it unique. The example of the Italian Hill does not show that such a neighborhood can be created amid adverse conditions out of the unpromising material of most city slums. But the experience of the Muslims and the Puerto Rican evangelicals provides ground for hope that even there trust and order can be brought into being. Perhaps this seems surprising only because we have forgotten that the early Christian church was a kind of guerrilla government ministering to slaves, outcasts, and even criminals in the rotting structure of the Roman Empire. Clearly such a force provides stronger political medicine than the laissez-faire, civil-libertarian individualism our Republican and Democratic parties are prepared to administer.

The question is whether the city can halt its present path toward becoming an "Indian reservation"—a poor house, with a set of suburbanized keepers (cops, school teachers, welfare workers, and other municipal bureaucrats), that surrounds a central business district protected by barbed wire—with anything less than a renewed social structure of committed citizens. Failing that, the path toward the "reservation" is the line of least resistance and greatest gain for those having a vested interest in what our brick-and-mortar and welfare politics represent. Can a coalition of black, Puerto Rican, and ethnic neighborhoods be built to support a city leadership that can master the brick-and-mortar coalition in the interest of the city's inhabitants? Can such leadership program both the local and the federal vested interests to restore a viable community political economy? These questions can only be answered by those who must fashion concrete answers out of the materials of their cities. What such leaders can do is to demonstrate that they understand the nature of the job and the form answers will have to take, and that they will make the lifelong commitment required to turn their cities around.

A Marshall Plan for cities will need much more than sunshine patriots. We have learned that the new states of the world require nation building. We have to learn this also applies to us: Our cities and their citizenship require renewing, as well as brick and mortar. This will require city builders whose job is as important as the nation builders of the new countries. In fact, the rebuilding of our cities is the rebuilding of our nation—though, incredibly, we do not realize it. Until we do, a Marshall Plan for cities is likely to come, however disguised, as an act of federal compassion or guilt or worse, as an intervention through the masterminding of an urban Vietnam, rather than as a diagnosis of our collective condition and a concerted, pluralistic effort to put the nation's economic and spiritual house in order. The mayors will find that seriously addressing the problems of our cities requires a politics of civic and moral reconstruction that far transcends central-business-district renewal, mass transit, low-interest loans, or the shifting of the burden of welfare to the shoulders of the federal government.

QUESTIONS FOR DISCUSSION

1. Would the Universal Local Income Tax ease the urban crisis?
2. What are the problems involved in establishing a Universal Local Income Tax?
3. What are the differences between the Marshall Plan for Western Europe and a Marshall Plan for the cities? Are these differences significant in solving the social and economic problems of American cities?
4. What are the points of agreement between Porter and Long?
5. Have federal governmental programs to aid cities helped or hindered the solution of urban social and economic problems?

SUGGESTED READINGS

Banfield, Edward C. *The Unheavenly City Revisited.* Boston: Little, Brown, 1974.

Brown, Claude. *Manchild in the Promised Land.* New York: The New American Library, 1965.

Glazer, Nathan, and Daniel Patrick Moynihan. *Beyond the Melting Pot.* Cambridge: The M.I.T. Press, 1963.

Jacobs, Jane. *The Death and Life of Great American Cities: The Failure of Town Planning.* New York: Random House, 1961.

Long, Norton. *The Unwalled City: Reconstituting the Urban Community.* New York: Basic Books, 1972.

Marmor, Theodore R. "Banfield's 'Heresy.'" *Commentary,* July 1972, pp. 86–88.

National Advisory Commission on Civil Disorders. *Report.* Washington, D.C.: Government Printing Office, 1968.

Piven, Frances F., and Richard A. Cloward. *The Politics of Turmoil: Essays on Poverty, Race, and the Urban Crisis.* New York: Pantheon, 1974.

———. *Regulating the Poor.* New York: Random House, 1971.

Sowell, Thomas. "Patterns of Black Excellence." *The Public Interest* 43(Spring 1976):26–58.

Should the Government Regulate the Sale and Ownership of Guns?

YES

EDWARD KENNEDY
We Need to Control Guns*

Mr. President, I am pleased to introduce the Federal Handgun Control Act of 1975. This bill has been designed to effectively curb the violence, the deaths, and the injuries that are caused by excessive numbers of handguns in the civilian society.

My bill requires:

First, the registration of all handguns.

Second, licensing of all handgun owners.

Third, a ban on the domestic manufacture, distribution, and sale of all handguns with a barrel less than six inches in length.

In past years, I have consistently introduced legislation to control all civilian-owned firearms, both handguns and long guns. Yet, despite the overwhelming statistical demand for effective controls, neither the Congress nor the administration has acted decisively to curb firearms violence. Each year, the nation's morgues receive more and more bullet-torn bodies.

In 1973, about 21,000 Americans died from gunfire. During 1974, the gun death tally rose to 25,000. And during 1975, we can expect that 26,000 to 27,000 Americans will be killed by gunfire. All firearms are lethal and potentially dangerous. But the national toll of gun deaths clearly shows that handguns disproportionately account for an uncommon percentage of gun deaths. Nationwide, handguns account for 54 percent of all murders. Yet, handguns number less than 20 percent of all firearms in civilian hands.

It is because of this vastly disproportionate relationship that I seek to enact legislation that is designed to primarily focus upon the problems caused by too many handguns. Handguns are clearly the

* From U.S., Congress, Senate, Committee on the Judiciary, *Handgun Crime Control*, Hearings, before the Subcommittee to Investigate Juvenile Delinquency, 94th Cong., 1st sess., 1975, vol. 1, pp. 871–878.

biggest single source of the firearms problem in America. And I intend to work diligently for a firearms control system that can eliminate the problems they cause.

Even though handguns account for 54 percent of all murders, these small deadly devices of infamy that we hear about so much in these times are as easy to buy as flashlights. Strong and effective restraints against the easy availability of handguns are the best insurance against more violence. Any weapon that has no valid justification beyond its use in crime should be strictly controlled. My interest in the need for effective firearms legislation goes back at least to 1963. I have introduced firearms bills in the Senate on several occasions. I offered gun control amendments to pending legislation on the Senate floor. I have observed much of the testimony presented by nearly 200 witnesses, during more than 40 days of hearings on gun control since I have been in the Senate.

The issues never change. The arguments never vary. The statistics never recede.

In 1963, handgun murders totaled 4,200. Eleven years later in 1974, handguns were used to murder 11,000 Americans. The tragic toll of handgun suicides and accidental handgun deaths pushes the annual figures well beyond reasonable limits for a society that claims to revere life and personal security. . . .

Gun manufacturers produce more guns each year, and American gun deaths increase right along with the output of firearms. Critical observers, like Robert Sherrill in *The Saturday Night Special,* warn the nation to arrest the headlong rush to the horrible logical conclusion that this trend suggests. As more and more of our loved ones and neighbors are killed with guns, each American is provoked or frightened into buying a gun for protection against other gun owners. If we as legislators fail to realize that the current toll of gun deaths is morally and socially excessive and must be curbed by law, we will have failed in our responsibility to insure the safety of the citizens of our nation. . . .

When our high schools must be policed against armed students, it is clear our society makes it too easy to obtain a handgun.

When jobless people can rent a weapon to hijack a taxi or rob a bank, the handgun industry has overproduced.

Seven years ago, I heard a member of the Chicago police force insist that young people who want laws changed must seek change through the due process of law. Our system of government he said, responds when change is necessary, and the proper way to make it respond is through legislative action, not through street demonstrations.

Today, I think of the fight for gun controls, a fight which has lasted through six Congresses and seven attorneys general, a fight which has never been taken to the streets, but has been pursued lawfully and quietly in the hearing rooms, committee rooms, and Chambers of this Capitol, a fight supported by over 80 percent of the American people, and even by two thirds of the nation's gun owners, but a fight which has not yet produced results.

What lesson, I wonder, have we taught our young and our dissatisfied in this history? They have seen the flood tide of gun tragedies proceed on unabated, while the legislative channels have been damned at every turn by obstruction, obfuscation, and delay. They have watched in horror as the facts of gun violence and bloodshed are reproved daily, while the enemies of change respond only with an effort to brainwash the Congress and the people into inaction. . . . So today, protecting the people of our nation from the lawless misuse of handguns, remains an important item on the list of our national social crises.

For that reason, I am proposing legislation to install a uniform nationwide system that will begin to control the widespread misuse of hand-held firearms. . . .

The principal purpose of the first requirement [of the Handgun Control Act of 1975]—that all handguns must be registered—is to provide an improved system for law enforcement agencies to trace those who commit crimes with handguns. This provision covers handguns already in private ownership and those to be acquired in the future. . . .

Registration will tell us how many guns there are, where they are, and in whose hands they are held.

Under my bill, registration information will be referred to the National Crime Information Center maintained by the Federal Bureau of Investigation, thus enabling enforcement officers throughout the country to trace immediately the ownership of any handgun. A person who carries a handgun must have a certificate of registration, to be exhibited upon the demand of any law enforcement officer.

Under the terms of the proposals, a violation of the registration provisions is punishable by imprisonment for up to five years, a fine of up to $10,000, or both. The secretary has authority to declare periods of amnesty during which previously unregistered handguns may be registered without penalty. Any purposeful falsification or forgery of registration information is punishable by imprisonment for up to ten years, or a fine of up to $25,000 or both.

The second feature of my bill requiring every handgun owner to obtain a license before he may be entrusted with a handgun is fundamental in guarding against the hazards of indiscriminately allowing criminals to obtain handguns. . . .

Under the provisions of my bill, if a state does not adopt a handgun permit system that meets minimum standards specified in the bill, federal licensing will become effective until the state adopts an adequate permit system. No person—whether a licensed dealer or a private individual—may sell ammunition to an individual who does not have either an adequate state permit or a federal handgun license. To qualify as having an adequate permit system, a state must restrict the issuance of permits applied for by convicted felons, fugitives from justice, mental defectives, alcoholics, juveniles, and drug addicts, and must adequately investigate applicants prior to the issuance of permits.

In states that do not enact adequate permits systems, federal handgun licenses, valid for up to three years, will be issued by federally licensed dealers upon receipt—from both the chief law enforcement officer of an applicant's locality and a licensed physician—of information bearing upon his eligibility for a federal license.

The sale or possession of ammunition in violation of the licensing and permit provisions of the bill carries a maximum sentence of imprisonment of five years and a fine of $5,000.

The purpose of the third provision of my bill—banning the domestic output of hand-held firearms with a barrel less than six inches in length—is to get at the heart of the problem of those guns used in crime. Handguns with a barrel of two, three, four, or five inches are so easily concealed that the weapons can be flashed at a moment's notice to intimidate, or overpower and then to wound or to kill. The handgun's role in crime is disproportionate to its number in comparison with long guns in the commission of homicide, aggravated assault, and armed robbery. . . .

Under the system that I have proposed uniform standards of handgun control will be proscribed by the federal government. Each state will be governed by the minimum requirements for a registration and licensing system. With such a comprehensive and uniform system of controls of handguns, we can eliminate the controlled flow of handguns from state to state. . . .

The arguments used to oppose gun controls are old and hackneyed. The same lament has been used in one of the following forms time and time again:

First, gun control cannot limit the supply of guns enough to reduce violence.

Second, the Constitution protects the citizen's right to bear arms.

Third, there is no need to ban guns because guns are not killers; people do the killing.

Fourth, criminals will always find a way to obtain a gun. Thus, controls will only disarm those who obey the law.

Fifth, registration and licensing procedures are so cumbersome and inconvenient that they would create unfair burdens for legitimate gun owners.

Opponents of effective gun controls believe that these objections are firmly rooted in substance. But a thorough examination of each of these claims reveals that not one of them is well founded.

First, can laws limit the supply of guns enough to reduce violent crime?

Of course such laws, properly enforced, can reduce the availability of handguns. In 1968, when importers anticipated enactment of a new gun law, about 1.2 million handguns were rushed into the American market. Then in 1969, pistol and revolver imports fell to less than 350,000 and have not risen substantially above that total since then.

Today, nearly 3 million new handguns enter the American market because handgun parts are still legally imported and because U.S. manufacturers are still authorized to produce them. The legislation I am introducing would not only reduce the number of handguns assembled from imported parts, but it would also drastically curtail the output of domestically manufactured handguns.

In June 1934, President Roosevelt signed the National Firearms Act which outlawed civilian ownership of machineguns. Perhaps, it is the law that best illustrates the way in which legislation can effectively restrain the availability of firearms. Since enactment of that measure over forty years ago, machine guns have been virtually eliminated from the scene. Obviously, that weapon has no legitimately useful place in a civilized society. Easily concealable pistols and revolvers are also out of place in today's highly urbanized and complex society.

Opponents of handgun control insist that it is impossible to prevent the criminal from obtaining a handgun. But, if the criminal has to steal a gun before he can use a gun, he will use a gun much less frequently.

I believe we can reduce the awesome rate of death, and injury caused by fire from pistols and revolvers. And I believe an effectively enforced ban on the output of these deadly devices is the most direct way to accomplish that goal.

Second, it is claimed that the Second Amendment to the Constitution protects the citizen's right to bear arms. Anyone who believes "the right to bear arms" is borne in the Constitution has conveniently ignored the language of the Second Amendment. For, the Second Amendment provides that "A well-regulated militia, being necessary to the security of a free state, the right of the people to keep and bear arms shall not be infringed."

The U.S. Supreme Court has repeatedly said that this amendment has nothing to do with the right to personal ownership of guns but only with the right of a state to establish a militia.

In its historic perspective, the purpose of the Second Amendment emerges clearly. Debates in the First and Second Congresses were naturally affected by the recently won independence of the new government. And in Massachusetts it was bitterly recalled that the British Crown had quartered its troops but forbade the organization of a colonial militia. Reported congressional debates from those times support the view that the Second Amendment was designed to protect and preserve the state militias. No mention was made of any individual "right" to possess, carry, or use arms, and there is no indication of any concern with the need to do so. The new government was much more interested in maintaining state militias to defend the hard won liberty. That fledgling government feared the establishment of a federal standing army as a threat to the basic authority of the several states.

Indeed, all but one of the fourteen states of the Union in December 1791, when the Bill of Rights was ratified, adopted a constitution or a declaration of rights, under which their people were governed.

Rhode Island still operated under its charter of 1663, which authorized the colony to organize a militia. But there was no mention of any "right" to bear arms.

Eight states—Delaware, New Jersey, Connecticut, Georgia, South Carolina, Maryland, New Hampshire, and New York—operated under constitutions that made no mention of any "right" to bear arms, though each authorized a state militia.

Three states—Massachusetts, North Carolina, and Virginia—expressly recognized the right of the people to bear arms for the defense of the state.

Two states—Pennsylvania and Vermont—included language in their constitutions which acknowledged that "the people have a right to bear arms for the defense of themselves and the State." However, that sentence was included in a paragraph that was concerned with the prohibition against a standing army and guarantee of civilian control of the militia.

Considering the history of this problem, reason defines the phrase "defence of themselves" as referring only to collective defense. That phrase did not include individual defense.

It appears, therefore, that both the states and the Congress were preoccupied with the distrust of the standing armies and the importance of preserving state militias. It was in this context that the Second Amendment was written and it is in this context that it has been interpreted by the courts.

Third, one other common refrain against firearm controls is that "guns do not kill, people do." This argument contends that people who use guns should be dealt with severely. But efforts to control the weapons are not necessary. Yet, a quick look at the statistics and common sense tell us that it is when guns are in hand, that two thirds of the people who kill other people do so; and it was when guns were in hand that over 250,000 robberies were committed in 1973; and it was when guns were in hand that one quarter of the nation's 400,000 aggravated assaults were committed in 1973.

Murder is usually committed in a moment of rage. Guns are quick and easy to use. They are also deadly accurate, and they are all too often readily accessible. Some estimate that there are over 35 million handguns in private ownership in this country. Each year, 2.5 million new handguns are introduced for civilian use into the marketplace. Because handguns are available, people use them.

Rarely does an attacker make a deliberate choice of a gun over a knife. But because the fatality rate of knife wounds is about one fifth that of gun wounds, it may be concluded that using a knife instead of a gun might cause 80 percent fewer deaths.

Fourth, others make the argument that because criminals have guns, gun control will simply disarm law abiding citizens. Lawless citizens, according to that argument, will feel unobliged to be bound by gun restrictions.

Perhaps there is something to that. And for that reason, I am convinced that gun restrictions can be effective in limiting the wholesale misuse of firearms. Strict gun restrictions will aid in disarming any who fail to register their weapons or obtain a license for ownership. Indeed, the enforcement of licensing and registration laws serves to isolate precisely those citizens who flaunt the law. For enactment of such legislation makes it a crime merely to possess an unregistered firearm. Commission of a crime with such a weapon compounds the wrong of any illegal act.

Fifth, it may be the greatest number who protest gun controls do so on the basis that the administrative requirements for registration are cumbersome and inconvenient. Since 1969, the Congress has attempted several times to remove the recordkeeping requirements of the 1968 gun control law, regarding sales of .22 caliber ammunition.

I have repeatedly objected to any move that would repeal

provisions of the requirement to record sales of such ammunition. Between 6 billion and 7 billion rounds of ammunition are produced in this country each year. At least 85 percent of those bullets are .22 caliber. Records maintained to control the sales of ammunition may be useful in restricting access only to those gun owners who intend to use their weapons for legitimate purposes.

I believe that any measure we might adopt which will substantially reduce the misuse of firearms will at the same time enhance whatever pleasures that may be derived from the so-called recreational pursuits of gun ownership.

If the only price of firearms recordkeeping requirements is the inconvenience to gun users, then with my bill, the American people will have been delivered a special bargain.

Should the Government Regulate the Sale and Ownership of Guns?

NO

ROBERT J. KUKLA
Gun Control Is a Hoax *

I believe in the kind of freedom for which America stands, a freedom of individual rights exercised within a context of individual responsibility under the law. I further believe that personal freedom is precisely what the American heritage is all about, and that the Constitution and Bill of Rights are its guarantee.

One of the distinctive characteristics of a free society is the right of every law-abiding citizen of good repute to exercise a broad variety of value judgments, among which are included the decision as to whether or not they desire to own a firearm, including handguns, for any one of a number of traditionally legitimate purposes.

The only kind of gun control laws which are justifiable are those

* From U.S., Congress, House, Committee on the Judiciary, *Firearms Legislation*, Hearings, before the Subcommittee on Crime, 94th Cong., 1st sess., 1975, Serial No. 11, Part 8, pp. 2708–2713.

that concern themselves with the improper or criminal use of firearms, as opposed to those affecting the firearms themselves. I am opposed to the latter category of gun laws because of three basic reasons: (1) they do not work against the criminal class, and they constitute an unjustifiable burden on the law-abiding citizen; (2) they are philosophically repugnant to the traditional freedoms upon which this nation was founded two centuries ago; and (3) they contradict the spirit and letter of the U.S. Constitution and Bill of Rights.

I believe that the right to keep and bear arms is a basic right, and that it is an individual right, not one that is collective in nature or limited to any concept of the militia as an organization. Although the Bill of Rights is a fundamental part of our constitutional heritage, there have been very few Supreme Court cases dealing with the Second Amendment and none which can be considered a definitive, or even binding, interpretation today. Moreover, it must be understood that fundamental human rights, including property rights and the right to an effective means of self-defense, are not created by any constitution or bill of rights, but exist independently of mere man-made documents, arising as they do out of the very nature of humanity and natural law. It must never be forgotten that a constitution or bill of rights is not the cause of personal and political freedom, but, rather, the consequence thereof. It is the function of constitutional guarantees to acknowledge and affirm the existence of basic human rights, and to sanctify and enshrine them for the enlightenment of the uninformed.

In general, it is probably fair to state that there are three primary reasons why gun control laws in the United States have consistently failed to work as they were intended; namely: (1) the extreme difficulty of drafting gun legislation on a federal level that will not offend some one of several constitutional safeguards; (2) the nearly insurmountable difficulties attendant upon the prosecution of many kinds of very common gun-law violations due to the legal requirements imposed by the so-called exclusionary evidence rule; and (3) the general reluctance of courts to impose significant penalties against persons convicted for gun-law violations, thereby very seriously diminishing their potential deterrent effect among the criminally inclined.

Among the difficulties attendant upon any federal gun legislation are those which arise from the fact, often lost sight of by laymen, that the federal government is one of limited and delegated powers derived solely from the specific grants given it by the states, whose creation it is, under the Constitution and Bill of Rights. The federal government does not possess police powers, which are reserved to the individual states, and can legislate only through the exercise of its authority over interstate commerce, and its power to tax. Moreover, in exercising its specific powers it must do so within the constraints of the Second, Fifth, and Ninth Amendments, which, among other things, extend their respective mantles of protection over the right to keep and bear arms, the right to be secure in the possession of personal property, the right to an effective means of self-defense, and the right against self-incrimination.

The historic problems inherent in federal gun legislation can be briefly illustrated by citing two examples where important segments of the National Firearms Act of 1934 were held to be unconstitutional. The first instance related to what was originally regarded by many of its sponsors as the single most significant provision of the act, namely, a provision that the mere possession of a firearm or ammunition was presumptive evidence that such firearm or ammunition had been transported in interstate commerce. When the U.S. Supreme Court subsequently declared that subsection unconstitutional only a few years after enactment, it effectively emasculated the core of the statute, leaving intact, for all practical purposes, only the requirement that certain kinds of gangster-associated weapons, such as machineguns and sawed-off shotguns, among others, be registered with the federal government under heavy penalty of law for failure to do so. However, in 1968, in the so-called *Haynes* case, the U.S. Supreme Court effectively neutralized that statutory provision when it held, in effect, that a timely plea of self-incrimination, under the Fifth Amendment, would constitute a complete defense to a prosecution for failure to register such illegally held firearms.

The second major federal statute, the Federal Firearms Act of 1938, did not fare very much better, albeit for somewhat different reasons. There had never been a single conviction under its major provision in the entire thirty years of its existence.

The problems inherent in the federal government's excursions into gun control are comparatively minuscule and insignificant when compared with the obstacles faced by the states in their attempt to regulate the use of firearms under their constitutionally reserved right of the police power. Chief among the impediments in this regard is the exclusionary evidence rule. It is my considered opinion that no other single factor is as responsible for the failure of gun control regulations to function effectively as is the exclusionary evidence rule.

The Fourth Amendment to the Constitution provides that people are to be secure against unreasonable searches and seizures of their persons, papers, houses, and effects. The remedy for the violation of these rights is called the *exclusionary* evidence rule. Simply stated, the exclusionary evidence rule provides that reliable evidence of a crime cannot be admitted in court, and cannot be considered by the judge or jury to decide the guilt of the defendant, if a law-enforcement officer obtained that evidence by what a court later decides was an unreasonable search and seizure. In effect, the exclusionary evidence rule blocks ascertainment of the truth, causes false verdicts, frees defendants who are clearly guilty, and affords protection only to the guilty.

The exclusionary evidence rule was created by judicial decision of the U.S. Supreme Court in the apparent belief that it would deter unlawful police conduct, unreasonable searches and seizures, by removing the incentive through the exclusion of improperly obtained evidence from court. The rule was first adopted by the U.S. Supreme Court in 1914 to exclude from federal courts evidence improperly obtained by federal agents. It did not then apply to the states. However, in 1961, the year that approximates the beginning of the burgeoning crime rate, the U.S. Supreme Court extended the exclusionary evidence rule to all states.

The particular significance of the exclusionary evidence rule to weapons cases becomes obvious when it is realized that the great bulk of arrests for gun-law violations involves defendants who are caught in the act of carrying concealed a handgun on or about their person. As a direct consequence of the application of that rule, the overwhelming majority of those persons easily escape conviction because of minor technical deficiencies involved in the circumstances surrounding their arrests. For example, it is not at all uncommon in the city of Chicago for anywhere from 8,000 to 10,000 persons to be arrested in any recent year for the violation of one or more gun laws, including among others, the carrying of concealed weapons, failure to register guns in their possession, and failure to possess a state gun-owners identification card. However, only a very small fraction of such persons are ever convicted of their offense, usually because the firearms involved are excluded from use as lawful evidence.

Although the exclusionary evidence rule was conceived out of the most laudatory motives, its indiscriminate application over recent years has exacted an incalculable toll from society by suppressing the truth in criminal trials, freeing obviously guilty criminals, destroying respect for law and the courts, and generally undermining the effectiveness of the criminal justice system. It has also produced a loud clamor for yet additional and far more stringent gun laws from among those persons who do not as yet comprehend the nature of the problem.

Fortunately, an eminently suitable alternative to the exclusionary evidence rule can be achieved merely by the enactment of a law which abolishes the exclusionary evidence rule and substitutes in its place the right of a civil action for ordinary damages, plus attorney's fees, for unlawful searches and seizures, and providing for punitive damages and criminal prosecution, where applicable, against any officers guilty of malicious, fraudulent, or oppressive conduct. In this way, a remedy is provided to innocent victims, while enabling the courts to return to the emphasis of truth finding in criminal trials.

The final barrier to effective regulation of the illegal use of firearms arises out of the extraordinary reluctance of courts to impose meaningful penalties even in those comparatively few cases where solid convictions for criminal acts have been obtained. This general phenomenon is clearly reflected by the experience of the three major states of Illinois, New York, and California.

In 1935, Illinois had a population of approximately 8 million people, and there were some 16,000 convicts committed to the state penitentiary system. This year, 1975, with a population that has increased to 11.5 million people, Illinois now has some 6,000 convicts assigned to the Department of Corrections, a decrease of some 10,000 convicts, and, of those, half are out of jail on parole, probation, supervision, furloughs, and work-release programs. During the seven-year period from 1968 (when the Illinois firearms license law and the Chicago gun registration ordinance took effect) through 1974, serious crimes in Illinois increased by 52 percent, while prison sentences dropped 26 percent, and the number of inmates in the penitentiary system decreased by 22 percent.

The typical scenario of the Chicago gun court's failure to function effectively was outlined by the Chicago Crime Commission in the following case history:

 In 1969 the defendant was sentenced to one year in the House of Corrections for theft (reduced from burglary charges).

In 1970, 1971, 1972, and 1974 he was arrested for unlawful use of a weapon and freed without a trial.

Then in August of this year (1974), a Cook County grand jury indicted him for murder.

It is appropriate at this point to comment briefly on the myth currently being advanced by certain proponents of gun control that the great majority of murder victims are killed by persons with whom they are acquainted, or to whom they are related in some social sense. This misleading contention is apparently intended to convey the impression to the American public that their mere possession of a firearm, particularly a handgun, increases the likelihood that they, or some member of their family or circle of friends will be the victim of its use in a moment of uncontrollable passion or outrage. Such an assumption is false and unsupported by the known facts, except as among those persons who customarily maintain a close or intimate association with individuals possessing psychopathic and/or established criminal tendencies. For example, an analysis of the 970 murders committed in Chicago during 1974 revealed that 61 percent of the known murderers had a prior criminal record, and 45 percent of all murder victims had a prior criminal record.

The Chicago experience confirms the 1964 findings of the Senate Judiciary Subcommittee following its special study of the backgrounds of murderers from the 120 major population centers of the United States. The latter study of firearms homicides disclosed that 80 percent of those who used a gun had a prior criminal record; that 78 percent of all murderers studied had criminal records; that the gun killer had an average of six prior arrests before his first murder; and that 60 percent of the gun killers had been arrested for a crime of violence before the murder indictment.

Clearly, society's murderers are not the average hard-working, tax-paying, law-abiding citizen. In those instances where they are described as being acquainted with, or socially related to, their victims, then it is primarily in the sense that drug addicts are acquainted with their drug pushers, that habitual gamblers are acquainted with their loan sharks, that thieves and burglars are acquainted with their fences, that prostitutes are acquainted with their procurers and clientele, that adulterers are related to their spouses and are acquainted with their paramours, that deranged persons are related to their immediate family, and that various kinds of drunkards, perverts, and petty hoodlums are acquainted with their usual companions.

It is an undisputed fact that New York City has the most stringent statutory sanctions against the illegal possession of handguns anywhere in the nation. In light of this circumstance, the results of a recent survey by the New York City Police Department of the court disposition of cases where individuals were arrested under the Sullivan Law for illegal possession of handguns is extremely enlightening.

There were two studies undertaken. The first covered the latter part of 1972, and the second covered the first half of 1973. The analysis of the results of these studies focused only on those cases in the surveys which had resulted in convictions. The object of the studies was to determine whether or not the sentences imposed bore any meaningful relationship to the severity of the crimes committed.

In the first survey, there were 164 cases involving the arrest of 208 individuals. No cases involving juveniles under the age of sixteen were selected for purposes of the survey. The local criminal courts processed 138 of these defendants, of which 121 cases resulted in a final disposition. Of these 121 cases, 69 (57 percent) resulted in a conviction; however, only 11 (15 percent) of these 69 defendants who were convicted received a sentence involving any incarceration. Approximately 85 percent of the defendants received no prison sentence. The majority of the defendants convicted received only a fine. In these cases where a grand jury handed down indictments, 37 resulted in conviction; however, only 4 (10 percent) of the 37 received any prison sentence.

In the second survey, 342 defendants were chosen for study. A total of 120 (35 percent) defendants were convicted in the local criminal courts with the result that only 16 (13 percent) received terms of imprisonment. Here, again, approximately 85 percent of the defendants received no prison sentence at all.

A total of 108 defendants were indicted by a grand jury and 62 (57 percent) of these individuals were convicted. Of the 62 convictions, only 13 (21 percent) received terms of imprisonment.

These studies revealed an appalling pattern with respect to gun crimes which speaks for itself. The fact is, as clearly demonstrated by these surveys, that very few defendants received jail sentences even though in every one of these cases the defendants could have received a sentence of up to seven years in the penitentiary.

Subsequent to the survey of the New York City Police Department, a public commission, disturbed by the results, undertook an independent study. The commission scrutinized the sentencing practices in felony gun cases in Kings County during March 1973. It was determined from court records that there were 90 cases where defendants were sentenced on the felony charge of illegal possession of a loaded handgun. In only four (4 percent) cases were sentences of one year or more imposed. There were only eight (9 percent) cases where terms of imprisonment were imposed for a year or less. However, the vast majority of these cases, seventy-eight (87 percent) resulted in noncustodial sentences such as fines, probation, unconditional and conditional discharges.

It has been exactly this kind of sentencing practice that also prompted the FBI [Federal Bureau of Investigation] to conduct its own study with regard to the kind of person typically involved in the murder of police officers. According to FBI records, there were a total of 1,084 offenders identified in connection with the killing of 786 law enforcement officers over the ten year period from 1963 to 1972. Of that number, 825 had records of prior criminal arrests; 641 of that number had been convicted of those prior offenses, and 391 of those who were convicted received leniency in the form of parole or probation. More incredible yet, fully 178 of those police killers were actually out of jail either on parole or probation at the very moment that they killed a police officer.

An extraordinarily similar pattern of the judiciary's widespread preference for probation instead of prison sentences was also found to exist in California by the 1973 Governor's Select Committee on Law Enforcement Problems. The committee found that this policy had almost totally eliminated the deterrent effect of prison by reducing the rate of prison sentences so that less than one out of fourteen defendants convicted of crimes punishable by prison are sent to prison.

In 1971, out of the 56,000 defendants who were finally convicted in superior court of the state of California, fewer than 10 percent were sentenced to prison, compared to 70 percent that were granted probation. The prison commitment figure of less than 10 percent takes on additional significance in light of the fact that 78 percent of the defendants had prior criminal records and 35 percent of them were already on parole or probation or in an institution. From 1960 through 1971, the crime rate in California increased by 122 percent, while prison sentences decreased by 59 percent. Of those persons charged with FBI index crimes in 1960, 24 percent of those convicted were sentenced to prison, as compared to only 7 percent during 1971.

The sale of heroin is a felony in California, punishable by five years to life in prison, but imprisonment is frequently avoided by probation. In 1971, of all defendants convicted of selling opiates, only 18 percent were sentenced to prison, with 34 percent committed to a rehabilitation center, while 32 percent were granted probation with minimal jail time, and 12 percent were granted straight probation or no penalty whatsoever. Moreover, 22 percent of those convicted had a prior prison record. More shocking yet is the fact that over 41 percent of the defendants were already on parole or probation at the time they were arrested for their current offense.

Similarly, possession of heroin is also a felony in California, but only 8 percent of all defendants convicted of possession of opiates in 1971 were actually sentenced to prison.

The extraordinary extent to which California courts have repudiated prison sentences as punishment, in preference for awarding probation, is graphically illustrated by the table disclosing the percentage of defendants who were granted probation *again* after the conviction of a felony in 1971 while they were *already* on probation for a *previous* offense.

Gun control, as that term is commonly used today, constitutes nothing more than a monumental hoax and a fraud upon the American public. Although gun control proposals pretend to be directed towards the laudatory objective of reducing the incidence of violent crime, they tend in fact to aggravate the very conditions fostering crime by diverting attention away from the dismal failure of the criminal justice system to adequately cope with criminality. As a society we simply have failed

Convicted Offense	Probation Granted Again (Percent)
Robbery	33
Assault	68
Burglary	57
Theft (nonauto)	68
Car theft	63
Rape	29
Sale of opiates	34
Sale of dangerous drugs	67
Sale of marijuana	73

to provide for an efficient means whereby criminals can be apprehended, speedily prosecuted, reliably convicted, jailed, and kept in jail. In turn, that failure, or lack of resolve, to treat crime and the people who commit criminal acts for what they really are, stems primarily from a philosophical repudiation of, and retreat from, the traditional American concept of an egalitarian social order based upon individual freedom exercised within a context of individual responsibility. . . .

America does not have a "gun problem," and gun control does not equal crime control. We have a crime problem. But for those who take the trouble to examine the facts and are both psychologically and politically free to interpret them fairly and objectively, it is abundantly clear that the problem with crime has nothing whatsoever to do with guns but, rather, lies squarely upon the manner in which criminals are regarded and treated by the institutions upon which society must rely for law enforcement and the administration of justice.

America does not need any more gun control laws. Improved law enforcement and the reduction of crime can and must be achieved without either developing an oppressive state, or curtailing basic and essential liberties. Effective law enforcement guarantees individual freedom; it does not restrict it.

What America desperately does need is the immediate restoration of the judicial system to its proper constitutional role, namely, the ascertainment of truth and the application of the law to that truth. Those practices which contribute to court delay, or which abuse legal technicalities and thereby encourage law breaking must be eliminated and replaced with an effective mechanism to assure fair, speedy, and certain administration of criminal justice. Finally, the correctional process must be reformed so as to insure that these persons who violate the privilege of parole or probation are held strictly accountable and immediately returned to imprisonment.

QUESTIONS FOR DISCUSSION

1. Would strong gun-control laws reduce the number of deaths caused by handguns?
2. Is the Second Amendment to the Constitution (protecting the citizen's right to bear arms) a legal impediment to gun control?
3. Is advocacy of gun control a liberal or conservative view?
4. Would gun-control laws restrict gun owners who intend to use their weapons for legitimate purposes?
5. Does the evidence from individual states with strong laws regulating the possession of guns support or weaken the advocates of strong federal gun-control laws?

SUGGESTED READINGS

Bakal, Carl. *No Right to Bear Arms*. New York: Paperback Library, 1968.

Block, Irvin. *Gun Control: One Way to Save Lives*. New York: Public Affairs Committee, 1976.

Bruce-Briggs, B. "The Great American Gun War." *The Public Interest* 45(Fall 1976):37–62.

"Controversy over Proposed Federal Handgun Legislation." *Congressional Digest,* December 1975.

Davidson, Bill. *To Keep and Bear Arms*. New York: Arlington House, 1969.

Greenwood, Colin. *Firearms Control: A Study of Armed Crime and Firearms Control in England and Wales*. London: Routledge & Kegan Paul, 1972.

Hays, Stuart R. "The Right to Bear Arms: A Study in Judicial Misinterpretation." *William and Mary Law Review* 2(1960):381–406.

Hunter, George. *How to Defend Yourself, Your Family and Your Home*. New York: David McKay, 1967.

Kennett, Lee B., and James La Verne Anderson. *The Gun in America: The Origins of a National Dilemma*. Westport, Conn.: Greenwood Press, 1975.

Sherrill, Robert. *The Saturday Night Special*. New York: Charterhouse, 1973.

Wills, Garry. *The Second Civil War: Arming for Armageddon*. New York: New American Library, 1968.

Should the Government
Restrict the Development
of Nuclear Power?

YES

MIKE GRAVEL
*The Hazards of Nuclear Power**

Our government and the electric power industry hope to commit the
United States to nuclear-generated electricity within the next decade.
But there are profound and inherent hazards connected with nuclear
power—hazards so far-reaching that we must carefully contemplate the
consequences of a nuclear power future.

Here are a few facts you should know:

ABOUT RADIOACTIVE WASTES

Nuclear power reactors produce deadly radioactive wastes like fallout.
Each year, a large reactor accumulates the radioactive poisons of 1,000
Hiroshima bombs. These poisonous wastes must be isolated from the
natural environment for centuries. If they are released accidentally into
our air or water, they can enter the food chain to be distributed and
concentrated uncontrollably.

The intense radioactivity of reactor wastes can lead to cancer and
genetic damage. With burial grounds of reactor waste, we leave to
future generations an unprecedented threat to life and health. In the
words of Dr. Hannes Alfven, Nobel laureate in physics, "The fission
reactor produces both energy and radioactive waste; we want to use
the energy now and leave the radioactive waste for our children and
grandchildren to take care of."

In a fully developed nuclear economy, overwhelming amounts of
radioactive waste would be generated. The release of as little as a
fraction of a percent of these wastes would threaten human health. And
yet, even though the United States is proceeding with nuclear plant

* From a letter to constituents, n.d.

construction, *we do not have any program for the ultimate safe disposal of the hazardous wastes.* And in our nuclear weapons program, 500,000 gallons of high-level wastes have already leaked from storage tanks.

ABOUT REACTOR SAFETY

A study by the Atomic Energy Commission said the worst accident at a power reactor could kill 45,000 persons and cause more than $17 billion in property damage. An area the size of Pennsylvania could be contaminated.

The Emergency Core Cooling System [ECCS], a device meant to prevent such a catastrophe, has been proven only by computer. The ECCS failed six out of six semiscale tests, and full-scale testing is several years behind schedule. In a fire at the Browns Ferry reactor in March 1975, the ECCS failed to operate when called upon.

Even though damage could reach billions of dollars in a nuclear accident, insurance companies provide only $125 million in liability coverage, and the government protects the nuclear industry from claims beyond that amount. *Industry refused to "go nuclear" until it was given this protection from full liability.* In a nuclear catastrophe, a total of $560 million would be available to victims—mostly in taxpayer funds.

ABOUT PLUTONIUM

Plutonium, an element created in the fission reactor, is one of the most poisonous substances known. It is also the material that makes atomic bombs. *One* pound of plutonium represents the potential for billions of lung cancers. Less than *twenty* pounds is needed to construct a nuclear bomb. But by 1985, world production of plutonium may exceed *200,000* pounds *per year*. Plutonium remains dangerous longer than 100,000 years.

By spreading nuclear reactors around the world, we are spreading nuclear weapons capability. With a large reactor, even the most unstable country will be able to produce plutonium for a nuclear arsenal.

Terrorists with stolen plutonium could threaten huge areas. They might threaten to release the plutonium into the air—or they could construct a bomb. Atom bomb technology is now public property, and it has been proven that laymen can design a credible weapon from public reference works. The terrorist menace also implies a threat to our civil liberties—what rights would we not forego to avoid nuclear terrorism?

ABOUT OUR ENERGY PRIORITIES

Our nation's first energy priority is currently the fast breeder reactor, which is to produce large quantities of plutonium (to be used as reactor fuel) while it generates electricity. The breeder will be even more dangerous than today's reactors. Total costs for the breeder program are now estimated at $10 billion, up from original estimates of less than half that amount. Cost estimates for a breeder prototype have gone from $700 million to $1.95 billion. A breeder facility in Washington state now is to cost $933 million, up from $87 million.

U.S. reserves of uranium are small, only about enough to fuel the reactors we already have throughout their lifetimes. Thus, if America turns to nuclear electricity, we will become dependent on foreign uranium, and we could find ourselves at the mercy of another energy cartel. Nuclear energy would harm the U.S. economy in the long run because it would produce less energy for each dollar of investment it requires. In other words, if we use reactors to supply the energy we need, this will draw away job-producing capital from other sectors of the economy. We should quickly develop the nonhazardous energy alternatives which are available to us, especially solar energy. These are our best long-term investments.

For many years, nuclear energy has not received sufficient public scrutiny. Today, as the hazards of nuclear power become better known, it is clear that many citizens believe that the risks of this technology outweigh the benefits.

In California, an initiative that would have severely limited the nuclear industry won the approval of about a third of the state's voters, and three bills which restrict nuclear growth in the state have been signed into law. In Oregon and Colorado, initiatives like California's are on the November ballot, and signatures are being gathered to present similar measures to voters in about a dozen other western states. In Vermont, state legislature approval is now required for nuclear plants. And more than 300,000 persons have signed the national clean energy petition asking that nuclear power be kept out of their lives.

Our citizens need to become fully aware of the hazards of nuclear power before we find ourselves irrevocably committed to the nuclear option. My office provides free information about nuclear energy and about the nuclear debate in Congress. Write to me at 3317 Dirksen Building, U.S. Senate, Washington D.C., 20510.

I urge you to examine this issue carefully and critically. Arnold Toynbee, the historian, has pointed out that man's nuclear fire can destroy life on this planet—both through war and through radioactive waste. The question before us is as important as that—and we must give our answer soon.

Should the Government Restrict the Development of Nuclear Power?

NO

MIKE McCORMACK
Controversy over the Safety of Nuclear Energy Production *

Understanding the nature of the energy crisis and the role that nuclear energy will play in providing energy for the present and the future is a matter of supreme importance, for our nation is truly in mortal danger. Our national security, the stability of our economic systems, and even our political institutions may well depend on our ability to develop responsible energy policies and to implement rational programs to carry them into effect.

The stark realities are that our oil production is down about 10 percent in the last three years; our natural gas production is down almost as much; our coal production has increased less than 10 percent in this period; the percent of petroleum we import has increased from about 35 percent at the time of the Arab oil embargo to about 41 percent today; more railroads have gone out of business, the situation in the Middle East remains unstable; and a handful of antinuclear activists are advocating a moratorium on nuclear energy production—our only hope, along with coal, for energy self-sufficiency, economic stability and national security, during this century.

We cannot afford the luxury of basing our energy policies on

---

* From an address to the Wisconsin Energy Coalition's Conference on Energy Supply and Economic Life, March 19, 1976, Milwaukee, Wisconsin. Reprinted by permission from *Congressional Digest*, February 1977, pp. 48 ff.

fantasies, such as assuming that solar energy or geothermal energy or some suppressed carburetor design, or some magic will bail us out of our problems.

Nor can we base policies on anti-public-power or anti-utility-company or anti-Israeli or anti-Arab or anti-oil-company or anti-nuclear prejudices or obsessions. Nor can we base our energy policies on hopes, such as the hope that we will keep finding enough gas or petroleum to keep us going, or the hopes of some that the people of this country will, in the name of conservation, voluntarily and in blind ignorance, accept still higher unemployment, and severely reduce their standard of living, when indeed, it is not necessary for anyone to suffer if we adopt responsible policies to produce the energy required for full employment.

While we cannot afford the excesses which marked some industrial development of the past, raping our land and polluting the atmosphere, we cannot expect to have energy production without some impact on the environment, no matter how benign the source may seem to be from a distance; and we certainly cannot expect to have jobs for the American people unless we produce more energy.

So, we have several "environments" to protect all at the same time. There are, for instance, those that we classically think of in terms of air, land, and water, but there is also the environment of the job market, and an industrial capacity that will maintain this nation's national security and economic stability. Finally, there is the environment of our homes, and those of millions of low-income Americans, where we must have enough energy for a decent standard of living. Our national energy policy must strike this dynamic balance in a rational manner.

One of the most important realities that the American people must understand is that this nation has, since 1970, truly passed from one major historical era into another. We have passed from an era of cheap, abundant fuels, energy, and materials into an era of shortages and high costs which will, at best, be with us for many decades.

That reality is exceedingly difficult to accept, for us who have lived all our lives in a culture built on cheap mobility and the assumption that American affluence was endless. Nevertheless, we must face the fact that we have, almost certainly, already burned up more than half of all the petroleum, and almost half of all the natural gas we have ever discovered, or ever will discover, on this continent or off its shores, and that it will be gone, insofar as a significant supply of fuel is concerned, by about the end of this century, no matter what price—within reason—we pay for it today.

Remember, this will be happening while our demand for energy is doubling, even with a successful and spartan conservation program.

As our supplies of petroleum and natural gas dwindle, this nation will become dependent for most of its energy on coal and nuclear fission. However, even these sources of energy are, in the long range perspective, only transitional. Although we must increase our reliance upon them from now until sometime in the twenty-first century, we must also make plans for phasing them out in the more distant future, and replacing them with other, still-to-be-developed resources.

As responsible citizens sort out the facts with respect to our energy future, it becomes more and more obvious that one of the greatest strokes of good fortune this nation has experienced is to have our nuclear industry as well advanced as we find it today, ready now to provide much of the energy this nation will need during the next fifty to seventy-five years.

Nuclear energy is the safest, cleanest, cheapest, most reliable source of energy available, with the least environmental impact of any significant option. If we did not have a large block of nuclear energy available to us for the coming decades, this country would be in critical danger, even if we succeed in tripling coal production by the year 2000.

Today, there are fifty-nine nuclear plants licensed to operate in the United States. During 1975, nuclear energy produced about 8.5 percent of this nation's electricity, with a higher reliability factor than comparably sized coal plants of the same age. Had this amount of energy been generated by fossil-fired plants, 60 million tons of coal or 250 million barrels of oil would have been required. This is equivalent to two thirds of a million barrels of oil a day, about 2 percent of our total energy production, and 4 percent of our total oil consumption. This nuclear energy production saved more than 2 billion dollars in generating costs in 1975.

Eleven more plants are scheduled to be on the line within the next twelve months. In addition to these 70 plants, there are 158 more nuclear plants which are under construction or committed. If these plants are all on the line by 1985, and they can be if we simply eliminate unnecessary delays and provide for construction capital, then this nation will have a nuclear capacity of about 226 thousand megawatts—about 30 percent of our electric generating capacity—by 1985.

One can appreciate the importance of such progress in view of the fact that each new nuclear plant, operating at 64.4 percent capacity, saves the equivalent of more than 10 million barrels of oil a year. It would require more than six million barrels of oil a day to produce the same electricity that these 228 plants would generate. This is approximately the same as the amount of petroleum products that the United States imports today.

With the nuclear breeder program in place in the 1990s, the advantages of nuclear energy will significantly increase, particularly with respect to establishing this nation's energy independence. At the present time we are in the midst of an extensive research, development, and demonstration program involving nuclear breeder technologies and are focusing on learning essential engineering facts related to the liquid metal fast breeder. Our demonstration programs will have reached the point by about 1990 that licensing of commercial breeders should be in order. Unfortunately we are already far behind France, England, Germany, Russia, and probably Japan in the commercialization of this technology.

A breeder is a nuclear power plant which produces more fuel than it consumes. With a breeder program, this nation can convert our large stockpile of Uranium 238, already mined and in purified form, into a nuclear fuel of extraordinary value. This will give our nation a chance at energy independence. The energy that can be produced from the otherwise useless Uranium 238 can, with a breeder program, produce as much electricity as would be produced by more than five times all the oil possessed by all of the OPEC [Organization of Petroleum Exporting Countries] nations combined.

Statements that the breeder program presents some sort of special safety problem are simply not true. All nuclear plants produce plutonium. The breeder simply produces more than it uses. This new fuel will, in turn, be used to provide for concurrent energy requirements. Nuclear wastes from breeder plants are no different from the wastes of today's nuclear plants.

There is no moral or intellectual justification for becoming so obsessed with hypothetical hazards of nuclear energy that one refuses to deal in facts.

The most important fact is that the campaign to undermine nuclear energy is, in effect, a campaign to cause additional unemployment. Cutting back on nuclear energy production will mean increased unemployment among American workers, not only those involved in the construction of the nuclear plants themselves, but, far more important, those involved in permanent industries which will require the energy produced.

Of course, the nuclear industry, just as any other, does have some hazardous aspects, and we must assume that at some time in the future there will be some accident causing property damage, injuries, and even deaths. It is crucial, however, to ask how likely these accidents are, and how this risk compares to that associated with other everyday activities.

While it is essential that every reasonable precaution be taken to guard against every conceivable accident—and this is being done—there is a point beyond which imagining wildly unlikely nuclear accidents becomes meaningless at best. Obsession with such antinuclear fantasies, while ignoring the much greater hazards of the real world around us, does a great disservice to the people whom we elected public officials are expected to represent.

The fact is that not a single radiation death or injury has resulted from the operation of any licensed nuclear power plant in the United States, or anywhere else in the free world, nor has any member of the public been exposed to any radiation in excess of internationally approved standards as the result of the operation of all the fifty-nine nuclear power plants and their supporting activities, and the more than one hundred U.S. military nuclear reactors now in service.

QUESTIONS FOR DISCUSSION

1. Are the safety hazards from nuclear power greater than those from other energy sources?
2. What are the dangers to United States foreign policy of exporting nuclear reactors?
3. What effect would a decision by the United States to stop building nuclear power reactors have on other technologically advanced countries capable of producing similar reactors?
4. What effect would a decision to stop building nuclear power reactors have on the American economy?
5. What is the environmental impact of nuclear energy compared to that of other sources of energy?

SUGGESTED READINGS

Berger, John J. *Nuclear Power—the Unviable Option: A Critical Look at Our Energy Alternatives.* Foreword by Mike Gravel. Introduction by Linus Pauling. Palo Alto, Calif.: Ramparts Press, 1976.

Dawson, Frank G. *Nuclear Power: Development of a Technology.* Seattle: University of Washington Press, 1976.

Garvey, Gerald. *Nuclear Power and Social Planning: The City of the Second Sun.* Lexington, Mass.: Lexington Books, 1977.

Hunt, Stanley Ernest. *Fission, Fusion and the Energy Crisis*. New York: Pergamon Press, 1974.

Murphy, Arthur W., ed. *The Nuclear Power Controversy*. Englewood Cliffs, N.J.: Prentice-Hall, 1976.

Myers, Desaix B. *The Nuclear Power Debate: Moral, Economic, Technical, and Political Issues*. New York: Praeger, 1977.

Novick, Sheldon. *The Careless Atom*. Boston: Houghton Mifflin, 1969.

Patterson, Walter C. *Nuclear Power*. Harmondsworth, England: Penguin, 1976.

Union of Concerned Scientists. *The Nuclear Fuel Cycle: A Survey of the Public Health, Environmental, and National Security Effects of Nuclear Power*. Cambridge, Mass.: MIT Press, 1975.

Webb, Richard E. *The Accident Hazards of Nuclear Power Plants*. Amherst: University of Massachusetts Press, 1976.

14.

Is The United States Meeting Its Global Challenges in National Security and Foreign Policy?

Security is the key factor motivating the foreign policy of most nations. Nearly every American is in favor of national security. Since the end of World War II, however, heated debates have surrounded the fundamental problems of security: What are the dangers facing American security? What are the best methods of achieving security? How should security be reconciled with other considerations? The answers to these questions have depended upon the changing global role of the United States and upon the ideas of policy makers and citizens alike about world politics and the position of the United States.

From the end of World War II to the present, the United States has experienced many changes in the conduct of foreign policy. Immediately after World War II, this country abandoned its traditional isolationist position. No longer was the United States able to stand aside and let the leading nations in Europe and Asia play balance-of-power politics. Several factors contributed to the United States' active participation in world politics in a way unprecedented in its peace-time history.

First, by the end of the war, the United States had become the strongest military power in the world. Its armed forces, moreover, had triumphed both in the Pacific and in Europe. Importantly for the future, the United States invented atomic bombs and used them in the last days of the war against Japan.

Second, in addition to its extraordinary military power, the United States had a strong economy. Most of the industrial powers of the world had been severely hurt by the war. Germany, France, the Soviet Union, Japan, and Britain had suffered heavy damage to their industrial plants. The United States, in contrast, did not experience the same kind of fate.

Third, in the years immediately after the war, policy makers in the United

States and Western Europe feared the Soviet Union. Stalin had led that country to victory over Germany, and now Soviet military power extended throughout Eastern Europe.

Fourth, Europe's colonies in Africa and Asia were struggling for independence. The outcome of these struggles would strongly affect the balance of power in the world.

Because of the changing landscape of world politics, then, America began to play a strong internationalist role. That role came to be marked over the years by high defense budgets, alliances, foreign-aid programs, and war.

Historically, military spending in time of peace had been low in the United States. The coming of the Cold War, which pitted the Soviet Union against the United States, put an end to low military budgets as Congress appropriated money to develop and produce nuclear and conventional weapons.

The United States abandoned its isolationism and entered into multinational alliances. The North Atlantic Treaty Organization (NATO) and the South East Asian Treaty Organization (SEATO) were two important components of its multilateral approach to alliances. Special bilateral arrangements with Nationalist China, Japan, and other countries offered an alternative approach to alliances.

In addition to rearmament and alliances, the United States relied on foreign-aid programs. Since the end of World War II, this country has sent funds to every continent and has spent more than $100 billion in foreign aid. Aid was an important feature of American foreign policy under the Marshall Plan, which was designed to strengthen the economies of European countries. Aid also became an essential component of America's Vietnam policy.

The most controversial aspect of American foreign policy since the end of World War II has been war. The United States has fought two undeclared wars—one against North Korea and the other against North Vietnam. Both wars were costly in terms of lives and property. Both, moreover, were accompanied by controversy over the way the wars were fought and even over the necessity in these cases of engaging in combat at all.

The world has changed much since America assumed a superpower role in 1945. No longer is United States military power as superior to that of other nations as it was. The Soviet Union, too, has nuclear weapons and the means to deliver them against the United States. Other countries—Britain, France, Communist China, and India—have exploded nuclear devices, and there is every likelihood that many more nations will have nuclear capability by 1985. The invention of the cruise missile with its nuclear warhead, moreover, has given a potential nuclear weapons capability to many nations because of its low cost.

In addition to the relative military decline of the United States, American economic power has been challenged by the rise of other nations. West European countries and Japan have expanded their industrial production. Oil-producing nations have strengthened their economic power. The peoples of the Third World, moreover, have won their wars for independence, and their economies in some cases have become stronger.

Another important change affecting United States foreign policy, in addition to its relative decline in both defense capabilities and in economic power, has been America's decreased fear of the communist world. Communism no longer appears to be monolithic. Until Joseph Stalin's death in 1953, communism looked more united throughout the world than it does today. Because of the predominance of Soviet military power in Eastern Europe, Stalin was able to establish communist regimes friendly to the Soviet Union in this area of the world. Mainland China sought support from the Soviet Union, moreover. The assertion of independence by Tito in Yugoslavia in 1948, followed by the rise of the Sino-Soviet rivalry, have made many in the West less alarmed about the danger of communism today than they were in the early years of the Cold War. In Italy and France, moreover, communist parties profess a belief in Eurocommunism that, its supporters contend, is a new form of communism committed to political democracy and to independence from the Soviet Union.

The world of American foreign policy, then, has changed since World War II. Debate over security matters, however, continues as sharply as in the immediate post-World War II years. This chapter deals with some of the more vital issues affecting American national security and foreign policy. Specifically, four questions are considered: (1) Is the United States defense establishment strong enough to cope with Soviet military threats? (2) Does détente favor the Soviet Union? (3) Should the United States adopt an activist policy regarding human rights in other nations? (4) Should the United States impose economic sanctions on the South African government in order to promote majority rule?

DEFENSE

A major problem of security is defense. "How much is enough for defense?" is asked in every budget year. Defense spending is a function of available resources, popular willingness to make sacrifices, and assessment of threats. One view is that the United States is spending too much for defense. According to this perception, the reasons for this unnecessarily high expenditure are diverse: inaccurate assessment of Soviet defense spending, bureaucratic pressures by the United States military for higher budgets, and the demands of American industry and labor for defense contracts. David Cortright and Robert Borosage, two authors who have specialized in national security matters, argue the "dovish" case that the United States is spending too much for defense.

Another view often expressed is that the United States is not spending enough for defense. Evidence is presented to indicate that the Soviet Union is continuing its aggressive activities in the world and that the Soviet defense budget is increasing more rapidly than its American counterpart. Eugene V. Rostow, Sterling Professor of Law and Public Affairs at Yale University, argues the "hawkish" case.

DÉTENTE

Although an easing of tensions between the Soviet Union and the West was the stated policy of Soviet Premier Nikita Khrushchev during the late 1950s, a policy of détente did not become widely accepted until the Nixon and Ford Administrations. The word *détente* has been used to signify a movement away from a policy of Cold War tension between the United States and the Soviet Union and toward a policy of negotiation and accommodation.

The opinion that détente serves the interests of the United States is challenged by Alexander Solzhenitsyn, a Soviet exile and well-known writer and Nobel laureate. Solzhenitsyn contends that détente is a trick being used by the Soviet Union to lull the West into a false feeling of security. He criticizes Soviet actions in Angola and in the Middle East and argues that the Soviet Union has not abandoned its goal of world domination. He condemns the United States for pursuing policies that strengthen the economic and political position of the Soviet Union.

Henry Kissinger, first as National Security Adviser to the President and later as Secretary of State, was an advocate of détente. In the selection following, Kissinger posits that détente is the only feasible policy for the United States to pursue. He argues that both the United States and the Soviet Union must act cooperatively because of the danger of nuclear war. Arms control and improved economic ties will contribute to a feeling of mutual trust, according to Kissinger's view. The benefits of détente to the United States far outweigh the losses.

HUMAN RIGHTS

Solzhenitsyn and others have often criticized Soviet violations of human rights. In Helsinki in 1975, the Soviet Union and other powers agreed to protect human rights. When Jimmy Carter became president, he called for an activist policy to promote human rights around the world.

Such a call evoked criticism from the Soviet Union and other countries. They complained that the United States was interfering in the internal affairs of other nations. Human rights as a major motivating factor in the conduct of foreign policy became a subject of considerable debate at home and abroad. People wondered, "Should the United States push the human-rights issue even against its friends?" Political scientist Susan M. Davis argues that the United States should pursue an activist policy regarding human rights abroad, while fellow political scientist Ryan Barilleaux contends that such a policy works against American security interests.

Davis asserts that foreign policy, like domestic policy, must conform to the ideals and principles of the nation in order to gain popular support. The United States is a significant presence in the world, and its actions and inactions have a strong impact on the international system. The United States, moreover, has a long-term commitment to peace and support of free people everywhere.

According to Davis, the human-rights policy should avoid assuming a missionary purpose. It must also distinguish between desirable and legitimate human rights. Although the United States record on human-rights violations is not perfect, it should not be indifferent to human-rights violations abroad. Conflicts with other national policy objectives will arise, moreover, but human rights should remain a goal.

Barilleaux regards the Carter initiative as a moral crusade. The danger of a moral crusade lies not in its motives but in its effects. The worst effects of the Carter program are that it alienates other nations, is counterproductive, and draws emphasis away from vital security interests. Security, not human rights, ought to be the major consideration of America's foreign policy.

SOUTH AFRICA: ECONOMIC SANCTIONS?

One of the most controversial issues of African affairs is the future of apartheid ("separateness"), the means by which the white minority of South Africa pursues racist policies against the black majority. Black African countries have denounced South Africa and have called for the nations of the world to use force if necessary to impose majority rule.

The system of apartheid is based upon race. Everyone in South Africa must carry identification cards indicating racial classification. Segregation exists in education, transportation, restaurants, and hotels. Better-paying jobs are held by white people. Whites also dominate the political and economic power of the country.

What should the United States policy be on South Africa? American presidents have frequently made statements against the treatment of blacks by the white government of South Africa. Problems, however, have arisen concerning how much pressure the United States should apply.

In his former capacity as a legislator (now United States ambassador to the United Nations), Andrew Young argues that economic restrictions should be imposed on United States corporations doing business in South Africa. Such a policy would be in accordance with the principles of justice and economics. Justice would be served because the nonviolent protest movement among blacks would be strengthened. He feels that the American economy would be aided because, potentially, black Africa represents a bigger market than South Africa.

Conservative writer Robert L. Schuettinger argues that the United States should not impose economic sanctions because South Africa strengthens Western security and economic interests. South Africa is in a strategic position on the sea lanes of the world, serving as a vital link to Western oil routes. Moreover, the South African economy offers enormous benefits to the West for trade. The best way to end apartheid, according to Schuettinger, is not to weaken the current regime, a move that might encourage Soviet imperialism, but rather to try to modify the position of the regime through persuasion.

Is the United States Defense Establishment Strong Enough to Cope with Soviet Military Threats?

YES

DAVID CORTRIGHT and ROBERT BOROSAGE
It's Budget Time Again: "The Russians Are Coming!" *

Over the last twenty years, Americans have been treated to an annual performance of *Sturm und Drang* in advance of Congressional hearings on the defense budget. A fusillade of press leaks on some new Soviet menace blends with the blare of the brass seeking additional weapons. The spectacle has had so many reruns that many in the legislative audience are now bored with it. This year, however, a much more intense and concerted performance has captured the attention of legislators and the national press alike.

The primary theme is the new National Intelligence Estimate [NIE] on Soviet military intentions, first leaked to *The New York Times* during the slow-news Christmas holidays and picked up by nearly every print and broadcast outlet since then. The estimate—a product of what is described as a "furious" debate between regular intelligence analysts and a special team of outside "experts"—gives a "grim" portrayal of Soviet aggressiveness. But the NIE is only one of many variations in a well-orchestrated performance by conservatives, designed to scare citizens about Soviet intentions. The entire movement poses a major policy challenge to President Carter, one which will tell much about the future directions of this administration.

Annual assessment of Soviet military intentions is the task of analysts within the $10 billion intelligence apparatus. Over the years,

* From David Cortright and Robert Borosage, "It's Budget Time Again: 'The Russians Are Coming,'" *The Nation*, February 19, 1977, pp. 205–208, Copyright 1977, The Nation Associates.

the views of the [Central Intelligence Agency] CIA's analysts have predominated, with conflicting views footnoted in the text, and often supported in appendixes. Clearly irritated by the moderate, unimpassioned findings of previous analyses, President Ford and CIA Director George Bush sought to influence the result by appointing an outside team to provide an "alternative" view. The panel was headed by Harvard Professor Richard Pipes and included retired Army Lieutenant General Daniel Graham, former director of the Defense Intelligence Agency; Paul Nitze, former deputy secretary of defense; Thomas Wolfe of the Rand Corporation; John W. Vogt, former air force general; William Van Cleave, a member of the SALT [Strategic Arms Limitation Treaty] delegation, and Foy Kohler, former U.S. ambassador to the Soviet Union—all known to hold gloomy views about Soviet designs. This outside group, designated Team B, was given access to raw data and told to debate its views with the regular analysts. In an exchange described as "bloody," the panel apparently succeeded in moving the accepted analysis closer to its own predilections. Team B was a stacked jury, chosen to deliver a predetermined verdict. The process gave very conservative voices official endorsement to attack intelligence community analysts.

Political leaders have ignored or rebuked disagreeable intelligence analysts since at least the time of Xerxes. The Greeks had to be warned against the folly of killing messengers bearing bad news. Modern practice is somewhat more subtle. The Pentagon Papers demonstrated that the Johnson administration repeatedly ignored CIA assessments of the bombing of North Vietnam. Walt Rostow (like his Nixon counterpart, Henry Kissinger) often preferred to get raw data directly, the better to fit them to his views. Instead of basing policy on assessments, estimates were created to fit the policy. The Pipes committee is another variation of the practice, in this case changing the analysts to get the desired result—that is, an official finding that the USSR seeks strategic "superiority" over the United States.

There is much less to support the claims of the Pipes panel than meets the eye. According to reports, it based its estimate on three primary charges: that the Soviet Union is improving its air defenses; that it is proceeding with a massive civilian defense program, and that it is improving the accuracy of its missiles. The USSR is improving its capabilities in each of these areas, but there is no evidence in the public domain to suggest that there has been a new surge of development. Moreover, none of these steps gives the USSR an edge over the United States, or substantially alters the present relationship between the two powers. For example, the Soviet program for low-level air defense may well be a response to American acquisition of the F-15 fighter-bomber and the likely procurement of the B-1. Low-level air penetration has always been an area of U.S. technological advantage over Russia. Are we to expect that buildups of American air power will simply be ignored by the Soviet Union? As for Moscow's embrace of civilian evacuation plans, Hedrick Smith, *The New York Times* correspondent in Moscow over the past three years, reports what most everyone suspects is true: the civilian defense program is a widely neglected irritant in the eyes of most Moscow residents. Secretary of Defense Harold Brown concludes that no meaningful civil defense program exists in either the USSR or the United States.

Improvement in Soviet missile accuracy is an important military advance, but again the Soviet program is part of a long-standing attempt to catch up. By 1980, it is claimed, the Russians will be able to drop an ICBM [intercontinental ballistic missile] within 300 feet of its target; the United States can already come nearly that close. Are these Soviet projects the stuff of strategic superiority? Representative Les Aspin is correct when he states the new claims are "75 percent bull."

In any case, the very concept of "superiority" is pretty much meaningless in the calculation of nuclear deterrence, which is based on convincing a potential adversary that an attack will be met with devastating response. Given the number and variety of nuclear warheads possessed by the United States, it hardly matters how many missiles the Russians have. No sane leader would launch a nuclear attack on the United States, and no level of armament would deter an insane leader from doing so. Those who feel secure under the theory of mutual destruction should rest easy. Henry Kissinger himself has reminded us that "the term 'supremacy,' when casualties on both sides will be in the tens of millions, has no . . . operational significance."

The United States has always led the grisly race for nuclear weaponry. It was the first country to possess (and the only one to use) the atomic bomb, the first to develop the hydrogen bomb, the ICBM, the independently targeted warhead (MIRVs [multiple independently targetable re-entry vehicle]). As Richard Barnet has noted, the recent Soviet initiative in strategic weaponry seems to be part of a decision, made in the wake of the Cuban missile crisis, to trim the American lead in this area. "We taught the Soviets what it means to be a great power in the nuclear age," remarks Barnet, "and they have learned their lesson well." Even with its recent gains, however, the USSR still has only 3,300 deliverable strategic warheads, compared to 8,400 for the United States.

However, the National Intelligence Estimate was not about capability but about intention. The Pipes panel therefore went beyond empirical evidence to examine the underlying motivations of Soviet policy. The panel apparently criticized the CIA analysts for relying too heavily on hard data rather than on Kremlin ideology. About this the members of the Pipes group had little doubt: the Soviet Union was the same implacable menace its members had first described in the 1950s, and they were not disposed to let facts change their minds.

The truth is that Soviet foreign policy seems increasingly moderate, in logical response to its current geopolitical situation. Most Soviet forces—unlike our own—are devoted to continental defense of the homeland. The USSR faces potential adversaries on all sides of its vast territory. On the east, at least half a million men guard the border with China; they face the largest land army in the world. On the west, hundreds of thousands of troops are stationed in East Europe, to police the restive "colonies" as much as to match NATO [North Atlantic Treaty Organization] forces. In the south, Iran continues to build a potent modern arsenal, and maintains its traditional antagonism toward the Soviet Union. These external factors impose major constraints on any Soviet adventurism.

Thus, in recent times the USSR has often exercised considerable restraint in international crises. During the Middle East war in 1973, it reacted to the military collapse of its allies with unusual moderation; the fissure in Soviet-Egyptian relations can be traced to this failure to act. Russia finds itself increasingly unable to paste together the cracks in the communist world, and has been unable to halt the emergence of a Eurocommunism that is hardly to its advantage. In Zimbabwe, the Soviet Union and the United States have acted in concert. Needless to say, the USSR does seek to increase its political influence in the world, and its formidable military power is a significant factor in international affairs, as demonstrated in Angola. But the realities of Soviet policy hardly justify the overheated fears peddled by the Pipes panel.

What, then, is all the gnashing of teeth about? Why a new Red scare? Some have dismissed the move as merely an attempt by some conservatives in the national security elite to gain support against an administration that would exclude them from policy circles. But this bureaucratic explanation ignores the context for the new argument about American policy.

The Pipes committee is noteworthy because its activities are but a small part of a broad scare campaign now being waged by members of the national security elite. Individuals who normally operate on the "inside" have joined together to go public. Thus, the impetus for the Pipes panel originated with the Foreign Intelligence Advisory Board [FIAB], a collection of aging conservatives selected primarily by former President Nixon. Several FIAB members are part of a new public group, the Committee on the Present Danger, which has become a major force in the call for increased militarization in the United States. Formally established in the fall of 1976, but in formation for two years, the committee's purpose is to convince the American people that the Soviet Union is bent on world domination and that nothing can save us but an immediate expansion of our military budget. Its membership includes representatives from business, labor and academia. The policy chairman of the committee, Paul Nitze, was one of the seven civilian members of the Pipes panel. Three of the seven are on the committee, as are six of the sixteen members of the FIAB.

The arguments made by the committee and the Pipes panel are part of the dispute that broke out two years ago in a public feud between then Secretary of Defense James Schlesinger and Henry Kissinger. Schlesinger, now serving as Carter's energy czar, used the occasion of the 1976 budget to call for a strategy of "limited nuclear war," and to propose initial funding for several new and very expensive strategic weapons programs. Donald Rumsfeld, Schlesinger's successor as defense secretary, extended the Schlesinger argument to conventional forces, and presided over the largest expansion of the defense budget since the war in Vietnam. Procurement and development of new military hardware shot up by more than $8 billion in the budget for fiscal 1977. But these steps, which promise to add tens of billions to military spending in the next years, seemed threatened by Carter's calls for budget cuts, and his flirtation with "populism." Moreover, public support for cuts in the military budget is at a modern high. Thus the conservative national security elite decided it was time to go public, to warn the public that "the Russians are coming."

Many of the fears of the conservative wing are shared across a narrow spectrum of opinion among national security insiders. It is generally agreed within established foreign policy circles that the relative position of the United States in the world has declined over the past decade, a decline symbolized by the defeat in Indochina. The ability of the United States to impose its will on Third World countries has been significantly impaired, and the emergence of these countries as potentially powerful economic factors has contributed to the changing balance. The growing scarcity of critical raw materials has already made OPEC [Organization of Petroleum Exporting Countries] a major actor in world politics; other cartels may become increasingly important.

External decline has been reinforced by the loss of domestic support for America's imperial role. The antiwar movement and a growing skepticism about government in general have stirred the public from the acquiescence that buttressed interventionist policy. The sense of purpose and of external threat necessary to support international adventure has been dissipated. Moreover, internal economic shortages have increased opposition to wasteful spending, with the polls showing stronger support for military budget cuts.

Faced with these reverses, the conservative wing of the national security elite has called for a return to Cold War intransigence. The new complexity of international affairs cannot be ignored in policy, but it can be slighted in rhetoric. Members of the Committee on the Present Danger clearly believe that traditional anticommunist bombast can help create a public consensus for larger military budgets and greater activity abroad. They also believe that only by a show of will and military strength can the United States hope to retain its position as the guarantor of a world order favorable to domestic commercial interests.

Thus the committee's publications evoke the image of a Russia intent on world domination, probing at every chink in the armor of the "free world." The United States is the "crucial moral difference," the only possible salvation for other countries. The way to restrain the voracious Soviet appetite is to increase American will and military might. In recent years, the percentage of our GNP [Gross National Product] devoted to the military has declined from approximately 9.5 percent in 1968 to less than 6 percent. The scaremongers hope to reverse this trend, shifting more resources to the military. In concrete terms, this means support for a new generation of strategic weapons, including the Trident submarine program, a new round of mobile ICBMs and procurement of the B-1. The cost of these and related programs is likely to reach into the tens of billions of dollars, on top of current outlays placed at about $112 billion in fiscal 1978.

The conservative campaign may be seen as a challenge to the Carter administration. The short-term effect has been to forestall even the minuscule promised cutbacks of $5 billion to $7 billion in the defense budget, a Carter campaign promise which Defense Secretary Harold Brown started backing away from immediately on appointment. The campaign may also influence early talks on strategic arms limitation agreements, complicating any bilateral moves toward further arms reductions. . . .

Is the United States
Defense Establishment Strong Enough
to Cope with Soviet Military Threats?

NO

EUGENE V. ROSTOW
What Is Our Defense Program For?*

. . . the mission of the American defense establishment is not only to defend the United States against nuclear blackmail, and invasion or bombardment from the sea or the air, but also to defend Western Europe, Japan, and many other countries in many parts of the world from being taken over as Soviet satellites under a variety of circumstances which cannot be cataloged in advance. In short, the mission of the American military establishment has inherent elements of uncertainty which can be minimized but never eliminated. . . .

It is extremely difficult for Western opinion to accept the notion that Soviet policy is still firmly fixed in what Professor Bernard Lewis has astutely called "the imperial mood" of the eighteenth and nineteenth centuries. In the West, that mood has given way everywhere to a sense of satiety, doubt, and guilt, reflecting the decent and well-meaning values of our prevailing liberalism. The idea of conquering another nation in order to rule it has been nearly unthinkable in the West for two generations. It would take a veritable earthquake, affecting the possibility of survival, to bring it back to life. But Soviet policy, like Russian policy before it, reflects an altogether different culture and system of values. It expresses the nearly instinctive quest for power which has made predators and depredation so important among the forces of history. History is pitiless. It makes no allowance for nations, however civilized they may be, if they refuse to recognize the prevalence of predators, and to protect themselves against attack. Virtue, innocence, and cultivation of the arts have never been sufficient in themselves to guarantee survival. The chronicles of the past are

* From Eugene V. Rostow, Foreword, in *Arms, Men, and Military Budgets: Issues for Fiscal Year 1978*, eds. Francis P. Hoeber and William Schneider, Jr. (New York: Crane, Russak & Co., 1977), pp. xxv–xxxvii. Copyright © 1977 by National Strategy Information Center, Inc. Reprinted with permission.

punctuated with the records of states and civilizations which lost their will and capacity to survive.

But, Westerners ask, do the Soviets really intend to conquer the world? The idea is incredible to us, and we reject it as fanciful. As a Rand Corporation study recently observed, however, this is the wrong question to ask, even about Marxists who believe that the victory of socialism over capitalism is assured by scientific laws of social development. The quest for power should be analogized to the quest for money, the Rand study remarked. We never ask ourselves whether a rich man is trying to gain possession of all the money in the world. But we know that however rich he may be, he rarely resists the opportunity to make a little more money. So it is with the Russians and their pursuit of power. They have always taken a long view and steadily pursued long-range goals, despite the inevitable setbacks of the moment. They never suffer from Hitler's disease—a romantic yearning for "the glorious excitement" of war in his own lifetime. Russians have always seen themselves as part of history; and that tendency in the Russian outlook has been intensified by their conversion to Marxism, and their acceptance of the mission of bringing the true faith to the heathen.

The Soviet policy of indefinite expansion is based upon the full but prudent exploitation of military power as an instrument of politics—not only through its direct application in wars, coups d'état, and revolutions, but, in what are nominally times of peace, as a credible coercive threat designed to induce change in the policies of other nations. In the eyes of the Soviet government, the whole of their foreign policy is thus directly based upon the Soviet military establishment.

That establishment has been growing in recent years at a rate without parallel in modern history, and growing not simply in mass, but in technological sophistication as well. For some years after 1945, the Soviet military establishment consisted of an army and an air force. This is no longer the case. The Soviet Union is today a world power, not a regional power only. By some measures, the Soviet navy is now larger than that of the United States, and has an impressive capacity to project power all over the world. Its presence both in the eastern Mediterranean and the Red Sea has already had an effect on the course of events. The denouement of the Yom Kippur War in 1973 might well have been different if the United States had not taken Soviet military threats more seriously than we took comparable threats in 1967. And one can well ask whether there would have been an oil embargo, and a 400 percent increase in the price of oil in 1973, if the Soviet naval presence in the Mediterranean and the Red Sea area had not been so formidable. Soviet airlift capacity is quite as impressive as the growth of Soviet power on the high seas. While the existence of Soviet airborne troops has not yet touched the public mind in the West, as Soviet seapower has, it is a fact which concerns Western governments and defense experts very seriously indeed.

Western experts differ as to whether the Soviet Union has already outstripped the United States in overall military strength. They agree, however, that if present trends continue, the Soviet Union will soon be in a posture of complete military superiority in every category. Soviet leaders and their spokesmen have consistently and carefully explained that the goal of their military build-up is to achieve a position of "military preponderance" vis-à-vis the United States and its allies. From that position, they say, Soviet policy should be able to determine the direction of world political development—indeed, "to transform the conditions of world politics."

Soviet military doctrine in all services is altogether consistent with this general view of the political mission of the Soviet armed forces. The Soviets stress surprise, deception, preemption, and winning wars quickly by massive, sudden, secret attacks. Our doctrine, on the other hand, is defensive and deterrent. It relies upon treaties and other public warnings, the deployment of defensive forces in being, and the development of a war-winning capacity through mobilization and a prolonged effort *after* we have been attacked. The model in our minds is our experience in both world wars; the model in the Soviet mind is that of Blitzkrieg, exemplified by the Middle East War of 1973, which they planned and supervised, and in which they participated to a significant extent.

The first priority of Soviet military-political policy is the Soviet arsenal of strategic and tactical nuclear weapons. While the United States and the Soviet Union are far ahead of all other nations in nuclear science and technology, and in nuclear weapons, the two nations have quite different doctrines with regard to the strategic and tactical use of nuclear weapons. Those differences reflect deeper differences between their foreign policies. The foreign policy of the United States is defensive in every respect; that of the Soviet Union, like the foreign policy of Russia under the tsars, is dominated by the idea of expanding the influence of the nation, decade after decade, in so far as expansion can be achieved without excessive risk.

In the United States, we argue about whether the security of the United States requires us to maintain our security commitments to the Philippines, Australia, Taiwan, South Korea, Israel, or even to Japan and Western Europe. Congress went into a state of near-hysteria when it realized that the Cold War had reached Angola. In the Soviet Union, on the other hand, the government is active in dozens of situations of conflict or potential conflict all over the world, seeking to bring about explosions—of war, politics, or revolution—which might permit an increase in Soviet influence. Its military forces routinely conduct themselves, on the high seas and elsewhere, in ways calculated to intimidate other nations. And its diplomacy corresponds to the pattern of its policy as a whole; it is designed to soothe and lull, to frighten, or to coerce, as the case may be.

With regard to nuclear weapons, the policy of the United States is and always has been extremely simple—namely, to prevent the use or the credible threat to use nuclear weapons in world politics. The policy of the Soviet Union, on the other hand, is to prepare to threaten, and if need be to wage, a successful nuclear war against the United States. In Soviet military thinking, nuclear war itself should be unnecessary. The Soviets believe that United States policy will become "cooperative" and "understanding" when the Soviet Union achieves a position of marked nuclear superiority over us, so that it becomes clear to American officials that the Soviets can eliminate our land-based missiles and still have enough missiles left to make American retaliation suicidal. In this deadly bridge game, the Soviets think, we will throw our hand on the table when we realize its weakness.

It is ironic, and revealing, to recall that no one ever supposed that the United States had the capacity to coerce the Soviet Union and to dominate its policy by parading our nuclear missiles during the period of our nuclear monopoly and, later, of our huge nuclear superiority. Save conceivably in moments of great stress, like the final period of the Korean War, the idea of an American nuclear threat was simply incredible; it is a comment on the realities of world politics to realize that the same cannot be said of Soviet nuclear strategy. It has been difficult for American opinion to believe that Soviet nuclear doctrine is what it is. We feel guilty and chagrined about the use of nuclear weapons at Hiroshima. And we conceive of nuclear warfare in the perspective of Hiroshima and Dr. Strangelove—as an affair of bombing cities and killing hundreds of thousands, or millions, or hundreds of millions of civilians. Our leaders frequently remark that nuclear warfare is "unthinkable," and would mean the end of civilization as we know it. And some of our leaders wonder, in public, what earthly use it can be to accumulate enough weapons to destroy the Soviet Union several times over.

The Soviet Union, however, takes an altogether different view. It orients its nuclear policy to the bombing not of cities, but of military installations, and particularly the hardened silos which house our land-based missiles. The Soviet plan is to establish a position from which they could destroy as much of our land-based nuclear capacity as possible, both in silos and on air fields. Perhaps they have plans for our submarine-based missiles as well. Such an initial attack would not kill large numbers of civilians. Land-based missiles and air fields are located in relatively remote places.

The threat of a first strike against a large part of our nuclear capacity becomes a potentially credible instrument of political coercion once the Soviet Union achieves what might be called effective "third-strike capacity"—that is, once it is in a position to carry out such a first strike, and to have enough missiles left to deter an American nuclear response. The latter has been the logic of "second-strike capability," on which our own nuclear policy has been based since 1945. The first objective of the American strategic forces has been to deter a Soviet nuclear attack on either the United States or its allies. To deter a Soviet first strike, our weapons must be sufficiently strong, numerous, and well-placed so that enough of them would survive to retaliate with such force that the Soviets could not hope to gain by the first strike. To be effective as a deterrent, American second strike (or Soviet third strike) capability must be clear beyond the shadow of a doubt.

In a world of changing technology, the tactics and the arithmetic of second- and third-strike capability keep changing. But the underlying concept is simple. American second-strike and Soviet third-strike capability are not only a matter of throw-weight and the numbers of ground-based, air-based, and submarine-based launchers on each side. The key issue for us is, and will remain, whether the Soviets can have any reasonable expectation of being able to destroy so large a number of our weapons by a first strike as to create doubt about our second-strike capacity or our willingness to respond to a nuclear attack as may be necessary. There are several ways of making such calculations. . . . A number of factors are of critical importance: the number of warheads on each side, as distinguished from the number of missiles or launchers; the accuracy of the warheads; the vulnerability of launchers, taking into account their number, location, and degree of protection; the availability of ABM [antiballistic missiles] and air defense, other defensive measures, and civil defense, and industrial decentralization and protective programs; and the vulnerability of each side to fall-out, particularly within its military forces.

Until the last few years, the American second-strike capability was clear and effective. Following the Cuban missile crisis of 1962, however, the Soviet Union stepped up its program of military expansion in all categories, but particularly in the field of long-range nuclear weapons. As that program has proceeded, and gained in momentum, our earlier view of the matter has become irrelevant.

Before 1970, our superiority in numbers of weapons and nuclear technology was such that we became accustomed to stereotyped thinking on the subject, and relied on a doctrine of deterrence which never made much sense, and now makes none. That theory held that we must have adequate forces to wreak "assured destruction" on the Soviet Union after its worst possible "out-of-the-blue" attack on our strategic forces. That is, we needed a retaliatory capacity capable of destroying so large a proportion of the population and industrial plants in their cities that no prize could be worth the punishment they would take in return for striking first. If both sides have this capacity, we thought neither would ever dare to attack. The balance of terror would become stable—the "two scorpions in the bottle" would both live, because neither could survive if it attacked the other.

This doctrine of "mutual assured destruction" has been called by its acronym, MAD, because it leaves no alternative to Armageddon if either side miscalculates and deterrence fails. But recent advances in the accuracy and numbers of strategic weapons have made it clear that this doctrine, dubious even in its heydey, is now obsolete. The Soviets will soon be able to launch a first strike that spares our cities but destroys a substantial portion of our strategic and conventional military forces. Indeed, according to some calculations, the Soviets may now be in that position. They are in any event close to it. After such an attack, it would be repugnant—and of doubtful utility—to respond by wiping out Soviet population centers. Moreover, if the Soviets should use only a portion of their growing strategic forces in such a first strike against military targets, they would retain the capacity to wreak havoc on our people if we should respond with a retaliatory attack on their cities. Soviet leaders might be willing in some circumstances to gamble with the lives of their people by launching a first strike against our military; but would we respond to such an attack by massacring the Soviet population—especially when our own people were in effect hostages to the possibility of a second Soviet nuclear attack? We would surely be reluctant to launch a spasm of nuclear bombs on Soviet cities if the Soviets were to attack our military forces in a selective, probing fashion. And we would be at least as reluctant to respond with an attack on the Soviet population if the Soviets were to launch their first strike against our allies, since to do so would insure the destruction of our own cities without doing anything to rescue those of our allies. Besides, as other nations acquire the bomb, there are not just two scorpions in the proverbial bottle, but several.

In response to this grisly predicament, Secretary of Defense Schlesinger moved from 1973 to 1975 to give our forces a greater range of options for meeting the variety of offensive possibilities the Soviets are now developing. We need not only the capability for a massive counterattack on enemy cities, but also the capability selectively to counterattack against enemy military targets. This must include the capacity to destroy "hard" targets, such as hardened missile silos, without expending all our forces. And we must be able to do this with a minimum of damage to nearby civilian populations. These developments are indispensable both to strengthen deterrence and to provide more rational military alternatives if deterrence fails.

In our present state of imminent or actual strategic inferiority,* it will require a crash program employing bombers and cruise missiles, as well as the more orthodox land- and submarine-based missile launchers, to restore a clearly adequate deterrent posture capable of checkmating the Soviet nuclear force, which is improving rapidly in both size and versatility. The goal of American nuclear policy is nuclear stalemate—the assurance that neither the Soviets nor any other power could effectively use or threaten to use nuclear weapons in world politics. But nuclear stalemate would be totally useless unless it were matched by equally effective deterrent policies at the conventional level. Nuclear peace can hardly be considered a license for Soviet expansion by conventional means.

At the conventional level, the military balance between the United States and its allies and the Soviet Union reveals the same pattern one sees in the field of nuclear arms: a strong and active Soviet push for superiority, an effort which has not yet been matched by the West. Here again, experts argue as to whether the Soviets have as yet achieved genuine "preponderance," taking into account the differing missions of the two forces; but they are in full agreement that Soviet preponderance will result very soon if present trends continue.

The rise of Soviet seapower represents the most fundamental change in the political relationship between the United States and the Soviet Union, except for the area of nuclear weapons itself.

In the field of sea power, the military missions and military doctrines of the United States and the Soviet Union are decidedly different. Freedom to use the seas at will is vital to the security of the United States, both in war and peace. The system of alliances on which our security depends cannot endure without the assurance that seaborne transportation will not be interrupted. We and our allies depend upon the network of world trade not only for our prosperity, but for our very survival. The first principle of the defense policy of the United States and its allies is that they must be capable of controlling the seas if their freedom on the seas is challenged.

---

* Paul H. Nitze, "Assuring Nuclear Stability in an Era of Détente," *Foreign Affairs* 54, no. (January 1976).

For the Soviet Union, on the other hand, sea power is an instrument not of defense, but of offense. The security of the vast land mass of the Soviet Union and its allies does not depend upon continued access to the seas. The Soviet economy participates only marginally in world trade, and its military potential is not now seriously affected by overseas imports. The huge Soviet effort to become a major naval power during the last twenty-five years is the clearest possible proof of its imperial will. The role of the Soviet navy is to permit the rapid and permanent projection of Soviet power to distant places, and not in any sense to protect the Soviet Union against possible attack. The Soviets themselves freely admit that the mission of their naval forces is to facilitate the advance of socialism prophesied by Marx, Engels, and Lenin. No other hypothesis can explain the spectacular and continuing increase in Soviet naval forces since 1945.

Recent controversies about the defense policies of the United States justify some emphasis on what has been, and should be, a self-evident truism, namely, that the object of sea power is to project influence on land. Indeed, as [Alfred Thayer] Mahan and other students of sea power have repeatedly written, sea power cannot be an effective military or political force without land bases. Soviet policy accepts this view as axiomatic.

In this area, too, the American and allied response to the Soviet bid for military superiority has been slow in coming, and is still inadequate. While the Soviet fleet is being increased each year by new and advanced vessels of modern design, ours has been reduced—in part as a result of the end of our participation in the Indochina War; in part because of our rapprochement with China and the new military planning guidelines adopted thereafter; and in part as a reflection of the general mood of pacifism and protest against all things military which characterized the period immediately before and immediately after the end of our involvement in Indochina. While the United States has begun to move, especially in the 1977 Defense Appropriations Act, an increase of $5.5 billion in appropriations for naval vessels and planes, and of twenty-two ships a year, hardly begins to redress the balance. . . .

America's slowness to realize the purpose and implications of the Soviet drive for military supremacy is difficult to understand or explain, save in the feverish context of the final phases of the war in Vietnam, and the political and psychological experience of the Nixon years. One factor lulling American consciousness of Soviet aims and capabilities during this period was President Nixon's emphatic claim to have achieved a condition of "détente" in Soviet-American relations—a claim which became a matter of great political importance to President Nixon in his struggle to survive the Watergate affair. An easing of tensions with the Soviet Union has been the aim of American policy since the time of President Franklin D. Roosevelt. "Détente" in this sense will always be among the principal goals of American foreign policy. President Nixon claimed that this aspiration for détente had become a reality. According to him and Secretary of State Kissinger, Soviet behavior had become more reasonable, confrontation had been replaced by negotiation, and the Cold War was over.

This claim was myth, but a myth very difficult to dispel as a political force. Few of President Nixon's political opponents were willing to deny his claims. To do so might have put them in the perennially unpopular role of Cassandra, and of "Cold Warriors" as well—a label particularly unpopular during the period of bitter controversy over Vietnam. Slowly, gradually, and almost without political leadership, American opinion has come to realize that the Cold War is far from over—indeed, that the pressures of Soviet policy have never been more intense, more diverse, more sophisticated in their orchestration, or more ominous. The leadership of the Soviet Union has never been bolder or more audacious than it was in supporting the North Vietnamese campaign of 1973–1975 against South Vietnam, Laos, and Cambodia, in breach of its promises to us in the Paris Agreements of March 1973; and in supporting the Arab attack on Israel in October 1973, a breach of its promises to President Nixon of May 1972. Soviet policy is bold, and becoming bolder, because it is backed by what it hopes will be perceived as the intimidating pressure of military forces which are formidable in themselves, and growing more rapidly than our own.

Unless these trends are promptly reversed, we shall soon lose the capacity to protect our national security through peaceful deterrence and concerted alliance diplomacy, rather than through war. There is still time for effective action to ensure the safety and prosperity of the nation in peace. If we perceive the world as it is, and restore our will, our strength, and our confidence in ourselves, we will be strong enough, and we will have friends enough, to assure the success of our diplomacy. The necessary predicate for such a policy is an aroused and realistic public opinion, supported by an allied defense posture capable of deterrence at every level and in every theater vital to our interests.

QUESTIONS FOR DISCUSSION

1. What evidence can be offered to show that the United States is spending too much for defense?
2. Is the Soviet Union planning a war against the United States?

3. Is the concept of military superiority meaningful in the nuclear age?

4. Who is responsible for the arms race: the United States or the Soviet Union?

5. What would be the response of the Soviet Union if the United States announced a major reduction in defense spending? What would be the response of the United States if the Soviet Union announced a major reduction in defense spending?

SUGGESTED READINGS

Cox, Arthur Macy. *The Dynamics of Détente: How to End the Arms Race.* New York: Norton, 1977.

Hoeber, Francis P., and William Schneider, Jr., eds. *Arms, Men, and Military Budgets: Issues for Fiscal Year 1978.* New York: Crane, Russak, 1977.

Holst, Johan J., and Uwe Nerlich. *Beyond Nuclear Deterrence.* New York: Crane, Russak, 1977.

Kahan, Jerome H. *Security in the Nuclear Age: Developing U.S. Strategic Arms Policy.* Washington, D.C.: The Brookings Institution, 1975.

Lee, William T. *The Estimation of Soviet Defense Expenditures, 1955–75: An Unconventional Approach.* New York: Praeger, 1977.

Luttwak, Edward N. "Defense Reconsidered." *Commentary,* March 1977, pp. 51–58.

McGovern, George. "The Russians Are Coming—Again." *The Progressive,* May 1977, pp. 17–23.

Pipes, Richard. "Why the Soviet Union Thinks It Could Fight and Win a Nuclear War." *Commentary,* July 1977, pp. 21–34.

Yergin, Daniel. "The Arms Zealots." *Harper's Magazine,* June 1977, pp. 64–76.

———. "The Terrifying Prospect: Atomic Bombs Everywhere." *Atlantic,* April 1977, pp. 46–65.

Does Détente Favor the Soviet Union?

YES

ALEXANDER SOLZHENITSYN
*Détente Is a Soviet Trick**

. . . the principal argument of the advocates of détente is well-known: All of this must be done to avoid a nuclear war. But after all that has happened in recent years, I think that I can set their minds at ease, and your minds at ease as well: There will not be any nuclear war. What for? Why should there be a nuclear war if for the last thirty years they have been breaking off as much of the West as they wanted—piece after piece, country after country and the process keeps going on. In 1975 alone four countries were broken off. Four. Three in Indochina plus India; the process keeps going on, and very rapidly, too. One should be aware of how rapid the tempo is. But let us assume that ultimately the Western world will understand and say, "No, not one step further." What will happen then?

Let me direct your attention to the following fact. You have theoreticians who say: "The United States must stop the process of nuclear armament. We have enough already. Today America has enough nuclear weapons to destroy the other half of the world. Why should we need more than that?" Let the American nuclear specialists reason this way if they want, but for some reason the nuclear specialists of the Soviet Union—and for some reason the leaders of the Soviet Union—think differently. Ask your specialists! Leaving aside their superiority in tanks and airplanes, where they surpass you by a factor of four, five, or seven, take the SALT [Strategic Arms Limitation Treaty] talks alone: In these negotiations your opponent is continually deceiving you. Either he is testing radar in a way which is forbidden by the agreement; or he is violating the limitations on the dimensions of missiles; or he is violating the limitations on their destructive force; or else he is violating the conditions on multiple warheads. As the proverb says, "Look before you leap, or you will have bruises to keep."

At one time there was no comparison between the strength of the

* Reprinted from the *AFL-CIO Free Trade Union News*, July–August, 1975, pp. 27–32.

USSR and yours. Then it became equal to yours. Now, as all recognize, it is becoming superior to yours. Perhaps today the ratio is just greater than unity, but soon it will be two to one. Then three to one. Finally it will be five to one. I'm not a specialist in this area, and you're not specialists either, I suppose, but this can hardly be accidental. I think that if the armaments they had before were enough, they would not have driven things further. There must be some reason for it. With such a nuclear superiority, it will be possible to block the use of your weapons, and on some unlucky morning they will declare: "Attention. We're marching our troops to Europe, and if you make a move, we will annihilate you." And this ratio of three to one, or five to one, will have its effect: You will not make a move. Instead, theoreticians will be found to say, "If only we can have that blessed silence. . . ."

To make a comparison with chess, this is like two players sitting at a chess board, one of whom has a tremendously high opinion of himself and a rather low opinion of his opponent. He thinks that he will, of course, outplay his opponent. He thinks he is so clever, so calculating, so inventive, that he will certainly win. He sits there, he calculates his moves. With these two knights he will make four forks. He can hardly wait for his opponent to move. He's squirming on his chair out of happiness. He takes off his glasses, wipes them, and puts them back on again. He doesn't even admit the possibility that his opponent may be more clever. He doesn't even see that his pawns are being taken one after the other and that his castle is under threat. It all seems to him, "Aha, that's what we'll do. We'll set Moscow, Peking, Pyongyang, Hanoi one against the other." But what a joke! No one will do any such thing! In the meantime, you've been outplayed in West Berlin, you've been very skillfully outplayed in Portugal. In the Near East you're being outplayed. One shouldn't have such a low opinion of one's opponent.

. . . a concentration of world evil, of hatred for humanity, is taking place and it is fully determined to destroy your society. Must you wait until it comes with a crowbar to break through your borders, until the young men of America have to fall defending the borders of their continent?

After my first address, as always, there were some superficial comments in the newspapers, which did not really get to the essence. One of them was as follows: that I came here with an appeal to the United States to liberate *us* from communism. Anyone who has at all followed what I have said and written these many years, first in the Soviet Union and now in the West, will know that I've always said the exact opposite. I have appealed to my own countrymen—those whose courage has failed at difficult moments, and who have looked imploringly to the West—and urged them: "Don't wait for assistance, and don't ask for it. We must stand on our own feet. The West has enough troubles without us. If they support us, many thanks. But to ask for it, to appeal for it—never."

I said the last time that two processes are occurring in the world today. One is a process of spiritual liberation in the USSR and in the other communist countries. The second is the assistance being extended by the West to the communist rulers, a process of concessions, of détente, of yielding whole countries. And I only said: "Remember, *we* have to pull *ourselves* up—but if you defend us you also defend *your own* future."

We are slaves there from birth. We are born slaves. I'm not young anymore, and I myself was born a slave; this is even more true for those who are younger. We are slaves, but we are striving for freedom. You, however, were born free. If so, then why do you help our slave owners?

In my last address I only requested one thing and I make the same request now: When they bury us in the ground alive (I compare the forthcoming European agreement with a mass grave for all the countries of East Europe)—as you know, this is a very unpleasant sensation: Your mouth gets filled with earth while you're still alive—please do not send them shovels. Please do not send them the most modern earthmoving equipment.

By a peculiar coincidence the very day when I was giving my address in Washington, Suslov was talking with your senators in the Kremlin. And he said, "In fact, the significance of our trade is more political than economic. We can get along without your trade." That's a lie. The whole existence of our slave owners from beginning to end relies on Western economic assistance. As I said the last time, beginning with the first spare parts used to reconstruct our factories in the 1920s, from the construction in Magnitostroy, Dneprostroy, the automobile and tractor factories built during the first five-year plans, on into the postwar years and to this day, what they need from you is economically absolutely indispensable—not politically but economically indispensable to the Soviet system. The Soviet economy has an extremely low level of efficiency. What is done here by a few people, by a few machines, in our country takes tremendous crowds of workers and enormous masses of materials. Therefore the Soviet economy cannot deal with every problem at once: war, space (which is part of the war effort), heavy industry, light industry, and at the same time the necessity to feed and clothe its own population. The forces of the entire Soviet economy are concentrated on war, where you won't be helping them. But everything which is lacking, everything which is needed to fill the gaps, everything which is necessary to feed the people, or for other types of industry, they get from you. So indirectly you are help-ing them to rearm. You're helping the Soviet police state.

To get an idea how clumsy the Soviet economy is, I'll give you the following example: What kind of country is it, what kind of great power, which has tremendous military potential, which conquers outer space, but has nothing to sell? All heavy equipment, all complex and delicate technology, is purchased abroad. Then it must be an agricul-tural country? Not at all; it also has to buy grain. What then can we sell? What kind of economy is it? Can we sell anything which has been created by socialism? No! Only that which God put in the Russian ground at the very beginning, that's what we squander and that's what we sell. What we got from God in the first place. And when all this will come to an end, there won't be anything left to sell.

The president of the AFL-CIO, Mr. George Meany, has quite rightly said that it is not loans which the United States gives to the Soviet Union, it is economic assistance. It's foreign aid. It's given at a level of interest that is lower than what American working men can get for their home mortgages. That is direct aid.

But this is not all. I said in my last address and would like to repeat it again, that we have to look at every event from the other point of view—from the point of view of the Soviet Union. Our country is taking your assistance, but in the schools they're teaching and in the newspapers they are writing and in lectures they are saying, "Look at the Western world; it's beginning to rot. Look at the economy of the Western world, it's coming to an end. The great predictions of Marx, Engels, and Lenin are coming true. Capitalism is breathing its last. It's already dead. And our socialist economy is flourishing. It has demon-strated once and for all the triumph of communism." I think, gentle-men, and I particularly address those of you who have a socialist out-look, that we should at last permit this socialist economy to prove its superiority. Let's allow it to show that it is advanced, that it is omnipo-tent, that it has defeated you, that it has overtaken you. Let us not interfere with it. Let us stop selling to it and giving it loans. If it's all that powerful, then let it stand on its own feet for ten or fifteen years. Then we will see what it looks like. I can tell you what it will look like. I am being quite serious now. When the Soviet economy will no longer be able to deal with everything, it will have to reduce its military preparations. It will have to abandon the useless space effort, and it will have to feed and clothe its own people. And the system will be forced to relax.

Thus, all I ask you is that as long as this Soviet economy is so proud, so flourishing, and yours is so rotten and so moribund—stop helping it, then. Where has a cripple ever helped along an athlete?

Another distortion appeared in your press with respect to my last address. Someone wrote that "one more advocate of the Cold War has come here. One more person has arrived to call on us to resume the Cold War." That is a misunderstanding. The Cold War—the war of hatred—is still going on, but only on the communist side. What is the Cold War? It's a war of abuse and they still abuse you. They trade with you, they sign agreements and treaties, but they still abuse you, they still curse you. In sources which you can read, and even more in those which are unavailable to you, and which you don't hear of, in the depths of the Soviet Union, the Cold War has never stopped. It hasn't stopped for one second. They never call you anything but "American imperialists." One day, if they want, all the Soviet newspapers could say that America wants to subjugate the world and our people would have nowhere to get any other information. Do I call upon you to return to the Cold War? By no means, Lord forbid! What for? The only thing I'm asking you to do is to give the Soviet economy a chance to develop. Do not bury us in the ground, just let the Soviet economy develop, and then let's see.

But can the free and varied Western system follow this policy? Can all the Western countries together say: "It's true, let us stop competing. Let us stop playing up to them. Let us stop elbowing each other and clamoring, 'Me, me, let me have a concession, please give it to me.' " . . . It's very possible that this could not be done. And if this sort of unity cannot be achieved in the West, if, in the frenzied competition of one company with another they will continue to rush in loans and advanced technology, if they will present earth-moving equipment to our gravediggers, then I'm afraid that Lenin will turn out to have been right. He had said: "The bourgeoisie will sell us rope, and then we shall let the bourgeoisie hang itself."

In ancient times trade would begin with the meeting of two persons who had come out of a forest or had arrived by sea. They would show one another that they didn't have a stone or club in their hand, that they were unarmed. And as a sign of this each extended an open hand. This was the beginning of the hand clasp. Today's word "détente" literally means a reduction in the tension of a taut rope. (What an ominous coincidence: A rope again!) So "détente" means a relaxation of tension. But I would say that what we need is rather this image of the *open hand*. Relations between the Soviet Union and the United States of America should be such that there would be no deceit in the question of armaments, that there would be no concentration camps, no psychiatric wards for healthy people. Relations should be such that the throats of our women would no longer be constricted with tears, that there would be an end to the incessant ideological warfare waged against you, and that an address such as mine today would in no way be an exception. People would simply be able to come to you from the Soviet Union, from China, and from other communist countries and would be able to talk freely, without any tutoring from the KGB [Soviet secret police], without any special approval from the Central Committee of the Party. Rather, they would simply come of their own accord and would tell you the truth about what is going on in these countries.

This would be, I say, a period in which we would be able to present "open hands" to each other.

Does Détente
Favor the Soviet Union?

NO

HENRY A. KISSINGER
*Détente with the Soviet Union**

THE CHALLENGE

Since the dawn of the nuclear age the world's fears of holocaust and its hopes for peace have turned on the relationship between the United States and the Soviet Union.

Throughout history men have sought peace but suffered war; all too often, deliberate decisions or miscalculations have brought violence and destruction to a world yearning for tranquility. Tragic as the consequences of violence may have been in the past, the issue of peace and war takes on unprecedented urgency when, for the first time in history, two nations have the capacity to destroy mankind. In the nuclear age, as President Eisenhower pointed out two decades ago, "there is no longer any alternative to peace."

The destructiveness of modern weapons defines the necessity of the task; deep differences in philosophy and interests between the United States and the Soviet Union point up its difficulty. These differ-

* From *Department of State Bulletin*, October 14, 1974, pp. 505–519.

ences do not spring from misunderstanding or personalities or transitory factors:

- They are rooted in history and in the way the two countries have developed.
- They are nourished by conflicting values and opposing ideologies.
- They are expressed in diverging national interests that produce political and military competition.
- They are influenced by allies and friends whose association we value and whose interests we will not sacrifice.

Paradox confuses our perception of the problem of peaceful coexistence: if peace is pursued to the exclusion of any other goal, other values will be compromised and perhaps lost; but if unconstrained rivalry leads to nuclear conflict, these values, along with everything else, will be destroyed in the resulting holocaust. However competitive they may be at some levels of their relationship, both major nuclear powers must base their policies on the premise that neither can expect to impose its will on the other without running an intolerable risk. The challenge of our time is to reconcile the reality of competition with the imperative of coexistence.

There can be no peaceful international order without a constructive relationship between the Unied States and the Soviet Union. There will be no international stability unless both the Soviet Union and the United States conduct themselves with restraint and unless they use their enormous power for the benefit of mankind.

Thus we must be clear at the outset on what the term "détente" entails. It is the search for a more constructive relationship with the Soviet Union reflecting the realities I have outlined. It is a continuing process, not a final condition that has been or can be realized at any one specific point in time. And it has been pursued by successive American leaders, though the means have varied as have world conditions.

Some fundamental principles guide this policy:

- The United States cannot base its policy solely on Moscow's good intentions. But neither can we insist that all forward movement must await a convergence of American and Soviet purposes. We seek, regardless of Soviet intentions, to serve peace through a systematic resistance to pressure and conciliatory responses to moderate behavior.
- We must oppose aggressive actions and irresponsible behavior. But we must not seek confrontations lightly.
- We must maintain a strong national defense while recognizing that in

the nuclear age the relationship between military strength and politically usable power is the most complex in all history.

- Where the age-old antagonism between freedom and tyranny is concerned, we are not neutral. But other imperatives impose limits on our ability to produce internal changes in foreign countries. Consciousness of our limits is recognition of the necessity of peace—not moral callousness. The preservation of human life and human society are moral values, too.

- We must be mature enough to recognize that to be stable a relationship must provide advantages to both sides and that the most constructive international relationships are those in which both parties perceive an element of gain. Moscow will benefit from certain measures, just as we will from others. The balance cannot be struck on each issue every day, but only over the whole range of relations and over a period of time. . . .

THE EVOLUTION OF DÉTENTE—
THE BALANCE OF RISKS AND INCENTIVES

The course of détente has not been smooth or even. As late as 1969, Soviet-American relations were ambiguous and uncertain. To be sure, negotiations on Berlin and SALT [Strategic Arms Limitation Treaty] had begun. But the tendency toward confrontation appeared dominant.

We were challenged by Soviet conduct in the Middle East ceasefire of August 1970, during the Syrian invasion of Jordan in September 1970, on the question of a possible Soviet submarine base in Cuba, in actions around Berlin, and during the Indo-Pakistani war. Soviet policy seemed directed toward fashioning a détente in bilateral relations with our Western European allies, while challenging the United States.

We demonstrated then, and stand ready to do so again, that America will not yield to pressure or the threat of force. We made clear then, as we do today, that détente cannot be pursued selectively in one area or toward one group of countries only. For us détente is indivisible.

Finally, a breakthrough was made in 1971 on several fronts—in the Berlin settlement, in the SALT talks, in other arms-control negotiations—that generated the process of détente. It consists of these elements: An elaboration of principles; political discussions to solve outstanding issues and to reach cooperative agreements; economic relations; and arms control negotiations, particularly those concerning strategic arms.

THE ELABORATION OF PRINCIPLES

Cooperative relations, in our view, must be more than a series of isolated agreements. They must reflect an acceptance of mutual obligations and of the need for accommodation and restraint.

To set forth principles of behavior in formal documents is hardly to guarantee their observance. But they are reference points against which to judge actions and set goals.

The first of the series of documents is the statement of principles signed in Moscow in 1972. It affirms: (1) the necessity of avoiding confrontation; (2) the imperative of mutual restraint; (3) the rejection of attempts to exploit tensions to gain unilateral advantages; (4) the renunciation of claims of special influence in the world; and (5) the willingness, on this new basis, to coexist peacefully and build a firm long-term relationship.

An Agreement on the Prevention of Nuclear War based on these principles was signed in 1973. It affirms that the objective of the policies of the United States and the USSR is to remove the danger of nuclear conflict and the use of nuclear weapons. But it emphasizes that this objective presupposes the renunciation of *any* war or threat of war by the two nuclear superpowers not only against each other but also against allies or third countries. In other words, the principle of restraint is not confined in relations between the United States and the USSR; it is explicitly extended to include *all* countries.

These statements of principles are not an American concession; indeed, we have been affirming them unilaterally for two decades. Nor are they a legal contract; rather, they are an aspiration and a yardstick by which we assess Soviet behavior. We have never intended to "rely" on Soviet compliance with every principle; we do seek to elaborate standards of conduct which the Soviet Union would violate only to its cost. And if over the long term the more durable relationship takes hold, the basic principles will give it definition, structure, and hope. . . .

AN ASSESSMENT OF DÉTENTE

Where has the process of détente taken us so far? What are the principles that must continue to guide our course?

Major progress has been made:

- Berlin's potential as Europe's perennial flashpoint has been substantially reduced through the quadripartite agreement of 1971. The

United States considers strict adherence to the agreement a major test of détente.

- We and our allies are launched on negotiations with the Warsaw Pact and other countries in the conference on European security and cooperation, a conference designed to foster East-West dialog and cooperation.

- At the same time, NATO [North Atlantic Treaty Organization] and the Warsaw Pact are negotiating the reduction of their forces in Central Europe.

- The honorable termination of America's direct military involvement in Indochina and the substantial lowering of regional conflict were made possible by many factors. But this achievement would have been much more difficult, if not impossible, in an era of Soviet and Chinese hostility toward the United States.

- America's principal alliances have proved their durability in a new era. Many feared that détente would undermine them. Instead, détente has helped to place our alliance ties on a more enduring basis by removing the fear that friendship with the United States involved the risk of unnecessary confrontation with the USSR.

- Many incipient crises with the Soviet Union have been contained or settled without ever reaching the point of public disagreement. The world has been freer of East-West tensions and conflict than in the fifties and sixties.

- A series of bilateral cooperative agreements has turned the U.S.-Soviet relationship in a far more positive direction.

- We have achieved unprecedented agreements in arms limitation and measures to avoid accidental war.

- New possibilities for positive U.S.-Soviet cooperation have emerged on issues in which the globe is interdependent: science and technology, environment, energy.

These accomplishments do not guarantee peace. But they have served to lessen the rigidities of the past and offer hope for a better era. Despite fluctuations, a trend has been established; the character of international politics has been markedly changed.

It is too early to judge conclusively whether this change should be ascribed to tactical considerations. But in a sense, that is immaterial. For whether the change is temporary and tactical, or lasting and basic, our task is essentially the same: To transform that change into a permanent condition devoted to the purpose of a secure peace and mankind's aspiration for a better life. A tactical change sufficiently prolonged becomes a lasting transformation.

But the whole process can be jeopardized if it is taken for granted. As the Cold War recedes in memory, détente can come to seem so natural that it appears safe to levy progressively greater demands on it. The temptation to combine détente with increasing pressure on the Soviet Union will grow. Such an attitude would be disastrous. We would not accept it from Moscow; Moscow will not accept it from us. We will finally wind up again with the Cold War and fail to achieve either peace or any humane goal.

To be sure, the process of détente raises serious issues for many people. Let me deal with these in terms of the principles which underlie our policy.

First, if détente is to endure, both sides must benefit.

There is no question that the Soviet Union obtains benefits from détente. On what other grounds would the tough-minded members of the Politburo sustain it? But the essential point surely must be that détente serves American and world interests as well. If these coincide with some Soviet interests, this will only strengthen the durability of the process.

On the global scale, in terms of the conventional measures of power, influence, and position, our interests have not suffered—they have generally prospered. In many areas of the world, the influence and the respect we enjoy are greater than was the case for many years. It is also true that Soviet influence and presence are felt in many parts of the world. But this is a reality that would exist without détente. The record shows that détente does not deny us the opportunity to react to it and to offset it.

Our bilateral relations with the USSR are beginning to proliferate across a broad range of activities in our societies. Many of the projects now under way are in their infancy; we have many safeguards against unequal benefits—in our laws, in the agreements themselves, and in plain common sense. Of course, there are instances where the Soviet Union has obtained some particular advantage. But we seek in each agreement or project to provide for benefits that are mutual. We attempt to make sure that there are trade-offs among the various programs that are implemented. Americans surely are the last who need fear hard bargaining or lack confidence in competition.

Second, building a new relationship with the Soviet Union does not entail any devaluation of traditional alliance relations.

Our approach to relations with the USSR has always been, and will continue to be, rooted in the belief that the cohesion of our alliances, and particularly the Atlantic alliance, is a precondition to establishing a more constructive relationship with the USSR.

Crucial, indeed unique, as may be our concern with Soviet power, we do not delude ourselves that we should deal with it alone. When we speak of Europe and Japan as representing centers of power and influence, we describe not merely an observable fact but an indispensable element in the equilibrium needed to keep the world at peace. The cooperation and partnership between us transcend formal agreements; they reflect values and traditions not soon, if ever, to be shared with our adversaries.

Inevitably, a greater sense of drama accompanies our dealings with the Soviet Union, because the central issues of war and peace cannot be other than dramatic. It was precisely a recognition of this fact and our concern that alliance relations not be taken for granted that led to the American initiative in April 1973 to put new emphasis on our traditional associations. We sought political acts of will which would transcend the technical issues at hand, symbolize our enduring goals, and thus enhance our fundamental bonds. Much has been accomplished. The complications attendant to adapting U.S.-European relations should not be confused with their basic character. We were tested in difficult conditions that do not affect our central purposes. Today relations with Europe and Japan are strong and improving. We have made progress in developing common positions on security, détente, and energy. The experience of the past year has demonstrated that there is no contradiction between vigorous, organic alliance relations and a more positive relationship with adversaries; indeed, they are mutually reinforcing.

Third, the emergence of more normal relations with the Soviet Union must not undermine our resolve to maintain our national defense.

There is a tendency in democratic societies to relax as dangers seem to recede; there is an inclination to view the maintenance of strength as incompatible with relaxation of tensions rather than its precondition. But this is primarily a question of leadership. We shall attempt to be vigilant to the dangers facing America. This administration will not be misled—or mislead—on issues of national defense. At the same time, we do not accept the proposition that we need crises to sustain our defense. A society that needs artificial crises to do what is needed for survival will soon find itself in mortal danger.

Fourth, we must know what can and cannot be achieved in changing human conditions in the East.

The question of dealing with communist governments has troubled the American people and the Congress since 1917. There has always been a fear that by working with a government whose internal policies differ so sharply with our own we are in some manner condoning these policies or encouraging their continuation. Some argue that until there is a genuine "liberalization"—or signs of serious progress in this direction—all elements of conciliation in Soviet policy must be regarded as temporary and tactical. In that view, demands for internal changes must be the precondition for the pursuit of a relaxation of tensions with the Soviet Union.

Our view is different. We shall insist on responsible international behavior by the Soviet Union and use it as the primary index of our relationship. Beyond this we will use our influence to the maximum to alleviate suffering and to respond to humane appeals. We know what we stand for, and we shall leave no doubt about it.

Both as a government and as a people we *have* made the attitude of the American people clear on countless occasions in ways that have produced results. I believe that both the executive and the Congress, each playing its proper role, have been effective. With respect to the specific issue of emigration:

- The education exit tax of 1971 is no longer being collected. We have been assured that it will not be reapplied.

- Hardship cases submitted to the Soviet Government have been given increased attention, and remedies have been forthcoming in many well-known instances.

- The volume of Jewish emigration has increased from a trickle to tens of thousands.

- And we are now moving toward an understanding that should significantly diminish the obstacles to emigration and ease the hardship of prospective emigrants.

We have accomplished much. But we cannot demand that the Soviet Union, in effect, suddenly reverse five decades of Soviet, and centuries of Russian, history. Such an attempt would be futile and at the same time hazard all that has already been achieved. Changes in Soviet society have already occurred, and more will come. But they are most likely to develop through an evolution that can best go forward in an environment of decreasing international tensions. A renewal of the Cold War will hardly encourage the Soviet Union to change its emigration policies or adopt a more benevolent attitude toward dissent.

AGENDA FOR THE FUTURE

Détente is a process, not a permanent achievement. The agenda is full and continuing. Obviously the main concern must be to reduce the sources of potential conflict. This requires efforts in several interrelated areas:

- The military competition in all its aspects must be subject to increasingly firm restraints by both sides.

- Political competition, especially in moments of crisis, must be guided by the principles of restraint set forth in the documents described earlier. Crises there will be, but the United States and the Soviet Union have a special obligation deriving from the unimaginable military power that they wield and represent. Exploitation of crisis situations for unilateral gain is not acceptable.

- Restraint in crises must be augmented by cooperation in removing the causes of crises. There have been too many instances, notably in the Middle East, which demonstrate that policies of unilateral advantage sooner or later run out of control and lead to the brink of war, if not beyond.

- The process of negotiations and consultation must be continuous and intense. But no agreement between the nuclear superpowers can be durable if made over the heads of other nations which have a stake in the outcome. We should not seek to impose peace; we can, however, see that our own actions and conduct are conducive to peace.

In the coming months we shall strive:

- To complete the negotiations for comprehensive and equitable limitations on strategic arms until at least 1985;

- To complete the multilateral negotiations on mutual force reductions in Central Europe, so that security will be enhanced for all the countries of Europe;

- To conclude the conference on European security and cooperation in a manner that promotes both security and human aspirations;

- To continue the efforts to limit the spread of nuclear weapons to additional countries without depriving those countries of the peaceful benefits of atomic energy;

- To complete ratification of the recently negotiated treaty banning underground nuclear testing by the United States and USSR above a certain threshold;

- To begin negotiations on the recently agreed effort to overcome the possible dangers of environmental modification techniques for military purposes; and

- To resolve the longstanding attempts to cope with the dangers of chemical weaponry.

We must never forget that the process of détente depends ultimately on habits and modes of conduct that extend beyond the letter of agreements to the spirit of relations as a whole. This is why the whole process must be carefully nurtured.

In cataloging the desirable, we must take care not to jeopardize what is attainable. We must consider what alternative policies are available and what their consequences would be. And the implications of alternatives must be examined not just in terms of a single issue but for how they might affect the entire range of Soviet-American relations and the prospects for world peace.

We must assess not only individual challenges to détente but also their cumulative impact:

- If we justify each agreement with Moscow only when we can show unilateral gain,
- If we strive for an elusive strategic "superiority,"
- If we systematically block benefits to the Soviet Union,
- If we try to transform the Soviet system by pressure,
- If, in short, we look for final results before we agree to any results, then we would be reviving the doctrines of liberation and massive retaliation of the 1950s. And we would do so at a time when Soviet physical power and influence on the world are greater than a quarter century ago when those policies were devised and failed. The futility of such a course is as certain as its danger.

Let there be no question, however, that Soviet actions could destroy détente as well:

- If the Soviet Union uses détente to strengthen its military capacity in all fields,
- If in crises it acts to sharpen tension,
- If it does not contribute to progress toward stability,
- If it seeks to undermine our alliances,
- If it is deaf to the urgent needs of the least developed and the emerging issues of interdependence, then it in turn tempts a return to the tensions and conflicts we have made such efforts to overcome. The policy of confrontation has worked for neither of the superpowers.

We have insisted toward the Soviet Union that we cannot have the atmosphere of détente without the substance. It is equally clear that the substance of détente will disappear in an atmosphere of hostility.

We have profound differences with the Soviet Union—in our values, our methods, our vision of the future. But it is these very differences which compel any responsible administration to make a major effort to create a more constructive relationship.

We face an opportunity that was not possible twenty-five years, or even a decade, ago. If that opportunity is lost, its moment will not quickly come again. Indeed, it may not come at all.

QUESTIONS FOR DISCUSSION

1. Does détente serve American interests?
2. Does the danger of nuclear war make détente a necessity?
3. Will improved trade and cultural ties between the United States and the Soviet Union lead to a relaxation of tension between the two superpowers?
4. Has the Cold War ended?
5. Is political liberalization in the Soviet Union a prerequisite for détente?

SUGGESTED READINGS

Barghoorn, Frederick C. *Détente and the Democratic Movement in the USSR*. New York: The Free Press, 1976.

Coates, Ken, ed. *Détente and Socialist Democracy: A Discussion with Roy Medvedev*. New York: Pathfinder Press, 1976.

Cox, Arthur Macy. *The Dynamics of Détente: How to End the Arms Race*. New York: Norton, 1976.

Draper, Theodore, et al. *Defending America: Toward a New Role in the Post-Détente World*. New York: Basic Books, 1977.

Goldman, Marshall I. *Détente and Dollars: Doing Business with the Soviets*. New York: Basic Books, 1975.

Pranger, Robert J., ed. *Détente and Defense: A Reader*. Washington, D.C.: American Enterprise Institute for Public Policy Research, 1976.

Solzhenitsyn, Alexander. *Warning to the West*. New York: Farrar, Straus & Giroux, 1976.

Urban, G. R., ed. *Détente*. New York: Universe Books, 1976.

Weeks, Albert L. *The Troubled Détente*. New York: New York University Press, 1977.

Whetten, Lawrence L. *The Political Implications of Soviet Military Power*. New York: Crane, Russak, 1977.

Should the United States
Adopt an Activist Policy
Regarding Human Rights
in Other Nations?

YES

SUSAN M. DAVIS
Human Rights: More Than Mere Rhetoric*

Shortly after his election, Jimmy Carter announced that human rights
would be an "all-pervasive" consideration for U.S. foreign policy
under his administration. Although this activist human-rights stance
began primarily out of a rhetorical atmosphere, the Administration has
attempted to formulate a human-rights foreign policy that can be justified and based on fundamental American values and the wide range of
American interests. Granted, the Administration has made many mistakes undertaking this new initiative without having first defined and
formulated a comprehensive human-rights policy to guide its actions in
the early weeks. Nevertheless, the United States should pursue an
activist human-rights policy based on fundamental values. This policy
should be consonant with domestic policy and values, and should recognize the United States' position in the world, the significance of its
moral reputation, and finally its long-term commitment to peace and
freedom. Consider each reason.

Foreign policy, like domestic policy, must conform to the ideals
and principles of the nation in order to be supported by the populace.
Deputy Secretary of State Warren Christopher recognizes the fact that
"domestic support for our policies will falter if they do not reflect
traditional American values." But, he goes on to say, this is not "a
policy of convenience, adopted because of its popularity at home. A
commitment to human rights protects the domestic vitality of these
values, keeping clear our image of ourselves and encouraging us to
make the democratic system work."[1] In the conduct of its foreign
policy, the United States should act consistently with its principles

* This article was written expressly for *Point-Counterpoint*.

"and not do things which require us to participate in violations of our morality."[2] In other words, the United States must be true to itself. It should not attempt to play a missionary role, conduct a moral crusade, or try to export democracy and Western principles, but it simply should not sell out its own principles or compromise them.

A second consideration in pursuing an activist human-rights foreign policy is recognizing that the United States is a significant presence in the world, and its action or inaction has a strong impact on the international system. This point is reiterated by Ray Cline, former deputy director of the Central Intelligence Agency (CIA): "Whatever the United States does or refrains from doing abroad materially affects the fate of nations and peoples whose welfare is tied to the fortunes of the strongest country in the world."[3] Thus, policymakers must realize that the alternative to an activist human-rights foreign policy—a passive policy—will affect the United States and the world with perhaps more detrimental consequences than would the activist policy. Robert Osgood, dean of the Johns Hopkins School of Advanced International Studies, presents a cogent argument by saying that

> the strength of America's moral reputation is as vital a factor in the power equation as planes, ships and tanks. But because the United States is unavoidably thrust into a position of global leadership, her standards of conduct must, inevitably, have a great influence in setting the moral tone of international relations in general.[4]

A final consideration in adopting an activist human-rights stance can be attributed to the United States' long-term commitment to peace and support of free people and their struggles to become free. Carter stated in his inaugural address and reiterated in his letter to Soviet dissident Andrei Sakharov, "Because we are free, we can never be indifferent to the fate of freedom elsewhere." He also asserted that "our moral sense dictates a clear-cut preference for those societies that share with the United States an abiding respect for individual human rights."[5] In his view, the undertaking to promote human rights helps the United States to "maintain leadership of the free societies that share similar values, and it serves as a pole of attraction to other states and peoples."[6] If the United States does not pursue an activist human-rights foreign policy, it will suffer a serious loss of prestige and appear hypocritical, to say the least. According to Henry Kissinger,

> Human rights are the very essence of a meaningful life and human dignity is the ultimate purpose of civil government. Respect for the rights of man is written into the founding documents of almost every nation of the world. The world needs to know what this country stands for.[7]

The problem, however, is discovering how to implement American convictions into action and to achieve both an enhancement of human rights and other national objectives. For a foreign policy to be successful, it is absolutely essential to maintain this balance between self-interest and ideals. Several considerations, therefore, emerge for policy makers formulating a human-rights stance: (1) the United States must recognize and respect differences among nations and carefully avoid a missionary role; (2) the United States must distinguish between *desirable* and *legitimate* international human rights; (3) the United States must not be indifferent to human-rights violations abroad, even though its human-rights record is not unblemished; and (4) the United States must recognize that conflicts among national-policy objectives will necessarily arise because human rights is just one factor in the foreign-policy formula.

The need to put human rights in the perspective of a realistic foreign-policy framework rather than that of a moral crusade should be recognized in making policy. As Charles Frankel, a former State Department official, notes: "To draw up a list of moral demands on the world and to pursue a policy designed to make the world accede to them is stupidity, not courage, arrogance, not intelligent principle."[8] Indeed, the rest of the world should not be expected to adhere to every one of America's Western principles concerning political freedom and democratic government. Likewise, the United States should not attempt to convert or impose its values on them. It is fundamentally important that the United States recognize and respect differences among nations.

A similar idea was expressed by Jimmy Carter in his Statement to the World on January 20, 1977: "We will not seek to dominate or dictate to others."[9] What the United States should do and is doing is to renew its commitment and concern for international human rights. The United States cannot issue "global report cards" and decide on friend or foe by evaluating a country's values or system of government. An activist human-rights foreign policy does not require a world of American-model governments; it does not preclude diversity. Indeed, diversity is genuinely fostered as an American value in its pluralistic society.

The United States, in its support of international human rights, must also distinguish a desirable claim or "right" from a legitimate one. In the past few decades, the list of "rights" has grown so much that often what people are claiming as a "right" is actually a desirable goal. Walter Laqueur, in a recent article in *Commentary,* illustrates this distinction.

Article 7 of the International Covenant on Civil and Political Rights states that "no one shall be subjected to torture or cruel, inhuman, or degrading treatment or punishment." This is an absolute right which can and should be enforced today! Article 7 of the International Covenant on Economic, Social and Cultural Rights, on the other hand, imposes on every country the duty to grant its citizens periodic holidays with pay and remuneration for public holidays. . . . The attempt to equate universal moral rights that need to be observed here and now with the introduction of social services is simply part of the endeavor to belittle the importance of human rights, to reduce them from the level of inalienable human requirements to the level of ideals that might, or might not, be achieved at some future date.[10]

Americans have not invariably lived by such "universal morals." The United States' record is far from unblemished, as the Soviets rightly point out. However, the United States is not emancipated from expressing its national values because of an imperfect record. The Soviets, in fact, expect it to do so, as Georgi Arbatov, Director of the Institute of U.S. and Canadian Studies in Moscow, points out:

Nobody in the Soviet Union expects President Carter not to speak about his own values. Of course, it is his right to do so. It is difficult, however, for us to take the United States as a teacher who has a moral right to give the Soviet Union lessons all the time.[11]

The United States should, therefore, avoid playing a self-righteous role in promoting its values concerning human rights, as well as a role of passive indifference to human-rights violations. When the United States is indifferent to direct violations of human rights and its values, it does "violence to itself and destroys a principal source of its own power in the world."[12]

The complexity of the human-rights challenge is exacerbated when conflicts in policy necessarily arise. Indeed, human rights do not exist in a vacuum but instead must be weighed with economic, military, strategic, and other considerations in making foreign-policy decisions. Deputy Assistant Secretary of State for Human Rights Mark L. Schneider says that

the major difficulty is that human rights is a new policy which is hard to define, and it cuts across the entire range of interests that the United States has with other governments. Therefore, these interests have to be integrated with human rights and taken into consideration.[13]

Instead of facing charges of "selective morality" or "double standards" as a result of supporting authoritarian regimes like those of South Korea or Iran because of overriding security considerations, the

United States should know and let the world know what it prefers. Kissinger maintains on this subject that "morality without security is ineffectual; security without morality is empty. To establish the relationship and proportion between these goals is perhaps the most profound challenge before our government and our nation."[14]

The result of openly making human-rights considerations an integral part of foreign-policy decisions would be a "greater candor, clarity, and consistency."[15] The United States must not pursue an activist human-rights foreign policy based on rhetoric or as a front for a moral crusade. Instead, the Carter Administration has been developing a series of questions to serve as guidelines or points of reference in plotting the direction of policy and to make it "surer of its basic course and less likely to be driven from it by the force of a particular circumstance."[16] Deputy Secretary of State Warren Christopher commented on this point when he outlined these questions before the Subcommittee on Foreign Assistance of the Senate Committee on Foreign Relations on March 7, 1977:

1. Will our action be useful in promoting the cause of human rights? Will it actually improve the human rights situation at hand? Or is it likely to make it much worse?

2. What will be the most effective means of expressing our views? Quiet diplomacy? A public pronouncement? Withdrawal of aid or other tangible sanctions?

3. Even when there is only a remote chance that our action will be influential, does our sense of values, our American ethic, prompt us to speak out or take action?

4. Will others support us? Can we expect the aid of national and international organizations dedicated to furthering human rights?

5. Have we steered away from the self-righteous and strident, remembering that our own record is not unblemished?

6. Finally, have we remembered our national security interests and kept our sense of perspective, realizing that human rights cannot flourish in a world impoverished by economic decline or ravaged by armed conflict?

Christopher concludes by stating that

the administration alone cannot take all the actions that should be part of this government's efforts on behalf of human rights. The Congress has a unique role to play by reflecting public concern for human rights in the laws it passes and monitoring their implementation, by forming and funding assistance programs, and by assuring that our domestic law is in conformity with our international obligations.[17]

In the campaign for human rights, the Carter Administration has utilized several means, from shrill publicity as in the first few weeks of 1977 (the letter to Soviet dissident Andrei Sakharov), to quiet diplomacy (the September 30, 1977, talk with Soviet Foreign Minister Andrei Gromyko). In the talk with Gromyko, Carter repeated what he had said publicly on June 13: that the charge of high treason against Soviet dissident Anatoly Shcharansky as a United States spy is without foundation. He asked Gromyko to convey his strong personal hope to President Leonid Brezhnev that Shcharansky be set free. Carter's September 30 approach to human rights was dramatically different from the soap-box treatment of the early days of his presidency.

The effect was beneficial at that time, too.* Also, the Kremlin has suddenly permitted increased Jewish emigration, which reached more than 1,600 in September—higher than in any other month in 1977.

The United States has taken a number of steps to advance the cause of human rights around the world—from speaking out in international forums, such as the current Belgrade Conference on implementing the 1975 Helsinki accords on European security and cooperation, to making rights a factor in the granting of military and economic assistance. Mark Schneider warns, however, that even though some of these actions have resulted in modest gains, it is only a beginning. In some countries only cosmetic efforts have been taken to lessen external pressure, rather than a substantial change in the pattern of repression and human-rights violations.[18] Arthur Goldberg, heading the United States delegation at the Belgrade Conference, insists that the United States is not courting confrontation with the Soviets or any other nation, but maintains that the Belgrade Conference is a proper forum for discussion of abuses of human rights both past and present. The United States and its Western allies are divided on the best way to pursue the sensitive human-rights issue, but all agree on the fundamental importance and significance of their effort.

The means by which a nation promotes human rights may be disputed, but not the fact that it should promote them. The alternative to an activist human-rights foreign policy is a passive policy—one that would be detrimental to the United States both on an international and national level.

The posture of the United States toward the rest of the world should reflect the moral principles that Americans are supposed to

---

* Although Shcharansky was later sentenced to thirteen years in prison for treason, the Carter Administration has taken steps, such as cancelling the sale of a sophisticated computer and threatening to stop some future technological transfers to the Soviets, that may result in his early release. Also, a deal might be worked out that would free him in return for economic concessions or the release of Soviet agents arrested in our country. If so, our activist human-rights policy would have served to promote freedom in the Soviet Union.

honor in their private lives and acknowledge in public policy. The erosion of America's influence abroad in recent years has been caused, in part, by a decline in our moral credibility. The President's evident aim to reclaim a position of respect in the world and to promote a more just world order is a most welcome and necessary change in United States public policy.

Should the United States Adopt an Activist Policy Regarding Human Rights in Other Nations?

NO

RYAN J. BARILLEAUX
*Human Rights and American Security Interests**

In his inaugural address, President Carter proclaimed a foreign policy that would champion human rights throughout the world. The nation's commitment to that policy, he said, "must be absolute." Mr. Carter's belief was that the American tradition of promoting human rights demanded such a crusade. In this belief, he was mistaken.

The American tradition of human rights, found in the eloquent writings of John Locke, Thomas Paine, and Thomas Jefferson, does not make the moral crusade a national imperative. That Mr. Carter reaffirmed the nation's commitment to such rights is totally appropriate, and even necessary, after the mass disillusionment of the past few years, but his approach to achieving that ideal is flawed. The danger of a moral crusade lies not in its motives, which are good, but in its effects: it alienates other nations; it is counterproductive, and it draws emphasis away from vital security interests. Consider each of these effects individually.

It should not be surprising that evangelical moralism would alienate other nations. The self-righteousness embodied in such a crusade is offensive in itself, and especially to countries whose record on human

---

* This article was written expressly for *Point-Counterpoint*.

rights is less than perfect, in other words, all nations.[19] Beyond this offensiveness to other nations, however, lie more practical considerations affecting American relations with communist and Third World countries.

The Soviet Union has reacted to American statements by cooling relations,[20] as is illustrated by the Soviet rejection of United States arms-control proposals in March 1977. At that time, the Soviet Union condemned the American human-rights campaign as interference in Soviet internal affairs.[21] This alienation is not, however, confined to the Soviet bloc. American allies in the Third World have also rejected United States human-rights activism. Although Iran and South Korea have remained silent on the subject, Brazil has denounced President Carter's statements on human rights.[22] Uruguay and Argentina have even gone so far as to refuse future American aid.[23] While such aggravation of world divisions may not trouble the moral crusader, it is counterproductive in that it ultimately causes the further suppression of rights.

The record of recent history demonstrates how counterproductive is an activist human-rights policy. Nations alienated by moral crusades tend to become more oppressive internally, rather than to liberalize their political systems in response to outside interference. Two examples may be cited to prove this point. When the Jackson-Vanik amendment to the 1972 Soviet-American trade agreement linked normalization of trade to emigration of Soviet Jews, such emigration decreased drastically.[24] Furthermore, suppression of dissidents by the Soviet Union intensified after President Carter's early pronouncements concerning human rights.[25] A policy accomplishes nothing if those it intends to save are only subjected to greater suffering.

Beyond counterproductive effects of this sort lie the problems of implementing a strong human-rights policy. If the advancement of human rights is sought through a policy that bends every effort to promote those rights, then that policy can ultimately lead to war.[26] The link between John Kennedy's inaugural pronouncement to "bear any burden, meet any hardship, support any friend, or oppose any foe to assure the survival and success of liberty" and the American involvement in Vietnam is still fresh in American minds.[27] Yet, war is so frightening to contemporary America that moralists are unwilling to consider it as a practical policy.[28] The refusal to go to war in the cause of human rights means that the rights of some could be sacrificed because of lack of resolve. The resultant loss of rights is an effect contrary to that intended by moralists. The human-rights policy is thus undermined by the unwillingness to take the measures of war, which might be essential to promote rights around the world.

Another contrary effect arising from such a policy is the problem of assertions of moral principles as immediate policy goals. Human rights sound like an admirable objective, but so, too, do national self-determination and liberation.

If other countries were to make their moral goals—such as self-determination and liberation—immediate objectives of their foreign policies, then the effects of such policies on world stability would be disastrous. Hitler's Germany used the principle of national self-determination in this way to justify its territorial expansion into the Sudetenland,[29] just as the Soviet Union portrayed itself as a liberator in order to justify the domination of Eastern Europe.[30] Such twistings of ideals can only be detrimental to the cause of human rights.

Finally, a strong human-rights policy is counterproductive in that it creates expectations that cannot be achieved. Such expectations, when encountering the shortcomings and failures of the human-rights policy, lead to disillusionment, bitterness, and even contempt for the government that cannot fulfill the promises of moralism. Short of war, which American moralists are not allowed to consider, the promises of the human-rights policy can only lead to greater problems for the moralist.

The greatest problem that arises from an activist human-rights policy is that emphasis is taken away from vital security interests. Since all nations are imperfect on the record of human rights, it is inevitable that the United States has allied itself with countries that are subject to criticism on moral grounds. Such criticism, however, can severely damage relations with those nations that are of vital strategic significance, such as Iran and Chile.

Iran, under authoritarian rule, is strategically located on the periphery of the Soviet Union between the Middle East and South Asia. Harsh criticism of this regime on the basis of human-rights violations could easily provoke an anti-American response, and the vital flow of oil from the Persian Gulf region to the West would be severely threatened.[31]

It is also important to avoid an anti-American government in Chile. In the past, United States policy has been constructed so as to keep Chile and other Latin American nations out of the Soviet sphere of influence,[32] but harsh attacks on the military government of Chile because of human rights violations could provoke a hostile response.

Unless "selective morality" is used to criticize only those nations not of strategic value, then alienation of countries like Iran and Chile will occur. It would be a compromise of the human-rights program, however, to apply strict moral standards in this way. Indeed, such selectivity would in itself be a form of immorality.

Because of the importance of the superpowers in a nuclear age, a foreign policy tilted toward human rights damages United States ties with the Soviet Union. Recall the cooling of relations by the Soviet Union when President Carter made his first pronouncements on human rights. In adopting a human-rights policy, the United States automatically placed itself at a disadvantage in negotiating with the Soviet Union.

So, one might ask, what if the United States is not in the good graces of the Soviet leadership? There are two answers to this question. First, cooperation is necessary for the purpose of confronting such global issues as scarcity of resources and economic development.[33] The oil crisis of 1973 underscored the scarcity of resources among industrial nations, just as the chronic poverty of many Third World countries illustrates the need for international cooperation in economic development.[34] Problems of this sort are reaching crisis proportions, and hostility between the two major world powers dashes hopes for their solution.

Second, and more important to matters of security, poor relations between the United States and the Soviet Union make agreements on strategic issues difficult, if not impossible. Arms-limitation talks have little chance of success in an atmosphere of hostility, as is illustrated by the Soviet reaction to Carter arms-limitation proposals in March 1977. Moreover, such hostility has ramifications outside of the conference room. As economist Samuel Pisar has observed: "If not handled with care, the fragile thaw that came over Soviet-American relations in the last five years would freeze over again."[35]

It is this issue of security that marks the frontier of United States foreign policy. That policy should tilt in the direction of security interests. Such a statement does not mean that security matters should be the only concern of foreign policy; rather, it signifies that security should receive primary attention. For without the proper emphasis on security interests, the United States will not be in a position to conduct any sort of campaign to promote human rights, nor will it be able to help its allies.

A security-oriented foreign policy is an affirmation that cooperation and communication between the United States and the Soviet Union is imperative.[36] It is also a recognition of the importance of American relations with all other nations,[37] and an acknowledgment of the fact that such relations are of extreme complexity.[38] It therefore disassociates itself from simplistic policies that cannot achieve the goals for which they are intended.

Consider the logic of a security-oriented policy. By aiming not to offend but to insure security, this policy would allow for the expediting of necessary arms talks. Furthermore, it would not promote the tensions that a human-rights policy would, and therefore not lead to the undesired expansion of Soviet activities that such tensions encourage.

Beyond these concerns, a policy tilted toward security interests would also avoid the various problems of human-rights activism. It would not alienate other nations through its arrogance, for all nations share some basic security interests.

A security-oriented policy is also not counterproductive as is a human-rights policy. A moral crusade in itself generates problems, especially in the measures of war that would be necessary to advance rights. The ultimate action necessary under a security-oriented policy is the defense of the nation when its very survival is threatened. Moreover, it would not matter if another nation adopted a policy of security. Nations are expected to be concerned for their security. Of course, it is possible that the concept might be twisted to justify an attack on the United States, but having a security-oriented policy would lead the nation to prepare itself for such an occurrence. Furthermore, as noted above, such a policy would allow for the promotion of cooperation between nations, rather than the aggravation of tensions. Operating under a policy similar to the one advocated here, the United States was able to raise the level of emigration of Soviet Jews to a high of about 35,000 in 1973.[39] (This level dropped drastically in the following year, as stated earlier, when the Jackson-Vanik amendment to the 1972 trade agreement linked trade normalization to such emigration.) A policy tilted toward security would allow a concentration on results and would not be by its nature counterproductive.

In applying such a security-oriented policy, the United States would also not be subject to charges of "selective morality." Nations with less than admirable records on human rights would only be supported if they were vital to security. This, of course, implies that there would be a reassessment of whether supporting a nation such as Iran, for example, is absolutely essential. If the reassessment indicates that Iran is vital to American security, however, then the United States would support such a country only to the extent of the demands of security. Moreover, American influence on such nations could be applied in the cause of human rights, ever mindful of the dangers of a crusade.

This is the logic of a policy of security. It would recognize international imperatives and seek to realize them. It would not encounter the problems of a moral crusade. Finally, it would even have certain advantages.

The first of these advantages is, of course, the maintenance of security interests. National security would always be of fundamental concern. By not having a crusading spirit, the United States would not have to alienate or abandon nations vital to security, especially traditional allies. Moreover, this restraint from evangelism would not stimulate threats to security, as would a crusade.

A second advantage lies in the fact that concern for security will allow for increased cooperation between nations. Such cooperation could be used to promote peace through communication, trade, and cultural exchange.[40] The Soviet bloc and South Africa illustrate the advantages of cooperation. In the early 1970s, American trade with the Soviet bloc led to a reduction of tension between the nations involved, and increased prosperity induced the Soviet client-state of Hungary to institute economic and political reforms.[41] Furthermore, recent history has demonstrated that economic development in South Africa presents the best way for blacks there to improve their lives.[42] Development of international cooperation is thus the most feasible way to bring about the expansion of human rights.

The most important advantage of adopting a policy of security, however, would be the promotion of human rights. By capitalizing on the mutual interests of nations, by increasing international trade and cooperation, and by making it clear to the Soviet Union that American intent is to have a positive effect in the interest of people, thus could human rights be promoted. As illustrated earlier, to impose or even suggest a threat to a government will evoke a negative response. On the other hand, American experience has shown that cooperation and the relaxation of tensions made possible by a security-oriented policy will do more to advance the cause of human rights than a crusade.

As George Kennan has observed, foreign policy "begins at home—the first requirement of a successful foreign policy is that one places oneself in a favorable position for its conduct.[43] By invoking a moral crusade to achieve human rights, President Carter has made a grave error. Tilting foreign policy toward security interests would correct that mistake and promote human rights much more effectively.

NOTES

1. Warren Christopher, "Human Rights: An Important Concern of U.S. Foreign Policy," *U.S. Department of State Bulletin,* March 28, 1977, p. 289.
2. Charles Frankel, former Assistant Secretary of State for Cultural Affairs and currently Old Dominion Professor of Philosophy and Public Affairs, Columbia University, in an address at Georgetown University on September 21, 1977.

3. Ray Cline, *World Power Assessment 1977* (Washington, D.C.: Center for Strategic and International Studies, 1977), p. 1.

4. Robert E. Osgood, *Ideals and Self-interest in America's Foreign Relations: The Great Transformation of the Twentieth Century* (Chicago: University of Chicago Press, 1953), p. 420, and in an address at Georgetown University on September 28, 1977.

5. *A Chronicle of Human Rights in the USSR,* (New York) 25(January–March 1977), p. 3.

6. Ibid.

7. Henry Kissinger, "Morality and Power: The Role of Human Rights in Foreign Policy," excerpt from the Arthur P. Salomon Lecture, September 19, 1977, New York University's Graduate School of Business Administration and reprinted in *The Washington Post,* September 25, 1977, p. C3.

8. Frankel, Address, p. 60.

9. Jimmy Carter, Statement to the World, January 20, 1977, quoted in John W. Sewell, *The United States and World Development: Agenda 1977* (New York: Praeger for Overseas Development Council, 1977), p. xiii.

10. Walter Laqueur, "The Issue of Human Rights," *Commentary,* May 1977, p. 30.

11. *U.S. News & World Report,* March 14, 1977, in an interview with Georgi Arbatov, quoted in *A Chronicle of Human Rights in the USSR,* (New York) 25(January–March 1977), p. 5.

12. Frankel, Address, p. 60.

13. "White House Assailed as Too Zealous, Too Timid on Rights," *The Washington Post,* October 26, 1977, p. A10.

14. Kissinger, "Morality and Power," p. C3.

15. Frankel, Address, p. 61.

16. Christopher, "Human Rights," p. 291.

17. Ibid.

18. "White House Assailed," *The Washington Post,* p. A10.

19. Michael Reisman, "The Pragmatism of Human Rights," *The Nation,* May 7, 1977, p. 558.

20. Samuel Pisar, "Let's Put Détente Back on the Rails," *The New York Times Magazine,* September 25, 1977, p. 31.

21. "Carter vs. Brezhnev: The SALT Standoff," *Time,* April 11, 1977, p. 11.

22. "Moral Policeman to the World?," *U.S. News & World Report,* March 14, 1977, p. 20.

23. Ibid.

24. Pisar, "Let's Put Détente Back on the Rails," p. 111.

25. "Moral Policeman to the World?," *U.S. News,* p. 17.

26. Hans J. Morgenthau, *Politics Among Nations* (New York: Alfred A. Knopf, 1955), p. 528.

27. Stanley Karnow, "Carter and Human Rights," *Saturday Review,* April 2, 1977, p. 7.

28. Ibid.

29. Morgenthau, *P itics Among Nations,* p. 87.

30. Louis Halle, *The Cold War as History* (New York: Harper & Row, 1967), p. 45.

31. U.S., Congress, House, Committee on International Relations, *The Status of Human Rights in Selected Countries and the U.S. Response,* by the Congressional Research Service, Library of Congress, Committee Print, 95th Cong., 1st sess., 1977, p. 21.

32. Stanley Hoffmann, "The International System and U.S. Policy Toward Latin America" in *The Americas in a Changing World,* ed. Sol Linowitz (New York: The New York Times Book Co., 1975), p. 89.

33. William R. Kinter, "A Program for America: Freedom and Foreign Policy," *Orbis* 21(Spring 1977):147.

34. George Ball, *Diplomacy for a Crowded World* (Boston: Little, Brown, 1976), p. 321.

35. Pisar, "Let's Put Détente Back on the Rails," p. 33.

36. George F. Kennan, *The Cloud of Danger* (Boston: Little, Brown, 1977), p. 188.

37. Ibid.

38. Inis L. Claude, Jr., "Prospects for an American Renewal," *Orbis* 20(Spring 1976):145.

39. Pisar, "Let's Put Détente Back on the Rails," p. 114.

40. Kennan, *The Cloud of Danger,* pp. 233–234.

41. Pisar, "Let's Put Détente Back on the Rails," p. 110.

42. George F. Kennan, "Hazardous Courses in Southern Africa," *Foreign Affairs* 49(January 1971):225.

43. Kennan, *The Cloud of Danger,* p. 26.

QUESTIONS FOR DISCUSSION

1. What is meant by human rights? What is meant by security interests? Do these articles suggest that the two are mutually exclusive?

2. Can a human-rights policy harm American relations with other countries?

3. Does a human-rights policy merely project American values on world society, or are human rights favored by most people throughout the world?

4. Does the United States have such a good record on human rights at home that it can in good conscience call upon other nations to promote human rights?

5. What effect does an activist human-rights foreign policy by the United States have on the plight of dissidents and political prisoners abroad?

SUGGESTED READINGS

Fraser, Donald M. "Freedom and Foreign Policy." *Foreign Policy* 26(Spring 1977):140–156.

Kennan, George F. *The Cloud of Danger*. Boston: Little, Brown, 1977.

Kinter, William. "A Program for America: Freedom and Foreign Policy." *Orbis* 21(Spring 1977):139–156.

Laqueur, Walter. "The Issue of Human Rights." *Commentary*, May 1977, pp. 29–35.

Morgenthau, Hans J. *Politics Among Nations*. New York: Alfred A. Knopf, 1947.

Moynihan, Daniel P. "The Politics of Human Rights." *Commentary*, August 1977, pp. 19–26.

Pisar, Samuel, "Let's Put Détente Back on the Rails." *The New York Times Magazine*, September 25, 1977, pp. 31–33, 108–117.

U.S. Congress. House. Committee on International Relations. *Human Rights in the International Community and in U.S. Foreign Policy, 1945–1976*. By the Congressional Research Service, Library of Congress, Committee Print, 95th Cong, 1st sess., 1977.

U.S. Congress. House. Committee on International Relations. *Soviet Union: Human Rights and Détente*. Joint hearings before a Subcommittee of the Committee on International Relations, 93rd Cong., 2nd sess., 1974.

U.S. Congress. Senate. *Human Rights and Their Relationship to Foreign Assistance Programs*. Hearings before a Subcommittee of the Committee on Foreign Relations, 95th Cong., 1st sess., 1977.

> Should the United States
> Impose Economic Sanctions
> on the South African Government
> in Order to Promote Majority Rule?

YES

ANDREW YOUNG
The Case for Sanctions*

. . . I would like to talk not just about South Africa but return to the whole problem of southern Africa. I would like to talk about it from the perspective of the interests of the United States and how those can best be protected and preserved in southern Africa.

I think we have a choice now in southern Africa as to just which side we are going to be on. It looks to me as though there are possibly four sides.

There is a side of white supremacy and racism bordering on fascism—in fact, not bordering on fascism; in fact fascism, and growing worse every day. There is also a struggling independence movement of peoples in various countries that simply want to share in determinations of the destiny of their lands.

We do, and perhaps this is one of the reasons why it became such a current focus for us, we do also have the possible presence of Soviet intervention and influence, which, I think in order to be on their side, the only thing we have to do is nothing. That foresight probably is doing nothing, becoming a part of the kind of inevitable chaos and dislocation that will rage in that region because of forces that we helped to create.

I have said to this committee before that in no sense should the ferment in southern Africa be attributed to outside Soviet influence; but, rather, to the kind of spirit of freedom and the dignity of human-kind which we have been the foremost exponents of verbally through-out the rest of the world.

We are now faced, I think, with trying to find something tactically

---

* From U.S., Congress, Senate, Committee on Foreign Relations, *South Africa—U.S. Policy and the Role of U.S. Corporations,* Hearings, before the Subcommittee on African Affairs, 94th Cong., 2nd sess., 1976, pp. 137–140.

and strategically to do in a situation where we have allowed our options to disintegrate drastically over the last ten years. I almost approach this moment with more despair and confusion than at any time before; for I, for one, have always been an optimist about the possibilities of progress and a rational transition to majority rule in southern Africa.

Four years ago I thought it was going to be maybe five years in Mozambique and ten years in South Africa. It ended up being two years in Mozambique and three years in South Africa.

I think that if we are honest in our portrayal and understanding of the situation, we will realize that the dominant force in the southern Africa scene is the movement amongst African people themselves for self-determination.

U.S. RECOGNITION, SUPPORT FOR SELF-DETERMINATION MOVEMENT

I would say our policies must begin with the recognition and support of those movements at the point where we begin to deny them.

I would go back then to the question of the recognition of the existing government in Angola and the beginning of support by this nation for a stable, orderly government in Angola. And I feel that concerning the problems of South Africa and the problems of southern Africa, the only positive resources that we have there right now are the resources of black people themselves; that not only do our moral interests lie with them, but our economic interests lie with them, for the volume of trade with Nigeria alone is twice the volume of trade of South Africa and even the illegal trade of Rhodesia thrown in; that the future of investment potential and market availability and resource availability is so much greater in the rest of black Africa that we are now being forced to choose which side we are going to be on.

I would think that we can choose to be on the side of the forces of liberation and independence in southern Africa, and that in fact it is also in the best interest of the white minority for those forces to be supported; that the only thing that I see that can insure the destruction and bloodshed which we all fear in South Africa is a continued support and propping up of a government whose policies are leading only to bloodshed and destruction; that the alternative, starting with support of the government in Angola and the recognition of that government by our government and the beginning of orderly relations with that government, would clearly declare us on the side of freedom and independence in southern Africa.

That would be read throughout southern Africa as a very positive move which is in everybody's best interests.

I think, following that, we would then be in a position through our relationships with Angola and with Zambia and with Tanzania and Mozambique, when those relationships are stable and positive relationships, we then will have in fact the bargaining chips to see to it that Rhodesia or Zimbabwe or Namibia or Southwest Africa undergo some rational transition.

Once we begin the process of orderly, rational transition in Namibia and Zimbabwe, I think the possibility of some reasonable survival of freedom and democracy throughout southern Africa, and even in South Africa, then becomes a possibility.

I think that is probably, as I see it, the limit of our governmental options, except insofar as our government policies have contributed to a climate of positive investment in southern Africa.

U.S. POLICY OF PRIVATE INVESTMENT

I would think that regarding those policies, though they never were formally policies of this government, there ought to be distinct steps taken to say to the business community which conducts its own foreign policy in relationship to southern Africa that the interests of the United States of America are such that we can no longer give any support either by tax incentives or tax credits or any other kind of encouragement to the investment of funds and resources and especially technology in the white regime in South Africa.

Frankly, I think this is just good business, as well as good politics. Were it not for the support that the South African government receives from United States and British banks, they would not be able to continue these policies.

The presence of the fluctuations in the gold market dropping from a high last year of $200 an ounce down to $103 an ounce, with $220 million lost in South Africa's balance of payments, the government revenues from gold have been reduced by more than $130 million in recent months is a clear case.

That certainly is not the kind of climate that American industry ought to be supporting and investing in. When we have problems getting American business to invest in New York City or in Washington, D.C., or in downtown Chicago, the thought of investing in Johannesburg is ridiculous. Any government policies which allow that to happen become equally as ridiculous.

The beginning, I think, of that kind of respectful relationship to the forces of freedom would also, I contend, give encouragement to the forces of freedom in South Africa, which I happen to believe are both black and white; that hard liners are in control because good people are doing nothing and feel as though there is no support for an accommodation to black majority rule.

Let me correct myself. I don't mean black majority rule. I think we know from majority rule that people can determine best those who represent them, and they may determine that those people need not be black.

But there are forces in South Africa that are prepared to work out a government that would include participation, if not immediately on a one-man-one-vote basis, certainly beginning to work toward a solution to the problems of exclusions of blacks, Asians, and coloreds from the political and economic order.

From my own limited experience in movements in this country, I would say that what we see happening in the black townships of South Africa is very similar to the kind of spirit that we had in our own movement here in the 1960s when nobody had to tell people in another place that the time for throwing off the chains is there; that there comes a time in a people's life when they will sing together, "Before I will be a slave, I will be buried in my grave."

I think that is what is now being sung by black people in South Africa and throughout southern Africa.

NONVIOLENT DEMONSTRATIONS

In South Africa, interestingly enough, it still is amazingly nonviolent. I think we should correct the record of our American press which tends to talk in terms of riots. In fact, what is called in the press, riots, is really a peaceful demonstration by young people that are then fired upon by the police.

This morning's news accounts talk of demonstrators marching, singing "Onward Christian Soldiers" with no weapons, and yet three people were reported killed. This is a police riot. This is not a violent uprising. This is a peaceful uprising on the part of freedom-loving people.

That is what this country has stood for throughout our 200-year history. If we back down off that commitment as it relates to southern Africa, I think we will be doing severe violence to our own commitment at home to maintain support of freedom-loving people. . . .

I think that because American investment has been so much in support of the evils of southern Africa, that they should be encouraged to use this time on their own to have an impact, an influence, on that government. If U.S. corporations didn't do anything but deal with the questions of torture and imprisonment of many of the legitimate leadership of black people in South Africa, that, for me, would be important. One of the criteria for the legitimacy of a government is whether or not it survives by torture.

That gets to be maybe an oversimplistic criterion at times. But it is one which I think when applied to South Africa would declare them not a legitimate government.

I think insofar as American influence can be used to give support and recognition for black leadership which is now imprisoned, which I think when I testified at this subcommittee before I reminded the committee that these are perhaps the last generation of men and women in South Africa that were educated in the Judeo-Christian tradition, this would be helpful. In fact, if there is a rational solution to the problems of southern Africa, it is going to have to be worked out with those men who are now imprisoned or detained or now being destroyed.

The young leadership which is now emerging, I think if that leadership were given a chance to develop, then we could minimize the violence in southern Africa.

But as soon as leadership emerges, if it is imprisoned, what we are doing then by those kinds of policies is contributing to chaos, not establishing order. I think order can only come through some recognition of legitimate black leadership in southern Africa. I frankly think American business could have a great deal of influence on that possibility.

Should the United States
Impose Economic Sanctions
on the South African Government
in Order to Promote Majority Rule?

NO

ROBERT L. SCHUETTINGER
*South Africa and United States Security Interests**

United States foreign policy has always faced a quandary in deciding
what its attitude should be toward nations that have domestic policies
different from or even repugnant to the democratic ideals of the American people. It is an unhappy fact that only about 20 of the 140 or so of
the world's nations can properly be called democracies. Of necessity,
therefore, we have often found ourselves allied with nations with whom
we share common security interests but who are different from us in
many ways. Without the alliance with the Soviet Union in World War
II, for example, it is likely that the war against Hitler would have gone
on longer and might not even have ended in victory for the Western
Allies. Today, we are closely allied with the Republic of South Korea,
which has some internal restrictions on liberty but is still far freer than
its old enemy, the so-called "Democratic Republic of (North) Korea."
Even Israel, while doubtless the most democratic nation in that part of
the world, has security laws that make it less than a perfect democracy.

  I would like to discuss one such contemporary case in this essay:
the Republic of South Africa, a nation that has fought beside us in three
wars but with whom relations have become increasingly strained.
Many Americans advance the view that we can bring about reform in
that country by imposing sanctions and trade boycotts. Others who are
no less dedicated to democratic rights for all the people of South Africa
hold the view that such a policy would be counterproductive, that it
would drive the white South Africans into more and more repressive
measures. This latter group of Americans argue, and I share that view,
that steady pressure on the South African government, combined with

* From Robert L. Schuettinger, ed., *South Africa—The Vital Link* (Washington, D.C.: Council on
American Affairs, 1716 New Hampshire Ave., N.W., 1976), pp. 7–16, as revised for *Point-
Counterpoint*. Reprinted by permission of Council on American Affairs.

assurances that we will stand beside them in the event of any Soviet- or Cuban-led invasion of their territory (out of our own self-interest) will lead to an era of greater racial harmony in South Africa and to the rapid admission of all its people to political rights.

I hope to demonstrate in this essay that the strategic and economic importance of South Africa makes it crucial to the survival of Western Europe and to the continued safety and prosperity of the United States. For this reason alone, we should take pains to remain on friendly terms with a government of which we do not wholly approve just as we must continue to negotiate with the Soviet Union on a wide range of issues even though we may deplore their internal acts of repression against their own people.

It must be said at the outset that the Republic of South Africa (like all too many other nations in the world, ranging from the United Kingdom to India to Nigeria to the Soviet Union) has serious internal problems. Indeed, the reconciliation of different ethnic, cultural, and religious groups has occupied the talents and energies of statesmen in almost every country of the world. There can be no doubt that South Africa is not as homogeneous as Sweden or Denmark, and it therefore has problems yet to be resolved. It would be foolish, in any study of the subcontinent, to ignore these obvious facts.

Yet, it must also be emphasized that the primary concern of American foreign policy must be with South Africa's external relations with us, with her neighbors, and with the rest of the world, including Cuba and the Soviet Union.[1] Having stressed this point, I must also add that I, in company with almost all Americans, have absolutely no sympathy with the system of racial segregation now in force in South Africa. It is true that it is changing and that barriers are gradually breaking down, but it is not changing fast enough to suit many "enlightened" white South Africans or the outside world. . . .

In a major speech on August 13, 1976, Dr. Hilgard Muller, then South Africa's foreign minister, reiterated his government's desire for peace and goodwill with its neighboring states. He also stressed that South Africa stood ready to demonstrate its "commitment to Africa"[2] by giving full support for a peaceful outcome in Rhodesia. He added that rapid progress was being made in Southwest Africa toward the independence of that territory in the near future.

This was not a new policy on South Africa's part; for years it has been trying to play a constructive role in a troubled continent. The meeting between Secretary Kissinger and Prime Minister Vorster in Germany was a major step in a continuing policy and, hopefully, other high-level meetings between South Africans and Americans will occur again in the near future.

Over the past decade South Africa has been practicing quiet and patient diplomacy to bring about greater understanding and cooperation with the black states of Africa. The policy of "détente,"[3] as it is called, has so far had modest, though not spectacular success. At the Lusaka Conference of 1969, the black nations gathered there recognized South Africa as an African nation and affirmed that the white citizens were as much Africans as the blacks. The South African head of government has exchanged several fruitful visits with black African heads of government in an atmosphere of mutual concern and respect.

The foreign minister of the Ivory Coast, Mr. Arsene Assouan Usher, in a speech before the Organization of African Unity in April 1975, declared that

> South Africa is an African country and the whites of South Africa are Africans. We have confirmed this in the Lusaka manifesto. The social structure in South Africa is an internal affair, as also declared by this manifesto. As Africans, the South African Government must therefore in its own interests (as we do in ours) promote this policy of absolute neutrality in Africa while achieving the conditions for internal peace.[4]

South Africa has also been building closer relations with several important nations outside of Africa, including Israel and Iran. The Israelis (who state clearly that they do not approve of South Africa's internal policies) are reportedly arranging to sell to South Africa small ships and jet planes and to buy from the South Africans coal and other needed raw materials for Israeli industry.[5] There is some indication, as a matter of fact, that a new alliance of anticommunist nations may be forming (possibly including the Republic of China) among states who are increasingly reluctant to rely for their security on the United States and its NATO [North Atlantic Treaty Organization] allies.

These nations have adopted the position that relations between states should be based on mutual self-interest and security considerations and should be governed by the basic rule of international law of the equality of states and noninterference in the internal affairs of other nations.

There is little doubt that a growing number of influential Americans and Europeans are realizing that good relations with South Africa (and a peaceful solution to problems there which will maintain the stability of the region) are very much in the economic and strategic interests of the United States and of the West as a whole.

It might be useful to review briefly the concrete reasons why South Africa is important to the United States (and the West in general) in these two main areas: the economic and strategic.

The year of 1974 stood out as the year when U.S. exports to the Republic of South Africa reached the billion dollar mark. Totalling 1.15

billion dollars it represents a 55.4 percent increase over the previous
year's figures. Indeed, South Africa is the single most important market for U.S. imports on the whole of the African Continent. Though
South Africa represents less than 5 percent of the total population of
the African Continent, and only 4 percent of its land mass, South Africa
takes more than 30 percent of total U.S. exports compared to the rest
of that continent's other fifty-two countries and territories. . . .

The trading relationship between South Africa and the United
States goes back to the earliest days of the American Republic when
American ships were frequent callers at Cape Town. But it was not
until after World War II that American exports to South Africa began
to grow as South Africa's needs for sophisticated equipment, machinery and other goods produced in the United States, increased with
its own dynamic economic development.

The magnitude of these needs becomes understandable when one
realizes that South Africa yields more than 60 percent of Africa's total
industrial output and that South Africa's sophisticated economic infra-
structure includes such advanced developments as the world's only
viable commercial installation for the conversion of coal into liquid
fuels. South Africa also has one of the world's most highly sophisticated mining industries, comparable to that of the United States and
Germany. These and many other highly developed industrial projects
in South Africa make it the fifth largest industrial complex in the world
(and the largest south of Milan, Italy).

American exports to South Africa must be seen not only in terms
of their gross value but also in terms of the overall trading relationship.
The United States exports far more to South Africa than it imports
from that country. In 1973, the favorable trade balance earned in
American trade relation with South Africa amounted to more than $300
million. In 1974 this figure is expected to show a considerable increase.
When looking at these figures it should be kept in mind that South
Africa has no access to the U.S. arms market due to the official U.S.
arms embargo.

Apart from direct exports of goods to South Africa, the United
States also has an important stake in the invisible exports to that country through the participation of American investments in South Africa.
More than 400 American companies, among them 50 of the top 100
U.S. companies, operate in South Africa. The South African Government is hospitable to foreign capital, know-how, and specialized skills.
Total American investments amount to a book value of over $1 billion
with an average return of about 17 percent. Special incentives are
offered to foreign investors to develop industry in certain parts of the
country.

Further U.S. earnings in South Africa come from equity investments by U.S. citizens in South African companies, particularly in the gold mining industry, and from commercial loans negotiated on the American market by official and private South African institutions.

South Africa has an exemplary record in the servicing of these loans, and it has never asked for or accepted financial assistance from any foreign country.

While the phenomenal growth in the U.S. exports to South Africa is understandable in view of that country's vigorous economic growth, it is, nevertheless, remarkable for there are a number of U.S.-imposed restraints on both trade and investments in South Africa.

In a statement made to the U.S. House of Representatives Sub-committee on Africa on 27 March 1973, the Assistant Secretary of State for African Affairs outlined U.S. policy on economic relations with South Africa. He said that the agencies of the U.S. government responsible refrain from any promotion of either investment or trade of the type carried out in other countries. He went on to say that despite the fact that the U.S. has a major balance-of-payments problem and that South Africa is a major economically attractive market, the U.S. limits its commercial activities in South Africa to low-key services. The U.S. does not participate in special promotions in trade missions or trade fairs. Nor are the credit facilities of the U.S. Export/Import Bank extended to South Africa.

Although South Africa is sharing its expertise in the conversion of coal into liquid fuel, chemicals, petrochemicals and fertilizers with the United States, the U.S. Export/Import Bank refuses to make credit facilities available to contractors wishing to place upwards of $500 million in orders for machinery, equipment, services, and material in the United States for the second oil from coal plant in South Africa. The availability of a project loan from the Export/Import Bank could translate into upwards of 25 million badly needed U.S. manufacturing labor man-hours having a value of approximately $250 million.

Despite the U.S. Export/Import Bank's refusal to extend credit facilities to South Africa, and despite the unwillingness of the U.S. to participate in special promotions in trade missions or trade fairs, the prospects for American exports to South Africa in the coming years should be excellent considering the vast investment and development program underway in that country.

Also in the nuclear field is the Valindaba project designed to produce enriched uranium, a mineral with which South Africa is well endowed. The cost of this project is expected to be more than $800 million.

South Africa, with a unique process for enriching uranium that is far cheaper then conventional processes, is in the forefront of international commercial competition for the highly profitable enriched uranium market of the future. West Germany and Japan are reportedly among the major industrialized nations seeking active cooperation with the fledgling South African nuclear industry.

These and many other projects offer good opportunities for U.S. economic participation—as exporters, as well as investors—in a favorable climate.[6]

Most important of all, however, from the point of view of the U.S. is the *strategic* position of South Africa and its role as "the Vital Link." The Cape Sea Route, for centuries the waterway carrying the riches of the East to the old countries of Europe, has in more recent years maintained its position as a vital mercantile route for the industrialized giants of Europe in a world becoming more and more dependent on international trade in which between 95 percent and 99 percent of world commerce by volume is carried by sea. The oil crisis has highlighted the strategic importance of the Cape Sea Route.[7]

This importance lies in the fact that the route is one of the major oil lines from the Middle East and the Persian Gulf whose fuel output dominates the world energy structure. Of the world's proven oil reserves of about 100,000 million tons (estimated reserves are in the vicinity of 300,000 million tons) 53 percent are in the Middle East. Saudi Arabia alone has estimated oil reserves of at least 150,000 million barrels (more than any other oil-producer) followed by Iran with 65,000 million barrels. Both Iran and Saudi Arabia use the Cape Sea Route heavily for supplying Northern Hemisphere markets.

The Cape Sea Route is currently transporting about seven million barrels of oil a day—equivalent to about one third of the combined output of the six major Persian Gulf producers of Saudi Arabia, Iran, Iraq, Kuwait, Abu Dhabi and Qater. Half of the world's tanker fleet regularly passes the Cape. Of the tankers currently at sea, about 27 percent could only use the Suez Canal when empty, and 40 percent could not use it at all. By the year 1980 about 1 billion tons of oil will have to be transported by sea. It is clear that even with the enlargement of the canal, barely one fifth of the oil from the Persian Gulf would be able to pass through Suez. If pipelines and the Suez Canal could cope with a total of 400 million tons a year, this would leave a balance of 600 million tons, to be transported by an alternative route—the Cape sea route.

Today the great bulk of West Europe's oil requirements and 25 percent of its food supplies pass via the Cape route.

Despite the increasing importance of the Cape Sea Route when considered in a peace-time context and despite the vital strategic position that the Cape and Southern Africa in general assume against the background of an aggressive Soviet naval buildup in the Indian Ocean and its littoral states, the British government has decided to terminate the Simonstown Agreement, which was the only meaningful security agreement in existence in a vast strategic area.

Despite the termination of the Simonstown Agreement by the British government, South African military planners, faced with the withdrawal of active British cooperation, are maintaining a high level of preparedness in ensuring that the Cape Sea Route—a major lifeline of the Western world—is secured against aggressive intent from external forces.

Whereas there were no Russian naval ships in the Indian Ocean in 1967, in 1975 the Russian presence in the Indian Ocean was nearly twice that of the United States.

A Guest Scholar of the Brookings Institution in Washington, D.C., Captain Paul R. Schratz (USN-Ret.), recently surveyed the strategic situation at the tip of Africa and summed up his report as follows:

> The strategic need in southern Africa is largely independent of domestic policy, a consideration which is not being given sufficient weight in our policy. The recent crumbling of the Portuguese colonial empire in Africa has created major security problems in the tier of states surrounding South Africa, from strife-ridden Angola on the Atlantic Coast to Marxist-led Mozambique on the Indian Ocean. The Soviet influence is prominent in all the unstable societies of black Africa. If South Africa were controlled by a hostile power, Western security interests would be gravely endangered. We cannot continue to expect that they can carry the responsibility for defense. The desire of the South Africans, for instance, to purchase U.S. aircraft for ecological, safety-at-sea or environmental reasons merits serious consideration. They favor the U.S. but Western European countries are interested. The fact that the sea surveillance aircraft also have a military role, albeit wholly defensive, should be viewed as a potentially fortuitous dividend and a direct contribution to strategic defense of the West.[8]

In conclusion, I hope I have made it clear that the new Soviet imperialism is the greatest threat to both peace and democracy on the African continent today. This is not only the view of many Americans and West Europeans, it is held by at least half of the heads of government of African states.

The good offices of the United States and its influential West European allies, especially Britain and West Germany, should be used to bring about peaceful and lasting reform in South Africa. At the same time, the power of the West should align itself against any attempt of the new Soviet-Cuban alliance to expand its sway over the people of Southern Africa.

NOTES

1. In fairness to South Africa, it must also be said, as our own ambassadors to the United Nations have noted on numerous occasions, that all too many of the critics of South Africa are not without a touch (or more) of hypocrisy. A good many notorious police states with all their (previously) active opposition locked up securely, with only government-run newspapers, and often with racial persecution rampant in their territory, have shed crocodile tears over conditions in South Africa.

2. *The New York Times,* August 14, 1976, p. 8.

3. For an extended discussion of this policy, see O. Geyser, "Détente in Southern Africa," *African Affairs* (Journal of the Royal African Society, London) April 1976.

4. *Africa Institute Bulletin,* 13, no. 5 (1975), 180.

5. *The New York Times,* August 18, 1976, p. 9.

6. There is, of course, a large literature on the economic importance of South Africa. One useful article, however, is entitled "South Africa's Mineral Resources: How Russia Can Hit the West," *To The Point,* June 25, 1976, p. 7.

7. See "The Security of the Cape Oil Route" published by the Institute for the Study of Conflict (London) and included in the volume edited by Patrick Wall, MP, entitled *The Indian Ocean and the Threat to the West,* London, 1975.

8. Paul R. Schratz, "Strategic South Africa," *Shipmate* (US Naval Academy Alumni Association) April 1976, p. 4. Dr. Schratz was former Director of International Studies at the University of Missouri and has taught at the Naval and National War Colleges.

QUESTIONS FOR DISCUSSION

1. Would the black people of South Africa benefit from the imposition of economic sanctions by the United States against South Africa?

2. Would the Soviet Union improve or weaken its security position if the United States instituted economic sanctions against South Africa?

3. What is the best way to end apartheid in South Africa?

4. Would a policy of imposing economic sanctions against South Africa because of its internal policies be consistent with a similar policy towards the Soviet Union or Cuba because of their internal policies?

5 If black majority rule is established in South Africa, would United States security interests in that area of the world be maintained?

SUGGESTED READINGS

Brotz, Howard. *The Politics of South Africa.* New York: Oxford University Press, 1977.

Carter, Gwendolen M., and Patrick O'Meara. *Southern Africa in Crisis.* Bloomington: Indiana University Press, 1977.

"Controversy in Congress over U.S. Policy Toward Southern Africa: Pro & Con." *Congressional Digest,* January 1977.

Hahn, Walter F., and Alvin J. Cottrell. *Soviet Shadow over Africa.* Washington, D.C.: Center for Advanced International Studies, University of Miami, 1977.

Johnson, R. W. *How Long Will South Africa Survive?* New York: Oxford University Press, 1977.

Nyerere, Julius K. "Africa and Southern Africa." *Foreign Affairs* 55(July 1977):671–684.

Rogers, Barbara. *White Wealth and Black Poverty.* Westport, Conn.: Greenwood Press, 1976.

Schuettinger, Robert L., ed. *South Africa—The Vital Link.* Washington, D.C.: Council on American Affairs, 1976.

U.S. Congress. House. Committee on International Relations. *Resource Development in South Africa and U.S. Policy.* Hearings before a Subcommittee on International Resources, Food, and Energy, 94th Cong., 2nd sess., 1976.

U.S. Congress. Senate. Committee on Foreign Relations. *South Africa—U.S. Policy and the Role of U.S. Corporations.* Hearings before the Subcommittee on African Affairs, 94th Cong., 2nd sess., 1976.

Contributors

Ryan J. Barilleaux is a political science student at the University of Southwestern Louisiana. He has also served as a legislative assistant to United States Senator J. Bennett Johnston.

Robert Borosage, Director of The Center for National Security Studies and a practicing attorney, is coeditor of *The CIA File* (Grossman) and coauthor of *The Lawless State* (Viking).

Frank Church is a United States senator from Idaho.

Dick Clark is a United States senator from Iowa.

William E. Colby was Deputy Director of Plans, the Central Intelligence Agency's covert operations division, and served as Director of the agency.

David Cortright, author of *Soldiers in Revolt* (Doubleday), is an associate of The Center for National Security Studies.

Robert A. Dahl is Sterling Professor of Political Science at Yale University. He is the author of *A Preface to Democratic Theory* (University of Chicago), *Who Governs?* (Yale), *Polyarchy: Participation and Opposition* (Yale), and other works.

Susan M. Davis is a recent graduate in political science from Georgetown University.

Peter DeLeon is a political analyst for the Rand Corporation.

Martin Diamond, a political scientist who taught at the University of Chicago and Claremont Graduate School, is the author of numerous works on the Founding Fathers.

Daniel J. Elazar is Professor of Political Science and Director of the Center for the Study of Federalism at Temple University. He is the author of *American Federalism: A View from the States* (Crowell), *American Partnership: Intergovernmental Cooperation in Nineteenth Century United States* (Chicago), and other works.

Sam J. Ervin, Jr., is a former United States senator from North Carolina.

Norman Goldfarb is a cochairman of the Citizens Council on Human Relations in Buffalo, New York.

Barry Goldwater, a United States senator from Arizona, was the Republican presidential candidate in 1964.

Walter Goodman is an editor for *The New York Times.* He is author of *The Committee* (Farrar, Straus, & Giroux) and *A Percentage of the Take* (Farrar, Straus, & Giroux).

Mike Gravel is a United States senator from Alaska.

Morton H. Halperin, formerly a senior staff member of the National Security Council and Deputy Assistant Secretary of Defense, is a senior fellow in foreign policy at the Brookings Institution in Washington, D.C. He is the author of *Defense Strategies for the Seventies* (Little, Brown), *National Security Policy-Making* (Lexington), and other works.

Michael Harrington is a socialist writer. His best-known book, *The Other America* (Macmillan), provided the intellectual stimulus underlying the national antipoverty programs of the Kennedy and Johnson Administrations.

Jacob Javits is a United States senator from New York.

Peter Jenkins is a British journalist.

Edward M. Kennedy is a United States senator from Massachusetts.

Henry A. Kissinger served as National Security Adviser and Secretary of State in the administrations of Presidents Richard Nixon and Gerald Ford.

Kenneth Kofmehl is Professor of Political Science at Purdue University in Indiana. He is the author of *Professional Staffs of Congress* (Purdue).

Irving Kristol is coeditor of the quarterly *The Public Interest.* He is the author of *On the Democratic Idea in America* (Harper & Row) and other works.

Robert J. Kukla is the author of *Gun Control* (Stackpole).

League of Women Voters, a voluntary organization of women citizens, has as its purpose "to promote political responsibility through informed and active participation of citizens in government."

W. Duane Lockard is Professor of Political Science at Princeton University and is the author of *Toward Equal Opportunity* (Macmillan), *Politics of State and Local Government* (Macmillan), and other works.

Norton E. Long is Curators Professor of Political Science at the University of Missouri, St. Louis. He is the author of *The Unwalled City: Rebuilding the Urban Community* (Basic) and other works.

Eugene J. McCarthy is a former United States senator from Minnesota.

Mike McCormack, a United States representative from Washington, is a ranking member of the Joint Committee on Atomic Energy.

George McGovern is a United States senator from South Dakota and was the Democratic party candidate for president in 1972.

Marvin Maurer is Professor of Government at Monmouth College in New Jersey. His articles have appeared in *New Leader, New America, Midstream,* and other journals.

Wallace Mendelson is Professor of Government at the University of Texas. He is the author of *Justices Black and Frankfurter: Conflict in the Court* (Chicago).

C. Wright Mills was Professor of Sociology at Columbia University. He is author of *The Power Elite* (Oxford), *Sociological Imagination* (Oxford), *White Collar: American Middle Classes* (Oxford), and other works.

Stanley Mosk is a Justice of the Supreme Court of California.

George Novack, a Marxist theoretician in the United States, has written and lectured on Marxist theory, philosophy, and politics. He is the author of *Empiricism and Its Evolution: A Marxist View* (Pathfinder), *Humanism and Socialism* (Pathfinder), and other works.

Nelson W. Polsby is Professor of Political Science at the University of California, Berkeley. He is the author of *Community Power and Political Theory* (Yale), *The Modern Presidency* (Random House), and other works.

Michael Parenti is a political scientist who has lectured and taught at various colleges and universities. He is author of *The Anti-Communist Impulse* (Random House) and *Democracy for the Few* (St Martin's).

Paul R. Porter served in various diplomatic posts in Europe and was an administrator for the Marshall Plan.

Kenneth Prewitt is Professor of Political Science at the University of Chicago. He is author of *The Recruitment of Political Leaders: A Study of Citizen-Politicians* (Bobbs-Merrill) and coauthor of *The Ruling Elites* (Harper & Row), among other works.

Ron Randall is a political scientist at the University of Toledo.

Austin Ranney is a former president of the American Political Science Association. He is author of *The Doctrine of Responsible Party Government* (University of Illinois), *The Governing of Men* (Holt), and other works.

Michael D. Reagan is Dean, College of Social and Behavioral Sciences, University of California, Riverside. He is author of *The New Federalism* (Oxford), *Science and the Federal Patron* (Oxford), and *The Managed Economy* (Oxford).

Eugene V. Rostow is Sterling Professor of Law and Public Affairs at Yale University. He served as Under Secretary of State for Political Affairs, 1966–1968; and since 1973 he has been president of the Atlantic Treaty Association.

Arthur Schlesinger, Jr., is Schweitzer Professor of Humanities at the City University, New York, and author of *A Thousand Days* (Houghton Mifflin), *The Age of Jackson* (Little, Brown), *The Imperial Presidency* (Houghton Mifflin), and other works.

Herbert S. Schlosser, a former president of the National Broadcasting Company, is an executive vice-president of the RCA Corporation.

Robert L. Schuettinger is Director of Studies at the Heritage Foundation in Washington, D.C., and editor of its quarterly journal of public policy, *Policy Review.* He was formerly a foreign policy aide in the United States House of Representatives.

Alexander Solzhenitsyn, a Nobel laureate, is the author of *The Gulag Archipelago* (Harper & Row), *Cancer Ward* (Dial), and other books.

Theodore Sorensen was an adviser to President John Kennedy. He is the author of a biography on Kennedy and *Watchman in the Night: Presidential Accountability After Watergate* (MIT).

Sam Steiger, a former Republican congressman, represented Arizona's Third Congressional District and was a member of the Interior and Insular Affairs Committee and the Government Operations Committee.

Gay Talese, a former writer for *The New York Times,* is author of *The Kingdom and the Power* (World) and *Honor Thy Father* (World).

Nick Thimmesch is a columnist whose articles have appeared in national newspapers and magazines.

Matthew O. Tobriner is a Justice of the Supreme Court of California.

John Tower is a United States senator from Texas.

Ernest Van Den Haag is a psychologist and Adjunct Professor of Social Philosophy at New York University. He is author of *The Jewish Mystique* (Stein & Day), *Punishing Criminals* (Basic), and other works.

Sidney Verba is Professor of Government at Harvard University. He is coauthor of *The Civic Culture* (Princeton) and *Participation in America: Democracy and Social Equality* (Harper & Row), among other works.

Ben J. Wattenberg has written extensively on demographic and political matters. He is coauthor of *This USA* (Doubleday) and *The Real Majority* (Coward, McCann & Geoghegan).

J. Skelly Wright is a judge, United States Court of Appeals for the District of Columbia Circuit.

Andrew Young served as congressman from Georgia. He is currently the United States Ambassador to the United Nations.